Mindfulness-integrated CBT has made a unique contribution to evidence-based approaches in health care – centrally relevant for those interested in teaching or learning mindfulness and those who practice Cognitive Therapy. The evidence shows that it helps people with some of the most serious physical and emotional difficulties, as well as working well to enhance flourishing and well-being. This manual for therapists and teachers is a very welcome step forward to make MiCBT even more available across the world.

Professor Mark Williams, PhD
Emeritus Professor of Clinical Psychology, University of Oxford
Co-author of Mindfulness-based Cognitive Therapy for Depression

It is an investment when you buy a book (both time and money). I recommend that you invest in the best authors. There is none better for MiCBT than Cayoun, Francis and Shires.

Professor Bruce A. Stevens, PhD
Clinical psychologist, Wicking Chair of Ageing and Practical Theology,
Charles Sturt University Canberra
Author of Happy ever after? A Practical guide to relationship counselling
for clinical psychologists

Dr. Bruno Cayoun and his colleagues Drs. Francis and Shires have written the most comprehensive book to date integrating mindfulness and CBT in a framework successfully designed to give therapists practical guidance to foster well-being in clients with an array of difficulties. Highly recommended.

Arthur P. Ciaramicoli, Ed.D.,Ph.D.,
Clinical psychologist
Author of The Stress Solution: Using Empathy and Cognitive Behavioral
Therapy to Reduce Anxiety and Develop Resilience

Bruno Cayoun developed a concise and effective mindfulness program in Mindfulness-integrated Cognitive Behaviour Therapy. Now, Dr. Cayoun and his colleagues have offered a valuable companion book for clinicians and clients that brings compassionate care into the lives of therapists and their clients as co-participants in mindfulness. It is a privilege for me to have known Dr. Cayoun as friend and colleague and to appreciate deeply the precision of his thinking and practice. This clinical handbook reflects not only his talent and insights, it highlights his d... tion to colleagues who can join him in providing an important level of ethical ... therapeutic care to others.

Psychologist, Directo...
Co-author of Mindfulness Starts Her...
Guide to Ethics and M...

MiCBT integrates the principal evidence-based methods of tradit... ...ndfulness meditation with seamless grace and an ability to preserve the importa... ...of both. I highly recommend this comprehensive and helpful clinical handbook to me... health professionals.

Shauna Shapiro, PhD
Professor of counseling psychology, Santa Clara University
Author of The art and science of mindfulness and Mindful Discipline

This important work is a masterful integration of mindfulness meditation training and clinical science for individual and group therapy. It fills a gap in the literature by linking the essence of mindfulness practice—equanimity—with carefully articulated behavioral change strategies. The authors explain the theoretical foundation of MiCBT, followed by generous, session-by-session instructions for every aspect of treatment. Almost 2 decades in the making, MiCBT is an innovative, transdiagnostic approach to clinical care that will surely inspire and inform clinicians for years to come.

Christopher Germer, PhD
Lecturer (part-time), Harvard Medical School
Author, The Mindful Path to Self-Compassion
Co-editor, Mindfulness and Psychotherapy

The Clinical Handbook of Mindfulness-integrated Cognitive Behavior Therapy

The Clinical Handbook of Mindfulness-integrated Cognitive Behavior Therapy

A Step-by-Step Guide for Therapists

Bruno A. Cayoun
Sarah E. Francis
Alice G. Shires

WILEY Blackwell

This edition first published 2019

Registered Offices
John Wiley & Sons, Inc., 111 River Street, Hoboken, NJ 07030, USA
John Wiley & Sons Ltd, The Atrium, Southern Gate, Chichester, West Sussex, PO19 8SQ, UK

Editorial Office
111 River Street, Hoboken, NJ 07030, USA

For details of our global editorial offices, customer services, and more information about Wiley products visit us at www.wiley.com.

Wiley also publishes its books in a variety of electronic formats and by print-on-demand. Some content that appears in standard print versions of this book may not be available in other formats.

Library of Congress Cataloging-in-Publication Data

Names: Cayoun, Bruno A., 1961– author. | Francis, Sarah E., 1951– author. | Shires, Alice G., 1963– author.
Title: The clinical handbook of mindfulness-integrated cognitive behavior therapy : a step-by-step guide for therapists / Bruno A. Cayoun, Sarah E. Francis, Alice G. Shires.
Description: Hoboken, NJ : Wiley-Blackwell, 2018. | Includes bibliographical references and index. |
Identifiers: LCCN 2018018086 (print) | LCCN 2018021975 (ebook) | ISBN 9781119389620 (ePub) | ISBN 9781119389644 (Adobe PDF) | ISBN 9781119389637 (paperback) | ISBN 9781119389644 (ePDF)
Subjects: | MESH: Mindfulness–methods
Classification: LCC RC489.C63 (ebook) | LCC RC489.C63 (print) | NLM WM 425.5.C6 | DDC 616.89/1425–dc23
LC record available at https://lccn.loc.gov/2018018086

Cover image: ©MiCBT Institute
Cover design by Wiley

Set in 10/12pt Sabon by SPi Global, Pondicherry, India

10 9 8 7 6 5 4 3 2 1

MIX
Paper from responsible sources
FSC® C013604

I slept and dreamt that life was joy.
I awoke and saw that life was service.
I acted and behold, service was joy.

—Rabindranath Tagore

Contents

About the Authors

Bruno Cayoun is a clinical psychologist and the principal developer of Mindfulness-integrated Cognitive Behavior Therapy (MiCBT), which he and his colleagues have been teaching to mental health professionals since 2003. He is also the founder and Director of the MiCBT Institute, a leading provider of training and professional development services in MiCBT to mental health services and professional associations internationally. Dr. Cayoun keeps a private clinical practice in Hobart, Australia, and undertakes mindfulness research at the MiCBT Institute and in cooperation with universities in various countries. He has practiced mindfulness meditation in the Burmese *Vipassana* tradition of Ledi Sayadaw, U Bah Kin and S. N. Goenka, and undergone intensive training in France, Nepal, India and Australia since 1989. He is the author of research articles and books, including *Mindfulness-integrated CBT: Principles and Practice* (Wiley, 2011), and *Mindfulness-integrated CBT for Well-Being and Personal Growth: Four Steps to Enhance Inner Calm, Self-Confidence and Relationships* (Wiley, 2015).

Sarah Francis is a registered psychologist trained in a number of mindfulness-based therapies. She specializes in Mindfulness-integrated Cognitive Behavior Therapy (MiCBT) and has been implementing it since 2006. In addition to her work in clinical psychology, Sarah has worked in a number of professional contexts including education, human resources, and business consulting. She is the author of *Workplace Communication: A Teacher's Guide* (Pitman, 1993). She is the convenor of the Melbourne MiCBT Interest and Research Group and a senior trainer for health professionals who train through the MiCBT Institute. Sarah's research interests include the measurement of mindfulness and the differential efficacy of MiCBT and treatment-as-usual in clients with a range of mental health disorders at Monash University.

Alice G. Shires is a clinical psychologist and Director of the Psychology Clinic and senior lecturer at the Graduate School of Health, University of Technology, Sydney (UTS) and was a founding Board Member of the Australian Clinical Psychology Association. Alice is a teacher, trainer and supervisor of clinical psychologists and has worked in acute and specialist mental health services in the United Kingdom. She has developed an interest in mindfulness and its integration with cognitive and behavioral therapies and has established a mindfulness-integrated research clinic at UTS. Her research includes the efficacy of MiCBT in chronic pain, the process of supervision and assessment of competencies in clinical psychology, and the inclusion of mindfulness training in the clinical psychology training process. Alice is a senior teacher of MiCBT for mental health professionals and supervises clinicians during the course of their MiCBT training.

Foreword

Discover real peace and harmony within yourself, and naturally this will overflow to benefit others.

—S. N. Goenka

As clinicians, we are continually looking for best practices that assist our clients to decrease their suffering. We begin by holding awareness of the certainty that a reduction in suffering *is* possible. Mindfulness-integrated Cognitive Behavior Therapy (MiCBT) supports us in the ensuing process of making meaningful change manifest for clients. It does this through the skillful integration of equanimity cultivated in meditation practice and cognitive behavior therapy-based exposure techniques. The authors of this manual accompany us step-by-step through the four stages of MiCBT, anticipating challenges and providing demonstrable advice and strategies for optimizing skill development.

I first met Bruno through our common commitment to precision and proficiency in meditation practice, and clarity of underlying theoretical frameworks, in an effort to optimize the rigor and effectiveness of mindfulness-based interventions. Alice, Bruno and Sarah bring decades of combined clinical wisdom across the full range of mental health conditions to this practical guide. They integrate their personal meditation experience within the Burmese *Theravada Vipassana* tradition of U Ba Khin with a structured therapeutic approach that can be adapted to a wide variety of clinical issues. The authors' integrity and embodiment of insights gained through meditation imbue both the explanations of the theoretical framework of MiCBT and the associated clinical examples with lucidity; this assists the clinician in merging the personal and experiential with the interpersonal and clinical.

This guide is an essential resource for therapists in that it provides an accessible, structured approach to applying MiCBT principles in both individual and group settings. It provides demonstrations of how to assist clients to identify clear treatment goals, including specific behavioral changes, and develop awareness of the benefits they will experience as motivation to establish and sustain a twice-daily meditation practice. The theoretical framework underpinning MiCBT emphasizes that it is automatic reactions to the hedonic tone of co-emerging sensations in the body, fueled by identification with experience, that in large part drive clients' symptoms and habitual behaviors. Therapists will find a refreshingly clear rationale for each stage of the therapy process, along with suggested methods for adjusting the treatment protocol based on clinical progress and need.

One of the challenges we repeatedly face as clinicians is skillfully selecting and applying the most appropriate components of mindfulness to meet the immediate needs of the client in the room. The content of this book, as carefully crafted by Alice, Bruno and Sarah, addresses this by clearly outlining the links between the various facets of mindfulness and their clinical effects. For instance, they explain *how* practicing mindfulness of breath develops metacognitive awareness, which, in turn, generalizes into daily life, resulting in decreased rumination. Importantly, they also provide examples of effective ways to explain these mechanisms to clients, serving as a further source of motivation for their daily mindfulness practice.

Throughout the book, considerable attention is devoted to problem-solving specific clinical situations, illustrated by clinical vignettes. With forethought to the challenges our clients may face in their CBT and meditation practices, such as difficulty accepting unpleasant bodily sensations or managing intrusive thoughts, the authors recommend specific practice modifications. By providing a comprehensive, yet adaptable, in-session and at-home therapeutic framework, while also clearly explicating the rationale for progression of practice as taught in MiCBT, this manual enables the clinician to adjust the treatment for each clinical case.

Having this handbook when I was first eagerly implementing MiCBT would have saved me much time in determining how to summarize succinctly the purpose of each practice for clients and how most effectively to bring together the mindfulness and CBT components. Most importantly, this manual empowers us to carry the insights gained in our personal mindfulness practice into the therapeutic relationship, equipping our clients with the skills not only to reduce their own suffering but also to express their full and unique potential.

Andrea Grabovac, MD, FRCPC
Vancouver, Canada, 2018

Acknowledgments

We express our gratitude for the traditional teachings and teachers of Vipassana meditation, which have inspired and taught us and from which this program is developed. We thank Gabrielle Cayoun for her assistance with figures, and Karen Cayoun and Dr. Glenn Bilsborrow for their reviews of drafts. We are also grateful to our colleagues and past clients for their permission to include their experience in the book, and to the entire team at Wiley for their patience and support. We would also like to express our gratitude to all mindfulness researchers who endeavor to remain true to the original teaching of mindfulness and provide an invaluable support to the clinical field and assist in the modern understanding of this ancient approach to cultivating well-being.

Introduction

> *The faculty of voluntarily bringing back a wandering attention, over and over again, is the very root of judgement, character and will. An education which should improve this faculty would be an education par excellence. But it is easier to define this ideal than to give practical instructions for bringing it about.*
>
> —William James, 1890

As we become more insightful in our therapeutic work, we progressively direct our interest to methods that best suit our personality and approach to life in general because we feel more at ease with these methods. Additionally, as we grow as human beings, becoming wiser over time, we choose what we believe are genuinely wholesome therapeutic tools. A wiser mind is more attracted to tools that promote wisdom, such as mindfulness. Since mindfulness is the art of being objective about subjectivity, many therapists from various disciplines choose to use mindfulness-based interventions as their primary toolset.

Over the past 15 years, there has been a surge of interest and requests for training in mindfulness-based therapies all around the globe. Among the most cited approaches that include mindfulness meditation are Mindfulness-Based Stress Reduction (MBSR; Kabat-Zinn, 2014) and Mindfulness-Based Cognitive Behavior Therapy (MBCT; Segal, Williams & Teasdale, 2002), but there are many more. Some of these approaches are associated with a second generation of mindfulness-based interventions, partly because they preserve skills that have been traditionally integral to mindfulness training, such as ethics and compassion training, and require extended education and mentoring (see Van Gordon, Shonin, & Griffiths, 2015, for detailed description). Second generation mindfulness-based interventions include Mindfulness Based Symptoms Management (Monteiro & Musten, 2013), Meditation Awareness Training (Shonin, Van Gordon, Dunn, Singh, & Griffiths, 2014), Mindfulness-Based Positive Behavior Support (Singh et al., 2014), Mindful Self-Compassion (Neff & Germer, 2013), Compassion Focused Therapy (Gilbert, 2009), and Compassion Cultivation Training (Jazaieri et al., 2013).

Mindfulness-integrated Cognitive Behavior Therapy or MiCBT (pronounced M-I-C-B-T) has become an important contributor to this growing field. Despite some inevitable overlap with other mindfulness programs, MiCBT differs in several key areas, which are discussed in Chapters 1 and 2. It offers a practical set of evidence-based techniques derived from mindfulness training in the Burmese *Vipassana* tradition of Ledi Sayadaw (1965/1999), U Ba Khin (1995/2011) and Goenka (2000), and the principles of Cognitive Behavior Therapy (CBT) to address a broad range of psychological disorders. Its increasing popularity may be best attributed to its novel ability to address both crisis and chronic conditions as well as help prevent relapse.

This book reflects 17 years of effort to develop, implement, research and teach MiCBT as an efficacious transdiagnostic approach to address a wide range of conditions, including those with complex comorbidity. We have written this volume to offer therapists a trusted guide that informs and assists them in their group and individual applications of this unique approach, across a wide range of disorders. Two volumes have already been written on the topic. One was written for professionals with a focus on the scientific basis and mechanisms of action of MiCBT (Cayoun, 2011). The other (Cayoun, 2015) was written as a step-by-step self-implementation to assist clients in therapy and provide an opportunity for the general public to use MiCBT for well-being and personal growth. These books have since been translated in several languages and continue to be widely used. However, there was no comprehensive guide to assist therapists in clinical settings until now. This book was written to fill this gap and provide a detailed week-by-week implementation of MiCBT.

When our publisher suggested that we write a workbook for therapists, it was important to us that the book serve therapists in the best possible way, so we conducted a survey of 233 clinicians known to use or to be interested in using MiCBT as their primary approach to therapy, to probe their format preference. About 15 % preferred a book written for clinicians only, the large majority (74 %) responded in favor of a workbook for clinicians that includes information for clients as well, and 11 % didn't mind. We went with the majority, which resulted in this book that guides both the therapist and their clients. This is because not all clients are able or willing to read, or can afford the self-implementation guide (Cayoun, 2015)—although we highly recommend it if they can, as it has proven to be an excellent resource for clients undergoing MiCBT.

Part 1 of the book contains three chapters that will provide you with important information about MiCBT, including a clear explanation of its origins and development, its structure and content, the scientific underpinnings and empirical evidence. Part 2 of the book contains ten chapters, called "sessions" to fit with the delivery of the ten-session program. It will guide you through the entire program, using an easy, conversational and engaging style which will encourage you to engage clients in the program. Your clients will learn about themselves in three complementary ways: through psychoeducation, through questioning their own views, and through their own experience. This clinical handbook contains precise guidance for each session, including suggestions on ways to overcome common difficulties, and worksheets and handouts that can be photocopied or downloaded and given to clients to assist them as they progress through the program. With this book, you and your clients are also given free access to the entire set of audio instructions for mindfulness training, which can be streamed online or downloaded in MP3 format. Appendix 2 also contains the scripts for these instructions, which include basic and more advanced methods given by the first author, an experienced *Vipassana* meditator and mindfulness teacher.

As you will notice, occasional references are made to Buddhist psychology and sometimes to the historical Buddha. The reason for this inclusion is simply good writing practice and ethics. One would expect responsible authors to include sources of their information, especially when the phenomena and methods they discuss are well established and documented. While some authors of mindfulness-related books may not acknowledge the source of the teachings they discuss, we feel grateful for having received this rich source of knowledge and are bound by good and ethical academic practice. However, this does not make this book a "Buddhist" book, nor does it make MiCBT a "Buddhist" therapy. Irrespective of the place, culture, or period from which psychological frameworks originate, "Psychology is the science of mental life, both of its phenomena and of their conditions" (James, 1890, p. 1). In our perception, 2 + 2 = 4 for Buddhists, Christians or atheists. As long as the information is validated, we do not discriminate between cultures, and we are transparent about its source and original meaning. We hope that these occasional references to Buddhist psychology will be perceived in the light of our intention and will be a useful and enriching source of additional information.

References

Cayoun, B. A. (2011). *Mindfulness-integrated CBT: Principles and practice*. Chichester, UK: Wiley.

Cayoun, B. A. (2015). *Mindfulness-integrated CBT for well-being and personal growth: Four steps to enhance inner calm, self-confidence and relationships*. Chichester, UK: Wiley.

Gilbert, P. (2009). *The compassionate mind: A new approach to life's challenges*. Oakland, CA: New Harbinger.

Goenka, S. N. (2000). *The discourse summaries*. Onalaska, WA: Vipassana Research Publications.

Hart, W. (1987). *The art of living: Vipassana meditation as taught by S. N. Goenka*. San Francisco: HarperCollins.

James, W. (1890). *The principles of psychology*. New York: Holt.

Jazaieri, H., McGonigal, K., Jinpa, T., Doty, J. R., Gross, J. J., & Goldin, P. R. (2014). A randomized controlled trial of compassion cultivation training: Effects on mindfulness, affect, and emotion regulation. *Motivation and Emotion*, *38*, 23–35. Doi:10.1007/s11031-013-9368-z

Kabat-Zinn, J. (2014). *Full catastrophe living: Using the wisdom of your body and mind to face stress, pain, and illness* (Revised ed.). New York: Random House.

Monteiro, L., & Musten, F. (2013). *Mindfulness starts here: An eight-week guide to skillful living*. Victoria, BC, Canada: Friesen Press.

Neff, K. D., & Germer, C. K. (2013). A pilot study and randomized controlled trial of the mindful self-compassion program. *Journal of Clinical Psychology*, *69*, 28–44. doi:10.1002/jclp.21923

Sayadaw, L. (1965/1999). *Manuals of Dhamma*. Onalaska, WA: Vipassana Research Publication.

Segal, Z. V., Williams, J. M. G., & Teasdale, J. D. (2002). *Mindfulness-based cognitive therapy for depression: A new approach to preventing relapse*. New York: Guilford.

Shonin, E., Van Gordon, W., Dunn, T., Singh, N., & Griffiths, M. (2014). Meditation awareness training (MAT) for work-related well-being and job performance: A randomized controlled trial. *International Journal of Mental Health and Addiction*, *12*, 806–823.

Singh, N., Lancioni, G., Winton, A., Karazsia, B., Myers, R., Latham, L., & Singh, J. (2014). Mindfulness-Based Positive Behavior Support (MBPBS) for mothers of adolescents with autism spectrum disorder: Effects on adolescents' behavior and parental stress. *Mindfulness*, *5*, 646–657.

U Ba Khin, S. T. S. (1995–2011). *The essentials of Buddha Dhamma*. Kandy, Sri Lanka: Buddhist Publication Society.

Van Gordon, W., Shonin, E., & Griffiths, M. (2015). Towards a second generation of mindfulness-based interventions. *Australian & New Zealand Journal of Psychiatry*, *49*, 591–592. Doi:10.1177/0004867415577437

About the Companion Website

This book is accompanied by a companion website:

www.wiley.com/go/Cayoun/Mindfulness-integrated

The website includes:

- Handouts
- Audio

Part 1

The MiCBT Approach, Theory and Validation

1
Principles of MiCBT

The real voyage of discovery consists not in seeking new lands but seeing with new eyes.

—Marcel Proust, 1923

This chapter describes the origins and development of Mindfulness-integrated Cognitive Behavior Therapy (MiCBT), as well as the core principles and theoretical basis for this integrated transdiagnostic approach. The chapter also discusses how we can conceptualize "suffering" in a way that productively guides our attitude and approach to using MiCBT. It also provides a brief description of the four stages of MiCBT, including the therapeutic mechanisms and supporting research evidence. We begin by describing our operational definition of mindfulness to ensure that the term used with regards to MiCBT is accurately understood.

Definition and Purpose of Mindfulness

Origins and Common Confusions

Mindfulness has a double meaning in the English language. The online *Oxford English Dictionary* defines mindfulness in its common meaning outside the meditative context as "The quality or state of being conscious or aware of something." As you can imagine, this can lead to all sorts of misinterpretations of the term when trying to apply it to the Buddhist teaching of mindfulness. In modern day Western psychology, mindfulness has progressively become an umbrella term related to purposeful sustained attention in the present moment. This understanding is not only inaccurate, but it also misleads newcomers to mindfulness training. For example, a cat sitting attentively in front of a mousehole, ready to jump on its prey, sustains attention from moment to moment; however, it is not a mindful cat. Similarly, a sniper paying purposeful attention in the present moment, ready to

The Clinical Handbook of Mindfulness-integrated Cognitive Behavior Therapy: A Step-by-Step Guide for Therapists, First Edition. Bruno A. Cayoun, Sarah E. Francis, and Alice G. Shires.

Companion website: www.wiley.com/go/Cayoun/Mindfulness-integrated

kill in the context of following orders without making judgments, is attentive but not mindful. Unfortunately, this initial misunderstanding of the construct engenders low construct validity in both mindfulness measurement tools and the studies that use them, but a discussion on these issues is beyond the scope of this chapter.

In the Buddhist psychological context, the term "mindfulness" is a translation of the Pali term *sati*. Pali was the common language used in northern India during the time of the Buddha, over 25 centuries ago. *Sati* has been interpreted by various monastic and lay teachers as "awareness" (Goenka, 2000, p. 135), "mindfulness or awareness" (Narada, 1988, p. 183; Rahula, 1974, p. 48), and as "remembering or bearing in mind" (Rhys Davids, 1881, p. 107; Sharf, 2014, p. 942;). The British Buddhist scholar Rupert Gethin explains that *sati* should be understood as that which allows us to be aware of the full range and extent of phenomena—as an awareness of phenomena and their relative value—and is therefore what causes the mindfulness practitioner to "remember" that any experience exists in relation to a whole variety of experiences that may be skillful or unskillful, wholesome or unwholesome, ethical or unethical (Gethin, 1992). The traditional purpose of mindfulness practice, since its origination in Buddhist teaching, is to develop wisdom and reduce suffering.

Unlike some of the current Western teaching models, the traditional approach teaches mindfulness as a quality of mind to be cultivated at all levels of experience. In particular, it involves developing our mindfulness skills across four modalities so that mindfulness permeates through all domains of functioning. This encompasses "the constant mindfulness with regard to body (*káyánupassaná*), feelings (*vedanánupassaná*), thoughts (*cittánupassaná*), and mind objects (*dhammánupassaná*)" (Narada, 1988, p. 182). Note that "feeling" (*vedana*) is meant to signify "interoception" and the associated pleasant, unpleasant or neutral hedonic tone, and is frequently used interchangeably with "body sensations" in the literature (e.g., Rahula, 1974, p. 48). Hence, *vedana* has more to do with "feeling" (the verb) than with "feelings" (the noun). Although it is not necessary to explain these details to clients, it is helpful for therapists to know the original purpose of mindfulness training and understand clearly the definition of mindfulness, as some clients will ask about it.

In particular, it is important that clients understand the differences between attentiveness, awareness and mindfulness. In brief, we understand attention to be the mental effort that directs awareness to an object or stimulus and awareness is the action of conscious apprehension of the object. While mindfulness requires both attentional effort and awareness of what is occurring in the present moment, it must be free from any bias, such as liking or disliking what we attend to, and the propensity to desire or resent the object. The attentive cat in the aforementioned example craves the appearance of the mouse, and the sniper may resent the target or crave a successful shot. Mindfulness meditation needs to be understood as a training in *unbiased* attention to our ongoing experience, preventing any personal interpretation or interference with the object of observation. Mindfulness must, therefore, include a sense of detachment from, and non-identification with, the object that we attend to.

For this reason, mindfulness practice must be accompanied by equanimity (*upekkha* in Pali), which is *a detached, neutral and balanced mental state that is neither elated nor depressed, which enables a non-reactive attitude irrespective of the type of experience being encountered*. Researchers are starting to express the importance of equanimity in mindfulness practice (e.g., Desbordes et al., 2015). Mindfulness practice requires mental neutrality, which allows us to investigate safely, objectively and with a healthy curiosity. Hence, to use the term mindfulness accurately, it must be understood as a tool, *not as a goal*. As we progressively acquire the ability to stabilize attention, our observation deepens and we notice that all things change, including our thoughts, emotions, physical body and the entire world around us—nothing remains the same, including what we call "the self." Thus, mindfulness is a tool for both self-investigation and "self-desensitization" through direct exposure to whatever we call "I," "my," or "mine" while preventing the reinforcement of a sense of self, as is discussed in the next chapter and revisited in Part 2 as we implement the stages of MiCBT.

Operational Definition

Most teachers agree that mindfulness practice requires paying attention to our present experience, without adding or subtracting any aspect to the experience, while preventing biased judgment, reactivity and identification with the experience. When gathering the essence of traditional and modern descriptions of mindfulness, we can summarize a mindful mental state as *a heightened sensory and metacognitive awareness of the present-moment experience, free from reactivity, biased personal values and self-referential evaluation*. Training in mindfulness meditation requires *deliberate sustained attention to sensory and cognitive processes with unconditional acceptance of the experience*. This necessitates a deliberate effort to inhibit one's learned reactions (craving and aversion) and develop greater objectivity, acceptance and detachment with each experience.

MiCBT applies mindfulness training in the Vipassana tradition of the Burmese teachers lineage of Ledi Sayadaw, Saya Tetgyi, Sayagyi U Ba Khin and, later, S. N. Goenka. Accordingly, MiCBT may be defined as *a theoretically congruent and technically complementary integration of traditional mindfulness training and CBT, which provides a transdiagnostic approach to address emotional distress across a wide range of disorders*.

Origin and Development

MiCBT, originally called Mindfulness-based CBT (MCBT) until 2005, was initially conceptualized between 1989 and 1997 and developed by the first author between 2001 and 2003 to address a range of moderate to severe psychiatric symptoms (Cayoun, 2003). It was then piloted in several clinical and community settings (e.g., Cayoun, Sauvage, & van Impe, 2004; Lindsay, 2007) and progressively modified until 2010, which led to the first publication of a comprehensive book on the principles and practice of MiCBT (Cayoun, 2011). Since then, the MiCBT approach has been studied across a range of disorders, age groups and contexts, as will be discussed in the next chapter, and only minimal adjustments have been necessary despite a wide range of applications. Clinician training in MiCBT has also been piloted through the supervision of numerous therapists undertaking courses in various countries since 2003.

In contrast with an increasing number of mindfulness-based interventions (MBIs) over the past 20 years, MiCBT was not derived from Jon Kabat-Zinn's (1990) Mindfulness Based Stress Reduction (MBSR) approach, which was not well-known outside America at the time. Rather than integrating an existing adaptation of the original teaching of mindfulness, MiCBT was independently composed of the core mechanisms underlying cognitive and behavioral therapies (Barlow, 2002; Beck, 1976; Hawton, Salkovskis, Kirk, & Clark, 1989) and traditional *Vipassana* (insight) meditation, taught in Northern India over 2500 years ago by Siddhartha Gautama, better known as the historical Buddha, who was also the prince of the Sakya province situated in current Southern Nepal. This doesn't mean that MiCBT is a "Buddhist" approach. It simply makes use of the profound phenomenological wisdom that the early teachers of mindfulness described in their approach to human psychology, henceforward referred to as "Buddhist psychology."

For most mindfulness-informed therapists, what makes the Buddha's story interesting is that he shunned a theistic approach (Hindu religion) and embraced a psychological perspective with the aim of reducing human suffering. The uniqueness of his approach was twofold: he only believed in verifiable and replicable phenomena and he only taught systematically applicable methods that showed evidence of efficacy in the reduction of human suffering. Of course, unlike today, the only means of gathering evidence then was through the direct experience of phenomena. Hence, the methods he taught were passed on through the science of phenomenology, which is the study of consciousness and the objects of one's direct experience through introspection.

The early pioneers of Western psychology were also known as "introspectionists." As with the Buddha's approach to psychology, they used introspection to examine the nature of consciousness and experiential phenomena. One of the fathers of Western psychology, the introspectionist William James, stated very similar realizations to those reported by the Buddha 2400 years earlier. Some of the most strikingly similar realizations found in James' seminal book *Principles of Psychology* (James, 1890), still commonly cited today, are that "A man's ME is the sum total of all that he can call his," and that "Thought is in constant change." These phenomenological realizations are not limited to Buddhist and modern Western psychologies, as many similar observations were made by Greek philosophers, especially Heraclitus, whose fundamental doctrine was that everything is in a state of flux, and that perpetual change is the fundamental nature of life. This understanding is not only shared by traditional teachers of mindfulness, it is also an important characteristic of human experience that mindfulness training helps us understand and accept.

Of note, Albert Ellis' Rational Emotive Behavior Therapy (REBT) has been frequently associated with elements of Buddhist philosophy, partly because of its common emphasis on unconditional self-acceptance. Ellis wrote that the approach of the Buddha and other ancient philosophers, which stated that "people are disturbed not by things but by their view of things", became the basis of REBT (Ellis & Drysden, 1997, p. 2). In the early days of MiCBT (then called MCBT), Henry Whitfield in the UK corresponded with one of us (BC) and saw much value in combining the basic elements of MiCBT with REBT, which resulted in a hybrid model of therapy combining these two approaches (Whitfield, 2006). Whitfield's mindfulness-based REBT seems to already be a common practice among REBT therapists (David, Lynn, & Lama Surya Das, 2013).

Over the past 17 years, the growth of MiCBT has been steady, and has been purposefully and carefully controlled because MiCBT was initially developed for clinical purposes, which necessarily places restrictions on who may use it and whom to use it with. Our understanding of professional ethics and our prudence with therapist training inclusion criteria made the overall research and dissemination of MiCBT slower than MBSR-based MBIs, which have historically been more compromising in this regard. One important point of the code of ethics for psychologists in Western countries is to abstain from teaching therapeutic methods to individuals who lack the professional background that enables them to use the methods safely and appropriately. We have remained continually aware of the importance of limiting access to MiCBT training courses to only those clinicians that have the appropriate professional qualifications and experience. We have also carefully monitored their levels of competency using MiCBT in clinical settings.

The first 10 years of research following MiCBT's initial piloting comprised a majority of convincing but unpublished research theses. Before the first book on MiCBT was published (Cayoun, 2011), we also discouraged MiCBT studies where the researchers were not formally trained in MiCBT because of the risk of poor implementation validity and low representativeness. MiCBT research is now blooming, including teams in India and Iran who have been industriously exploring the effects of MiCBT across a range of conditions, providing some indications of its transcultural efficacy.

Basic Principles

Approach to Learning

Learning from someone else can be engaging, but it relies on faith in another person's knowledge or experience and is limited to one's beliefs in someone else's view or knowledge. Our personal engagement in the learning process is minimal. In the therapy context, this would involve simply practicing the therapy methods that we have been taught without questioning their validity, just because we trust our teacher. People who train to be teachers of mindfulness are not immune to this exclusively devotional approach to learning. The same applies to clients, some of whom might engage in a mindfulness-based intervention because a friend, sibling or medical doctor they trust suggested it.

Critical thinking, on the other hand, requires more personal involvement in the process of learning. We question, verify the evidence beneath the assumed validity of a phenomenon, and eventually decide for ourselves on the basis of our findings. In the context of therapy, we verify whether the rationale for an approach makes sense, we may check the evidence in the literature, and ask questions with an open mind and healthy rationality. This learning process requires greater personal engagement than relying on faith and hearsay. Nonetheless, research evidence today is easily invalidated tomorrow. New findings cancel the previous, and what we thought made sense for a while has to be put into question; this is the nature of science and its evolution. The same applies to long-term clients, some of whom might have been told that a certain therapeutic approach was the "gold-star" evidence-based treatment 15 years ago and are now told that other treatment methods that lacked research backing 15 years ago have progressively been shown to be more efficacious than the original "gold star" treatment.

In contrast to belief and critical thinking, direct experience is by far the most personally engaging approach to learning, especially when learning about ourselves. During experiential learning, what is happening in the present moment is undeniably factual to a person; it is not hypothetical or based on others' experience. Meditation practice is the most profound and reliable method to learn about personal phenomena, including the experience of our sense of self. For this principal reason, therapists learning about MiCBT are required to meditate. However useful a manualized guide may be, it will not suffice for the successful implementation of MiCBT. Without our personal experience of what we teach our clients, it is very difficult to understand our clients' experiences during meditation and to guide them accurately. Again, the same applies to clients, many of whom are depressed or anxious because they have not had the benefit of directly experiencing rapid change in their symptoms by just noticing the ephemeral nature of experience, including that of profound sorrow or panic symptoms. It is through sitting quietly, observing objectively, and accepting the experience equanimously, that the ensuing relief teaches clients about the true nature of their predicament.

Approach to Therapy

Psychological therapies have been categorized in various groups of approaches (Corey, 1991). Among these, the "common factors" approach proposes that the efficacy of different approaches to therapy and counseling is enabled by factors that are inherent in all evidence-based therapies (e.g., Dollard & Miller, 1950). These factors include the therapeutic relationship, empathy, and active listening skills, but the factor that seems unequivocally present in effective therapies is learning (Tryon & Tryon, 2011). It has been proposed that mindfulness is also a common factor across various therapy approaches. Martin (1997, p. 291) has suggested that mindfulness is a "core psychotherapy process," on the basis that the development of mindfulness promotes access to new perspectives and disengagement from habitual response sets, including automatic thoughts and behavior. The "technical eclecticism" approach to therapy (e.g., Lazarus & Beutler, 1993) selects convenient techniques from various approaches, including mindfulness skills, according to the therapist's perception of the client's needs. This approach is inevitably limited by the client and therapist's insight into the origins and maintenance of symptoms. The "theoretical integration" approach to therapy (Norcross & Goldfried, 2005) aims at putting diverse theoretical systems together under a greater metatheoretical framework.

MiCBT uses a "theoretical integration" approach which incorporates the most central common factors, including learning, acceptance, self-awareness, disengagement from habitual response sets and therapeutic relationship. It is based on a multidisciplinary metatheoretical framework that integrates essential elements of Buddhist and Western psychologies into a single step-by-step manualized intervention. Specifically, MiCBT tightly weaves learning theory through the co-emergence model of reinforcement (Cayoun, 2011), cognitive and exposure techniques, affective and social neuroscience, the natural law of impermanence and its effects on one's sense of self, mindfulness, equanimity, and existential components through the theory of non-self directly experienced during mindfulness practice.

One advantage of working with a clinical intervention that is based on an established theory is that we operate from a clear understanding of mechanisms of action. We can then more easily understand and resolve difficulties commonly encountered in clinical practice. For instance, if the theory that we integrate in our therapy model is learning theory (operant conditioning; Skinner, 1953), we can easily case-conceptualize an unhelpful behavior and understand the maintaining or reinforcing factors at play, irrespective of the therapy techniques used. In contrast, an eclectic orientation tends to encourage using any potentially useful method from "our toolbox." The downside of this is an over-reliance on empirical findings with little understanding of how underlying mechanisms of action function to alter behavior. This can result in a lack of depth and grounding in the science underlying a therapeutic model.

The notion of theoretical integration lends itself to encouraging a scientist-practitioner approach to therapy. Being based on theory also prevents future modifications from jeopardizing the efficacy of the approach, since any model adaptation (e.g., for children) must remain in line with the underlying theoretical framework. As will be discussed in the next chapter, the central theoretical framework for MiCBT is the co-emergence model of reinforcement (Cayoun, 2011; Cayoun & Shires, submitted for publication), which is a neurophenomenological extension of operant conditioning. Although MiCBT is constructed with a tight integration of mindfulness and CBT, the level of integration varies according to the level of expertise. Our observation over years of providing professional training is that therapists initially tend to *juxtapose* CBT and mindfulness methods and perceive them as two different systems, and then *integrate* them and perceive them as various methods of the same system as their expertise increases.

Approach to Symptomatology

It is not easy for clients to understand that our mental and emotional difficulties arise not only from *within* our mind, but also because of our *attitude* toward our mind. As will be described in some detail in the next chapter, when we give thoughts personal importance, even subconsciously, body sensations co-emerge with them, quickly intensifying to produce an emotion, irrespective of the disorder. Mindfulness practice develops better understanding of these and other mental processes, so that the mechanisms, and not just the content, of cognition can be altered. The purpose for which mindfulness was taught over the past 2500 years is to develop the necessary wisdom to perceive, understand and abandon our tendency to maintain suffering, as well as to promote a sense of well-being. It is possible that this description differs from what your client may have previously read about mindfulness.

One of the fundamental needs for human beings is to grow and evolve. Unknowingly guided by suffering, people feel the need to change for the better. When we avoid discomfort, we miss the teachings inherent in suffering. Therapists are primarily students of suffering. They examine its multiple facets and their consequences, and eventually learn enough from it to develop means of reducing its unpleasant effects. What we mean by "suffering" is *an experience that leads to, or maintains, dissatisfaction or emotional reactivity following an unfulfilled expectation*. Buddhist psychology provides a profound understanding of suffering that supports the application of a transdiagnostic intervention. It helps us understand the common factors of suffering across all emotional disorders, as well as in life dissatisfaction in general. Human suffering can be divided into three types: (1) common suffering, such as physical pain and illness; (2) the effects of change; and (3) the effects of conditioning (Bodhi, 2000). Of course, these three types continually interact and cannot really be separated, but the way people learn and condition their mind is by far the most complex type to understand and is the principal reason for which they see a therapist.

It is useful to operationalize conditioned suffering in behavioral terms within the MiCBT theoretical framework, to demonstrate that the intervention is theoretically congruent with the problem. The *precipitating factor* (the trigger) for suffering is the fact that things change all the time, impacting all aspects of our life; this includes our sense of self, because of our attachment to our views, our senses, and our body and possessions. The *reinforcing factor* for suffering is our reactivity. Because of our attachments, we react with craving for the things we don't have and want, and we react with aversion to the things we don't want and have. As explained through the model of reinforcement in Chapter 2, our reactive behavior is positively reinforced when we obtain what we crave, and negatively reinforced when what we resent subsides. Our conditioned mind is extremely restricted by this ongoing, yet subconscious mental habit. As a consequence, our unawareness of these phenomena constitutes the principal *maintaining factor* for suffering because it prevents us from understanding these underlying mechanisms and correcting our habits accordingly.

Thus, the *mechanisms* of suffering, rather than their symptoms, form the transdiagnostic target of MiCBT. We make use of these mechanisms as a tool for growth, and not just "therapy," as will be explained in Part 2 of the book. Based on the understanding that unawareness can be replaced with insight, developing insight allows us to outgrow the factors of suffering. To the best of our knowledge, mindfulness is the most productive tool a therapist can offer clients to develop this kind of insight. Over the past 25 centuries, the main purpose of cultivating mindfulness through the long chain of traditional teachers, including our own, has been to develop insight and wisdom to alleviate suffering in people from all cultures and walks of life.

Approach to Comorbidity

It is now well-established that core mindfulness principles can be used for a wide range of symptoms and conditions (Keng, Smoski, & Robins, 2011). MiCBT was developed for clinical purposes as a transdiagnostic approach, partly to address the problem of comorbidity—between 60% and 85% of clinical cases contain one or more comorbid conditions, which makes diagnostic-specific therapies sub-optimal. Transdiagnostic interventions have recently been developed using exposure as the principal mechanism of action and are increasingly appealing to clinicians in general because they can address comorbidity more easily.

For instance, a standard diagnostic-specific therapy deemed efficacious to treat depression is not necessarily as useful when depressive symptoms are accompanied by panic or OCD symptoms. Transdiagnostic CBT is generally showing either equivalent or superior results to current evidence-based gold-standard diagnosis-specific CBT for most common anxiety disorders (Norton & Barrera, 2012), they tend to show a smaller dropout rate (Barlow et al., 2017), and the size of their effects is not affected by comorbidity (Pearl & Norton, 2017). Transdiagnostic interventions are also very useful in addressing barriers to the dissemination of evidence-based treatments. Thus, using one protocol instead of multiple single-disorder protocols can be a more effective way of treating most commonly occurring emotional disorders, and certainly easier to teach and learn.

Randomized controlled studies show that addressing crisis and comorbidity with MiCBT is possible when clients commit to sufficient frequency, duration and accuracy of mindfulness practice and integrate CBT skills, even in non-Western cultures (e.g., Bahrani, Zargar, Yousef-Ipour, & Akbari, 2017; Yazdanimehr, Omidi, Sadat, & Akbari, 2016). A brief review of MiCBT study outcomes is provided in Chapter 2.

Structure and Content of MiCBT: The Four Stages

MiCBT teaches mindfulness according to the original fourfold establishment of mindfulness (*Mahasatipatthana Sutta*; see Walshe, 2012, for translation), which includes mindfulness of body (posture and movement/physical activity), body sensations (including those associated with emotions), mental states (including emotional states) and mental content (thoughts, images, etc.) (Brahm, 2006; Hart, 1987; see also Thanissaro Bhikkhu, 2011, for a translation of the *Satipatthana Sutta*, and Goenka, 1990, for discourses and useful commentaries on the *Satipatthana Sutta*). Of course, MiCBT is not presented to clients as a "Buddhist approach," and this information is intended for you, the therapist, to know the components of MiCBT and their origins.

MiCBT is composed of four learning stages grouped into "internalizing" and "externalizing" phases that enable change at a systemic level. The stages are designed to develop mindfulness, cognitive and behavioral skill-sets across the main domains of functioning: intrapersonal ("personal stage"), situational ("exposure stage"), interpersonal ("interpersonal stage"), and transpersonal ("empathic stage"), typically denoted as Stages 1, 2, 3, and 4, respectively. The stages are usually delivered hierarchically, although the program can be delivered more flexibly when necessary. The purpose of this hierarchical integration is first to teach clients to internalize attention in order to regulate attention and emotion, and then externalize these skills to the contexts in which their psychological condition is triggered or maintained.

As will be discussed in Chapter 3, MiCBT is used in individual and group therapy with equivalent clinical efficacy (Roubos, Hawkins, & Cayoun, 2011) and usually requires between eight and twelve sessions for effective treatment of most emotional and behavioral disorders, but at least twice as long for moderately

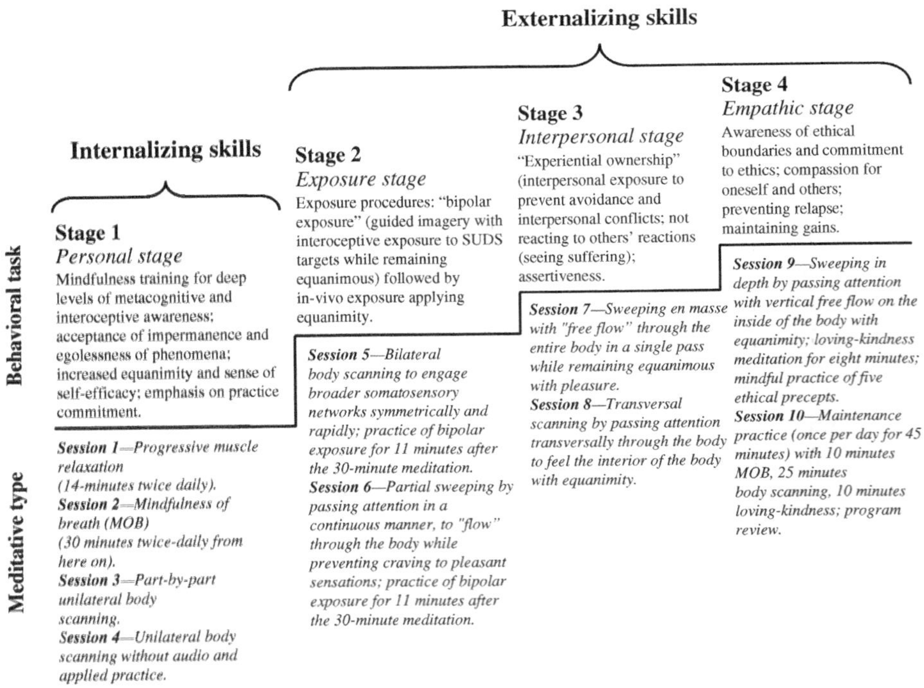

Figure 1.1 The four-stage model of Mindfulness-integrated Cognitive Behavior Therapy. (Adapted from Cayoun, 2011.)

severe personality disorders—though there are no controlled studies confirming the ideal program duration and long-term efficacy of MiCBT for personality disorders. Let us now examine the stages in some detail. Figure 1.1 summarizes the four stages of MiCBT within a typical 10-session format, which is also the delivery model through which you will be guided in Part 2 of this book. Note that this schedule is only an approximate indication of standard delivery. Each stage can be extended for a longer duration, depending on the patient's needs and requirements for progressing to the next stage.

Stage 1: Personal Stage: Attention and Emotion Regulation

In Stage 1, mindfulness meditation training is taught to internalize attention in a way that decreases emotional reactivity and promotes deep levels of experiential awareness and acceptance. An emphasis is placed on the internal context of experience to equip clients with an increased sense of agency and self-efficacy in handling thoughts and emotions before addressing the life difficulties for which they sought therapy.

Following standard intake assessment and contractual agreement on therapeutic goals (described in Session 1; see Part 2 of the book), clients begin with the practice of progressive muscle relaxation (PMR) and mindfulness of body posture and movement. Besides its potential relaxing effect, PMR provides an initial and reassuring sense of agency over stress-related muscle tension, which assists in reinforcing the client's initial effort to commit to a daily practice. However, PMR is only used for the first week in most cases, as a preparatory measure. This is because clients can inadvertently use relaxation as a means of experiential avoidance, which is incompatible with the aims and acceptance-based features of mindfulness. Mindfulness of body (posture and movements) in daily actions introduces the notion of present-moment awareness, which is a relatively easy introduction to mindfulness principles and practice, as commonly used in other integrations, such as Dialectical Behavior Therapy (Linehan, 1993).

Clients are then taught to practice mindfulness of breath (described in Session 2) for one to two weeks and basic (unilateral) body scanning for the following two weeks (described in Session 3 and Session 4). People who use these methods show an increased ability to detect and withstand distress, which leads progressively to brain reorganization in just a few weeks, both in grey matter (Hölzel et al., 2011) and white matter (Tang, Lu, Fan, Yang, & Posner, 2012). Increased efficacy of self-regulation networks produced by neuroplasticity provides an invaluable biological apparatus to facilitate emotion regulation during exposure tasks implemented in the following stages (exposure and interpersonal stages).

For instance, imaging research using functional MRI shows that mindfulness of breath can produce a generalized reduction in amygdala response to emotional stimuli that is maintained during non-meditative states (Desbordes et al., 2012). Anatomical MRI also shows rapid decrease in grey matter volume of the right basolateral amygdala during a standard eight-week MBSR program (Hölzel et al., 2010). The emphasis on interoception as the locus of reinforcement places body-scanning methods at the heart of twice-daily MiCBT practice. This is partly because interoceptive awareness and acceptance are central to the Vipassana approach to mindfulness training (Hart, 1987; Kerr et al., 2013), and partly because the last 15 years of affective and cognitive science have reliably shown that people with emotional disorders have impaired interoceptive capacity; i.e., a reduced ability to feel common body sensations (Khalsa et al., 2017). The effort to decrease the habit of identifying with moment-to-moment experience trains clients to process information in a less self-referential, more objective manner (Farb et al., 2010), as will be discussed in the next chapter.

To maximize training efficacy, clients learn to adhere to three fundamental practice principles: *sufficient frequency* (usually twice daily), *sufficient duration* (usually 30-minutes per session) and *sufficient accuracy* of practice (conscious effort to decrease identification with, and reacting to, emerging experiences). MiCBT research shows that clients who adhere to this protocol benefit most (e.g., Scott-Hamilton & Schutte, 2016). The first two principles permit the third, which specifically increases equanimity by reducing the need to react with craving or aversion, irrespective of the type of experience. Generalizing awareness and acceptance of thoughts and body sensations in everyday situations occurs as a spontaneous consequence of neuroplasticity.

In addition, clients are taught to apply equanimity in daily life. They learn to monitor body sensations as continually as possible in everyday situations and identify typical patterns of sensations experienced during stressful events while increasing their capacity to prevent learned responses (i.e., via increased equanimity). Hence, interoceptive awareness, developed during formal meditation practice, becomes a skillful means for preventing the reinforcement of unhelpful reactive habits in daily life. In chapter 2, we will cover the theory underpinning MiCBT and the crucial relevance of interoception and the reasons for surveying ("scanning") the body during mindfulness meditation to develop equanimity.

Stage 1 requires between three and five weeks (typically four weeks), depending on personal and clinical factors, such as symptom severity and adherence to treatment. Normalizing and psychoeducation about potential early difficulties of mindfulness practice are important at this early stage; these are discussed throughout the first four sessions in Part 2 of the book. Completion of Stage 1 is largely determined by enhanced interoceptive awareness and equanimity during practice and a better sense of agency in daily life. Clients must have developed a reliable ability to accept and "stay with" (expose to) most types of body sensations with some equanimity (i.e., the tendency to avoid aversive experiences is markedly decreased). Accordingly, clients are invited to start Stage 2 as soon as they can feel sensations in about 80 % of the body. They also begin to learn more efficient (faster and more global) ways of scanning the body, as taught by the Burmese *Vipassana* tradition, and develop ability for rapid distress-cue detection. The detailed delivery is in Session 3 and Session 4 of the book.

Stage 2: Exposure Stage: Behavioral Regulation

Meditating well, even for long periods, does not necessarily translate to behavior change when avoidance habits are well-established (see Toneatto & Nguyen, 2007, for a review of controlled research). For example, personal isolation when sitting with closed eyes on a cushion may be relieving or even pleasurable for socially anxious or avoidant clients, but in and of itself may not result in skill transfer allowing them to confront fears in social contexts. Stage 2 is the first "externalizing" stage, during which attention is partly directed outward to regulate behavior by applying Stage 1 skills (interoceptive awareness and equanimity) in contexts of avoidance. Clients learn to remain "equanimous" with external targets to extinguish their conditioned avoidance of stressful situations. Hence, mindfulness skills are now at the service of CBT, and CBT skills are used to extend mindfulness skills in contexts of avoidance.

There is neurological evidence that mindfulness meditation in novices produces a down-regulation of the left amygdala during emotional processing (Farb et al., 2015; Hölzel et al, 2010), and that the progressive acquisition of mindfulness skills induces a deactivation of brain areas associated with self-referential processing called the "default mode network" (medial prefrontal and posterior cingulate cortices) across all induced emotions (Taylor et al., 2011). Increasing one's ability to deactivate the default mode network (i.e., taking things less personally) is a function of one's ability to not identify with the experience, which in turn increases one's ability to extinguish a learned response. These findings are in line with the imagery-based exposure method called "bipolar exposure," which is the first procedure used with clients during Stage 2. The term "bipolar" in this context means two extreme poles; it has nothing to do with bipolar depression. Bipolar exposure is an MiCBT-specific technique based on interoceptive desensitization that lasts about 11 minutes. It is implemented following each 30-minute practice of mindfulness meditation for two days (i.e., four times) prior to commencing exposure *in vivo*.

Once the client has identified a set of varied avoided situations and listed them hierarchically as a function of subjective units (percentage) of distress, they begin the practice of bipolar exposure. This consists of imagining the worst-case scenarios that could happen when *in vivo* exposure takes place while remaining equanimous, and then repeat the procedure with best-case scenarios. This is fully described in Part 2 of the book (Session 5 and Session 6). Because interoception (feeling body sensations) is considered to be the locus of reinforcement in MiCBT (Cayoun, 2011; Cayoun & Shires, submitted for publication), exposure is applied to body sensations co-emerging with the imagined unpleasant and pleasant scenarios. As a result, bipolar exposure helps reduce the intensity of learned aversion and craving before exposure *in vivo* commences. Exposure to neutralize negative as well as positive expectations is important in order to develop equanimity, irrespective of the outcome—hence "bipolar" exposure.

Stage 2 is usually implemented over two to three weeks across a list of avoided situations, depending on client needs and commitment. Because exposure is also directed to body sensations during exposure *in vivo*, the increase in distress tolerance transfers to multiple unrelated situations that would habitually lead to some avoidance. This phenomenon of generalization and the entire procedure are explained in detail in Session 5 and Session 6. Thus, Stage 2 makes exposure non-context-specific. It helps generalize self-confidence and, as emphasized in the Acceptance and Commitment Therapy approach (Hayes et al., 1999), it helps clients follow their valued directions.

Stage 3: Interpersonal Stage: Interpersonal Regulation

For a therapeutic approach to be transdiagnostic, it needs to address interpersonal dynamics. There is evidence that amygdala volumes correlate with the size and complexity of social networks in adults, and this association does not seem to be present for other subcortical structures (Bickart, Wright, Dautoff, Dickerson, & Feldman Barrett, 2011). Neuroplasticity research also shows evidence that post-institutionalized children with distressing early childhood experiences who had been adopted at about 15 months of age showed larger amygdala volumes and decreased volumes in the hippocampus and prefrontal cortex eight years later (Davidson & McEwen, 2012). This further demonstrates that exposure to aversive social influences leads to developing a more emotionally reactive brain configuration. Moreover, socially driven neuroplasticity may be an important factor for personality development in childhood that may persists well into adulthood.

Although some clients will need more interpersonal skills than others, the social network of clients with chronic conditions or personality disorders is generally negatively affected by the client's symptoms. These include social withdrawal and other avoidant behavior, low mood, lack of motivation, agitation and reactivity, anxiety and addictive behavior. The sense of disconnectedness during and following an episode of emotional disturbance can be a maintaining factor for maladaptive behavior, such as substance abuse, and often precipitates relapse. In addition, the client's lack of social intelligence (Goleman, 2006) may also be a precipitating factor for crises. As we often hear in clinical practice, poor interpersonal boundaries, seeking validation in the wrong context or in destructive ways, reinforcing guilt about one's needs or one's rights, or using a passive/aggressive style of communication, often contribute to the client's interpersonal difficulties. Hence, the next stage of MiCBT employs mindfulness skills to cultivate interpersonal insight and interpersonal regulation.

Stage 3 of MiCBT requires externalizing mindful attention further towards others by dividing the focus of attention between self and others. In the first week of Stage 3, clients learn a mindfulness-based interpersonal skill called "experiential ownership" which uses a form of exposure to understand and accept others' ways of communicating and reacting. Clients learn to inhibit their value-based judgments by considering others' emotional experiences non-judgmentally and by not reacting to others' reactivity. Clients apply Stage 1 and Stage 2 skills during communication with others, knowing that others' emotional reactivity is a function of their lack of awareness and skill in managing body sensations. Recent behavioral and brain studies provide evidence that the experience of body sensations activates approach-avoidance behavior independently of what we may be thinking consciously (Krieglmeyer, Deutch, De Houwer, & De Raedt, 2010; Rogers-Carter et al., 2018). Clients learn to "see suffering" in others, rather than judge them for their reactions.

In the second (and perhaps the third) week of Stage 3, clients learn to combine assertive communication with experiential ownership and mindfulness skills in as many situations as possible (two at the very least). Awareness of interpersonal boundaries and assertiveness skills are more likely to develop if the client is able to contain his or her own arousal and is able to allow time for the other's reactivity to diffuse. Hence, mindfulness skills are again at the service of CBT. The detailed procedure for Stage 3 is explained in Session 7 and Session 8.

Stage 4: Empathic Stage: Transpersonal Insight and Relapse Prevention

One of the most common experiences shared by clients with an emotional, behavioral or personality disorder is a sense of separation from others. This may be in the form of feeling (or fear of being) judged, avoided, rejected or unloved by others, or through being uninterested in connecting with others and avoiding them. Sometimes, this is associated with a sense of lack of purpose. The result of such disconnectedness is a lack of perceived well-being and an increased probability of relapse. Stage 4 of MiCBT extends Stage 3 skills to a more global awareness of how we can overcome the perpetuation of unnecessary suffering and influence each other for the better. Stage 4 promotes self-acceptance and compassion, which helps clients to reduce their tendency to overidentify with their experiences and increase their ability to accept their perceived shortcomings and distress. In so doing, Stage 4 assists in the prevention of relapse. Through normalizing suffering in terms of it being a human condition, rather than a personal flaw or misfortune, clients learn to minimize unhelpful judgments about themselves and others and develop a sense of connectedness within themselves and with others. They do so by producing wholesome and pleasant mental states, such as kindness and compassion, rather than focusing solely on decreasing destructive emotions.

There is behavioral and neurological evidence that compassion can be learned through meditation practice (e.g., Jazaieri et al., 2012; Lutz, Brefczynski-Lewis, Johnstone, & Davidson, 2008). There is also evidence that becoming more compassionate helps clients remain more resilient when exposed to common stressors (Neff, Kirkpatrick, & Rude, 2007). In particular, people who learn to adopt a more self-compassionate perspective seem to be more able to acknowledge their role in negative events without feeling overwhelmed with emotions, and can more easily attenuate their reactions (Leary et al., 2007). This stage of MiCBT teaches empathic skills grounded in bodily experience and in genuine respect for ethical boundaries in daily actions.

Stage 4 of MiCBT is usually delivered over two weeks. In the first week, clients are taught "Loving-Kindness" meditation (*metta bhavana* in Pali), which has been taught as part of mindfulness training ever since mindfulness has been a feature of Buddhist teachings (Hart, 1987; Salzberg, 1995). It combines a set of simple positive affirmations that are paired with the pleasant body sensations produced by advanced body-scanning methods to create or enhance compassion toward oneself and others. This includes (but is not restricted to) producing thoughts of acceptance while pairing pleasant body sensations with memories of people with whom clients may have been in conflict or with whom they expect to be in conflict in the future, in a way that acts as a counterconditioning method. The practice lasts approximately eight minutes and is performed at the end of each mindfulness meditation session. Hutcherson, Seppala and Gross (2008) demonstrated that just a few minutes of loving-kindness meditation can increase one's sense of social connectedness on both explicit and implicit levels, which may help decrease social isolation. The implementation and practice of loving-kindness meditation are explained in Session 9.

Moreover, in traditional teachings of mindfulness, taking mindfulness training without initially committing to ethical conduct is simply inconceivable. It is theoretically unsound and technically unsuccessful (see Cayoun, 2017, for comprehensive discussion). Indeed, in the therapy context, actions that are harmful to oneself or others tend to maintain or reinforce an existing psychological condition and are counterproductive to therapy. Taking this into account, the second week of Stage 4 teaches clients to materialize their sense of connectedness and empathy with others through making an effort to prevent harm to themselves and others. Note that this is done out of compassion, rather than being based on culture, religious duty or guilt. Whereas empathy involves sensing other people's emotions and imagining what they could be thinking or feeling, compassion involves "*the will to extend oneself for the purpose of minimizing one's own or another's suffering*" (Cayoun, 2017, p. 177). Compassion can be experienced through a genuine *intention* and propensity for action, or through a fully-fledged *action* if the intention is sufficiently intense. Other program developers, such as our colleagues Drs Lynette Monteiro and Frank Musten at the Ottawa Mindfulness Clinic, have made mindfulness-based ethical training and compassion the essence of their program (Monteiro & Musten, 2013).

In MiCBT, clients develop compassion by "grounding" their developing empathy for others into ethical awareness, performing ethical actions and preventing unethical ones for an entire week as a behavioral experiment. Specifically, clients are asked to pay effortful attention to their motivation in daily actions to prevent harmful intentions and actions toward themselves and others, including basic acts such as using deceitful and other types of harmful speech, taking what is not given, intoxicating, performing harmful sexual acts, and taking lives (e.g., killing insects). These are presented as experiments and a means of education, rather than as a dogmatic moral protocol. Clients are asked to monitor body sensations co-emerging with harmful intentions preceding harmful actions, examine the nature of the sensations, inhibit the learned response (craving or aversion), let the sensations pass in their own right, and acknowledge that their conscious effort has successfully prevented harm. This procedure is explained in some detail in Session 9.

Clients are also asked to keep a record of such effort and how it made them feel about themselves, and the type of influence that this effort may have had on their environment. As clients learn to generate helpful thoughts and perform worthwhile actions out of compassion, they gradually internalize their locus of self-worth. Since there is less reliance on external factors in order to feel worthy and deserving of acceptance from others, the likelihood of relapse is lessened. Clinicians often report that clients make decisions regarding significant life changes during Stage 4, often mentioning that they now value their life and happiness more. Thus, the probability of relapse is further reduced.

Stage Structure

There is evidence to suggest that the ordering of the four stages in their current format is an advantage. For example, an electroencephalographic investigation of prefrontal alpha-asymmetry in previously depressed individuals showed that responses to type of meditation (mindfulness of breath and loving-kindness) was moderated by the degree of ruminative brooding (Barnhofer, Chittka, Nightingale, Visser, & Crane, 2010). Although both forms of meditation practice had beneficial effects on prefrontal alpha-asymmetry, individuals high in ruminative brooding tended to respond to mindfulness of breath (taught in Stage 1 of MiCBT) but not loving-kindness meditation (taught in Stage 4), whereas those low in ruminative brooding showed the opposite pattern. Another study, with novice meditators, showed that participants in the mindfulness-of-breath condition reported greater ability to not identify with emerging thoughts relative to loving-kindness meditation (Feldman, Greeson, & Senville, 2010). Moreover, people in the loving-kindness condition showed more repetitive thoughts and negative reactions to thoughts than those in the mindfulness-of-breath condition.

Both these studies support the view that clients who ruminate need to develop skills to address unhelpful thoughts first, before being able to benefit from producing more helpful ones, such as those produced by loving-kindness meditation. Since the majority of the clients we see in clinical practice ruminate, the MiCBT program places mindfulness of breath earlier and loving-kindness meditation later, once skillful means to address ruminative and other unhelpful thoughts have been developed. Although the sequential positioning of core CBT skills across the stages is based on their level of complexity (Stage 2 skills are less complex to learn than Stage 3 skills), this order of implementation has not been specifically researched.

We propose that the four-stage conceptualization of MiCBT has two significant advantages: (1) it permits a systemic application of mindfulness and CBT methods, and (2) facilitates a transdiagnostic application that helps address comorbidity. This broad development and application of skills is more likely to target the varied factors contributing to a client's condition, across life domains and symptomatology.

References

Bahrani, S., Zargar, F., Yousef-Ipour, G., & Akbari, H. (2017). The effectiveness of mindfulness-integrated cognitive behavior therapy on depression, anxiety, and stress in females with multiple sclerosis: A single blind randomized controlled trial. *Iranian Red Crescent Medical Journal*. e44566. doi:10.5812/ircmj.44566

Barlow, D. H. (2002). *Anxiety and its disorders: The nature and treatment of anxiety and panic* (2nd ed.). New York: Guilford Press.

Barlow, D. H., Farchione, T. J., Bullis, J. R., Gallagher, M. W., Murray-Latin, H., Sauer-Zavala, S., ...& Cassiello-Robbins, C. (2017). The unified protocol for transdiagnostic treatment of emotional disorders compared with diagnosis-specific protocols for anxiety disorders: A randomized clinical trial. *JAMA Psychiatry*, 74, 875–884. doi:10.1001/jamapsychiatry.2017.2164.

Barnhofer, T., Chittka, T., Nightingale, H., Visser, C., & Crane, C. (2010). State effects of two forms of meditation on prefrontal EEG asymmetry in previously depressed individuals. *Mindfulness*. doi:10.1007/s12671-010-0004-7

Beck, A. T. (1976). *Cognitive therapy and the emotional disorders*. New York: International University Press.

Bickart, K. C., Wright, C. I., Dautoff, R. J., Dickerson, B. C., & Feldman Barrett, L. (2011). Amygdala volume and social network size in humans. *Nature Neuroscience*,14, 163–164.

Bodhi, B. (2000). *The connected discourses of the Buddha: A translation of the Samyutta Nikaya*. Boston: Wisdom Publications.

Brahm, A. (2006). *Mindfulness, bliss, and beyond: A meditator's handbook*. Boston, MA: Wisdom Publications.

Cayoun, B. A. (2003). Advances in mindfulness training integration: Towards a non-dualistic Cognitive Behaviour Therapy. *Newsletter of the Australian Psychological Society*, 2, 6–10.

Cayoun, B. A. (2011). *Mindfulness-integrated CBT: Principles and practice*. Chichester, UK: Wiley.

Cayoun, B. A. (2017). The purpose, mechanisms, and benefits of cultivating ethics in Mindfulness-integrated Cognitive Behavior Therapy. In L. M. Monteiro, J. Compson, & F. Musten (Eds.) *Practitioner's guide to ethics and Mindfulness-Based Interventions*, pp. 163–192. Cham: Springer. doi:10.1007/978-3-319-64924-5_7

Cayoun, B. A., Sauvage, V., & Van Impe, M. (2004). A non-diagnosis-specific application of Mindfulness-based Cognitive-Behaviour Therapy: A pilot study. *Annual report to The Hobart Clinic*. Rokeby, TAS, Australia (available from the first author, see also Cayoun, 2011, for a summary of transdiagnostic effects).

Cayoun, B. A., & Shires, A. (submitted for publication). Co-emergence reinforcement: A proposed transdiagnostic mechanism in emotional disorders and their remediation through mindfulness and cognitive-behavioral interventions. Manuscript submitted for publication.

Corey, G. (1991). *Theory and practice of counselling and psychotherapy* (4th ed.). Belmont, CA: Brooks/Cole.

David, D., Steven, J. L., Das, L. S. (2013). Self-acceptance in Buddhism and psychotherapy. In M. E. Bernard (Ed.), *The strength of self-acceptance: Theory, practice and research*. Cham: Springer. doi: 10.1007/978-1-4614-6806-6_2

Davidson, R. J., & McEwen, B. S. (2012). Social influences on neuroplasticity: Stress and interventions to promote well-being. *Nature Neuroscience*, 15, 689–695.

Desbordes, G., Gard, T., Hoge, E. A., Hölzel, B. K., Kerr, C., Lazar, S. W., Vago, D. R. (2015). Moving beyond mindfulness: Defining equanimity as an outcome measure in meditation and contemplative research. *Mindfulness*, 6, 356–372. doi:10.1007/s12671-013-0269-8

Desbordes, G., Negi, L., T., Pace, T. W. W., Wallace, B. A., Raison, C. L., Schwartz, E. L. (2012). Effects of mindful-attention and compassion meditation training on amygdala response to emotional stimuli in an ordinary, non-meditative state. *Frontiers in Human Neuroscience*, 6, doi:10.3389/fnhum.2012.00292

Dollard, J., & Miller, N. E. (1950). *Personality and psychotherapy: An analysis in terms of learning, thinking, and culture. McGraw-Hill publications in psychology*. New York: McGraw-Hill.

Ellis, A., & Dryden, W. (1997). *The practice of rational emotive behavior therapy* (2nd ed.). New York: Springer.

Farb, N. A. S., Anderson, A. K., Mayberg, H., Bean, J., McKeon, D., & Segal, Z. V. (2010). Minding one's emotions: Mindfulness training alters the neural expression of sadness. *Emotion*, 10, 25–33.

Feldman, G., Greeson, J., & Senville, J. (2010). Differential effects of mindful breathing, progressive muscle relaxation, and loving-kindness meditation on decentering and negative reactions to repetitive thoughts. *Behaviour Research and Therapy*, 48, 1002–1011.

Gethin, R. M. L. (1992). *The Buddhist path to awakening: A study of the Bodhi-Pakkhiȳa Dhammā. BRILL's Indological Library*, 7. Leiden and New York: Brill.

Goenka, S. N. (1990). *Discourses on Satipatthana Sutta*. Igatpuri, India: Vipassana Research Institute. Retrieved online from: http://www.vridhamma.org/Printversion/Discourses-on-Satipatthana-Sutta (accessed February 7, 2018).

Goenka, S. N. (2000). *The discourse summaries: Talks from a ten-day course in Vipassana meditation condensed by William Hart*. Onalaska, WA: Vipassana Research Publications.

Goleman, D. (2006). *Social intelligence: The new science of human relationships*. New York: Bantam Dell.

Hart, W. (1987). *The art of living: Vipassana meditation as taught by S. N. Goenka*. New York: Harper Collins.

Hawton, K., Salkovskis, P. M., Kirk, J., & Clark, D. M. (Eds) (1989). *Cognitive Behaviour Therapy for psychiatric problems: A practical guide*. New York: Oxford University Press.

Holzel, B. K., Carmody, J., Vangel, M., Congleton, C., Yerramsetti, S. M., Gard, T., & Lazar, S. W. (2011). Mindfulness practice leads to increases in regional brain grey matter density. *Psychiatry Research*, 191, 36–43.

Holzel, B. K., Carmody, J., Evans, K. C., Hoge, E. A., Dusek, J. A., Morgan, L., …& Lazar, S. W. (2010). Stress reduction correlates with structural changes in the amygdala. *Social Cognitive and Affective Neuroscience*, 5, 11–17.

Hutcherson, C. A., Seppala, E. M., & Gross, J. J. (2008). Loving kindness meditation increases social connectedness. *Emotion*, 8, 720–724.

James, W. (1890). *The principles of psychology*. New York: Holt.

Jazaieri, H., Geshe Thupten Jinpa, McGonigal, K., Rosenberg, E. L., Finkelstein, J., Simon-Thomas, E., & Goldin, P. R. (2012). Enhancing compassion: A randomized controlled trial of a compassion cultivation training program. *Journal of Happiness Studies*. doi:10.1007/s10902-012-9373-z

Kabat-Zinn, J. (1990). *Full catastrophe living: The program of the Stress-Reduction Clinic at the University of Massachusetts Medical Center*. New York: Delta.

Keng, S., Smoski, M. J., & Robins, C. J. (2011). Effects of mindfulness on psychological health: A review of empirical studies. *Clinical Psychology Review*, 31, 1041–1056. doi:10.1016/j.cpr.2011.04.006

Kerr, C. E., Sachet, M. D., Lazar, S. W., Moore, C. I., Jones, S. R. (2013). Mindfulness starts with the body: Somatosensory attention and top-down modulation of cortical alpha rhythms in mindfulness meditation. *Frontiers in Neuroscience*, 12. doi: 10.3389/fnhum.2013.00012

Khalsa, S. S., Adolphs, R., Cameron, O. G., Critchley, H. D., Davenport, P. W., Feinstein, J. S., ... & Interoception Summit 2016 Participants. (2017). Interoception and mental health: A roadmap. *Biological Psychiatry: Cognitive Neuroscience and Neuroimaging*. doi:10.1016/j.bpsc.2017.12.004

Krieglmeyer, R., Deutch, R., De Houwer, J., & De Raedt, R. (2010). Being moved: Valence activates approach-avoidance behavior independent of evaluation and approach-avoidance intentions. *Psychological Science*, 21, 607–613. doi:10.1177/0956797610365131

Lazarus, A. A., & Beutler, L. E. (1993). On technical eclectism. *Journal of Counselling and Development*, 71, 381–385.

Leary, M. R., Tate, E. B., Adams, C. E., Batts Allen, A., & Hancock, J. (2007). Self-compassion and reactions to unpleasant self-relevant events: The implications of treating oneself kindly. *Journal of Personality and Social Psychology*, 92, 887–904.

Lindsay, M. (2007). *Mindfulness-integrated Cognitive Behaviour Therapy: A pilot program for developing Mindfulness-based self-efficacy and self-compassion for people with type 2 diabetes mellitus*. Unpublished Master Thesis, The University of Auckland, New Zealand.

Linehan, M. M. (1993). *Cognitive-behavioral treatment of borderline personality disorder*. New York: Guilford Press.

Lutz, A., Brefczynski-Lewis, J., Johnstone, T., & Davidson, R. J. (2008). Regulation of the neural circuitry of emotion by compassion meditation: Effects of meditative practice. *PLoS ONE*, 3, e1897.

Martin, J. R. (1997). Mindfulness: A proposed common factor. *Journal of Psychotherapy Integration*, 7, 291–312.

Monteiro, L., & Musten, F. (2013). *Mindfulness starts here: An eight-week guide to skillful living*. BC, Canada: Friesen Press.

Narada Mahathera (1988). *The Buddha and his teachings* (3rd ed.). Kandi, Sri Lanka: Buddhist Publication Society.

Neff, K. D., Kirkpatrick, K. L., & Rude, S. S. (2007). Self-compassion and adaptive psychological functioning. *Journal of Research in Personality*, 41, 139–154.

Norcross, J. C., & Goldfried, M. R. (2005). *Handbook of psychotherapy integration* (2nd ed.). New York: Oxford University Press.

Norton, P. J., & Barrera, T. L. (2012). Transdiagnostic versus diagnosis-specific CBT for anxiety disorders: A preliminary randomized controlled non-inferiority trial. *Depression and Anxiety*, 29, 874–882. doi:10.1002/da.21974

Pearl, S. B., & Norton, P. J. (2017). Transdiagnostic versus diagnosis specific cognitive behavioural therapies for anxiety: A meta-analysis. *Journal of Anxiety Disorders*, 46, 11–24. doi:10.1016/j.janxdis.2016.07.004

Proust, M. (1923). *Remembrance of things past: La Prisonnière* (Vol. 5). Paris: Gallimard.

Rahula, W. (1974). *What the Buddha taught* (Revised ed.). New York: Grove Press.

Rhys Davids, T. W. (1881). *Buddhist Suttras*. Oxford: Clarendon Press.

Rogers-Carter, M. M., Varela, J. A., Grobbons, K. B., Pierce, A. F., McGoey, M. T., Ritchey, M., & Christianson, J. P. (2018). Insular cortex mediates approach and avoidance responses to social affective stimuli. *Nature Neuroscience*. doi:10.1038/s41593-018-0071-y

Roubos, L., Hawkins, R., & Cayoun, B. A. (2011). *A comparison of group-enhanced and individual implementations of Mindfulness-integrated Cognitive Behaviour Therapy (MiCBT): An effectiveness study*. Unpublished Master Dissertation, James Cook University, Cairns, Australia.

Salzberg, S. (1995). *Loving-kindness: The revolutionary art of happiness*. Boston, MA: Shambala.
Scott-Hamilton, J., & Schutte, N. S. (2016). The role of adherence in the effects of a mindfulness intervention for competitive athletes: Changes in mindfulness, flow, pessimism and anxiety. *Journal of Clinical Sport Psychology*, 10, 99–117. Doi:10.1123/jcsp.2015-0020
Sharf, R. (2014). Mindfulness and Mindlessness in Early Chan. *Philosophy East and West*, 64, 933–964. doi:10.1353/pew.2014.0074.
Skinner, B. F. (1953). *Science and human behavior*. London: Collier-Macmillan.
Tang, Y., Lu, Q., Fan, M., Yang, Y., & Posner, M. I. (2012). Mechanisms of white matter changes induced by meditation. *PNAS*, 109, 10570–10574.
Taylor, V. A., Grant, J., Daneault, V., Scavone, G., Breton, E., Roffe-Vidal, S., & Beauregard, M. (2011). Impact of mindfulness on the neural responses to emotional pictures in experienced and beginner meditators. *Neuroimage*, 57, 1524–1533.
Toneatto, T., & Nguyen, L. (2007). Does mindfulness meditation improve anxiety and mood symptoms? A review of the controlled research. *Canadian Journal of Psychiatry*, 52, 260–266.
Tryon, W. W., & Tryon, G. S. (2011). No ownership of common factors. *American Psychologist*, 66, 151–152. doi:10.1037/a0021056.
Thanissaro Bhikkhu (2011). *Maha-satipatthana Sutta: The great frame of reference (DN 22)*, translated from Pali by the author. Access to Insight. Retrieved online from http://www.accesstoinsight.org/tipitaka/dn/dn.22.0.than.html (accessed 20 January 2018).
Walshe, M. (2012). *The long discourses of the Buddha: A translation of the Digha Nikaya*. Boston: Wisdom Publications.
Whitfield, H. J. (2006). Towards case-specific applications of mindfulness-based cognitive behavioural therapies: A mindfulness-based rational emotive behaviour therapy. *Counselling Psychology Quarterly*, 19, 205–217.
Yazdanimehr, R., Omidi, A., Sadat, Z., & Akbari, H. (2016). The effect of mindfulness-integrated cognitive behavior therapy on depression and anxiety among pregnant women: a randomized clinical trial. *Journal of Caring Sciences*, 5, 195–204. doi:10.15171/jcs.2016.021

2

Theoretical Framework and Empirical Findings

If we fancy some strong emotion and then try to abstract from our consciousness of it all the feelings of its characteristics of bodily symptoms, we find we have nothing left behind, no "mind–stuff" out of which the emotion can be constituted, and that a cold and neutral state of intellectual perception is all that remains.

—William James, 1884

This chapter describes the co-emergence model of reinforcement, which is the principal theoretical foundation of Mindfulness-integrated Cognitive Behavior Therapy (MiCBT). We contextualize this underlying theoretical framework within the clinical domain to emphasize the importance of focusing treatment on present experience, and demonstrate how doing so yields more ecological validity and clinical benefit than contemplating the origins of psychopathology in order to better understand it. The chapter also provides a summary of the empirical evidence supporting the clinical and subclinical applications of MiCBT across a range of conditions.

Over the past 20 years, there has been an extraordinary exponential growth in mindfulness research publications, with over 3000 studies published, as shown in Figure 2.1. During this short period, mindfulness studies have been carried out in numerous life domains, including emotional processes, general and mental health across age groups, pain management, sleep, memory and age-related cognitive decline, personality and attitude, parenting skills and attachment issues, teaching and learning competence, brain mapping and neuroplasticity, DNA, and workplace and organizational contexts. The list is too large and references are too numerous to be mentioned here. This enthusiasm for mindfulness research and applications is not due to a single factor or person. Rather, it seems that rapid technological advances enable us to relate scientifically to what may have been in gestation for a while. Some authors refer to it as "the mindfulness revolution" (Boyce, 2011).

The Clinical Handbook of Mindfulness-integrated Cognitive Behavior Therapy: A Step-by-Step Guide for Therapists, First Edition. Bruno A. Cayoun, Sarah E. Francis, and Alice G. Shires.

Companion website: www.wiley.com/go/Cayoun/Mindfulness-integrated

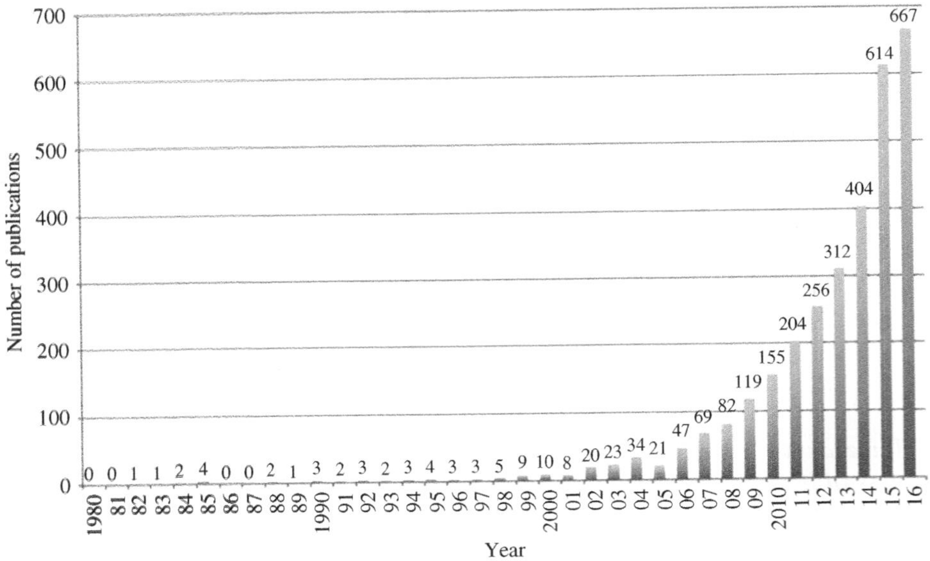

Figure 2.1 Exponential growth rate in mindfulness research over the past 20 years. (Source: © American Mindfulness Research Association. Reproduced with permission.)

The Co-emergence Model of Reinforcement: A Rationale for MiCBT

The co-emergence model of reinforcement (Cayoun, 2011; 2017; Cayoun & Shires, submitted for publication) is an integrative conceptualization of the interactive processing of cognition, emotion and behavior. It emphasizes the neurophenomenology of experience by integrating elements of cognitive and affective neuroscience, learning theory, schema theory and the "five aggregates" (*pancakkhandha* in Pali), which are the essential information-processing components of human experience in Buddhist psychology (see Bodhi, 2000, for an easily readable translation of the original teachings [*Khandhasamyiutta*]).

Basic Mechanism

The co-emergence model of reinforcement is presented briefly here by means of four generic functional components (see Cayoun, 2011 for a comprehensive description; also Cayoun & Shires, submitted for publication). The generic functional components of the model are represented in Figure 2.2.

Stimulus.

Stimuli are generated internally in the form of body sensations, thoughts, and images or sounds from imagination or memory. They are also generated externally by the environment. Basically, they are everything that comes in contact with our senses.

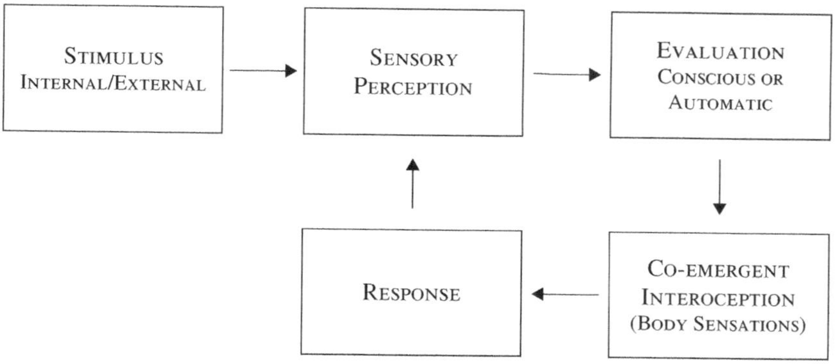

Figure 2.2 The co-emergence model of reinforcement in a state of equilibrium in information processing. (Adapted from Cayoun, 2011.)

Sensory perception.

Once a stimulus occurs, it triggers our perception. We experience stimuli through hearing, smelling, seeing, tasting and touching when they originate from the external environment, and as body sensations, thoughts, images or sounds from imagination or memory when they originate from inner experiences.

Evaluation.

Once a stimulus is perceived, we need to make sense of the information. The Evaluation component filters sensory information spontaneously, a process which often occurs subconsciously when the categorization of a stimulus has been learned and has become "automatic." Evaluative processes take place on a continuum of personal relevance, where stimuli are perceived as being more or less relevant and important to oneself. Toward one end of the continuum, information is treated as more factual, neutral and the least personally important (e.g., thinking that 3 plus 2 equals 5, or seeing an ordinary taxi passing by when we don't need one). In contrast, toward the other end of the continuum, information is evaluated as being increasingly relevant to our sense of self (e.g., one's values, needs, beliefs and schematic models, autobiographical memories, expectations, personality traits and culture; seeing a taxi go by when we really wanted one so that we won't be late) and contains personal judgment, such as likes and dislikes. Activation of filters of self-referential relevance often involves thoughts or expressions that include pronouns such as "I," "my," "me," "ours," as well as "you," "your," "yours," and "theirs" when comparisons with others or their attributes are made. Self-referential processing is associated with the activation of brain pathways forming the "default mode network" (DMN), with activation of the medial prefrontal cortex (mPFC), posterior cingulate cortex, and lateral parietal cortex (Buckner et al., 2008; Fox et al., 2005). Some have called this neural system the "*me* network" (Schwartz & Gladding, 2011). The more we take things personally, the greater the activation in this network, leading to the activation of the third component, interoception.

Co-emergent interoception.

Interoception is the ability to feel sensations within the body (Craig, 2002). The important role of interoception in the processing of emotion is now well established (Menon & Uddin, 2010). Interoception was central to the theories of William James, who is credited as the father of American psychology. James published an important article in 1884 explaining how emotions rely on interoception (James, 1884). In his words:

> Without the bodily states following on the perception, the latter would be purely cognitive in form, pale, colorless, destitute of emotional warmth. We might then see the bear, and judge it best to run, receive the insult and deem it right to strike, but we could not actually feel afraid or angry (p. 190).

As James proposed, the co-emergence model also suggests that if body sensations were suppressed or removed, for example during a dissociative state, there would be no emotional experience—we see this with our clients in therapy. This has been attributed to a survival mechanism that helps address perceived imminent threats more effectively (Suls & Fletcher, 1985).

In addition to interoception, some brain studies suggest that there are other factors that contribute to moderating emotional experience (Dalgleish, 2004). Nonetheless, current emotion theorists and affective neuroscientists agree that James' theory is difficult to disprove (e.g., George et al., 2002). We propose that a lack of differentiation between *physiological* and *interoceptive* activation can explain some inconsistencies in emotion studies that examine James' theory. Whereas physiological activation can be detected by a measurement of visceral systems (Houghton, Calvert, Jackson, Cooper, & Worthwell, 2002) and does not always reflect as awareness of an emotional experience (e.g., Johnsen, Tranel, Lutgendorf, Adolphs, 2009), such as instances of somatization, interoceptive activation is best observed through the activation of the insular cortex, which has been observed to fire neurons every time an emotion occurs (Seth & Critchley, 2013; Uddin, 2014). The insular cortex is central to the detection of emotions and the mapping of physiological responses to emotions, and passes the information to other brain regions (Lutz, Brefczynski-Lewis, Johnstone, & Davidson, 2008). Because of varying levels of interoceptive awareness, visceral activation does not always equate with emotional reactivity. In other words, we do not systematically *feel* the brain's activation of emotion-related interoception, and therefore we may not react emotionally when the visceral signal does not reach our threshold of awareness. This understanding is shared by other authors and is the subject of much reconsideration of the most accurate ways of addressing emotional disorders, such as depression (Barrett, 2017; Khalsa et al., 2017).

This is relevant in mindfulness meditation approaches where surveying ("scanning") the body serves to increase interoceptive awareness of very subtle cues, because such an ability helps us detect early cues of emotional distress. Jeff Greeson and his colleagues showed that the more mindful we are, the more able we are to uncouple physiological and emotional reactivity (Feldman, Lavallee, Gildawie, & Greeson, 2015). In the co-emergence model, consistent with accumulating findings in emotion research (e.g., Garfinkel & Critchley, 2012; Seth, 2013), interoception is the experiential substrate of emotional experience. Body sensations are the basic building blocks of all emotions (Barrett, 2006).

Central to the model is that self-referential evaluations "co-emerge" simultaneously with interoception. The term "co-emergence" refers to the experience that thinking and feeling occur simultaneously, even though there may be a short and often indistinguishable neural firing delay between the two functions. Studies of the neurobiological bases of emotion provide evidence in support of the proposition that self-referential evaluation and interoception combine to guide behavior (e.g., Gerber et al., 2008; Lane et al., 1998). Whether an evaluation is slow and conscious, or rapid and subconscious, pathways in the mPFC associated with self-referential processing stimulate body sensations through the activation of the insula, as reflected neurologically in patients with chronic pain (Gard et al., 2011; Grant, Courtemanche, & Rainville, 2011; Mansour, Farmer, Baliki, & Apkarian, 2014) and with depression (Farb et al., 2007, 2010).

Note that body sensations that are not co-emergent also occur directly via sensory perception due to common experiences (e.g., kinesthetic feedback during movements, digestion and pain) and are not the consequence of Evaluation but pertain to the Stimulus component. This includes cases where the stimulus is an emotional memory that has not yet been consciously recognized and evaluated. However, the automatic evaluation of such body sensations may lead to additional ("co-emergent") body sensations, which are then activated through corticolimbic pathways (Farb, Segal, & Anderson, 2013; Zang et al., 2014; Zeidan & Vago, 2016). For example, if you walk barefoot on a sharp rock (Stimulus), you might easily feel a sharp pain on the area of physical contact with the rock (Sensory Perception). This pain experience is just caused by an external stimulus. However, as the nociceptive feedback to the brain (Sensory Perception) triggers an automatic perception of harm (subconscious Evaluation), unpleasant co-emerging body sensations, which have nothing to do with the skin in contact with the rock, arise elsewhere in the body. This co-emerging interoceptive experience is the emotional material needed to trigger a response (quickly look at possible skin damage, etc.), as will be discussed in more detail below. This also means that every personally-important memory since early childhood has been encoded and stored with a bodily experience (Cayoun & Shires, submitted for publication).

The model of co-emergence posits that self-referential evaluation co-emerges spontaneously with interoception in two ways: the more a stimulus is evaluated as being personally important (associated with "I," "me," and "mine"), the more intense the co-emerging body sensations. Similarly, the more the stimulus is evaluated as being disagreeable, the more unpleasant the co-emerging body sensations. This easily observed daily experience is supported by fMRI studies on how motivation shapes interoceptive inference (see Farb et al., 2015, for a review).

Reaction.

Once our (conscious or automatic) appraisal of a situation has produced a bodily experience, there is a push for a reaction. The reaction will depend on the intensity (salience) and type (pleasant, unpleasant or neutral hedonic tone) of body sensations. Unless one is trained to practice equanimity, the probability of a reaction is a function of interoceptive intensity. More intense body sensations trigger stronger reactions. Note that "dissociating" is also a reaction, since it is an experiential avoidance. Moreover, the type of reaction is a function of hedonic tone (the experience of pleasantness, unpleasantness or neutrality accompanying the sensation). Sufficiently intense pleasant sensations lead to craving reactions, such as repeated reward-seeking, and sufficiently intense unpleasant sensations lead to aversive reactions, such as avoidant behavior. Hence, the model advances that people react because of the hedonic tone of body sensations, which is the consequence of self-referent evaluation; *they do not react to the stimulus or to its evaluation*. Once a reaction has occurred, it becomes the stimulus for the next cycle. If a pleasant sensation is increased or maintained by the reaction, the reaction is positively reinforced. If an unpleasant sensation is decreased or removed by the reaction, the reaction is negatively reinforced. The understanding that *a person's reaction is reinforced by their own craving and aversion* is universally applicable and is not limited to a specific disorder; it is a transdiagnostic phenomenon. Importantly, the model suggests that the locus of reinforcement is interoception (body sensations). Consequently, it has significant implications for both our original conception of operant conditioning (Skinner, 1953) and for therapeutic interventions.

System in Disequilibrium and Psychopathology

During stressful experiences, whether due to craving or aversion, a state of disequilibrium between these four information-processing components takes place. Attention is depleted from our senses (Sensory Perception and Co-Emergent Interoception) and is reallocated to evaluating the situation and reacting (Evaluation and Reaction). This formulation is supported by several imaging studies, showing the over-activation of "a cognitively evaluative neural network responding to emotion challenge, accompanied by the simultaneous deactivation of a viscerosomatic-centered experiential network" (Farb et al., 2007, p. 31). Figure 2.3 shows a state of disequilibrium in the system, pictorially reflected by the disproportionate size of boxes representing each stage of the model.

From a survival perspective, this disequilibrium state allows the rapid (learned) evaluation of potential threats and (learned) defensive reaction. In turn, increased reactivity prevents full attentional access to sensory perception.

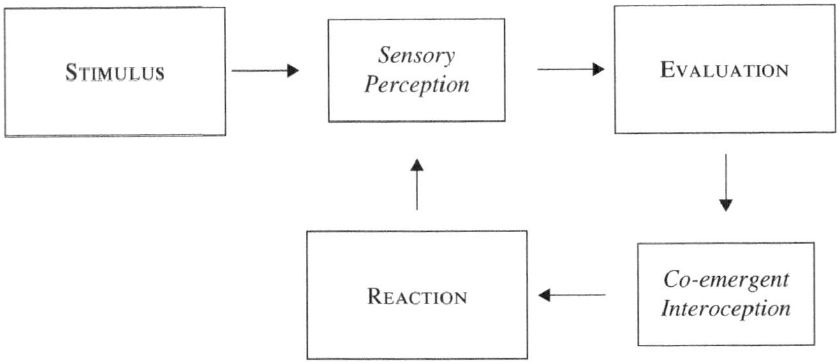

Figure 2.3 The co-emergence model of reinforcement during disequilibrium in information processing. (Adapted from Cayoun, 2011.)

Studies supporting this effect show that the greater our stress levels, the less able we are to process basic sensory information, and high-arousal negative emotions narrow the scope of attentional capacity (Friedman & Forster, 2010; Posserud et al., 2004). The reduced accuracy of perceptual abilities leads to an over-reliance on assumptions, such as schemas (Evaluation). For example, in the presence of an ambiguous stimulus, our mental representation of the stimulus replaces the more objective perception of the actual stimulus. As a consequence, our experience of the stimulus relies on mental representations stored in memory, and "what it is" is replaced by "what it is like," and often "what it is like *for me*." Although this schema-based evaluation produces spontaneously co-emerging body sensations, we barely pay attention to them and react immediately, being under the impression that the co-emerging body sensations are triggered by the stimulus and are an accurate perception of it. When this attentional bias is sustained or repeated sufficiently over time, the associated activation of neural structures in frontolimbic networks (including mPFC, insula and amygdala) strengthens and facilitates attitudes of being over-judgmental (inflated Evaluation) and over-reactive (inflated Reaction), at the cost of objectivity (depleted Sensory Perception) and interoceptive awareness (depleted Co-Emergent Interoception). As a result, the disequilibrium state progressively becomes our "new normal"—the new stable state of the system.

A depleted ability for interoception has also been recently identified by impaired insula function in all emotional disorders, especially when the condition is chronic (Khalsa et al., 2017; Farb et al., 2010; Farb et al., 2015). For example, Lackner and Fresco (2016) investigated the relative importance of interoceptive awareness in the emotional distress of 82 undergraduate university students. Their results showed that the highest levels of depression and anxiety-related distress were associated with high levels of ruminative brooding and low interoceptive awareness, whereas low levels of ruminative brooding coupled with high interoceptive awareness were associated with lower levels of depression and anxiety-related distress. Although an incidental disequilibrium state among the four components is a common way of responding to daily life's common stressors, disequilibrium can also be learned and express itself behaviorally in ways that clinicians assign to mental health disorders or problematic personality traits.

Recreating Balance in the System

Mindfulness training enables the resetting of the system to an equilibrium state. Evidence suggests that by learning to attend more objectively to all body sensations and co-emerging thoughts while minimizing Evaluation and Reaction, more attention is available for Sensory Perception and Interoception (Kerr, Sacchet, Lazar, Moore & Jones, 2013). This creates greater balance between components (as in Figure 2.2). Training to continuously and equanimously reallocate attention to our current experience enables a more "objective" or "realistic" appraisal of a situation and extinguishes conditioned responses (Hölzel et al., 2011; Hölzel et al., 2016). Accordingly, equanimity is considered to be the main active mechanism of change in MiCBT because it addresses the locus of reinforcement—interoception.

Rationale for MiCBT

Since learned disequilibrium is a transdiagnostic occurrence in chronic mental health conditions, it makes sense that therapy uses a method to decondition what maintains disequilibrium and recreate a flexible psycho-emotional state that can easily recover from schematic and reactive modes of functioning. Moreover, given that conditioned behavior is prescribed by the intensity and quality of body sensations, learning to become more aware of how we think (Evaluation) and more equanimous with how it spontaneously makes us feel (Interoception) decreases our need to react with craving and aversion (Hölzel et al., 2010; Hölzel et al., 2011). Furthermore, prolonged practice of mindfulness has been shown behaviorally and neurologically to decrease the emphasis on Evaluation and Reaction and increase the emphasis on Sensory Perception and Interoception, making us less judgmental and reactive, and more objective to what we experience in the present moment (Brewer et al., 2011; Farb et al., 2010; Ingram, Atchley & Segal, 2011; Taylor et al., 2011; Zeidan & Vago, 2016).

This understanding of how mindfulness training deconditions our reactive habits and recreates an equilibrium state among the four components is the guiding theoretical principle for the four stages of MiCBT. It has been proposed that MiCBT is efficacious in a range of conditions because it addresses the problem of systemic disequilibrium, the common factor in emotional disorders, *before* trying to modify behavior (Cayoun, 2011). Thus, the theoretical rationale underpinning MiCBT is that it uses mindfulness meditation to address learned disequilibrium and re-establish optimal executive functions, emotion regulations and insight, and then integrates mindfulness skills with Cognitive Behavior Therapy (CBT) to apply and maintain an equilibrium state across major life domains, and particularly in contexts where disequilibrium has been established. As described in Chapter 1, we start the MiCBT program with four weeks of mindfulness meditation *before* we introduce and integrate exposure tasks.

Relationship to Psychotherapeutic Orientation

It has been pointed out that "*therapists, and the therapeutic approaches that currently divide us, differ only with regard to what is to be learned and how it is to be acquired*" (Tryon, 2010, p. 10, italics in original), and that therefore "this makes learning and memory basic to our science and profession and should motivate us to search for mechanisms that underlie all effective psychological interventions" (Tryon & Tryon, 2011, p. 152). In terms of the co-emergence model, because emotional reactivity depends on the extent to which we identify with body sensations, whether in the presence or absence of a disorder, identifying with and reacting to body sensations is a common factor underlying suffering. Therefore, *interoceptive desensitization through equanimity (learning not to react to co-emerging sensations) is a transtherapeutic factor.*

Importance of Theoretical and Clinical Congruence

An important factor that differentiates various therapies is the choice of focus regarding the chronological development of symptoms. In MiCBT, although the past is considered an important source of information to understand the current difficulties, the emphasis of the intervention is on the present experience. This is because even if we are troubled by our past, our difficulty to cope with the experience occurs in the present. This is not always as straightforward as it may seem when it comes to clinical work. This may be partly because of past clinical education and partly due to our capacity for empathy. In MiCBT, the history of symptoms and behavior are useful for case-conceptualization purposes and for the understanding of the cause and effects of the learning process that has taken place since the onset of the problems. Understanding the past also provides an important means of triggering empathy in the therapist and evaluating the process, appropriateness and safety of the intervention. However, it does not address the client's present difficulties directly. Although we consider that psychodynamic issues do matter, the principal focus is on recreating an equilibrium state and preventing being "lost in the narrative."

For example, one of our clients, a traumatized woman who was raped 18 years ago, could not let go of her traumatic memories and related thoughts. She had been seeing a number of therapists over the past 11 years and was treated for depression and alcohol use disorder in various ways, but none of the therapeutic modalities were able to assist her. Some were aimed at assisting her to understand what had happened and acknowledge that this was the past and that it was sensible to stop ruminating. Others attempted to teach her to forgive the past and remain kind to herself. Yet another therapy attempted a form of exposure to her memory, to which she reacted strongly and left treatment. The MiCBT program taught her about how she had maintained a disequilibrium state for years and that fostering a less reactive nervous system was more important for recovery than what had initially triggered its dysregulation. She was able to realize that all she wanted was to not ruminate on intrusive thoughts, sleep without using alcohol, be around men without suspicion, and be intimate with her partner without dissociating. In short, she simply wished to be peaceful in the present, but her need for validation for what had happened, and justification for what had followed, drew her therapists to her past. The delivery of the rationale (see Session 3) was central to preventing her from feeling that her past was invalidated, and she was able to understand the concept and consequences of maintaining a state of disequilibrium. It took her only four months and three additional monthly follow-up sessions to unlearn unhelpful habits despite her comorbid depression, chronic pain, and self-medication with alcohol. Following completion of treatment, she was no longer drawn to thinking about her painful past and could perceive trauma-related memories as *just* memories. She only drank small amounts of alcohol when socializing, her sleep had significantly improved and she was able to enjoy fulfilling sexual intimacy with her partner.

The scientist-practitioner approach.

One of the strengths of MiCBT is that it ensures that the clinical approach is congruent with the theory. One of the many commonalities between CBT and Buddhist psychology is a reliance on demonstrated evidence for the application of behavior-modification methods. The approach to developing and applying MiCBT follows this perspective, making use of specific tools to gather clinical information throughout the program, as will be explained in Part 2 of the book.

Empirical Evidence

We now summarize some of the research findings on MiCBT in particular, although not all studies can be reviewed within the scope of this chapter. Let's begin by examining a typical approach to recreating an equilibrium state in MiCBT, using a chronic pain study by Cayoun, Simmons and Shires (2017) as an illustration of immediate and lasting unlearning of an established disequilibrium state. The participants had various types of moderate to severe chronic pain for the past six months to 20 years and most experienced at least one comorbid (mood, anxiety or both) clinical condition. All were asked to practice the mindfulness-based interoceptive exposure task (MIET), which is derived from MiCBT, where it is equally used for distress-reduction and emotion-regulation purposes (Cayoun, 2015). The task requires participants to focus mindful attention for 30 seconds (twice) at the center of the most intense area of pain sensation (Stimulus in Figure 2.3) while preventing any sort of self-referential judgment (Evaluation in Figure 2.3) or any sort of reactivity (Reaction in Figure 2.3), i.e., focusing with equanimity. In other words, they were asked to re-establish a state of equilibrium despite their old habit of catastrophizing and avoiding pain sensations.

To minimize the automatic emergence of self-referential evaluations and prevent identification with the pain experience (Evaluation in Figure 2.3), participants were asked to examine the interoceptive qualities of pain more "objectively" (Sensory Perception in Figure 2.3), in terms of four interoceptive characteristics: *mass*, *motion*, *temperature* and *fluidity/cohesiveness*. These four categories represent the experiential manifestations of the so-called "four elements" of physical life (earth, air, fire and water, respectively) in Buddhist psychology (Pa-Auk, 1998; see also Bodhi, 2000, for a comprehensive translation). Reappraising intense body sensations in terms of such impersonal characteristics decouples them from the sense of self and promotes a disidentification from sensations that are otherwise automatically categorized as "pain." This also allows a reduction in the arousal of additional sensations that would usually co-emerge with negative evaluation when identifying with pain. This very short interoceptive exposure task resulted in a statistically significant and large immediate decrease of pain severity, ranging from 30 % to 50 % reduction on several standardized pain measures.

In terms of the co-emergence model, participants reallocated attention from the over-inflated evaluative and reactive components to the depleted somatosensory components, and thus restored an equilibrium state to the best of their ability. Following this initial session with the experimenter, participants were asked to train themselves to use this task on their own every time pain would flare up, and systematically score the pre- and post-interoceptive exposure pain levels for the following two weeks. This led to significant reductions in pain anxiety ($p=.001$; $d=0.96$), pain duration ($p=.01$; d$=0.86$), and pain intensity ($p<.001$; $d=1.37$) after each 30-second exposure. These effects were maintained, and some further enhanced, at two-month follow-up. Large reductions in emotional distress (depression, anxiety and stress) were also observed ($p < .001$; $d = 0.81$), from moderate clinical severity at pre-intervention to the normal (community) range at two-month follow-up. A qualitative measure showed that participants found the task highly acceptable and some decreased their use of analgesic medication. No other psychotherapeutic treatment or meditation practice took place during the intervention.

In a randomized controlled trial (RCT) which investigated the effects of the MIET on induced pain using a cold-pressor task in 100 postgraduate students (Shires, Sharpe, & Newton John, submitted for publication), the MIET group reported a significantly higher pain threshold and pain tolerance than the control ($p < .005$, $d = 1.06$) and distraction ($p < .005$, $d = 1.42$) groups. These results show that effort to disengage the habitual self-referential evaluative and reactive components, while engaging the sensory/interoceptive components, is sufficient to decrease pain perception significantly more than distraction, which is often used in standard CBT for coping with pain.

Other Studies

Two studies investigating the effects of MiCBT on Type 2 diabetes and comorbid symptoms showed promising results, providing some evidence that the MiCBT program may be useful for supporting people with diabetes. In a quasi-experimental study (Lindsay, 2007), participants were assigned to either an MiCBT group or a standard care group. Compared to the standard care group, the MiCBT group had greater and clinically significant decrease in blood glucose reduction, greater increases in mindfulness, mindfulness-based self-efficacy, self-compassion, diabetes self-efficacy, and diabetes self-care behaviors, such as diet and exercise. Moreover, higher frequency of home mindfulness practice was associated with greater blood glucose reductions. MiCBT participants also reported an overall reduction in global impairment, and an increase in ability to manage symptoms. The other study was a recent randomized controlled trial examined the effects of MiCBT and treatment as usual (TAU) on depression, treatment adherence and control of blood glucose (Sohrabi, Sohrabi, Shams-Alizadeh, & Cayoun, submitted for publication). The results showed a significant decrease in depression and increase in diabetes-treatment adherence in the MiCBT group from pre- to post-treatment, with no differences found in the TAU group. The reduction in depression and gains in treatment adherence were maintained at six-week follow-up. There was also a statistically significant blood sugar reduction from pre- to post-treatment in the MiCBT group only, with medium-to-large effect size ($p = .012$; $\eta_p^2 = .19$).

MiCBT has been shown to be efficacious in treating anxiety and depression in pregnant women. In one RCT using a convenience sample of 80 pregnant women recruited from primary care health centers, the participants were randomly allocated to either an MiCBT group or a control group (routine prenatal care services). Post-treatment data showed a significant and large (about 50 %) reduction in both anxiety and depression in the MiCBT group, whereas no change occurred in the control group (Yazdanimehr, Omidi, Sadat, & Akbari, 2016). In another randomized controlled trial, the effects of MiCBT on comorbid symptoms of depression, anxiety and stress in 56 women with multiple sclerosis were compared with a treatment-as-usual control group (Bahrani, Zargar, Yousefipour, & Akbari, 2017). The results showed significant and large decrease (50 % to 63 %) in all the three variables from pre- to post-treatment in the MiCBT group, but none in the control group. Another study examined the effects of MiCBT on symptoms of post-traumatic stress disorder (PTSD) and major depression in women traumatized following a motor vehicle accident (Nazari-Kamal, Samouie, & Ghaebi, in preparation). Thirty participants were recruited three months after their accident and randomly assigned to an eight-week MiCBT group and a treatment-as-usual control group. Participants in the MiCBT condition reported a significantly greater reduction in both symptoms of PTSD and major depression than those in the control group at post-treatment and the benefits were maintained at three-month follow-up.

One study investigated the differential efficacy of MiCBT and Rational Emotional Behavior Therapy (REBT) in reducing procrastination, perfectionism and worry in university students who were referred to a university counseling center (Farzinrad & Nazari-Kamal, 2013). The participants were randomly assigned to two experimental groups (MiCBT and REBT). MiCBT and REBT were delivered over 13 weekly sessions, each lasting 150 minutes. The results showed that students in the MiCBT group reported a significantly greater reduction in behavioral procrastination, decision-making procrastination, negative perfectionism and worry than those on the REBT group, both at post-treatment and at three-month follow-up. No differences in positive perfectionism were found. Both approaches affected positive perfectionism equally. MiCBT has also been shown to help decrease OCD symptoms. Researchers examined the efficacy of MiCBT in 27 outpatients with predominant obsessions without prominent overt compulsions, who were recruited from a clinic specialized in OCD and from behavior therapy services of a tertiary care psychiatric hospital over 14 months (Kumar, Sharma, Narayanaswamy, Kandavel, & Reddy, 2016). The results showed an average reduction in obsessive severity of 56 % at post-treatment and 63 % at three-month follow-up on the *Yale-Brown Obsessive Compulsive Scale* (Y-BOCS) measure (Goodman et al., 1989). In total, 67 % of the participants achieved remission (55 % reduction in the Y-BOCS severity score) at three-month follow-up.

MiCBT has also been assessed in the context of sport. For example, Scott-Hamilton, Schutte, and Brown (2016) studied the effects of MiCBT on sport anxiety, pessimism and flow experience in 47 competitive cyclists. The participants were randomly assigned to the mindfulness components of the eight-week MiCBT program (excluding the behavioral components), which incorporated mindful spin-bike training or a wait-list control condition. All completed baseline and post-test measures of mindfulness, flow, sport anxiety and sport-related pessimistic attributions. Athletes in the MiCBT group reported significantly greater improvements in mindfulness and flow experience, and significantly greater decrease in pessimism than athletes in the control condition. Changes in mindfulness experienced in the MiCBT group were positively correlated with increased flow experience. In a second study using the same measures and athlete population, Scott-Hamilton and Schutte (2016) assessed the role that adherence to mindfulness practice may play on levels of mindfulness, flow, sport anxiety, and sport-related pessimistic attributions in athletes. Twelve athletes participated in an eight-week

MiCBT program (mindfulness components only), which incorporated a mindfulness focus on movement training. Athletes high in practice adherence showed significantly greater increases in mindfulness and aspects of flow, and significantly greater decreases in pessimism and anxiety than low-adherence athletes. Greater increases in mindfulness from baseline to post-training were associated with greater increases in flow and greater decreases in pessimism. Increases in flow were associated with decreases in somatic anxiety and pessimism.

Other studies have combined specific MiCBT skills that promote the equilibrium state with other mindfulness and acceptance-based methods (e.g., Senderey, 2017; Swain, Hancock, Dixon, Koo, & Bowman, 2013; Whitfield, 2006). One study of MiCBT comparing group with individual implementation to address depression and anxiety found no significant differences between the two types of implementation. MiCBT seems to be equally effective when implemented with individuals and groups (Roubos, 2011).

Research in MiCBT is being continually carried out in both clinical and non-clinical populations. We believe that an important step forward for mindfulness research is to evaluate the possible differential efficacy of existing mindfulness-based interventions (MBIs) in a range of disorders. This would assist clinicians in their choice of MBI methods, as it is currently unclear whether or not the transtherapeutic components of mindfulness are being used to their full potential across MBIs.

References

Bahrani, S., Zargar, F., Yousef-Ipour, G., & Akbari, H. (2017). The effectiveness of mindfulness-integrated cognitive behavior therapy on depression, anxiety, and stress in females with multiple sclerosis: A single blind randomized controlled trial. *Iranian Red Crescent Medical Journal*, e44566, doi:10.5812/ircmj.44566

Barrett, L. F. (2006). Valence is a basic building block of emotional life. *Journal of Research in Personality*, 40, 35–55. doi:10.1016/j.jrp.2005.08.006

Barrett, L. F. (2017). *How emotions are made: The secret life of the brain*. London: Macmillan.

Bodhi, B. (2000). *The connected discourses of the Buddha: A translation of the Samyutta Nikaya*. Boston, MA: Wisdom Publications.

Boyce, B. (2011). *The mindfulness revolution*. Boston: Shambhala.

Brewer, J. A., Worhunskya, P. D., Gray, J. R., Tang, Y., Weberd, J., & Kobera, H. (2011). Meditation experience is associated with differences in default mode network activity and connectivity. *Proceedings of the National Academy of Sciences USA*. doi:10.1073/pnas.1112029108

Buckner, R., Andrews-Hanna, J., & Schacter, D. (2008). The brain's default network: Anatomy, function, and relevance to disease. *Annals of the New York Academy of Sciences*, 1124, 1–38.

Cayoun, B. A. (2011). *Mindfulness-integrated CBT: Principles and practice*. Chichester, UK: Wiley.

Cayoun, B. A. (2015). *Mindfulness-integrated CBT for well-being and personal growth: Four steps to enhance inner calm, self-confidence and relationships*. Chichester, UK: Wiley.

Cayoun, B. A. (2017). The purpose, mechanisms, and benefits of cultivating ethics in Mindfulness-integrated Cognitive Behavior Therapy. In L. M. Monteiro, J. Compson, & F. Musten (Eds.) *Practitioner's guide to ethics and Mindfulness-Based Interventions*, pp. 163–192. Cham: Springer. doi:10.1007/978-3-319-64924-5_7

Cayoun, B. A., Simmons, A., & Shires, A. (2017). Immediate and lasting chronic pain reduction following a brief self-implemented mindfulness-based interoceptive exposure task: A pilot study. *Mindfulness*. 1–13. doi:10.1007/s12671-017-0823-x

Goodman, W.K; Price, L.H; Rasmussen, S.A; et al. (1989). "The Yale–Brown Obsessive–Compulsive Scale. I. Development, use, and reliability." *Archives of General Psychiatry*, 46, 1006–1011. doi:10.1001/archpsyc.1989.01810110048007

Craig, A. (2002). How do you feel? Interoception: The sense of the physiological condition in the body. *Nature Reviews Neuroscience*, 3, 655–666.

Dalgleish, T. (2004). The emotional brain. *Nature Reviews Neuroscience*, 5, 583–589. doi:10.1038/nrn1432. PMID 15208700.

Farb, N. A. S., Anderson, A. K., Mayberg, H., Bean, J., Mckeon, D., & Segal, Z. V. (2010). Minding one's emotion: Mindfulness training alters the neural expression of sadness. *Emotion*, 10, 25–33.

Farb, N., A. S., Daubenmier, J., Price, C. J., Gard, T., Kerr, C., Dunn, B. D., et al. (2015). Interoception, contemplative practice, and health. *Frontiers in Psychology*, 6, 763. doi:10.3389/fpsyg.2015.00763

Farb, N. A. S., Segal, Z. V., & Anderson, A. K. (2013). Attentional modulation of primary Interoceptive and exteroceptive cortices. *Cerebral Cortex*, 23, 114–126. doi:10.1093/cercor/bhr385

Farb, N. A. S., Segal, Z. V., Mayberg, H., Bean, J., McKeon, D., Fatima, Z., & Anderson, A. K. (2007). Attending to the present: Mindfulness meditation reveals distinct neural modes of self-reference. *Social Cognitive and Affective Neuroscience*, 2, 313–322.

Farzinrad, B., & Nazari-Kamal. M. (2013). *Comparison between Effectiveness of mindfulness integrated cognitive behavioral therapy (MiCBT) and rational emotional behavior therapy (REBT) on procrastination, perfectionism and worry in students*. Doctoral Dissertation, Tabtiz University of Medical Sciences, Iran.

Feldman, G., Lavallee, J., K., Gildawie, & Greeson, J. F. (2015). Dispositional mindfulness uncouples physiological and emotional reactivity to a laboratory stressor and emotional reactivity to executive functioning lapses in daily life. *Mindfulness*, 6. doi:10.1007/s12671-015-0487-3

Fox, M. D., Snyder, A., Vincent, J., Corbetta, M., Van Essen, D., & Raichle, M. E. (2005). The human brain is intrinsically organized into dynamic, anticorrelated functional networks. *PNAS*, 102, 9673–9678.

Friedman, R. S., & Forster, J. (2010). Implicit affective cues and attentional tuning: An integrative review. *Psychological Bulletin*, 136, 875–893. doi:10.1037/a0020495 doi:10.3389/fnhum.2013.00012

Gard, T., Hölzel, B., Sack, A. T., Hempel, H., Lazar, S. W., Vaitl, D., & Ott, U. (2011). Pain attenuation through mindfulness is associated with decreased cognitive control and increased sensory processing in the brain. *Cerebral Cortex*, 191, 36–43. doi:10.1093/cercor/bhr352

Garfinkel, S. N., & Critchley, H. D. (2012). Interoception, emotion and brain: new insights link internal physiology to social behavior. Commentary on: "Anterior insular cortex mediates bodily sensibility and social anxiety" by Terasawa et al. (2012). *Social Cognitive and Affective Neuroscience*, 8, 231–234. doi:10.1093/scan/nss140

George, M. S., Nahas, Z., Bohning, D. E., Kozel, F. A., Anderson, B., Chae, J. H., ...& Mu, C. (2002). Vagus nerve stimulation therapy: A research update. *Neurology*, 59, (6 supplement 4): S56–S61. doi:10.1212/WNL.59.6 suppl 4.S56

Gerber, A. J., Posner, J., Gorman, D., Colibazzi, T., Yu, S., Wang, Z., et al. (2008). An affective circumplex model of neural systems subserving valence, arousal, and cognitive overlay during the appraisal of emotional faces. *Neuropsychologia*, 46, 2129–2139. doi:10.1016/j.neuropsychologia.2008.02.032

Grant, J. A., Courtemanche, J., & Rainville, P. (2011). A non-evaluative mental stance and decoupling of executive and pain-related cortices predicts low pain sensitivity in Zen meditators. *Pain*, 152, 150–156.

Hölzel, B. K., Brunsch, V., Gard, T., Greve, D. N., Koch, K., Sorg, C., et al. (2016). Mindfulness-Based Stress Reduction, fear conditioning, and the uncinate fasciculus: A pilot study. *Frontiers in Behavioral Neuroscience*, 10, 124. doi:10.3389/fnbeh2016.00124

Hölzel, B. K., Carmody, J., Evans, K. C., Hoge, E. A., Dusek, J. A., Morgan, L., …& Lazar, S. W. (2010). Stress reduction correlates with structural changes in the amygdala. *Social Cognitive and Affective Neuroscience*, 5, 11–17.

Hölzel, B. K., Lazar, S. W., Gard, T., Schuman-Olivier, Z., Vago, D. R., & Ött, U. (2011). How does mindfulness meditation work? Proposing mechanisms of action from a conceptual and neural perspective. *Perspectives on Psychological Science*, 6, 537–559.

Houghton, L. A., Calvert, E. L., Jackson, N. A., Cooper, P., & Worthwell, P. J. (2002). Visceral sensation and emotion: a study using hypnosis. *Gut*, 51, 701–704. doi:10.1136/gut.51.5.701

Ingram, R. E., Atchley, R. A., & Segal, Z. V. (2011). *Vulnerability to depression: From cognitive neuroscience to prevention and treatment*. New York: Guilford Press.

James, W. (1884). What is an emotion? *Mind*, 9, 188–205. doi: 10.1037/ 10735-001

James, W. (1890). *The principles of psychology*. New York: Holt.

Johnsen, E. L, Tranel, D., Lutgendorf, S., & Adolphs, R. (2009). A neuroanatomical dissociation for emotion induced by music. *International Journal of Psychophysiology*, 72, 24–33. doi:10.1016/j.ijpsycho.2008.03.011

Kerr, C. E., Sacchet, M. D., Lazar, S. W., Moore, C. I., & Jones, S. R. (2013). Mindfulness starts with the body: somatosensory attention and top-down modulation of cortical alpha rhythms in mindfulness meditation. *Frontiers of Human Neuroscience*, 7, 12.

Khalsa, S. S., Adolphs, R., Cameron, O. G., Critchley, H. D., Davenport, P. W., Feinstein, J. S., …& The Interoception Summit 2016 Participants. (2017). Interoception and mental health: a roadmap. *Biological Psychiatry: Cognitive Neuroscience and Neuroimaging*. doi:10.1016/j.bpsc.2017.12.004

Kumar, A., Sharma, M. P., Narayanaswamy, J. C., Kandavel, T., & Reddy, Y. C. J. (2016). Efficacy of mindfulness-integrated cognitive behavior therapy in patients with predominant obsessions. *Indian Journal of Psychiatry*, 58, 366–371. doi:10.4103/0019-5545.196723.

Lackner, R. J., & Fresco, D. M. (2016). Interaction effect of brooding rumination and interoceptive awareness on depression and anxiety symptoms. *Behaviour Research and Therapy*, 85, 43–52. https://doi.org/10.1016/j.brat.2016.08.007

Lane, R. D., Reiman, E. M., Axelrod, B., Yun, L., Holmes, A., & Schwartz, G. E. (1998). Neural correlates of emotional awareness: Evidence of an interaction between emotion and attention in the anterior cingulate cortex. *Journal of Cognitive Neuroscience*, 10, 525–535.

Lindsay, M. (2007). *Mindfulness-integrated Cognitive Behavior Therapy: A pilot program for developing Mindfulness-based self-efficacy and self-compassion for people with type 2 diabetes mellitus*. Unpublished Master's Thesis, University of Auckland, New Zealand.

Lutz, A., Brefczynski-Lewis, J., Johnstone, T., & Davidson, R. J. (2008). Regulation of the neural circuitry of emotion by compassion meditation: Effects of meditative practice. *PLoS ONE*, 3, e1897.

Mansour, A. R., Farmer, M. A., Baliki, M. N., & Apkarian, A. V. (2014). Chronic pain: The role of learning and brain plasticity. *Restorative Neurology and Neuroscience*, 32, 129–139. doi:10.3233/RNN-139003

Menon, V., & Uddin, L. Q. (2010). Saliency, switching, attention and control: a network model of insula function. *Brain Structure and Function*, 214, 655–667. doi:10.1007/s00429-010-0262-0

Nazari-Kamal, M., Samouie, R., & Ghaebi, N. (in preparation). Effectiveness of MiCBT on post-traumatic stress disorder and major depression in women following a motor vehicle accident. Manuscript in preparation.

Pa-Auk, S. (1998). *Mindfulness of breathing and four-elements meditation*. Malaysia: WAVE. Retrieved from http://www.buddhanet.net/pdf_file/fourelements.pdf

Posserud, I., Agerforz, P., Ekman, R., Bjornsson, E.S., Abrahamsson, H., & Simren, M. (2004). Altered visceral perceptual and neuroendocrine response in patients with irritable bowel syndrome during mental stress. *Gut*, 53, 1102–1108. doi:10.1136/gut.2003.017962

Roubos, L. (2011). *A comparison of group-enhanced and individual implementations of Mindfulness-integrated Cognitive Behaviour Therapy (MiCBT): An effectiveness study*. Unpublished Master Dissertation, James Cook University, Cairns, Australia.

Schwartz, J., & Gladding, R. (2011). *You are not your brain: The 4-step solution for changing bad habits, ending unhealthy thinking and taking control of your life*. New York: Penguin.

Scott-Hamilton, J., & Schutte, N. S. (2016). The role of adherence in the effects of a mindfulness intervention on sports-anxiety, pessimism, and flow in competitive cyclists. *Applied Psychology: Health and Well-Being*, 8, 85–103. doi:10.1111/aphw.12063

Scott-Hamilton, J., Schutte, N. S., & Brown, R. F. (2016). Effects of a mindfulness intervention on sports-anxiety, pessimism, and flow in competitive cyclists. *Applied Psychology: Health and Well-Being*, 8, 85–103. doi:10.1111/aphw.12063

Senderey, E. (2017). Mindfulness and group cognitive behavioural therapy to address problematic perfectionism. *Athens Journal of Social Sciences*, 4, 49–66.

Seth, A. K. (2013). Interoceptive inference, emotion, and the embodied self. *Trends in Cognitive Sciences*, 17, 565–573. doi:10.1016/j.tics.2013.09.007

Seth, A. K., & Critchley, H. D. (2013). Extending predictive processing to the body: Emotion as interoceptive inference. *Behavioral and Brain Sciences*, 36, 227–228. doi:10.1017/S0140525X12002270

Shires, A., Sharpe, L. & Newton-John, T. (2018). The relative efficacy of mindfulness versus distraction: the moderating role of attentional bias. Manuscript submitted for publication.

Skinner, B. F. (1953). *Science and human behavior*. London: Collier-Macmillan.

Sohrabi, F., Sohrabi, A., Shams-Alizadeh, N., & Cayoun, B. A. (submitted for publication). Effects of mindfulness-integrated cognitive-behavior therapy (MiCBT) on depression, adherence, and blood glucose control of patient with Type 2 Diabetes Mellitus. Manuscript submitted for publication.

Suls, J., & Fletcher, B. (1985). The relative efficacy of avoidant and nonavoidant coping strategies: A meta-analysis. *Health Psychology*, 4, 249–288.

Swain, J., Hancock, K., Dixon, A., Koo, S., & Bowman, J. (2013). Acceptance and Commitment Therapy for anxious children and adolescents: study protocol for a randomized controlled trial. *Trials*, 14, 1–12.

Taylor, V. A., Grant, J., Daneault, V., Scavone, G., Breton, E., Roffe-Vidal, S., ...& Beauregard, M. (2011). Impact of mindfulness on the neural responses to emotional pictures in experienced and beginner meditators. *NeuroImage*, 57, 1524–1533.

Tryon, W. W. (2010). Learning as core of psychological science and clinical practice. *The Behavior Therapist*, 33, 10–11.

Tryon, W. W., & Tryon, G. S. (2011). No ownership of common factors. *American Psychologist*, 66, 151–152. doi:10.1037/a0021056.

Uddin, L. Q. (2014). Salience processing and insular cortical function and dysfunction. *Nature Reviews Neuroscience*. doi:10.1038/nrn3857

Whitfield, H. (2006). Towards case-specific applications of mindfulness-based cognitive behavioural therapies: A mindfulness-based rational emotive behaviour therapy. *Counselling Psychology Quarterly*, 19, 205–217.

Yazdanimehr, R., Omidi, A., Sadat, Z., & Akbari, H. (2016). The effect of mindfulness-integrated cognitive behavior therapy on depression and anxiety among pregnant women: a randomized clinical trial. *Journal of Caring Sciences*, 5, 195–204. doi:10.15171/jcs.2016.021

Zhang, S., Wu, W., Huang, G., Liu, Z., Guo, S., Yang, J., & Wang, K. (2014). Resting-state connectivity in the default mode network and insula during experimental low back pain. *Neural Regeneration Research*, 9, 135–142. doi:10.4103/1673-5374.125341

Zeidan, F., & Vago, D. R. (2016). Mindfulness meditation-based pain relief: A mechanistic account. *Annals of the New York Academy of Sciences*, 1373, 114–127. doi:10.1111/nyas.13153

3

Preparing for Implementation

The greatest obstacle to discovery is not ignorance—it is the illusion of knowledge.

—Daniel Boorstin, 1984

This chapter will assist you in preparing your implementation of MiCBT. We discuss the importance of the client's commitment to daily mindfulness practice, how to approach poor adherence, and a therapist stance that is congruent with MiCBT. We also describe the schedule of implementation with both groups and individual clients, and explain how to obtain and use the downloadable forms, client handouts and audio instructions for the practice of mindfulness meditation. Clinical situations in which use of MiCBT is contraindicated are reviewed.

Importance of Commitment

Therapist's Adherence

One of the recurring challenges of manualized interventions is poor therapist adherence to the method's protocol. This results in several problems affecting both the efficacy and dissemination of outcomes in the research literature. Inconsistencies are often observed in outcome studies because the clinical researcher lacked training in the investigated approach and over-relied on the implementation manual. In the case of mindfulness-based interventions (MBIs), this is all the more relevant because the method implemented is experiential and therefore cannot be learned adequately from a manual—one *has to sustain an accurate practice* to understand it. It is important that therapists using MiCBT adhere to the evidence-based protocol and obtain adequate training. We can only be confident about the efficacy of MiCBT if these two conditions are met. These are standards across therapy approaches and are not limited to MiCBT.

The Clinical Handbook of Mindfulness-integrated Cognitive Behavior Therapy: A Step-by-Step Guide for Therapists, First Edition. Bruno A. Cayoun, Sarah E. Francis, and Alice G. Shires.

Companion website: www.wiley.com/go/Cayoun/Mindfulness-integrated

Client's Adherence

With cognitive and behavioral therapies, homework exercises are an important part of treatment. In most MBIs, mindfulness practice at home is *the* most important mechanism of change. To achieve its transdiagnostic efficacy, MiCBT requires both exposure-based homework and mindfulness meditation. As described in Chapter 2, an important consequence of mindfulness meditation is its beneficial effects on the brain, which can be long-term if the practice is maintained (Farb et al., 2015; Hölzel et al., 2011). This includes neuroplasticity in areas associated with self-awareness, attention regulation and emotion regulation. However remarkable, this kind of brain reorganization does not happen, and cannot be maintained, without commitment to practice. The brain is part of the body and obeys the same rules: exercise it and it becomes fit, don't exercise it and it remains unfit—and when the brain is unfit, so is the mind.

There is evidence that the amount and accuracy of practice are neurologically and behaviorally correlated with the amount of benefit. For instance, Britta Hölzel and her colleagues found significantly greater grey matter volume in the expected brain areas of mindfulness (*Vipassana)* meditators compared to non-meditators, and the amount of practice predicted the amount of difference (Hölzel et al., 2008). Scott-Hamilton and Schutte (2016) implemented MiCBT in anxious professional athletes (cyclists) and also found those who adhered to the MiCBT protocol of 30 minutes, twice daily, in the specific way taught in the program, reported significantly more benefits. This amount of practice is necessary to address crisis and learn the method relatively quickly so that rapid positive changes act as a reward that reinforces commitment. Practice *frequency*, *duration* and *accuracy* can be compared to the three legs of a tripod; if any one doesn't contribute enough to holding the structure, it loses its balance. Note that once clients have completed the program, they are encouraged to practice only once daily, as that is sufficient to maintain their gains, promote well-being and prevent relapse.

Clients tend to rely on four main experiences and their corresponding motivational factors for commitment to daily practice. The locus of commitment may be internal or external to the client.

1. Faith in the therapist's personal competency and ability to understand and accept the client. Rapport is a significant factor for daily commitment.
2. Faith in the method's origins and proven efficacy. Psychoeducation and cost/benefit trade-offs are a significant factor for daily commitment.
3. Validation from the therapist. Reliance on the therapist's insight, empathy and ability to validate and reinforce effort, as well as reliance on the therapist for accountability are a significant factor for daily commitment.
4. Levels of suffering. Readiness for change is a significant factor for daily commitment.

Addressing Poor Adherence

Adherence to a therapy approach that requires experiential homework is never straightforward, and poor commitment is usually the first issue to address in

MBIs that require daily meditation practice. Although it is advisable for therapists to follow the MiCBT program as closely as possible, and to cover all the specific training tasks in the order presented, there may be times when a therapist will need to vary the delivery of the program or delay moving on to the next skillset. It is possible that your client may have practiced enough but remains unable to feel much in the body. In this case, it is important to discuss the accuracy of their practice, especially reducing the duration of being lost in thoughts. One useful approach is to discuss "the five hindrances" common to all meditation techniques (agitation, aversion, craving, drowsiness/fatigue and doubt) discussed in Session 2 of Part 2 of the book. This helps both the client and the therapist normalize the common challenges that all practitioners will encounter at some point. Part 2 will assist you in introducing to the client useful skills they can use to address these challenges.

If the issue is a lack of practice, you may wish to do a behavioral analysis of the client's day and together identify possible times that may be used for practice. For example, could they spend less time on social media? Could they get up half an hour earlier? Remember not to fall for the client's narrative. See avoidance as avoidance, while remaining compassionate and non-judgmental. For some clients, it is always too cold or too hot, too early or too late, they have too much or not enough energy, the house is too busy, or they are traveling. The list of reasons not to practice is long. Compassion does not mean losing our objectivity.

To encourage recommitment to practice it may be useful to review with the client their reason for commencing therapy. Once a therapy contract is done (see Session 1 in Part 2), looking back at their therapy contract's success indicators is a useful means to reviving adherence later on if needed. Using Socratic dialogue is more likely to promote an empathic and productive conversation (see example in Session 3).

Helpful Attitudes

Attitude to Outcome

Experienced therapists are usually careful not to take the client's results too personally, whether successful or not. In MiCBT, this is even more important because a "failure" is also considered to be a source of learning for both therapist and client, a set of causes and effects to be observed mindfully. We remain a student with the "beginner's mind," as Zen tradition would suggest. A scientist is primarily a student of what is being studied. Similarly, using the scientist-practitioner approach in MiCBT necessitates observing phenomena, whether successes or failures, merely as phenomena; they have their causes, the conditions in which they emerge, and they have their effects. This prevents us from feeling over-responsible for the outcome and allows us to see it as an opportunity to detect which skills are needed.

For example, a client with avoidant traits who did not start their practice and thinks about dropping out may perceive this as yet another failure in therapy. In MiCBT, we may ask clients to remember a situation in which they were prepared to practice but decided not to, examine the context through guided imagery, recall the type of thoughts and their co-emerging body sensations (see Chapter 2), and recall how avoidance relieved them of the unpleasant body-sensations. In short, we case-conceptualize the behavior, perform experiential (interoceptive) exposure to the discomfort they wanted to avoid by not practicing, and try again... smilingly! We have clearly observed over time that people's attitude to meditation is similar to their attitude in daily life; we carry the same brain connections in both contexts, after all. Accordingly, modeling acceptance of client outcomes will provide an opportunity to work in a more adaptive way with modifying the model, and it will also teach the client not to take failures personally in daily life.

To illustrate the above, let us take the example of a 27-year-old male client with an eating disorder and recurrent anxiety symptoms, whose fear of failure was a strong motivator for his high achievement in sport. He would overexercise while restricting his food intake, and then binge on sugar-rich food to maintain his energy. Midway through therapy, he and his therapist reviewed the progress made based on their prior therapy contract. While revisiting "targeted problems" and corresponding "success indicators," he began to feel disappointed about his achievements, to the extent that he soon after dropped out of therapy. The therapist was compassionate and technically very skilled, but she also tended to lack self-confidence and put a lot of pressure on herself. Being the head of a therapy team, she felt the pressure to perform and succeed clinically, and to lead others in the service. The fact that this client had dropped out triggered her self-doubt and she was concerned about her reputation. During a supervision session with one of us, it became apparent that the client's attitude to his "achievements" in therapy was a reflection of his attitude to his achievements in sport and other areas of his life. Subserved by a schema of failure, his habit of judging his self-worth according to his performance was activated, and he perceived his lack of change as an expression of failure and worthlessness. In this case, the therapist's own fear of failure was activated, and she took the client's departure a little too personally. This prevented her from accurately examining the client's unrelenting standards. Instead of attributing the client's decision to drop out of therapy to his embarrassment and his perfectionistic and controlling traits, she began to doubt her skills. As discussed in Chapter 2, taking things personally activates the brain's "me network," and what we perceive is automatically filtered through our sense of self, including our values. In the case of this therapist, the client's discontinuation of therapy activated these self-referential brain areas that prevented her from perceiving more factual information, such as the client's own fear of failure and avoidance. Hence, the more judgmental we are about therapy outcomes, the less we can see phenomena objectively.

Attitude Toward Clients

A good teacher is first a good student. In the therapy context of skills training, he or she doesn't always have to know the answers but always tries to ask the right questions, using Socratic questioning whenever it is appropriate. This applies to "teaching" mindfulness skills to our clients, whom we also consider to be "students" rather than "patients." Of course, working in clinical settings requires using a communication style that other clinicians can relate to, so we call people we train "clients," as in this book. However, MiCBT therapists avoid pathologizing people because they are aware that the underpinning theoretical framework for MiCBT is both transdiagnostic and applies to all human beings (see the co-emergence model in Chapter 2). We understand that numerous mental health conditions can easily be addressed with the improved brain connectivity produced by the effort to become more mindful and equanimous.

Another important aspect to consider is rapport. Though the notion of developing good rapport with clients may be common knowledge and required for all therapeutic systems, rapport matters most when we ask clients to do effortful homework. The more demanding the homework, the more trusting and strong the therapeutic alliance needs to be. Often, therapists new to MiCBT will initially try to remember everything they need to cover in each session, doing their best to adhere to the weekly implementation protocol. Although this is important, more important by far is that clients feel heard, understood and accepted.

Accordingly, active listening skills, unconditional positive regard and empathy must accompany the structured nature of this manualized implementation. We recommend that each individually delivered session starts with asking about the client's week, listening with empathy and showing genuine interest and care for about 15 to 20 minutes, or longer if a crisis has emerged. This gives the client an opportunity to share what happened and feel heard. We can focus on the homework and psychoeducation following that period. With groups, we cannot afford this amount of time for each person, but it is important to ask each participant how they are and how their week went.

Response to Clients Who "Did Mindfulness"

Given the exponential popularity of MBIs and available audio instructions on the Internet, an increasing number of clients who will seek your help will tell you that they have tried mindfulness training. It is important to clarify what they actually did, when, and for how long they did it, and who was the teacher, if there was one. As soon as you investigate a little further than the standard, "Oh, that's great, and did you feel that it was beneficial?" you will often be surprised about their poor understanding, the small amount of practice and the few skills they learned. How do we know this? Simply because most (though not all) people who come to see you on the basis that they cannot cope with life's stressors are doing so because whatever they learned was, or has become, insufficient to address their current concerns. For most, they are still taking their problems too personally and their equanimity is insufficiently developed to provide them with the resilience they need. Here is a typically recurring scenario from a recent exchange with a new client of the first author during the first session (Therapist = T, Client = C):

T: I read your doctor's referral and she says we'd be a good match because you've practiced mindfulness before. Is that right?

C: Yes, I heard about you from a friend and I checked you out on the Internet, and when I realized that you were doing therapy with mindfulness, I asked my doctor for a referral to see you.

T: I am very interested to hear about your experience of learning mindfulness. Can you tell me what you learned and where you learned it?

C: Different places... I read on it and I tried some of the things they say online.
T: Did someone suggest this?
C: Yes, my other therapist said it would be good for me to try mindfulness and she put me onto an app that you can download from the Internet, and some of the techniques helped.
T: This sounds good. Can you tell me what you did exactly?
C: Sure. Every time I got stressed, I listened to the instructions and focused on my breath and I calmed down very quickly. There's also another technique where you have to lay down and feel the whole body and relax, but I don't do that one very often because every time I tried, I fell asleep and I can get some nasty thoughts.
T: Yes, I understand. Do you do anything else in your mindfulness training?
C: Yes, I try to make time to meditate on my breath for a few minutes in the morning as often as I can.
T: OK, can you tell me roughly how many minutes you spent doing this practice in a week?
C: I mostly use it when I am stressed for 5 to 10 minutes, sometimes three or four times in the week.
T: Your doctor's referral says that you experience severe depression and anxiety, including panic attacks; is that right?
C: Yes, I've been depressed and anxious for many years, and then tried so many medications that we don't know what to do next.
T: Are you saying that the mindfulness you practiced did not resolve this?
C: Well, it helped decrease my stress, but it didn't fix my depression and worry.
T: I may be wrong, but it sounds as though the way you have learned and used mindfulness was more to relax than to change habits, which is why I believe it was not as productive as you were hoping.
C: I didn't know there was another way of practicing...
T: The way people learn mindfulness here is quite different, and certainly effective with depression and anxiety in general, but they need to be very committed to practicing enough and accurately. We can discuss this in our next session, next week, once we have agreed on what your goals are...

In the above case, the client tried a "mindfulness" practice entirely based on faith in the medical practitioner, without verifying and questioning the purpose, authenticity and validity of the method. The client's doctor was not trained in mindfulness meditation and was therefore unable to critically examine the validity of the methods. Given that the client used an online app without assistance during implementation, the methods were perceived and used as relaxation instructions. The consequences of these issues can be significant when a newcomer to mindfulness has clinical levels of symptomatology. In the current case, the client began to form the impression that mindfulness was a relaxation method and that feeling the body was a potential threat due to intrusive thoughts. As a consequence, avoiding feeling the body may have reinforced their overall avoidance, which strengthens the maintenance of symptoms. Nevertheless, the client's attempt and keenness to learn must be validated and recognized as a stepping-stone rather than a failure. Although the type of mindfulness they have learned has not produced the outcomes that they hoped for, they are receptive to learning MiCBT and may be well-motivated to fully engage with the program. It is fruitful for us to have some gratitude toward what may appear to be failed attempts. It is also helpful to provide referring agents with basic information on what you believe is a helpful mindfulness-based approach.

Program Delivery

Group and Individual Applications

MiCBT can be implemented in group or individual therapy; we recommend using the group application with clients with less severe symptoms. As a general rule, the more severe the symptoms, the more appropriate is individual delivery. Clients with social anxiety and avoidant personality disorders will do better in one-on-one therapy. Clients with a history of trauma with whom you choose to use MiCBT are also likely to benefit more in individual than group sessions particularly if their trauma involves social or interpersonal features and their trust in people is low. These decisions are best made on a case-by-case basis, relying on your clinical judgment.

Program Scheduling

Both group and individual sessions are best delivered weekly, at least for the first five sessions, which require more support while the skills learned are very new and clients still need a fair amount of support and an external means of accountability. After the first half of the program, we can be a little more flexible and extend the gap between sessions to two weeks—but avoid greater gaps or commitment to daily practice will decrease. MiCBT can be delivered in an eight-week to twelve-week program, depending on the purpose and client symptoms. Whereas eight sessions will usually suffice for clients with mild or remitting symptoms, more complex clients will usually need more sessions.

We recommend a generic ten-session implementation, as described in Part 2 of the book and in the client book (Cayoun, 2015). Although this is a relatively short period for a transdiagnostic application where crisis intervention is often required, a ten-session protocol provides sufficient flexibility for small delays and other alterations where needed. Sometimes, the program delivered individually with complex clients will require more time, and we recommend a series of follow-up sessions for about six months following treatment.

For individual delivery, a standard 50- to 60-minute therapy session is appropriate. Shorter sessions can be used but we don't recommend it, especially in the first half of the program. For group delivery, between 90 and 120 minutes usually suffices, depending on numbers and the potential additional assessment forms in the context of research. With group implementation, we recommend no more than 15 participants. Part 2 of the book will provide specific instructions.

Client Suitability and Contraindications

Despite the transdiagnostic nature of MiCBT, precautions must be taken to prevent the risk of harm. MiCBT works by principally increasing experiential awareness and decreasing emotional reactivity in most disorders—although more research is needed to examine the breadth of its applicability and efficacy. As a rule, MiCBT (and MBIs in general) is not recommended when a client's symptoms are too intense. In particular, it is contraindicated when the client is in a manic, psychotic, severely delusional or extremely anxious or depressed state.

One reason for these exclusions is that the more severe the symptoms, the less clients can understand or practice the skills accurately. In particular, equanimity is likely to be lacking, leading to a high likelihood of response reinforcement instead of response inhibition and desensitization. This includes periods of continual ruminative thinking. In this case, inaccurate meditation can cause harm. However, if the intense distress is, for example, due to Panic Disorder or Posttraumatic Stress Disorder, MiCBT provides a method called the "mindfulness-based interoceptive exposure task" (MIET), which is used to teach clients to reduce distress rapidly, whether it is caused by strong emotions or physical pain (Cayoun, Simmons, & Shires, 2017). The application of the MIET takes only three to five minutes and is an effective interoceptive desensitization method that can be used with distressed clients *before* they begin mindfulness training. An explanation and example of the MIET application is provided in Session 4 (Part 2 of the book). Once a client has learned to apply equanimity through the use of the MIET during distressing experiences, they are likely to undertake mindfulness training safely and confidently. This is because decreasing symptoms through one's own equanimity increases one's sense of self-efficacy.

MiCBT for Children

The adult protocol described in this book is not usually adequate for children. There is clinical experience, though no empirical data yet, that it is adequate for young teenagers. For children, given their developing brain and limited capacity for abstract thinking, the model needs to be modified. A generic child protocol already exists for the meditation components of MiCBT (Cayoun, 2012; Winney, Cayoun, & Shires, submitted for publication), but it does not include the rest of the program. Members of the MiCBT research team are currently working on the publication of an entire program for children, which we hope will be available in a handbook format in 2020. We also suggest that adults with pronounced symptoms of Attention Deficit Hyperactivity Disorder (ADHD) begin the MiCBT program using the child protocol before applying the standard adult program described in this handbook.

Professional Training and Ethics

Professional Training

Although this implementation handbook is a good guide, it cannot provide you with the experiential knowledge that MBI therapists need. The therapist's own practice of mindfulness meditation is a crucial element to successful implementation of MiCBT with clients. If you are using this guide, you may have already received some formal training in MiCBT, which will ensure your experiential understanding of each stage of the approach. You will also have established your own personal *Vipassana* meditation practice, consistent with the MiCBT methods. This will ensure experiential understanding of the practice, which differs from MBSR-based meditative techniques. This means that you have firsthand experience of mindfulness meditation and when your client encounters difficulties in their practice you will be more able to assist them, relying on your experience of having had (more often than not) similar difficulties in your own practice.

If you haven't had the opportunity to train in MiCBT, then we highly recommend that you do so, as we have observed the outcome differences produced by trained and untrained therapists over the past 15 years. Although it is certainly an asset to have already been trained in another MBI, it cannot substitute the MiCBT training. This is particularly important if you are interested in working with clients in crisis or with complex comorbidity and chronicity. Information about training can be found on the MiCBT Institute website: www.mindfulness.net.au

Professional Ethics

When misunderstood and mishandled, what is being taught as mindfulness meditation can harm, as is the case for most therapies. In addition, if the person implementing MiCBT with people who have a mental health condition is not a qualified mental health professional, adverse effects are more likely to arise. A typical poor approach to mindfulness training with mental health clients is the omission of a standard intake assessment, which includes history-taking and an evaluation of factors precipitating, reinforcing, maintaining, and contributing to the client's symptoms. This is not only standard practice in evidence-based therapies, it is also important in assessing the best approach for a mindfulness intervention.

For instance, suppose that a mindfulness group facilitator is not aware of a woman's unresolved past experience of having been sexually abused by several men whom she didn't know. There is a high likelihood that traumatic memories will be triggered by the context in which she is asked to practice—sitting closed eyes and immobile among male strangers. Taking a careful history will enable the therapist to avoid this kind of situation and suggest individual, rather than group, sessions. If the facilitator is not trained in dealing with mental health conditions, both the recognition and management of symptoms are likely to be either absent or inappropriate. This is also likely to result in the client dropping out of the program, thus remaining with untreated symptoms for some time and developing an inaccurate impression of mindfulness training.

Aversive experiences and skillful means in understanding and approaching these experiences have been well documented in 25 centuries of traditional teachings of mindfulness meditation, in terms of consequences of progressing through deeper "stages of insight" (e.g., Brahm, 2016; Grabovac, 2015). While strong discomfort is more likely to occur in retreat situations, where the intensity of practice increases, these effects can occur while people undergo MBIs that do not involve a retreat (Van Dam et al., 2017). Although discomfort is expected to emerge during mindfulness practice (as it is a metacognitive and interoceptive exposure approach), it might be difficult for a facilitator with insufficient clinical training to assess the type, severity and possible consequences of emerging symptoms. It would also be difficult for them to assess if some symptoms are due to good use of the practice or a misuse of it. For example, facilitators who are not clinically qualified may miss the cues of early onset of hypomania, simply because the client reports "wonderful experiences," especially if they don't understand this condition or didn't take a mental health history. Consequently, the facilitator will not be able to investigate the matter accurately by assessing the possible emergence of unusual symptoms or attitudes in daily life, such as increased impulsivity, reckless behavior or insomnia, and decide on a safe course of action. Although trainers are doing their best to improve training and implementation protocols (e.g., Grabovac & Burrell, 2017), non-clinical facilitators in the community are not likely to have access to the same training.

While MiCBT can be self-implemented or facilitated by a non-clinician for personal growth and well-being purposes (see Cayoun, 2015, for self-implementation guide), we would like to emphasize that only qualified mental health professionals should implement MiCBT with people who present with a mental health condition.

Resources

This book comes with a stock of resources, including downloadable forms to monitor clients' practice adherence and benefit, client handouts to provide them with the week-by-week relevant psychoeducation, summary checklists for quick review of session content (Appendix 1), free online access to the entire set of audio instructions for mindfulness training, downloadable in MP3 format, and scripts of these audio instructions (Appendix 2).

There are two reasons for which the scripts of audio instructions are provided. One is that they will facilitate translations into other languages. The other is that you may prefer to guide your clients with your own voice during group sessions once you feel more familiar with these methods. Using the scripts in your early days of implementation will assist you in preventing unintentional alterations to the original teaching, especially if you have previously been trained to guide clients using other mindfulness-based interventions, where instructions can vary greatly.

Clients can be given access to the online resource page and download the forms, psycho-educational handouts and audio instructions themselves. This will assist in the continuity of the program when clients or therapists are not available weekly.

All the forms and handouts can be freely downloaded from this link:

http://clinicalhandbook.mindfulness.net.au/handouts

All audio instructions are listed below and can be freely downloaded from this link:

http://clinicalhandbook.mindfulness.net.au/audio

Stage 1

1 General Introduction.mp3
2 Rationale for Training.mp3
3 Introduction to PMR.mp3
4 Progressive Muscle Relaxation.mp3

5 Introduction to Mindfulness of Breath.mp3
6 Mindfulness of Breath.mp3
7 Introduction to Body Scanning.mp3
8 Body Scanning.mp3

Withdrawing the Instructions.mp3

Stages 2, 3, 4

9 Introduction to Advanced Scanning.mp3
10 Symmetrical Scanning.mp3
11 Introduction to Partial Sweeping.mp3
12 Partial Sweeping.mp3
13 Introduction to Sweeping en masse.mp3
14 Sweeping en masse.mp3
15 Introduction to Transversal Scanning.mp3
16 Transversal Scanning.mp3
17 Introduction to Loving Kindness.mp3
18 Loving Kindness.mp3
19 Maintenance Practice.mp3

References

Bahrani, S., Zargar, F., Yousef-Ipour, G., & Akbari, H. (2017). The effectiveness of mindfulness-integrated cognitive behavior therapy on depression, anxiety, and stress in females with multiple sclerosis: A single blind randomized controlled trial. *Iranian Red Crescent Medical Journal*, e44566, doi:10.5812/ircmj.44566

Boorstin, Daniel J. (1984). Quoted by Edward Bond in "The 6 o'clock scholar: Librarian of Congress Daniel Boorstin and his love affair with books by Carol Krucoff." *The Washington Post*, January 29.

Brahm, A. (2006). *Mindfulness, bliss, and beyond: A meditator's handbook*. Boston, MA: Wisdom Publications.

Bodhi, B. (2000). *The connected discourses of the Buddha: A translation of the Samyutta Nikaya*. Boston: Wisdom Publications.

Cayoun, B. A. (2012). A protocol for mindfulness training in children with behavioral difficulties. Unpublished manuscript available from the MiCBT Institute, Hobart, Australia.

Cayoun, B. A. (2015). *Mindfulness-integrated CBT for well-being and personal growth: Four steps to enhance inner calm, self-confidence and relationships*. Chichester: Wiley.

Cayoun, B. A., Simmons, A. & Shires, A. (2017). Immediate and lasting pain reduction following a brief self-implemented mindfulness-based interoceptive exposure task: a pilot study. *Mindfulness*, 1–13. doi:10.1007/s12671-017-0823-x

Farb, N., Anderson, A., Ravindran, A., Hawley, L., Irving, J., Mancuso, E., ...& Segal, Z. V. (2017). Prevention of relapse/recurrence in Major Depressive Disorder with either Mindfulness-Based Cognitive Therapy or Cognitive Therapy. *Journal of Consulting and Clinical Psychology*. doi:10.1037/ccp0000266

Farb, N., Daubenmier, J., Price, C. J., Gard, T., Kerr, C., Dunn, B. D., ... & Mehling, W. E. (2015). Interoception, contemplative practice, and health. *Frontiers in Psychology*, 6, 763. doi:10.3389/fpsyg.2015.00763

Grabovac, A. (2015). The stages of insight: Clinical relevance for mindfulness-based interventions. *Mindfulness*, 6, 589–600. doi:10.1007/s12671-014-0294-2

Grabovac, A., & Burrell, E. (2017). Standardizing training in mindfulness-based interventions in Canadian psychiatry postgraduate programs: A competency-based framework. *Academic Psychiatry*, 1–7. doi:10.1007/s40596-017-0721-5

Hölzel, B. K., Lazar, S. W., Gard, T., Schuman-Olivier, Z., Vago, D. R., & Ött, U. (2011). How does mindfulness meditation work? Proposing mechanisms of action from a conceptual and neural perspective. *Perspectives on Psychological Science*, 6, 537–559.

Hölzel, B. K., Ott, U., Gard, T., Hempel, H., Weygandt, M., Morgen, K., ...& Vait, D. (2008). Investigation of mindfulness meditation practitioners with voxel-based morphometry. *SCAN*, 3, 55–61. doi:10.1093/scan/nsm038

Kuyken, W., Hayes, R., Barrett, B., Byng, R., Dalgleish, T., Kessler, D., ...& Byford, S. (2015). Effectiveness and cost-effectiveness of mindfulness-based cognitive therapy compared with maintenance antidepressant treatment in the prevention of depressive relapse or recurrence (PREVENT): a randomised controlled trial. *The Lancet*, 386, 63–73. doi:10.1016/S0140–6736(14)62222–4

Scott–Hamilton, J., & Schutte, N. S. (2016). The role of adherence in the effects of a mindfulness intervention for competitive athletes: Changes in mindfulness, flow, pessimism and anxiety. *Journal of Clinical Sport Psychology*, 10, 99–117. doi:10.1123/jcsp2015–0020

Teasdale, J. D., Segal, Z. V., Williams, J. M. G., et al. (2000). Prevention of relapse/ recurrence in major depression by Mindfulness-based cognitive therapy. *Journal of Consulting and Clinical Psychology*, 68, 615–623.

Van Dam, N. T., van Vugt, M. K., Vago, D. R., Schmalz, L., Saron, C. D., Olendzki, A., ...& Meyer, D. E. (2017). Mind the Hype: A critical evaluation and prescriptive agenda for research on mindfulness and meditation. *Perspectives on Psychological Science*, 1–26. doi:10.1177/1745691617709589

Walsh, M. (2009). *Dukkhata Sutta: Suffering* (SN 45.165). Access to Insight (BCBS Edition). Retrieved from http://www.accesstoinsight.org/tipitaka/sn/sn45/sn45.165.wlsh.html

Winney, L., Cayoun, B. A., & Shires, A. (submitted for publication). Effects of mindfulness practice on child and parent anxiety: A multiple baseline study. Manuscript submitted for publication.

Yazdanimehr, R., Omidi, A., Sadat, Z., & Akbari, H. (2016). The effect of mindfulness-integrated cognitive behavior therapy on depression and anxiety among pregnant women: a randomized clinical trial. *Journal of Caring Sciences*, 5, 195–204. doi:10.15171/jcs.2016.021

Part 2

Step-by-Step Application

Session 1: Therapy Contract and Commitment to Self-Care

Unless you change how you are, you will always have what you've got.
—Jim Rohn, 2010

In this chapter, we will assist you to introduce the MiCBT program structure as a whole and discuss the rationale for its use. You will also be guided in speaking to your clients about the need for commitment to a daily mindfulness practice in order to gain lasting benefits. This chapter contextualizes the program and includes a review of ways of learning about the world throughout our lives. We describe the rationale for setting up a therapy contract with success indicators and for teaching clients a pre-mindfulness relaxation method and mindfulness of the body to be used throughout the day. Your clients will learn about neuroplasticity and the importance of commitment to twice-daily practice in order to achieve their success indicators.

Writing a "Therapy Contract"

Rationale

As with most modern evidence-based therapeutic interventions, clinicians begin treatment with MiCBT by completing an intake assessment. Explaining how to perform an intake assessment, which is a foundational clinical skill, is outside the scope of this more specialized clinical guide. Therefore, we will limit our description to what usually follows an intake assessment in a cognitive-behavioral intervention: a therapy contract. Therapeutic contracting is an important component of therapeutic alliance (BACP, 2016; Center for Substance Abuse Treatment, 1999), and is described as involving three types of agreements: agreement on the goals of therapy, agreement on the tasks to be expected, and the therapeutic bond or rapport (Bordin, 1979). These are relevant and central to all therapeutic interventions, whether they include mindfulness components or not (Beutler, 2004).

The Clinical Handbook of Mindfulness-integrated Cognitive Behavior Therapy: A Step-by-Step Guide for Therapists, First Edition. Bruno A. Cayoun, Sarah E. Francis, and Alice G. Shires.

Companion website: www.wiley.com/go/Cayoun/Mindfulness-integrated

Accordingly, whether during the first appointment or, more often, during the next, it is important to discuss writing a "therapy contract." Introduce it as a guide that will help direct therapeutic decisions and actions over the next few weeks. It will also assist with determining whether the client's expectations are realistic within the context of therapy. Explain to your client that the "therapy contract" consists of three main parts: agreement on the problems or situations to be addressed, agreement on the indicators of success in addressing them, and agreement on the means to achieve them; the therapy model; and the rationale on which it is chosen.

Describe to your client that problems can be used as tools and that we can learn to benefit from the skills that we develop *because* of problems. The rationale for using "problems as tools" to develop skills is that skills can only be learned in the context where they are needed. Where skills are needed but absent, problems occur. If we see problems as mere reflections of the skills needed, we feel less distressed and less likely to perceive personal failures and we can maintain a level of creativity and faith in our abilities. Explain that during this program, we will use problems to develop important skills that could not be developed without the problems, and that these skills will benefit the client in the long term.

Targeted Problems and Situations

Ask your client to think honestly about what they would like to change. Help your client to find at least three things (more if possible) that they would like to change and list them in the Targeted Problems section in the Therapy Contract form ("Therapy Contract: Expectations from the Program" found in Handout 1.2*). Targeted problems can be issues such as overeating, chronic worry, depressed mood, poor motivation, chronic pain, relationship discord, poor anger management with the children, low sense of self-worth, loneliness, avoidance of change and new experiences, risk-aversiveness and anxiety symptoms. It is important not to change clients' wording. If they say, "I lose it with the kids" we may write "losing it with the kids" but not "poor anger management." This is because when we review progress at a later stage, it will be easier for clients to recall their targeted problems if these are worded using their terminology. The same principle applies to the wording of success indicators, discussed in the next section.

Help your client to understand that targeted problems need to be personal issues, such as lack of skill, poor self-management, addiction, etc. They are not solely external matters, such as "my partner is a bully" or "my work colleague is too competitive" or "my boss pushes the boundaries and gives me too much work," because clients cannot change what others choose to be or do. Help your client reformulate these issues by acknowledging *their* own suffering, behavior and limitations. For example, "I am scared of my partner" or "I let my partner control everything." Similarly, she or he could say "I let myself be affected by my colleague's competitiveness at work" or "I feel too anxious to talk to my boss about my workload." When formulated this way, change on your client's part becomes feasible.

---

* Handouts are all located at the end of their chapter.

Success Indicators

Next, you will need to help your client to find at least one "success indicator" (preferably more) for each targeted problem and record it in the Success Indicators section. You will need to help your client be specific. If the targeted problem is cited as "lack of assertiveness," it needs more precision. This is because your client may be relatively assertive in one context, such as work, but not in another, such as home. You may wish to discuss these examples with your client. If the targeted problem of a middle-aged male client is feeling powerless with his teenage children at home, a possible success indicator may be to be able to set better boundaries and say "no" comfortably, with less or no guilt or anxiety. Using success indicators to measure progress is much easier and more reliable when the indicators are specific.

Moreover, if your client is persuaded that the only way to resolve their sense of emotional neglect in the marriage will be for their partner to love them more, they might propose a success indicator such as "I will feel loved by him" or "She will spend more time with me." In this case, you can clarify that since the problem is feeling emotionally unfulfilled and having difficulty in handling a sense of abandonment when the partner is away, a possible success indicator could be "feeling emotionally satisfied" or "being able to handle aloneness comfortably." This will avoid establishing unrealistic expectations and help the client to take more responsibility for their experience.

Readiness for Change

Having identified clear goals and measures of success with your client, it is important to discuss their readiness for change (Handout 1.3). Are they prepared to engage in change towards a more peaceful, harmonious and fulfilling life? If they answer yes, then they will need to commit time and effort to achieve these success indicators. Ask if they would be prepared to commit half an hour of their time in the morning and half an hour in the evening to make it possible to achieve their success indicators. Ask them how much is their well-being worth: "Is it worth at least one twenty-fourth (four percent) of your time every day?" Discuss the use of time with your client. Time can be so precious that even the promise of well-being can be insufficient. Many people direct their time and effort outwards, toward serving or attending to others. Though it may make them feel generous, responsible and worthy as a friend, parent or employee, they tend to neglect their own needs in the process. This is worthwhile discussing with your client. Discuss also what unproductive habits may be taking up time, such as social media and other entertaining activities, even though they may be very attached to them.

It is useful to continue to stress the importance of time management during the course of treatment. You may wish to agree with the client that most of us would say we probably don't *have* time because when we have time, we proceed to occupy ourselves with some activity or another, which gives us the impression that we never have time, except for very immediately rewarding activities. Since you are introducing a new activity and your client has no evidence at this early stage that mindfulness training will be that rewarding, they are not likely to think that they have one hour a day to practice it. You will need to discuss with your clients the need to *make* time. Making time for themselves is a necessity for self-care and is also a gift to others on the basis that their well-being will benefit others, since we share our experiences with others—for better or worse.

Help your client to see that, with some creativity and good will, they will find it relatively easy to make time for self-care by getting up 30 minutes earlier in the morning and freeing 30 minutes in the afternoon or evening. The returns from this effort will be exponential. You can also take a moment to assure your client that the many therapists teaching MiCBT find that most problems are helped tremendously by the program, which requires a threefold effort: sufficient *frequency* of training (twice daily), sufficient *duration* of training (30 minutes per session) and sufficient *accuracy* of training (as per the guidance in this book and audio instructions). This threefold effort has been shown to make a marked difference in the therapeutic efficacy of MiCBT (Scott-Hamilton & Schutte, 2016).

Commitment

Stephen Hayes and colleagues conducted a study in the 1980s to identify the mechanisms responsible for observed "self-reinforcement" effects in two consecutive experiments (Hayes et al., 1985). In Experiment 1, using a studying task, self-reinforcement procedures did not work when they were private (i.e., when others were not aware of the goals or contingencies), but did work when they were public. The results showed that public goal-setting was the critical element in people's ability to commit to a task. In Experiment 2, goal-setting alone was effective in modifying studying behaviors of people with significant studying difficulties over a long period, but only when the goals were known to others. Overall, these two experiments demonstrated that commitment to difficult tasks is more feasible when we let others know of our goals and commitment to them. This is partly why having a clear therapy contract between client and therapist, where success indicators can be reviewed, is important. Additionally, it is useful to ask clients to show their targeted problems and success indicators to at least one person they trust and value.

Three Ways of Learning

Explain that long-term recovery and lasting well-being necessitates an improved understanding of ourselves and others. Since we learn about ourselves in various ways, some more fruitful than others, this section describes the three complementary ways of acquiring self-knowledge taught in Theravada teachings, from which mindfulness practice originated. According to this approach, we acquire self-knowledge through others' views (beliefs and faith in what others say), through our own views (intellectual evaluation and critical thinking) and through self-observation (direct experience of phenomena). Handout 1.4 will support your client's understanding of these learning methods.

Beliefs and Faith

Our views are often acquired through repeatedly hearing and internalizing the views of others. Progressively identifying with our acquired views inevitably shapes the neural configuration of corresponding brain pathways. Neuroscience research repeatedly shows that prefrontal areas of the brain are involved in this process, especially when the information we learn is related to ourselves and to whatever we identify with, including our view of reality (Farb et al., 2015). Repeatedly identifying with the world as it is presented to us subconsciously shapes the person we become. More often than not, we later discover that much of the information we received from our parents, teachers and others happens to be incorrect. This is because we are always learning new information that continually shapes our understanding of the world.

Nevertheless, such devotional learning is an important way of learning, including in adult life. For instance, trusting a medical doctor might save our life, trusting a psychologist might save our marriage, trusting a lawyer might bring justice in our conflicts, trusting a politician's promises might bring beneficial social change, and trusting a respected scientist can direct our research toward great discoveries. Nonetheless, blind beliefs can delay or even prevent the development of critical evaluation and rational thinking; we remain unable to question assumptions logically, jeopardizing our ability to grow into an independent thinker. We explain to clients that a good way of learning about ourselves requires us to question, investigate and evaluate the information at hand.

Intellectual Evaluation

Explain to your client that as we grow from children into adolescents, our brain physiology produces rapid changes that enable the growth of intellectual independence. Although this may take the form of a rebellious attitude at times, it reflects the ability to question, disagree and create a more independent understanding of reality, as we see it. When we engage in critical thinking we become more actively engaged in the learning experience. However, one of the limitations of over-reliance on intellectual evaluation is that most scientific findings change over time. New scientific technologies can significantly alter what was previously accepted as scientific fact.

Despite the increased ability to examine and question information about ourselves and the world we live in, this aspect of learning never seems to bring us tranquility and joy. Being a philosopher or scientist, with a great ability for critical thinking, does not translate to being happier than other people. Our faith in our own and others' views can also be a trap. In fact, we often remind clients who find themselves entangled in unhelpful arguments that "being right doesn't make us happy." We will return to this notion in Session 7 of the program, when we discuss the elements of the Interpersonal Stage (Stage 3) of MiCBT.

Direct Experience

Now explain that having first-hand experience allows us to access information in a way that is grounded and undeniable. It engages us fully in the learning experience and brings a sense of knowing what we can rely on. It marks the difference between intelligence and wisdom. Nonetheless, while direct experience is the most reliable way of learning, what we make of it largely depends on the accuracy and depth of our understanding. Although experiential learning is the most reliable means to acquire more accurate self-knowledge, it needs to be balanced with the other two learning vehicles: others' useful knowledge we are yet to learn (e.g., reading about what a phobia is) and our ability to make sense of the experience accurately (e.g., questioning if we would really die by walking or driving on this road). We can see that our direct experience needs to be balanced with a degree of faith in our trusted teachers and a degree of healthy skepticism.

While these ways of acquiring self-understanding are independently useful, they are most useful when integrated. The MiCBT program is structured in a way that combines these learning methods in an integrated way. A recent review of the research literature has shown that mindfulness increases self-knowledge of personality, emotions, thoughts, behavior and the ability to sense how other individuals perceive themselves (Carlson, 2013). Having discussed the three methods of acquiring knowledge, you can now introduce the four stages of MiCBT and the rationale for each.

Explaining the Four Stages of the MiCBT Program

Your client or group participants may have arrived at the first session with some ideas about what a mindfulness program is, based on what they have read or heard about mindfulness. You may need to take a few minutes to suggest that they put aside any preconceptions and be open to learning MiCBT, a program that integrates Eastern and Western psychologies to facilitate profound changes in our actions and in the way that we understand ourselves and others. It will be important for those who may already have a meditation practice to suspend it for the duration of the MiCBT program, to prevent being confused with different approaches. Your description of MiCBT needs to convey its systemic approach, addressing intrapersonal (Stage 1), situational (Stage 2), interpersonal (Stage 3) and transpersonal (Stage 4) factors of change. Below is a summary of each stage.

Stage 1: Personal Stage

Explain simply to your client how the MiCBT program is structured, in two broad parts. We suggest using either a whiteboard or pen and paper on which you can draw a staircase-like figure with four steps, as in Handout 1.5. A visual aid can be very helpful to some clients. Review Chapter 1 if it helps you to remember the accurate rationale for each stage. In brief, the first set of skills (Stage 1) requires focusing attention on our inner experiences in order to develop important personal skills. The second skillset (Stages 2, 3 and 4) requires focusing attention simultaneously on our inner and outer experiences in order to develop important relational skills. You need to ensure that clients conceptualize MiCBT accurately, in terms of its systemic approach and transdiagnostic efficacy (see Chapter 1 for detail).

Explain to your client that the mindfulness skills they will learn during Stage 1 are usually learned over a period of approximately four weeks. These skills help people decrease distractibility and the habit of being caught up in unhelpful thoughts. They will benefit from knowing that their new skills will help them pay attention better and be more in the present. They will also develop a better understanding of their emotions and a sense of control over their emotional reactivity. Sleep, work productivity and general coping skills are usually improved. Gaining a better sense of agency over thoughts and emotions is a typical outcome of Stage 1.

Stage 2: Exposure Stage

Then explain that once these valuable intrapersonal skills have been developed, they can be invested and applied into the second part of the program, Stage 2, with which they will continue to address the unresolved targeted problems identified at the start of the program. This is an important aspect to mention, as it helps clients perceive the various skills learned during the program as a coherent and integrated therapy approach of addressing their primary issues. Explain that the principal aim of Stage 2 is to teach clients to reduce the avoidance that creates anxiety and prevents them from moving toward their goals or living according to their (wholesome) values. Overcoming such avoidant habits develops self-confidence across a range of life domains, allowing clients to enjoy situations that they may have avoided to their detriment or to the detriment of others.

Stage 3: Interpersonal Stage

Now explain to your client that by the end of Stage 2, they will have sufficient skills to begin Stage 3, where exposure skills are applied to difficult situations with other people. Clients usually become very interested when we tell them that Stage 1 taught them not to react to their own thoughts and emotions, and now Stage 3 will teach them to apply these skills with others; they will now learn not to react to others' reactivity. They will acquire proficient interpersonal skills, such as mindfulness-based assertive communication and interpersonal insight, which increases patience and tolerance in difficult interactions. Learning these interpersonal skills enhances genuineness and friendliness in our relationships.

Stage 4: Empathic Stage

Explain that Stage 3 naturally promotes a transition to Stage 4, where people learn to be kinder to themselves and others. They will learn to remain objective about the true nature of their dissatisfaction and reactivity. It is also powerful to ask, "Would you like to learn to develop compassion instead of reacting to other people's reactivity?" Not many will answer no! Explain also that during Stage 4, the problems targeted before starting the program will be more easily dealt with, and that compassion and kindness will be developed sufficiently to make people feel more interconnected with others. We become more aware when we are about to perform an action that may be harmful to ourselves or to someone else and can prevent it effortlessly. In turn, this increases our sense of self-worth and decreases the probability of relapse.

Importance of Neuroplasticity

We frequently observe clients making profound transformations in their lives as they acquire the skills through the four stages of the program. However, we remind you that this relies heavily on three conditions to succeed: the *frequency*, *duration* and *accuracy* of your client's mindfulness practice. These are important conditions for brain changes to occur, and to occur in specific pathways. It is important for clients to hear this from you, so that they don't begin to assume that the discipline required in MiCBT comes from an attempt to cling to Buddhist traditions, as this is not the case. We simply know from research (e.g., Scott-Hamilton & Schutte, 2016) and through personal and professional experiences over the years (Cayoun, 2015) that this threefold effort is important for helpful neuroplasticity to occur.

Why neuroplasticity? Using a computer analogy, it is because just as you cannot easily install new and more sophisticated software on old hardware, you cannot easily learn to think differently using the old neural substrate that maintains dysfunctional beliefs. This is especially important with chronic conditions and dysfunctional personality traits. Though it may initially appear that practicing twice daily is a big ask, reminding clients that "we can't negotiate with the brain, we can't bargain with nature" tends to help them put the requirement for commitment into its proper context. Sometimes using the analogy of "bringing our brain to the gym everyday" can also facilitate understanding.

This Week's Practice

Progressive Muscle Relaxation (PMR)

When starting mindfulness training, it is a good idea to begin with a task that is easily achievable, even though making time for it can be a real challenge for people who have not been valuing self-care enough. If the task is "easy" and rewarding, the effort to make time for it will seem more acceptable. Moreover, starting mindfulness training without having developed relaxation skills can be too difficult for people with high levels of stress and motor agitation.

Stress reduction through the practice of PMR has been well demonstrated since the 1920s, through the work of American physician Edmund Jacobson. Its inclusion in clinical psychology was promoted by his 1938 book *Progressive Relaxation* (Jacobson, 1938), which made PMR, also called Jacobsonian Relaxation, popular among psychologists. In the early decades of its application, using PMR would take about two hours, requiring the practitioner to tense and relax every part of the body, starting with each toe. As you can imagine, this would be impractical to do in our busy lives today. Fortunately, the method was revised in the 1970s and its duration was significantly reduced by behavior therapists to about 20 minutes with no loss in efficacy (Bernstein, 1973). Since the seminal book of American cardiologist Herbert Benson, *The Relaxation Response* (Benson, 1975, 2001), PMR has become integral to addressing stress and anxiety in psychology, especially in behavior therapy. There is empirical evidence for its effectiveness as a short-term stand-alone technique in addressing discomfort associated with stress, muscle tension, headaches and anxiety (Hayes-Skelton et al., 2013).

This week, we introduce the daily practice of progressive muscle relaxation (PMR). Clients can sit comfortably in an armchair or sofa, but instruct them to avoid lying down or they are most likely to become too drowsy to benefit from the learning process. We need to learn to be relaxed while remaining alert. The practice of PMR requires clients to tense and relax 16 muscle groups in 14 minutes. While tensing a muscle group for a few seconds, the client feels the experience of muscle tension, and then "lets go" of the created tension without delay. The client is then asked to feel the effects of relaxing the muscle group, especially the difference between tension and relaxation, for a few seconds. She or he performs the same exercise with subsequent muscle groups, throughout the entire body.

The rationale for including this approach in MiCBT is that our progressive ability to recognize the difference between tension and relaxation during the practice is transferred to tense and stressful situations in our daily life. We become more able to recognize the early onset of a stress response through muscle tension, and therefore more able to address it (through relaxation) earlier than we usually do, when it is still manageable. We learn a "*relaxation response*," as Dr. Benson would say (Benson 1975, 2001). We have observed three benefits in using PMR at the start of MiCBT: (1) it creates a focus in present-moment experience while relaxing and restoring the connection between mind and body; (2) it gently and pleasantly initiates clients to make time for the practice twice daily while being rewarded with relaxation; and (3) it is an important and easily practiced act of self-care, enhancing an early sense of self-efficacy in dealing with stress.

Ask your clients to choose a quiet room where they won't be disturbed for about 25 minutes (which is the overall duration of tracks 1 to 4) for the first two days and then 15 minutes (track 4 only) for the following days. They will need to wear loose clothing to feel comfortable. The sooner they start the better, but they first need to organize their time. As you will know from personal experience, we don't *have time* to practice, simply because as soon as we have some time, we fill it in with some activity. Accordingly, we need to remind the client to *make time*, which is not always easy, and so some scheduling preparations may be helpful. Perhaps they could tell their partner or the people they live with that they will be busy or unavailable for certain times of the day. It is important that they reorganize their timetable so that they can make time for practice twice daily. This might include setting the alarm clock 30 minutes earlier in the morning from now on and deciding on what time of the afternoon or evening would suit them best for their second practice.

Mindfulness of Body

This week, in addition to spending 14 minutes twice a day practicing PMR, the client is asked to practice "mindfulness of body." This is not time-consuming and requires only their awareness of posture and movements throughout the day. They need to do their best to bring their attention to the present moment with each activity, using their body posture or movement as an anchor for attention. Though this doesn't sound very meditative, it is a powerful method if sustained during the day, each day—indeed, at night as well if awake.

Ellen Langer's early study showed that simply paying close attention to our daily activities, rather than functioning on "automatic pilot," can improve health and extend longevity (Langer, 1989). Above all, paying attention to whatever we are doing in the present moment prevents us from ruminating over the past and worrying about the future. Clients benefit from being reminded that the present is the *only* reality they live in; the past is gone, never to return, and the future doesn't yet exist. In other words, the present is the only place to be. The initial notion of present-moment awareness is thus materialized in daily life with a very simple focus that even children can apply. However, your client needs to be reminded that remaining aware of posture and movement throughout the day (and night when not asleep) is much more effortful than it may seem at first, and they will need to make a strong commitment to perform this task. This will be the first step toward the progressive acquisition of profound mindfulness skills.

Application with Individual Clients

Session Aim

Session 1 introduces MiCBT and aims to establish commitment to daily practice. The first session provides a basic understanding of the principles of mindfulness and a sense of direction for participants. There is more material to cover in this session than in all subsequent ones, so it is important to carefully monitor your timing of implementation.

Identifying and Setting Goals

Have your client identify their goals and write them down. Why did they come to therapy? What issues or problems do they wish to address? Be sure that they are clear about what they want to change. Discuss the types of issues to be targeted. Remember to guide your client to identify issues that are *theirs*, not those of others. For example, "I would like to change the way I react in arguments with my partner," not "I want my partner to be less argumentative."

Help your client to be clear about their success indicators. Explore how they will know if they have achieved their goals. How will they know when they have succeeded? What will be their objective indicators, their evidence, of a goal successfully achieved? You will need to record your client's targeted problems and success indicators in your notes for your progress review(s).

Explain the Three Ways of Learning and Introduce Experiential Learning

Describe the three complementary ways of learning about ourselves; through others' views (beliefs and values), through our views (intellectual evaluation), and through our own observation (direct experience). Explain that while learning from direct experience is the most reliable way of getting to know ourselves, it needs to be balanced with the other ways of learning. This requires us to question, investigate and evaluate the information at hand. This program will provide the opportunity to learn through the three complementary ways.

Introduce Mindfulness

Briefly introduce the concept of mindfulness and then present the following definition for the purposes of MiCBT:

> *Mindfulness is a mental state experienced as heightened awareness of the present moment, free from judgment, reactivity and identification with the experience.*

Explain that mindfulness facilitates the ability to let go of emotional reactivity. It is especially important to explain the difference between mindfulness and attention (you may find it helpful to review the explanation in Part 1). Handout 1.1 will provide your client with a simple explanation.

Describe the Structure of the MiCBT Program

Explain that mindfulness training and CBT are both evidence-based approaches, which MiCBT integrates into one therapy system to address both cognitive content and processing of information (both thinking and how we process thinking). MiCBT uses evidence-based techniques grouped in a unique way to help with a variety of issues that cause psychological distress. Explain that the MiCBT program has four stages and that you will probably be working together over about ten sessions for an eight- to twelve-week period. Briefly describe the rationale for each stage.

- Stage 1 teaches how to regulate where attention goes, what the mind is up to, and how to learn to let go of unhelpful thoughts and emotions. The exercises in this stage enable the development of deep levels of insight and equanimity as we realize that we do not have to react to every thought and feeling that arises.
- Stage 2 applies these "internal" self-regulation skills to the difficulties that the client tends to avoid because of associated feelings of discomfort.

- Stage 3 makes use of skills from Stages 1 and 2 to develop better interpersonal understanding and communication skills in the face of tense situations, and teaches skills that enable one not to react to others' reactivity.
- Stage 4 teaches compassion, including being kind to oneself and others, thus enhancing a sense of care and connectedness with people, and a foundation for the prevention of relapse.

Introduce the Need for Regular Practice

Introducing MiCBT requires that you are able to help motivate your client to commit to a significant amount of mindfulness practice—two half-hour practices per day. Making adjustments to their schedule will usually be necessary. If you have pre-existing experience in using the Socratic dialogue as part of CBT training, this is a good place to use it. You may assist your client to reappraise their perceived lack of time for practice and other erroneous or unhelpful beliefs that might contribute to early limitations. Handout 1.6 is designed to further inform your client.

Explain the practice requirements (30 minutes twice daily) and provide a good rationale for the amount of practice needed to create new neural pathways. Note that this week requires less practice time, as this version of PMR lasts only 14 minutes. Using an analogy of fitness training at the gym may help. Stress that they don't need to commit for weeks or months, but rather agree to commit fully for one week and see what sort of benefit they derive from this initial full commitment. Asking clients to commit one week at a time helps prevent fear of failure. It can also reassure clients and enhance their sense of control and choice. Ask participants to think about when they could practice and if they can find a suitable quiet space to use.

Introduce Progressive Muscle Relaxation (PMR)

Having provided some background information about the program, introduce the first of the exercises—progressive muscle relaxation (PMR). Explain that PMR is used in MiCBT because it creates a focus in present-moment experience while relaxing and restoring the connection between mind and body. Introducing PMR at the outset of the program helps to ground clients in a practice routine that, for most people, is not too challenging (use Handout 1.7). Clarify that PMR is not a mindfulness practice per se—mindfulness training will start next week with mindfulness of breath.

Introduce Mindfulness of Body

Explain to your client that in addition to daily practice of PMR, they will need to pay non-judgmental attention to both their body movements and posture, as often and as long as possible during waking hours. The rationale is that since most mental health issues are triggered, maintained or worsened through allowing our mind to wander in the past and future, being in the present decreases distress. We will be using the body "as a hook" for maintaining attention in the present moment. Explain that being aware of posture and movements as they take place keeps us in the present and is the first step toward preventing unhelpful thoughts. An awareness of posture and movement should also be practiced as your client falls asleep and gets out of bed.

Explain Homework Exercises

Distribute the handouts, including the Daily Record of Progressive Muscle Relaxation (Handout 1.9). Explain the usefulness of recording practice and bringing the form to the next session. We suggest that you use the handouts as part of your teaching aids as this improves adherence to program structure. It is important to encourage commitment and accountability. The client needs to do the following:

- Listen to the introductory tracks (1, 2, and 3) as well as PMR (track 4) on Stage 1 audio instructions (a CD version is available from the MiCBT Institute for people who prefer using a CD). Clients tend to find the rationale on track 2 to be very helpful; however, they don't need to listen to the three introductory tracks more than twice.
- Practice PMR *twice* daily using track 4. Ensure that clients understand that they should practice 14-minute PMR only *once* per practice session this week. The 30-minute-long practice starts next week.
- Practice mindfulness of body.
- Read the relevant handouts.
- Fill in all assessment and practice forms (if data collection is necessary).

Application with Groups

Session Aim

Session 1 introduces MiCBT and aims to establish commitment to daily practice. The first session provides sufficient understanding of the principles of mindfulness and a sense of direction for participants. There is more material to cover in this session than during all subsequent ones, so it is important to carefully monitor your timing of implementation.

Materials

- Whiteboard and markers;
- Audio instructions (tracks 1, 2, 3 and 4) and a computer or MP3 player on which to play them (a CD version is available from the MiCBT Institute for people who prefer using a CD);

- Copies of the Daily Record of Progressive Muscle Relaxation (Handout 1.9);
- Assessment forms for baseline data when necessary;
- Pen and paper for participants.

Method of Delivery

Set the chairs in a full or ¾ circle. This helps everyone to see and hear each other easily, which in turn will facilitate group cohesiveness. Keep your preferred arrangement each week for the entire program.

Explain the general structure of weekly sessions in order of delivery: group practice, participants' feedback on the past week, the topic of the week to learn, explanation of homework exercises, weekly reporting of practice and measurement of outcome (if you collect measurement data). Emphasize the need for three main commitments:

1 Attending each session
2 Doing home practice (reiterate making time rather than trying to find time). Make a point that the greatest benefit of the program will come from the homework exercises
3 Commit to confidentiality about, and respect for, other group participants.

Identifying and Setting Goals

Use the whiteboard to set goals. Brainstorm first, and then condense participants' overlapping goals into more generic ones so that there are at least five goals and no more than fifteen.

- Ask the participants to write their goals on a sheet of paper.
- Ask the group what each would like to change/improve through the program and tally each person's endorsement of a proposed improvement on the whiteboard (e.g., if a participant says "I want to feel less angry," ask if this goal would apply to other participants by show of hand, count the people concerned and report the number on the board next to the item).
- Record the list of goals and the number of participants who endorsed each of them on a notepad to allow future comparisons in Session 10.
- Collect participants' goal sheets.

Explain the Three Ways of Learning and Introduce Experiential Learning

Describe the three complementary ways of learning about ourselves; through others' views (beliefs and values), through our views (intellectual evaluation), and through our own observation (direct experience). Explain that while learning from direct experience is the most reliable way of getting to know ourselves, it needs to be balanced with the other ways of learning. This requires us to question, investigate and evaluate the information at hand. This program will provide the opportunity to learn through the three complementary ways.

Introduce Mindfulness

Briefly introduce the concept of mindfulness. Start with writing a definition on the whiteboard—you may ask participants how they define mindfulness and then present the following definition for the purposes of MiCBT:

Mindfulness is a mental state experienced as heightened awareness of the present moment, free from judgment, reactivity and identification with the experience.

Mindfulness facilitates the ability to let go of emotional reactivity. It is especially important to explain the difference between mindfulness and attention (you may find it helpful to review the explanation in Part 1). Handout 1.1 will provide participants with a simple explanation.

Describe the Structure of the MiCBT Program

Explain that mindfulness training and CBT are both evidence-based approaches, which MiCBT integrates into one therapy system to address both cognitive content and processing of information (both thinking and how we process thinking). MiCBT uses evidence-based techniques grouped in a unique way to help with a variety of issues that cause psychological distress. Explain that the MiCBT program has four stages and that you will probably be working together over about ten sessions for an eight- to twelve-week period. Briefly describe the rationale for each stage.

- Stage 1 teaches how to regulate where attention is, what the mind is up to and learn to let go of unhelpful thoughts and emotions. The exercises in this stage enable the development of deep levels of insight and equanimity as we realize that we do not have to react to every thought and feeling that arises.
- Stage 2 applies these "internal" self-regulation skills to the difficulties that the client tends to avoid because of associated feelings of discomfort.
- Stage 3 makes use of skills from Stages 1 and 2 to develop better interpersonal understanding and communication skills in the face of tense situations, and teaches skills that enable one not to react to others' reactivity.
- Stage 4 teaches compassion, including being kind to oneself and others, thus enhancing a sense of care and connectedness with people, and a foundation for relapse prevention.

Group Practice of This Week's Training (Stage 1): Progressive Muscle Relaxation (PMR)

- Guide the group into PMR using either Track 4 of the Stage 1 audio instructions or the script for PMR in Appendix 2.
- Briefly explain the practice and rationale for PMR in the first week.
- Explain setting-up for home practice.
- Distribute the Daily Record of Progressive Muscle Relaxation (Handout 1.9).

Introduce the Need for Regular Practice

Introducing MiCBT requires that you are able to help motivate clients to commit to a significant amount of mindfulness practice—two half-hour practices per day. Making adjustments to their schedule will usually be necessary. If you have pre-existing experience in using the Socratic dialogue as part of CBT training, this is a good place to use it. You may assist participants to reappraise their perceived lack of time for practice and other erroneous or unhelpful beliefs that might contribute to early limitations.

Explain the practice requirements (30 minutes twice daily) and provide a good rationale for the amount of practice needed to create new neural pathways. Note that this week requires less practice time, as this version of PMR lasts only 14 minutes. Using an analogy of fitness training at the gym may help. Stress that they don't need to commit for weeks or months, but rather agree to commit fully for one week and see what sort of benefit they derive from this initial full commitment. Asking clients to commit to one week at a time helps prevent fear of failure. It can reassure clients and enhance their sense of control and choice. Remind participants that next week is an important week and they must do all they can to attend the group even if a crisis has emerged. Ask participants to think about when they could practice and if they can find a suitable quiet space to use.

Introduce Mindfulness of Body

Explain to participants that in addition to daily practice of PMR, they will need to pay non-judgmental attention to both their body movements and posture, as often and as long as possible during waking hours. The rationale is that since most mental health issues are triggered, maintained or worsened through allowing our mind to wander in the past and future, being in the present decreases distress. We will be using the body "as a hook" for maintaining attention in the present moment. Explain that being aware of posture and movements as they take place keeps us in the present and is a very first step toward preventing unhelpful thoughts. An awareness of posture and movement should also be practiced as participants fall asleep and get out of bed.

Explain Homework Exercises

Distribute the handouts, including the Daily Record of Progressive Muscle Relaxation (Handout 1.9). Explain the usefulness of recording practice and bringing the form to the next session. We suggest that you use the handouts as part of your teaching aids as this improves adherence to program structure. This will encourage commitment and accountability. Participants need to do the following:

- Listen to the introductory tracks (1, 2, and 3) as well as PMR (track 4) on Stage 1 audio instructions. Participants tend to find the rationale on track 2 to be very helpful; however, they don't need to listen to the three introductory tracks more than twice.

- Practice PMR *twice*-daily using track 4. Ensure that clients understand that they should practice 14-minute PMR only once per practice session this week. Their 30-minute-long practice will start next week.
- Practice mindfulness of body.
- Read the handouts.
- Clients fill in all assessment and practice forms (if data collection is necessary).

Frequently Asked Questions

This section appears in this and all following chapters to help you normalize and work with the typical challenges that tend to arise at each of the stages of the program. It presents questions that have been frequently asked by therapists during supervision sessions, training courses and masterclasses. Since these exchanges were in simple, conversational language, this section preserves the same conversational style. All information has been de-identified to maintain confidentiality.

Question: My client reports that she feels anxious when she does her PMR practice. How can I best advise her?

Answer: The practice of PMR tends to be rewarding for most people. However, sometimes clients can find it initially a little challenging. For example, people who suffer from severe chronic pain have trained themselves to avoid relaxing on the basis that it allows them to feel the sensations they have continually tried to ignore. This is understandable, since pain sensations appear to be threats to most people. The threat of being hurt immediately triggers the brain's defense mechanism, which can produce some anxiety and we consequently react with fear and avoidance of relaxing.

This also applies to the experience of traumatic memories. For people who suffer from post-traumatic stress disorder (PTSD), relaxing can sometimes allow intrusive painful memories to reach consciousness, which they ordinarily tend to avoid. People with severe symptoms of PTSD can be very tempted to watch TV late into the night, work too much and too long, or intoxicate regularly. They do so to keep the mind busy and distracted in order to avoid fearful thoughts and the accompanying emotions.

During PMR, one of the fears that may arise is to sit with the eyes closed, because it feels like losing control. If your client experiences this, ask her to keep her eyes half open for the first few sessions and gradually close them as her confidence increases. If she happens to suffer from severe pain or trauma symptoms, in both fear of pain and fear of fear, PMR can produce a degree of relaxation-induced anxiety, which may manifest in the form of motor agitation, hyperventilation or nausea. Although unpleasant, these "side-effects" of relaxation are usually harmless and you can encourage your client to continue practicing, starting with open eyes, and perhaps their favorite calming music in the background. There are other cases where relaxing can be a little challenging initially, such as the intrusion of ruminative thoughts, being hyperactive, or simply being impatient; relaxing is a skill that needs to be practiced before it is developed. Paradoxically perhaps, it takes effort to learn to relax.

Question: My client has practiced other forms of relaxation in the past and it was suggested during these that he lies down. He wants to lie down for this method too. Is that a good idea?

Answer: It is better not to lie down for two main reasons. The first is about drowsiness and the need to learn to remain awake while relaxed, so that we can carry this ability into everyday life. The second reason is about this training as a whole. Using PMR is only the very first step of this program, which is to get the nervous system ready for mindfulness by training it to relax quickly. This will enable your client to rapidly develop deep states of calmness before he starts mindfulness training next week. In other words, while benefiting from 14 minutes of peaceful and efficient relaxation practice morning and evening this week, you are also preparing him for next week's training, which will capitalize on an ability to remain alert and attentive while deeply relaxed. If a client becomes drowsy and cannot establish and maintain a degree of alertness during PMR, which is commonly the case with relaxation practices that are carried out while lying down, he or she is likely to experience drowsiness next week too, when mindfulness of breath is commenced. This is why posture is important. Sitting will assist a client to maintain a wakeful mental state during the practice.

Question: My client has severe chronic pain in both knees and in her lower back. How do I instruct her to practice when she gets to those parts?

Answer: She just needs to be very gentle with those body parts when the instructions ask her to tense and release these muscles. If these body parts are injured, she may gently *stretch* those parts rather than *contract* the muscles. Also, when the instructions say "now relax this part" or "now let go of tension in your …" ask her to do her best to relax that body part in one go, instantly, just by *dropping* any muscle contraction that she has produced following the instructions to contract, or stretch. However, because your client has severe pain in her knees, she should not let go of her legs directly on the floor when the instructions say so; she should put them down very gently. The same applies to her lower back when she is asked to arch her back—always gently.

Question: My client is very busy; he travels a lot and has problems making time for practice. He asked me if he can just practice once instead of twice daily. What do you think?

Answer: The research literature on mindfulness shows that the more we practice, the better the results, so your client is likely to benefit more if he practices more. How much he practices is ultimately up to him, but you need to be transparent about the relationship between duration of practice and results. Telling him what he wants to hear will not help. Since he is engaged in this program and hopes to benefit from it, why not help him to reorganize his activities so that his essential needs for well-being don't come last. He might be committed to prioritizing others' needs, often out of a sense of duty or compassion, but this training is an opportunity for him to improve self-care. It might be useful to use Socratic questioning if you have training in it. Sometimes clients say that they will be on holiday or at a conference and won't be able to commit to their practice.

You could ask "Where will you sleep when you are there?" They may answer "In a hotel room." or "At my sister's." You could then ask, "Would anything prevent you from having a chair in your bedroom, getting up earlier than the others, putting some headphones on and doing your practice in the morning?" You could also proceed with a similar approach for the evening.

You may also do some task-scheduling with him, asking precisely at what time he wakes up and gets up, how long breakfast lasts, etc., and assist in scheduling time for practice. Sometimes adults need the sort of assistance that we would usually offer to disorganized children. In any case, restrain your own judgment and reactivity in the face of avoidance or resistance. It's amazing what a kind and compassionate (but assertive) approach can do!

Handout 1.1 What is Mindfulness?

Mindfulness involves paying attention to what is happening in the present, right now, without trying to change anything. The word "mindfulness" is a translation of the Indian Pali word *sati*, which means awareness. Some have translated it as "remembering," because to be aware of what is happening in the present moment, we need to remember to do so. Mindfulness refers to a way of noticing all the things that the mind gets involved with (including seeing and hearing, smelling, touching, tasting, sensing in the body and thinking and feeling things), in a calm and non-judgmental way, without needing to change things or react emotionally. This means that mindfulness involves "equanimity," which is the ability to remain calm and non-reactive, whatever our experience may be. This is another way of saying "keep your cool."

Handout 1.2 Therapy Contract: Expectations from the Program

At the end of the program, these are some things you would like to have improved or changed. Be specific—how will you know that these have changed?

Targeted Problems	*I will know that change was real and successful because…*
1	
2	
3	
4	
5	
6	

Signed: (client)..................................

Signed: (Therapist).............................. Date: ....

Handout 1.3 Readiness for Change and Requirement for Effort

Are you prepared to commit time and effort to achieve your success indicators? Are you prepared to commit half an hour of your time in the morning and half an hour of your time in the evening? How much is your well-being worth? Is it worth at least one twenty-fourth of your time every day?

It takes time to earn a living and to satisfy the expectations of family and friends. There are those not-so-useful activities that we are attached to that take time. It is also possible that a lot of your time is used in attending to others' needs, and you may feel that you are being generous and responsible; however, you can easily neglect your own needs in the process if you don't make time to practice what would genuinely benefit you. Making time for yourself is a gift to others as well as to yourself, because if you are less stressed, anxious or depressed, this will benefit others too.

With a bit of creativity and effort you will be able to prioritize time for self-care, perhaps by getting up half an hour earlier and freeing up time in the afternoon or evening. How often, how long and how well you practice is very important. Remember you are about to create new and very healthy connections in the brain and like learning any skill, it takes practice. Remember how long it took you to learn to drive, for example? You had to practice frequently and well, for a good amount of time under the guidance of an experienced instructor. This required a lot of effort! So, just to make things clear, the *frequency* of practice is twice daily, the *duration* is 30 minutes (the exception is there is only 14 minutes of practice in the last five days of Week 1), and the *accuracy* is following the audio instructions on the audio tracks given by your therapist. This commitment will bring about the changes in your brain that will lead to long-term benefits.

Handout 1.4 Three Ways of Learning

There are many ways to learn about ourselves. Here are the three most important ones:

1 *Believing*: Someone can "tell" you how things are. We have learned much of what we know in this way from parents and teachers or others we regard as experts.
2 *Rationalizing*: We can use our own problem-solving ability to "work it out." Physicists have worked out much about planets and stars without ever having "experienced" them. As we mature, we get better at working things out for ourselves using what we have learned and our own problem-solving skills. We can learn things that we may not be able to experience first-hand.
3 *Experiencing*: Learning that is based on our actual experience. First-hand experience is the most reliable way to learn because your own experience of something is the only real evidence that you have about that thing. It becomes true to you.

Making sense of our experience is very important. Direct experience of being bitten by a dog gives you reliable evidence that it hurts, but on its own, your experience may also lead to a lifelong fear of dogs, unless someone explains to you that not all dogs bite. Similarly, experiencing a difficult landing in an airplane may lead to a fear of flying unless we learn that the chance of this happening in the future is very low. Therefore, using the three types of learning together is the most useful, so that by believing others who have more experience than we do (someone who can explain to us that most dogs do not bite, for example) and using our logical mind, we can make sense of our experience so that we don't start avoiding situations (like patting dogs!). This program will give you direct experience of your potential for a more harmonious life through the practice exercises, and your therapist will help you make sense of that experience.

Handout 1.5 Program Structure: The Four Stages

The MiCBT program has four stages:

Stage 1: In this stage, you will learn to focus attention *internally* and observe internal events, such as thoughts, sensations in your body and the kind of mental states that you experience. Mindfulness skills will help you manage your thinking habits and emotional reactivity. In the first stage of this program, you will learn four helpful skills:

1 relaxing your body;
2 keeping your mind in the present by using your movements and posture;
3 attending to the way you think and preventing unhelpful thoughts;
4 attending to body sensations that form your emotions, and so reducing emotional reactivity.

Once you have developed these skills (usually in about four weeks) we proceed to Stage 2.

Stage 2: In this stage, because you will be more aware and "in charge" of your thoughts and emotions, you will be able to begin to pay attention *externally*, to challenging external situations or events, in a more constructive way. You will break habits of avoidance, such as avoiding socializing or taking healthy risks. You will learn advanced body-scanning skills and ways to handle emotional discomfort with more ease (exposure techniques).

Stage 3: In this stage, you will use the skills from Stages 1 and 2 to tackle unpleasant situations with other people, including those you may be avoiding because you might fear how you or the other person could react. By applying mindfulness and exposure techniques to these interpersonal situations, you will be able to tolerate your emotional discomfort and, at the same time, the reactions of other people. You will develop a mindful way of being more assertive while remaining non-reactive. Seeing people's negativity and emotional reactions in their true light is seeing their suffering. This is why we often call this stage "the art of seeing suffering."

Stage 4: In this stage, you will expand your focus even further, learning how empathy, compassion, personal values and ethics enhance and maintain your emotional well-being. Now that we understand how and why we behaved the way we did when we were distressed, we can understand that others operate in a very similar way. However, they may not have the understanding that you will have at this stage of the MiCBT program, so you will learn to remain kind and empathic. We also begin to understand that minimizing harm to oneself and to others is good for our well-being.

Handout 1.6 Why it is Important to Develop Regular Practice

The MiCBT program often involves an average of ten sessions, approximately a week apart, although this can be adapted with your therapist according to your needs. It is designed to allow you to practice between each session. In order to make the progress you want, you will need to commit to two 30-minute practice sessions each day, except in the last five days of week 1 where only two 14-minute practice sessions are needed for progressive muscle relaxation training. Practicing less than two 30-minute sessions a day can prevent you completing the program in the ten recommended sessions and will slow down your ability to achieve your goals.

Most effective mindfulness programs rely on regular home practice, because this is how you create healthy connections within your brain in a way that will help you manage thoughts and emotions more skillfully. This is called "neuroplasticity." Practice sessions that are too short will not leave much opportunity to develop and strengthen neural pathways. Research shows that a routine of two 30-minute sessions daily seems to be ideal for making good, rapid gains across the four stages of this program. When you are practicing, it may take a little time to calm the mind at the start, and sometimes you might find that you are less focused towards the end of practice. This is normal and it changes over time as your brain makes new connections to perform the tasks. It is a little bit like bringing your brain to the gym twice a day.

Occasionally, your therapist might suggest a variation to the amount of practice or the length of time scheduled for practice. Your therapist will be working with you as you establish your practice and will support you with any hurdles or difficulties that get in the way.

Common Difficulties with Commitment

"I need more sleep"

Some people worry about sleep and believe that they can't practice in the morning because of their sleep requirements. We develop all sorts of beliefs about how much sleep we need or what might happen if we have a little less sleep. Remember that the benefits of your mindfulness practice are very likely to outweigh the effects of sleeping 30 minutes less in the morning. This is because people tend to gain much deeper sleep when they practice mindfulness meditation, and deeper sleep is just as important (if not more) than the length of sleep. In other words, quality is just as important as quantity. The program assists us to question ourselves about the things that hold us back from doing what we value in our lives, and the fear of not sleeping enough could be a good fear to put to the test. Ask yourself if you would be willing to lose some sleep if you needed to catch a plane to Hawaii in the early hours of the morning!

Being Too Busy To Practice

We often feel we are too busy to make time to look after ourselves or to take steps towards positive change—change that would be beneficial for ourselves and for those around us. This program requires you to schedule valuable practice time for *yourself*. Your therapist will work with you to problem-solve prioritizing your time. The belief that you don't have time to practice is simply an opportunity to challenge your belief, because that's all it is. Ask yourself honestly if you would be willing to make time for 30 minutes of meditation practice twice daily if you were paid $1,000 for each session, or if the practice would save you from a deadly disease. Would you make time? If yes, then what holds you back from committing time is low motivation, rather than time limitations. This leads us to the next common hindrance.

Feeling Indulgent and Guilty

You may already take care of yourself by spending time on yoga, physical exercise or creative activities. If so, you might believe that adding time for mindfulness meditation would be indulgent because it would take too much of the time that you should spend on work or be with your family. Consider that your mental well-being needs attention too, and feeling better because of your mindfulness training will also benefit others. Remind yourself why you decided to do the program. When people are asked why they really want to change, they often reply that they wish to reduce some form of suffering. When we ask what would happen if they *didn't* reduce their worry, emotional pain or unhelpful habits, they often say "It would affect people around me in a bad way and I don't want this to affect my family." This is because most people feel compassionate toward the people they love. Once people have committed to twice daily practice, they report the many benefits that their commitment has brought to friends and family members.

Handout 1.7 Progressive Muscle Relaxation and Mindfulness of Body

Relaxation to prepare for mindfulness practice

For most people, when we are emotionally distressed, we are less able to actually feel the emotion (the sensations in the body) because we are reactive and "in our head," so to speak. When we are calm and peaceful, we can attend to what is going on in our body more easily. In MiCBT we use progressive muscle relaxation, or PMR, because it helps us to be aware of our body and relax the tension. PMR has been shown to be effective as a relaxation and stress-relieving technique since the 1930s. This practice also prepares you for a regular daily practice so that you will be able to commit to your twice a day 30-minute mindfulness practice next week.

Practice of Progressive Muscle Relaxation

With PMR, we learn to contract and relax 16 muscle groups. You will learn to feel and let go of muscle tension in a way that will help to make you feel more grounded, present and committed to self-care each day in preparation for the exercises next week. There are audio instructions to help as you start with the practice. The tracks for this week are tracks 1, 2 and 3 as introductions and explanations, and then track 4 to guide the PMR exercise. When you have listened to tracks 1, 2, 3 and 4 a couple of times you can simply use track 4 for the rest of the week. Record how much you practice on the Daily Record of Progressive Muscle Relaxation form (Handout 1.9) and bring it to your therapist in your next session.

Practice of Mindfulness of Body

For most people, not only those who seek therapy, being in the present moment is difficult. With a scattered and distracted mind, we can easily ruminate over the past or worry about the future. In this exercise, you will learn to keep your mind in the present, using your own body as an "anchor" or "hook" for your attention in the present moment. You will learn to stay focused by noticing your body posture and movements when you are walking, running, sitting, lying or standing.

Pay attention to your movements and posture as much as possible each day during the week. Apply this effort when you go to bed as well. Fall asleep with the awareness that your body is lying down, feeling its weight and pressure on the mattress. Focus on the body with interest and curiosity, without judging it. Avoid seeing the body as beautiful or ugly, or in any other way. Simply *observe* it for what it is, a body, a part of nature. When you are truly observing the body, you are in the present moment, and are a little more distant from the repetitive unhelpful thoughts. This is an important start in your development of skills to live in the present.

Remember also to pay attention to what you are doing throughout the day, so that you experience things more as they are in the present. You will be able to notice details on a friend's face and respond appropriately, the shapes of seeds inside an apple with interest, the taste of a familiar food with appreciation, etc.

Handout 1.8 Audio Tracks for the MiCBT Program

Please use the tracks listed below as instructed by your therapist. You can download all these audio instructions using this link: http://clinicalhandbook.mindfulness.net.au/audio

Stage 1

1 General Introduction.mp3
2 Rationale for Training.mp3
3 Introduction to PMR.mp3
4 Progressive Muscle Relaxation.mp3
5 Introduction to Mindfulness of Breath.mp3
6 Mindfulness of Breath.mp3
7 Introduction to Body Scanning.mp3
8 Body Scanning.mp3
 – Withdrawing the Instructions.mp3

Stages 2, 3, 4

9 Introduction to Advanced Scanning.mp3
10 Symmetrical Scanning.mp3
11 Introduction to Partial Sweeping.mp3
12 Partial Sweeping.mp3
13 Introduction to Sweeping en masse.mp3
14 Sweeping en masse.mp3
15 Introduction to Transversal Scanning.mp3
16 Transversal Scanning.mp3
17 Introduction to Loving-Kindness.mp3
18 Loving-Kindness.mp3
19 Maintenance Practice.mp3

Terms of Use of Audio Track and Forms

This license grants the right to stream and download the audio files for your private and domestic use only. For example, *you can*, for your private use, copy the recordings onto your iPod/ iPhone/ iPad or MP3 player, and copy the files onto a CD to play them in your stereo. *This license is limited to you.* This license does not grant the right to sell, give away, distribute, perform in public, or broadcast private copies, make private copies from an illegitimate recording (e.g., from a burnt CD or from peer to peer files), or share private copies online. Uploading or distributing the files via the internet without permission from the copyright owner (Dr. Bruno Cayoun) will infringe copyright.

Handout 1.9 Daily Record of Progressive Muscle Relaxation

For your convenience, you can download this form and all other forms used for this program using this link:
http://clinicalhandbook.mindfulness.net.au/handouts

Day	**Date**	**Morning** *(circle)*	**Duration**	**Efficacy rating in %** *How relaxing was it?*	**Evening** *(circle)*	**Duration**	**Efficacy rating in %** *How relaxing was it?*
Monday		I practiced Yes / No			I practiced Yes / No		
Tuesday		I practiced Yes / No			I practiced Yes / No		
Wednesday		I practiced Yes / No			I practiced Yes / No		
Thursday		I practiced Yes / No			I practiced Yes / No		
Friday		I practiced Yes / No			I practiced Yes / No		
Saturday		I practiced Yes / No			I practiced Yes / No		
Sunday		I practiced Yes / No			I practiced Yes / No		

References

BACP. (2016). *Good practice in action 055 Fact sheet resource: Making the therapeutic agreement in the counselling professions*. Leicestershire, UK: British Association for Counselling and Psychotherapy. Retrieved May 2, 2018 from http://www.bacp.co.uk/ethical_framework/documents/GPiA055.pdf

Benson, H. (1975/2001). *The relaxation response*. New York: Harper Collins.

Bernstein, D. A., & Borkovec, T. D. (1973). *Progressive relaxation training: A manual for the helping professions*. Champaign, IL: Research Press.

Beutler, L. E. (2004). The empirically supported treatments movement: A scientist-practitioner's response. *Clinical Psychology: Science and Practice*, 11, 225–229. doi:10.1093/clipsy.bph076

Bordin, E. S. (1979). The generalizability of the psychoanalytic concept of the working alliance. *Psychotherapy: Theory, Research & Practice*, 16, 252.

Carlson, E. N. (2013). Overcoming the barriers to self-knowledge: Mindfulness as a path to seeing yourself as you really are. *Perspective on Psychological Science*, 8, 173–186.

Cayoun, B. A. (2011). *Mindfulness-integrated CBT: Principles and practice*. Chichester: UK: Wiley.

Cayoun, B. A. (2015). *Mindfulness-integrated CBT for well-being and personal growth: Four steps to enhance inner calm, self-confidence and relationships*. Chichester, UK: Wiley.

Center for Substance Abuse Treatment (1999). *Brief interventions and brief therapies for substance abuse. Treatment improvement protocol (TIP). Series No. 34. HHS Publication No. (SMA) 12-3952*. Rockville, MD: Substance Abuse and Mental Health Services Administration.

Farb, N., A. S., Daubenmier, J., Price, C. J., Gard, T., Kerr, C., Dunn, B. D., et al. (2015). Interoception, contemplative practice, and health. *Frontiers in Psychology*, 6, 763. doi:10.3389/fpsyg.2015.00763

Hayes, S. C., Rosenfarb, I., Wulfert, E., Munt, E., Zettle, R. D., & Korn, Z. (1985). Self-reinforcement effects: An artifact of social standard setting? *Journal of Applied Behavioral Analysis*, 18, 201–214. doi: 10.1901/jaba.1985.18-201

Hayes-Skelton, S. A., Roemer, L., Orsillo, S. M., & Borkovec, T. D. (2013). A Contemporary view of applied relaxation in generalized anxiety disorder. *Cognitive Behaviour Therapy*, 42, 292–303.

Jacobson, E. (1938). *Progressive relaxation*. Chicago: University of Chicago Press.

Langer, E. J. (1989). *Mindfulness*. New-York: Addison-Wesley.

Rohn, J. (2010). *The treasury of quotes*. Lake Dallas, TX: Success Books.

Scott-Hamilton, J., & Schutte, N. S. (2016). The role of adherence in the effects of a mindfulness intervention for competitive athletes: Changes in mindfulness, flow, pessimism and anxiety. *Journal of Clinical Sport Psychology*, 10, 99–117. doi: 10.1123/jcsp.2015-0020

Session 2: Regulating Attention Through Mindfulness of Breath

Patience and time do more than strength or passion.

—Jean de la Fontaine, 1668

Introduction

This week's session focuses on the development of attention-regulation skills through the practice of mindfulness of breath (*anapanasati* in Pali) and addresses potential difficulties in adhering to a regular practice schedule. This chapter introduces the practice and purpose of mindfulness of breath, which is the first meditative method used in MiCBT. It provides guidance for your clients' practice of mindfulness of breath, which will assist them to gain a deeper understanding of their mental states and how these affect emotions and behavior. As clients become less judgmental, less reactive and relate more objectively to their thoughts, they also become less affected by them. Your clients will learn to notice and let go of unhelpful thinking, such as worrisome, ruminative or catastrophic thoughts, and instead, nurture helpful thoughts.

Checking Client Readiness

If you are following the standard delivery protocol, this is your client's second week of training. You need to check if they committed to the practice of progressive muscle relaxation (PMR) twice daily. If so, ask if they benefited from it. Although most people do benefit from PMR, many can be challenged by the practice because their mind remains distracted, or even agitated, while tensing and relaxing muscles. This is particularly the case when the person is used to being highly stimulated with daily activities, such as working, studying or worrying about things. Many people say that they can't stop thinking, which means that

The Clinical Handbook of Mindfulness-integrated Cognitive Behavior Therapy: A Step-by-Step Guide for Therapists, First Edition. Bruno A. Cayoun, Sarah E. Francis, and Alice G. Shires.

Companion website: www.wiley.com/go/Cayoun/Mindfulness-integrated

they may be *attached* to thoughts, in the same way that one is attached to other sensory stimulation. Just as a person can be addicted to sugar, one can be addicted to thinking. Despite the well-documented benefits of relaxation, it is not easy to learn when we are caught up in thoughts. Without specific skills, it can be difficult to disengage from unwanted thoughts. This is precisely what your client will be learning to do this week, unless we need to delay the next step.

Delaying the Next Step

If your client has had difficulties establishing a daily practice or has found that even PMR created significant difficulties, you will need to work with them at determining the cause of their difficulties to enable them to move forward without feeling like a failure. Sometimes, clients experience relaxation-induced anxiety. This is more likely to occur in people with a recent history or active symptoms of trauma. As they relax and their awareness threshold decreases, they become more aware of what is intermittently subconscious. They begin to remember the things they usually try to avoid. This also applies to some people with chronic pain. Even though they deeply wish they could relax their tormented body, relaxing also means feeling it more. In both types of cases, people resent what they feel and usually do all they can to avoid it, whether by means of medication, distraction or intoxication. As they begin to relax, they may initially feel a little anxious. They can practice PMR with open eyes to begin with, if it helps. If they need to, it is not detrimental to allow them to skip a few parts of the body, as we are not using PMR just to relax—but rather to commit to a daily practice in a way that is congruent with mindfulness—and a state of relaxation is not what we are ultimately attempting to achieve. Acceptance of the client's limitations is a priority.

When there is a problem with establishing a daily practice routine, you will need to assist your client to recommit and then repeat last week's practice before moving on to the practice of mindfulness of breath. It is important that they are able to establish a practice before moving on.

If they have been able to maintain a regular practice, now is the time to introduce mindfulness of breath. Since mindfulness of breath is a prerequisite for the next step of the program, your client will also need to commit to a daily mindfulness of breath practice. Without strong commitment, clinical improvement will be slow, and this can contribute to low motivation to continue with the program, with some clients eventually dropping out. Commitment to a task is most likely to occur if people benefited from the previous task, which positively reinforces the likelihood of effort and trust. We reiterate the importance of commitment to practice because benefits *depend* on practice.

Purpose of Mindfulness of Breath

This week, your client will start developing mindfulness skills using their breath. They will learn to practice mindfulness of breath to remain focused in the present moment, from moment to moment, whilst learning to inhibit their propensity to engage with thoughts that emerge spontaneously in conscious awareness. This is a concentration task that progressively calms the mind and provides the mental strength to prevent over-thinking (Kabat Zinn, 2013). Clients learn to observe the natural breath in order to anchor their attention on the interoceptive aspect of breathing while being exposed to such intrusive thoughts and preventing the usual reaction to thoughts. They develop some control over their response to intrusive thoughts. This is an attentional training which uses an already existing function (the breath) that is a natural part of the client's present-moment ongoing experience. Your client will progressively notice that the mind is anything but still from one moment to the next, wandering into the past or future, but hardly ever remaining in the reality that is taking place in the present. Monitoring these mental patterns without engaging in them or reacting to them progressively calms and stabilizes the mind (Hart, 1987). This method alone has been shown to reduce ruminative brooding in previously depressed clients (Barnhofer, Chittka, Nightingale, Visser, & Crane, 2010).

Practice Set-up

Environment and Material

Before starting, preparing a favorable environment for practice is important. The context must be conducive when people are new to the practice. The best environment for the practice of mindfulness meditation is one with the least amount of stimulation possible—indoors in a quiet room. Discuss where and when your client may be able to practice twice daily. As they start developing practice skills we want them to limit distractions as much as possible in order to minimize external sensory stimulation. Later on, when your client becomes skilled, they can practice anywhere, but this is a skill that takes time to develop. This means for now they will need to minimize seeing, hearing, smelling, tasting, touching, moving the body and voluntary thinking. If we are too stimulated by the environment, our attention will move from the intended object of practice to external stimuli, such as sounds and touch, instead of focusing internally on breath sensations. In other words, the external environment can create sensory input that prevents us from attending to the output, such as arising thoughts and body sensations, which would normally occur during practice.

Discuss the above with your client, including choosing a quiet room where they won't be disturbed for 30 minutes in the morning and 30 minutes in the evening. Some people think that they need somewhere special for meditation. This can sometimes create limitations to their practice. Some clients will say that they didn't or couldn't practice because the kids played in the next room or their partner was doing something in the room in which they usually practice. If this occurs with your client, it is useful to remind them that they can practice anywhere reasonably quiet. If they practice while sitting on a chair, they can put a kitchen chair in their bedroom and practice there.

Your client will need to play the audio instructions on an MP3 player, smart phone or CD player (if they choose to copy the tracks on to a CD). Room temperature is important, particularly at the start of the program. It will be helpful if the temperature is not too low or too high. Being too hot can make your client sleepy, while being too cold creates agitation. Noise level can be an issue when your client hasn't yet acquired equanimity skills, which help to prevent reactivity. Light is also important to consider. It can be useful to dim the lights, but having some light is better than practicing in the dark, as a dim or pitch-black room can induce drowsiness.

Mental and Physical States

The less food before practice the better. In the evening, it is best to practice before dinner or well after dinner if it is not too late. Practicing after a meal and with a full stomach is difficult. Digesting food depletes our energy and most people will feel drowsy.

If your client uses intoxicants, including alcohol at dinner, make sure that they don't use them *before* their practice. Alcohol, marijuana and other intoxicants have been shown to disinhibit prefrontal areas of the brain necessary for the kind of mental effort that is required in meditation practice. As a result, your client will not be able to control their response to what arises in the mind (e.g., Suchotzki, Crombez, Debey, van Oorsouw, & Verschuere, 2015; Smith et al., 2011). Once they have practiced mindfulness skills for 30 minutes, it is likely that they will need less substances later that day than they usually would, especially if they use substances to relax or sleep.

Posture

It is important to explain that we practice with eyes closed to minimize distraction from external stimuli and to allow better focus on inner experience. Some clients may have problems with closing their eyes because of a fear of becoming agitated or anxious due to past trauma or a fear of losing control. There are some ways to address this with your client. It might be useful to close their eyes halfway and to direct their gaze down to the floor, so that they don't see further than two and a half meters in front of their knees. As your client begins to feel safer and more comfortable, they can make progressive efforts to close their eyes further in each practice session.

Unlike the very comfortable sitting posture used during PMR, the posture needed from here on in for mindfulness practice involves keeping the neck and back straight, while not leaning against anything. Your client's knees are best positioned lower than their buttocks. This will open the angle between the torso and the thighs, allowing your client to safely sit straight without strain on their lower back. Sitting upright will also keep them more alert and attentive despite the lack of external stimulation. An example of comfortable sitting postures on a chair and on the floor is depicted in Session 2, Figure 1.

Practice may be undertaken sitting on a chair or on a very thick cushion on the floor. If your client uses a chair, ensure that they don't lean against the back. If they sit on the floor, ensure that they don't lean against anything either, such as a bed, sofa or wall. Being able to let the knees touch the floor will keep the back in an upright position with ease, without tiring. However, this is not always easy to do when we start practicing. Your client may choose to either work on it and

Session 2, Figure 1 Examples of sitting positions on a chair and on the floor.

get there progressively or simply sit on a chair. There is no need to use a complicated or painful posture with mindfulness training. In fact, creating pain intentionally can become a great distraction from the actual task. This is important to keep in mind if your client has a history of trauma or practices *asana yoga* and tends to want to strain the body. Doing so may be a means of avoidance of whatever else could be arising in consciousness if they were to simply relax into a comfortable upright posture. Ensure that your client does not go to the other extreme by lying on the floor, or it will soon become a snoring session!

Clothing

Your client will need comfortable clothing whether they sit on a chair or on the floor. When sitting on the floor, they will benefit from placing a thick blanket or mat on the floor that will be underneath their feet and knees, and then place a thick cushion on top to sit on. Meditators often use a shawl or blanket around their shoulders because they can feel a little colder when they sit still for some time. Covering the lower back and legs can make the practice more comfortable.

Practice of Mindfulness of Breath

The practice of mindfulness of breath (MOB) is carried out with closed eyes, whilst seated in a comfortable upright position. We begin by taking half a minute to relax the body, but this time without tensing and relaxing muscles as in the past week. We are only doing a quick "scan" through the body to let go of any possible tension. This resembles a very rapid PMR exercise, but without the tensing part. This is not to teach aversion to tension; it is simply to make it a little easier for people who are agitated and very new to meditation. The audio instructions accompanying this book provide the necessary guidance for the practice.

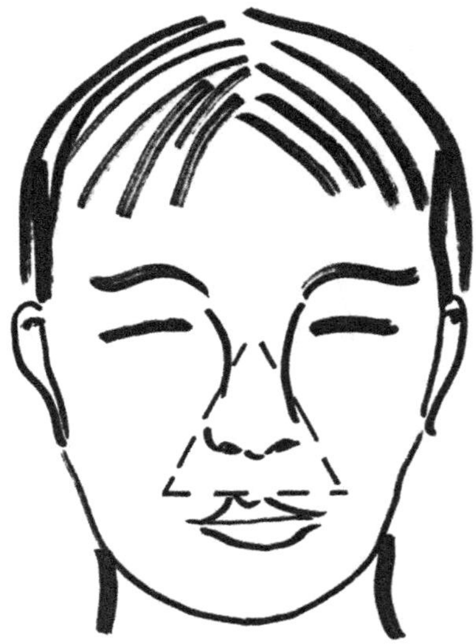

Session 2, Figure 2 Area of focus for mindfulness of breath.

MOB practice then starts with a calm mind, with the attention focused as much as possible on the entrance of the nostrils. Your client needs to bring their attention to a small triangular area of the face, covering the entire area of nostrils. The primary focus is on the breath entering and exiting the nostrils, creating temperature change and friction on the inner walls of the nostrils, the outer rings of the nostrils and the area just below the nostrils, above the upper lip. Session 2, Figure 2 illustrates the area in which to limit the focus of attention during mindfulness of breath.

Your client needs to learn to maintain the primary focus of their attention on sensations of breath at the nostrils. When other possible objects for their attention enter their conscious awareness, such as sounds, prominent sensations in other areas of the body, or thought content related to their recent or habitual concerns, they are instructed to continue to attend to sensations associated with normal, natural, non-controlled breathing. If their breath feels agitated to them (e.g., fast, deep or otherwise unpleasant), then they are instructed to just witness and accept the experience of agitation, but to do their best to remain non-reactive and mentally calm. If they are not mentally calm, they are asked to focus their attention on observing the breath and not their thoughts, and notice how thoughts can settle when we focus on the breath without wishing that things were different, with acceptance of the present experience. Trying to change aspects of the breath may occur because of a negative reaction to the experience of breathing, which can cause some further agitation. On the other hand, accepting that the breath is too fast or deep allows the mind to begin to relax. After a few days of committed practice, your client may become aware of subtle sensations in and around this area of the face, such as unexplained itching sensations. You may need to reassure your client by normalizing this experience, telling them that it is normal to feel these and to just notice the sensations without giving them any importance, acknowledging that they can initially be experienced as annoying. The same applies to sensations felt elsewhere in the body while monitoring the breath.

Explain to your client that it is not advisable to use imagery or any verbalization technique even though they may have used them previously. Mindfulness is *always* a practice of observing our experience of reality *as it is*, as it manifests itself from moment to moment. Visualization techniques and mantras are sometimes added to assist beginners, especially when the focus of practice is the concentrative aspect of meditation. However, because MOB (a concentration practice) is not our final practice, using visualization or imagery will become a hindrance in the next few weeks.

Skills Your Client will Learn

The skills your client will learn may not be familiar to them, but they are well understood in Western psychological science, where they are considered as "executive functions" skills (Cayoun, 2011; Chambers, Lo, & Allen, 2008). These are essential mental functions that we use to "govern" our lives every day (Cayoun, 2010). For instance, *the first skill* your client will develop is "metacognitive awareness," which is the ability to be aware of the presence and type of thoughts present in consciousness. They will learn to develop this skill with MOB through sustaining their attention on a selected focus (the breath) for increasingly longer periods of time. This alone is a great tool for focusing on daily activities.

A second skill that your client will acquire with MOB is the ability to observe thoughts emerging spontaneously in consciousness without identifying with them. In fact, your client does not choose to have these specific thoughts. We will provide an explanation for the dynamic emergence of thoughts a little later, when we discuss ways of normalizing intrusive thoughts. Using this explanation will also help your client to be more at ease with painful memories that could emerge during practice.

In traditional Eastern practice, observing thoughts without identifying with their content, and abstaining from using them to feed a narrative about self is one way to practice "egolessness." In recent Western terminology, this has been called "decentering" (Teasdale, Segal & Williams, 1995). You will need to help your client understand that thoughts are *just* thoughts, and there is no need to identify with them just because we experience them. Your client will develop the ability to perceive thoughts for what they are: *just* thoughts, just mental events and nothing else.

Observing thoughts when they intrude requires inhibiting the habitual reaction of engaging with 'thinking' the thoughts. What we habitually do when a thought enters our mind is to just go with it, without questioning whether or not this is what we want to do or whether it could be useful or harmful to proceed with thinking it, or even without realizing that we didn't actively choose to think this thought. Without the mental liberation that mindfulness training provides, we remain a prisoner of our own mind. Training in MOB will teach your client to be more assertive with their own mind and say "no" to thoughts.

If we consider MOB from a behavioral perspective, it largely consists of exposure (to thoughts and other stimuli) and response prevention (inhibiting the proliferation of thinking). When understood this way (i.e., strongly based on a sound theory), clinicians feel more confident about what they are doing and understand the mechanisms of action better. This also means that clinicians are more able to evaluate the risk of adverse effects occurring, such as potential abreactions with spontaneous trauma memories (Van Dam et al., 2017). For example, if you work with traumatized clients who have been stable for a while but have a history of strong emotional reactivity, letting them practice on their own for too long is not a good idea. If clients inadvertently reinforce strong emotions co-emerging with painful memories for more than two to three weeks (i.e., *not* applying equanimity to the co-emergent sensations), they may experience strong reactions, and this can increase the likelihood of dropping out of therapy. To prevent this, seeing clients who have had a complex or traumatic childhood history weekly or fortnightly is important. It provides sufficient opportunities to clarify the tasks, troubleshoot problems and provide validation and support—hence our strong recommendation in Part 1 of the book for accurate professional training in MiCBT and supervision by trainers who are well informed and experienced. We will discuss a useful way of addressing traumatic memories in Session 6.

A third skill developed with MOB is the ability to detach ourselves from thoughts and switch attention back to the task at hand, which in this case is the focus on our own breath. This third executive function is called attention-shifting. As soon as your client has recognized that a thought has arisen in the mind, their next step should be to return attention immediately to the nostrils without getting caught up in the thought. Doing this repeatedly, gently, will increase their cognitive flexibility, and make their mind more patient, tolerant and flexible in daily life too. This involves a strengthening of the brain connections necessary to prevent the old reaction from taking place and to choose a new response (Hölzel et al., 2011). Hence, these skills allow us to deal with the *process* of thinking, rather than its *content* (the meaning of the thought itself).

Differentiating Mindfulness from Attentiveness

For most newcomers to mindfulness-based therapies, instructing clients to just notice the breath from moment to moment seems rather straightforward, but the devil is in the detail. It is important to note that while being mindful always requires being attentive, being attentive per se does not mean being mindful. A couple of useful analogies to evoke with your client are a cat in front of a mouse-hole, very attentive, ready to catch the mouse, and a circus performer walking on a tightrope. One is paying full attention to its prey with a strong desire to catch it (craving), and the other is paying full attention to its physical balance to avoid falling (aversion). In both these examples where being fully concentrated in the "here and now" is essential, the mental state involves either craving or aversion. In contrast, paying attention mindfully requires being free from craving, free from aversion and free from identification with thoughts and other spontaneously emerging experiences. Therefore, paying attention to our breath during meditation is done without craving and without aversion toward any unwanted thoughts that may intrude in conscious awareness during practice.

The confusion about what constitutes mindfulness (Cayoun, 2017; see also Van Dam et al., 2017, for a review) often emerges when we lack a sound theoretical framework from which to understand constructs and mechanisms of action. For instance, if we understand mindfulness skills to be *attentional mechanisms enabling of exposure and response prevention*, then sustained attention is insufficient (Cayoun, 2011). As in all methods of exposure therapy, we need to prevent reactivity—in this case, in the form of craving and aversion. This is important for two reasons. One reason relates to practice benefits. If your client produces an attentional effort but succumbs to a craving attitude for future expectations or feels engulfed with resentment every time they encounter an unpleasant memory, they are not learning to neutralize the emotional load attached to (co-emerging with) the thought and are instead strengthening unhelpful habits (Cayoun & Shires, submitted for publication).

The second reason relates to the potential harmful effects of being attentive but not mindful. Since it is *highly likely* that during accurate practice your client will remember stressful events, a lack of objectivity and equanimity will allow a learned aversive reaction. In other words, if your client experiences a painful memory during practice and they don't clearly understand that memories are just combinations of thoughts and co-emerging sensations, impersonal mental and physical phenomena, they will pay attention to them in a way that involves reacting with aversion (e.g., avoidance, rumination, etc.). In this case, their learned response is being reinforced instead of being extinguished. Hence, in the name of mindfulness, a poor understanding of mechanisms of action can mislead clients, which may lead to adverse effects of mindfulness practice in some cases. It is for this reason that the whole of Chapter 2 was devoted to the theoretical framework underlying MiCBT.

Normalizing Intrusive Thoughts

One of the first phenomena encountered during MOB is the spontaneous emergence of thoughts and images. When people begin to practice, these are perceived as unwanted distractions or even frustrating events. This common experience needs to be normalized to prevent an incorrect perception of personal incapacity or failure and a resultant decrease in motivation. Just saying "it's normal, just refocus on the breath" is a fair suggestion, but it relies on "devotional learning," on faith in the therapist, and does not sufficiently make use of the three learning modalities (devotional, critical and experiential). Providing an explanation, even metaphorical, can engage critical thinking and boost effort. Below are three ways of normalizing intrusive thoughts.

Socratic Method

Socratic dialogue—the questioning approach often used in CBT and a communication style that the Buddha used about 500 years before Socrates—is always a good ally when it comes to normalizing clients' experiences. Since MiCBT is a tight integration of mindfulness and CBT, Socratic dialogue is often used throughout the program. Whether we are discussing a client's reactivity to intrusive thoughts or to another unpleasant experience, here is a typical interaction (T = therapist, C = client):

T: You seem to be very annoyed at all these thoughts that seem to interfere with what you are trying to do, which is to focus on the breath, right?

C: Yes, it became very frustrating after a few days, which is why I did it only for 15 minutes in the past three days; after that I get too distracted and it seems a bit pointless.

T: I completely understand how this can be frustrating. I wonder how you handle being distracted by people or unexpected tasks that interfere with what you are trying to achieve in your day-to-day life? Are you tolerant and very flexible or do you tend to be easily frustrated?

C: Yes, I get frustrated. I just hate it when you try to do something and you can't because something comes up or people keep wanting your attention…

T: Is it possible that your frustration with trying to focus on the breath and being distracted by thoughts is triggering a habitual reaction that you have in your daily life?

C: Mm…, it looks like it, doesn't it? I didn't think about that.

T: Since the brain you use for meditation is the same brain that you use in daily actions, doesn't it make sense that it responds in a similar way when you think in a similar way?

C: Yes, I guess this makes sense.

T: Our personality and the pathways in the brain that maintain our habits are not changed at this early stage of your training, so you react in your meditation just the way you react in daily-life, and *vice versa*. Would you like to change this habit in your daily life?

C: Yes, for sure, it would make my life easier. It would be nice if people would feel more relaxed around me too.

T: Great, now just imagine that you keep on training your mind to be not so reactive, to remain more peaceful, more detached and flexible every time a thought distracts you from focusing on the breath when you meditate. Do you think that this would influence your daily life?

C: Yes, possibly.

T: This is exactly what we observe with this program and in the research: because your mindfulness practice rewires your brain to be more focused, flexible and settled, you also experience it in daily life as you become more patient and less reactive. This means that we actually *need* these intrusive thoughts to develop these skills. Without having the opportunity to learn to handle intrusive thoughts peacefully, without identifying with them, we cannot develop these skills. Can you see why it is actually useful to have these thoughts when we start?

C: Yes, I guess they are a little bit like tools.

T: Exactly! It is useful to remember that the way you meditate is the way you live your life, and that this gives you the choice to make changes… Are you now willing to practice for the whole 30-minute in each session from now on?

C: I will certainly try. Now I understand this better…

This explanation can be sufficient, but it will be strengthened if followed (or replaced) by the following explanation.

Three Internal Causes of Intrusive Thoughts

There are external and internal contexts in which intrusive thoughts arise in conscious awareness. External contexts consist of all the external environmental stimuli: what we hear, see, smell, taste or feel. Sitting practice minimizes this external stimulation, as practice is with eyes closed, in a quiet place and sitting without moving. You can see why practicing indoors will be easier for your client as this reduces the amount of external stimulation. Internal stimuli (thoughts and body sensations) however, are not dependent on any external source. With some observation, it becomes increasingly noticeable that thoughts pertaining to topics that we have been thinking about recently or frequently tend to emerge more readily in consciousness. Based on neural networks theory (McClelland, Rumelhart, & The PDP Research Group, 1986), this can be explained in terms of the *strength* and *depth* of neural activation related to these thoughts (see Cayoun, 2011, for a detailed account).

Basically, the sets of neurons required to process these recent and frequent thoughts remain more activated than those used to process older and infrequent thoughts. As we relax and focus on the breath, neural networks with the greatest level of activation allow their corresponding thoughts to reach conscious awareness. This is best demonstrated with the activation of the so-called "default mode network," located on the midline of the prefrontal cortex. This part of the brain has repeatedly shown to activate during daydreaming and thinking thoughts related to ourselves, such as autobiographical memories and anticipation of future interactions with others; in fact, the typical thoughts we experience as we start to learn to meditate (Doll, Hölzel, Bouckard, Wohlschlager, & Sorg, 2015; Xu et al., 2014). In addition, spontaneous intrusive thoughts during practice are determined by the *depth* of their neural activation, i.e., the activation of neurons deep inside emotional pathways of the brain. Consideration of the co-emergence model of reinforcement (see Chapter 2) shows that the Evaluation component causes concomitant stimulation in the Interoception (body sensations) component and the intensity of the sensations is determined by the degree of judgmental thinking.

This is a little more complicated, but this explanation helps us understand and normalize what appear to be random thoughts and thoughts that can lead to strong reactions in your clients. During meditation practice, since one of the tasks is to minimize the production of new thoughts, frequently and recently activated thoughts are given the chance to intrude. As we inhibit reaction to these thoughts, they are not (or are only minimally) being reinforced because the attention is immediately shifted back to the breath. This weakens the strength of activation of these networks, hence weakening the associated thoughts. It is an *extinction process* that allows for older material to emerge into consciousness, and this explains why people often report re-experiencing old memories during meditation practice. This enables thoughts to be re-processed neutrally, in a way that is less personal. The process has been called "decoupling" by Daniel Siegel: detaching thoughts from their emotional aspect (Siegel, 2009b). However, recall does not appear to be impacted; in fact, it may be improved when co-emergent sensations have become conscious while the emotional reactivity usually associated with the memory is absent. Memories that are associated with more intense sensations are likely to have strong connections to emotional pathways and appear to be harder to extinguish. From an evolutionary perspective, this is advantageous as it means we remember things that caused great emotional reactivity and may have been a threat.

When we have an experience that evokes some emotion, the sensations underlying the emotion and the associated aspect of the cognitive memory are encoded and stored together. This means that when we feel sensations in the body that are sufficiently similar to those experienced at some earlier time, they can act as memory cues and cause memory recall. Hence, spontaneous thoughts that can appear random during meditation may not be random at all—for any event, there must be a cause. Note also that sensations triggered through a recent emotional experience can act as memory cues during or between meditation practices. This explanation may help clients normalize their experiences of intrusive thoughts during their mindfulness practice.

It follows from the above that trying to suppress thoughts is counterproductive, because they are maintained by body sensations. In contrast, addressing thought intrusions and their co-emerging body sensations with equanimity, non-reactively, supports the extinction process. It has been shown that although the duration of anxiety may be reduced during suppression, the anxiety is likely to be more severe and occur more frequently when thought suppression stops (Koster, Rassin, Grombez, & Näring, 2003). It is actually not productive to "not think" a thought that is emerging in consciousness. If you are asked "try not to think about a white bear" the first thing you do is think about a white bear before trying to suppress it. This is highly relevant to the treatment of anxiety disorders, where intrusive thoughts are central.

Keep in mind that all recency, frequency and co-emergence effects are part of an interactive dynamic system of cognitive processing and are not separate mechanisms. For example, this morning's experience of walking to work is more recent than a car accident that you witnessed yesterday afternoon, but thoughts that are likely to reach consciousness first when you meditate this evening are those related to the accident, even though these are less recent than this morning's walk. This is because the emotional load of these thoughts (co-emerging body sensations) is much "heavier" than that of this morning's peaceful walk. If these co-emerging sensations have not fully subsided since the accident (especially if you have thought about it frequently since), then the body sensations act as memory cues. In other words, interoception acts as a mediating variable between recency and frequency effects.

The Mind-fasting Metaphor

Some clients don't have the ability to assimilate the above neurophenomenological explanation of intrusive thoughts, even when the explanation is given in very simple terms. In this case, we suggest offering the "fasting metaphor" below, which is inspired from the discourses of one of our Vipassana meditation teachers, S. N. Goenka (Goenka, 1987). If we want to lose weight, we need to decrease the input of energy that we obtain from food or increase the output of energy ("burning fats") through physical effort, or both. If our body needs more energy than our food provides, it has to find it in the body's reserves—our stored fat. This is the main reason we lose weight. The same reasoning can be applied to the mind. What is the input for the mind? From an experiential perspective, mental inputs are mostly thoughts and images. When we focus attention on the breath, we are not focusing on thoughts or even thinking about the breath. We know that it is there just by feeling it. As such, we are not creating new mental input. Metaphorically speaking, the mind is "fasting" and needs to tap into its reserves to continue functioning, and the reserves for the mind are our memories. The less we feed the mind new thoughts, the more it "consumes" memories.

Certainly, our mind is not free from thoughts just because we choose not to think. This is because the mind always needs information to process. Much as the body stores food surplus in the form of fat, the mind stores our perception of events as memories. From this giant memory bank, millions of thoughts can emerge, both thoughts about the things we can remember and those we cannot. By refraining from creating new mental input (thoughts) during mindfulness meditation, we allow mental output to occur. A thought, image or even feeling in the body can arise in the mind.

If we don't get involved with a memory—even though we may not recognize the thought as a memory—and just notice it as it emerges, the value we may have given it in the past will be neutralized, along with any emotions associated with it. If we remain a neutral observer every time a thought emerges, it ceases to influence our daily life today and in the future. The more of our thoughts that are re-experienced in such a neutral way, the freer we are from our past.

Sometimes, it is not clear that thoughts arising during practice are from the past. How do we know a thought is a memory when we can't recognize it as such? Think of opening one of your kitchen drawers and finding a spoon in it. How can the spoon be there unless you have put it there in the past? Thoughts are just like anything else; they cannot be retrieved unless they were there in the first place. Moreover, thoughts about future topics that emerge during meditation are only memories of thoughts we had about the future. For example, if you have been worried about tomorrow's exam this morning, it is possible that you will experience some memories of this fear during your practice this evening. During your evening practice, spontaneous thoughts about tomorrow, the future, will emerge from yesterday's experience, the past. The same applies to having spontaneous thoughts while in bed, trying to sleep.

Application with Individual Clients

Session Aim

Session 2 introduces mindfulness of breath (MOB) and the rationale for it (developing metacognitive awareness, inhibitory control over intrusive thoughts and attention shifting) and provides a detailed explanation of thought intrusion (recency, frequency and co-emergence effects).

Review Homework Exercises and Progress

Welcome feedback on the home exercises set last week and clarify points as they arise. Ask your client how the week was in general. Did they notice anything different this week? Notice, value and validate small changes. This helps reinforce their practice. Encourage questions and clarify any aspect of the practice as necessary.

Deepening Motivation

Depressed and anxious clients often experience a fear of failure, which makes any new task appear difficult to commit to. Therapy-based expectations can become a new source of anxiety and a reason for dropping out. If they have struggled to commit to regular practice, you may wish to employ Socratic questioning: "If you were given the skills to change your condition, would you use them?" or "Out of a hundred, how much would you be prepared to change; zero being not at all and a hundred being completely?" If less than 100 %, clarify their reasons, which might include self-doubts, fear of failure or low motivation. Challenge their view using Socratic dialogue: "It may sound a bit strange, but could you tell me why you would like to change?" If you keep prompting with "...and what would be the purpose of that?" or a similar question, at some point, they might say, "I don't want to pass my depression (or anxiety, etc.) to my kids," or "I don't want my partner to suffer." At this point, emphasize that one reason for them to go through this program is compassion: "Did you realize how compassionate you can be? Much of what motivates you to go through all these efforts is your compassion and love for your (e.g., children or family), did you realize that?"

Ask, "What could happen if you don't change?" Emphasize the "cost" (homework), mentioning it is sometimes difficult to keep up with the practice. Emphasize the need for commitment: "When would you be prepared to spend 30 minutes in the morning and 30 minutes in the evening on your therapy? And where could you practice?"

Deliver a Rationale for Mindfulness of Breathing

Present a rationale for the practice of mindfulness of breath. The following is an experiential exercise using the "finger task" and rationale for the client's homework. It can also be used as an ad-hoc explanation for thought intrusion during practice if the information it contains has not been discussed prior to implementing MOB homework.

> Before you start your training of MOB this week, let's try it for a few minutes together here and make sure that you understand it, so you can practice confidently at home. First, sit with your neck and back straight, and rest the palms of your hands on your thighs. Now close your eyes and focus all your attention at the entrance of your nostrils whilst breathing naturally, without controlling your breath. Just feel the breath as it naturally passes through the nostrils. Try also to feel the touch of the breath on the inner walls and outer rings of the nostrils, and the small area below the nostrils above the upper lip, and pay attention to this part patiently and attentively for a minute, until I give you more instructions...

Wait silently for about thirty seconds allowing the client to experience some intrusive thoughts.

> Great! Keeping your eyes closed, as soon as you notice that a thought has just popped into your mind, slightly raise the index finger of your dominant hand, keeping your wrist on your thigh. Keep your finger raised until you are able to bring your attention back to your nostrils and then gently let it rest again on your knee. Do this with each thought that arises in your mind while you simply monitor your breath. You may have to do this many time in the next few minutes. This is not a problem and it is not a reflection of lack of skill. What really matters is that you

catch each thought as it arises, that you calmly and patiently release attention from the thought and redirect attention to the breath as soon as possible. Do your best for the next few minutes, remembering to use your finger to help me understand what your thoughts are doing... Note also that a sound is not a thought. The sounds of birds or cars outside the building are not thoughts unless you think about them, like how beautiful they sound or how noisy they are. So, don't raise your finger if you hear something and *don't* think about it. Raise your finger only if you are actually thinking about the sounds you hear. Do this for the next few minutes.

Observe the client's attitude, body language and frequency of thought intrusion for about one minute. Occasionally, some clients show little or no thought intrusions. If you think that the client displays some social desirability (i.e., tries to impress you), especially if they have meditated or done yoga before, gently clarify what you are looking for by reframing the task in terms of looking at the "ability to catch emerging thoughts." At other times, the client might be so caught-up in a stream of thoughts that he or she is unable to realize that they are actively engaged in the thinking process. A typical example of this is a concern about their posture or appearance while practicing with closed eyes. Even though this engages an ongoing assessment of how they present in front of you, especially if they are socially anxious, people new to MOB will often assume that these kinds of thoughts don't count as intrusive thoughts. Now ask the client to open their eyes and to discuss their experience.

Have you noticed how agitated the mind is? We try to rest our attention peacefully and quietly on the breath and our minds don't let us. There is no rest there, only busyness and agitation. Have you noticed how this is similar when you try to relax at home? Unless we have a drink, watch TV, read a book or use other distractions it is difficult to unwind and free our mind from thoughts, especially negative ones... is that right?... Let me give you some explanations for this by looking at what happens in the brain when we process information...

Now is a good time to explain how MOB is a method that trains three executive functions.

When we practice mindfulness of breath, we train ourselves to maintain our attention to the natural flow of breath. The first skill we develop is "metacognitive awareness," which enables us to detect intrusive thoughts and see them for what they are: just thoughts, just mental events. This helps us remain a more objective observer, rather than assuming that we *are* the thought. This is a very important skill because it gives us the option to respond in a way we choose, rather than reacting automatically. The second skill is to prevent the usual reaction to the thought, which is to think it. We learn not to engage with the thought. This is called "response inhibition." Basically, this means that we take control of our response. The third skill is to refocus attention on the target of attention, the breath at the entrance of the nostrils. To practice this, we disengage attention from the thought and systematically reallocate it back to the breath, gently, patiently, and without frustration. Through this continual effort of releasing and shifting attention, we develop "cognitive flexibility." These are the three main mental skills that allow us to be aware that we are over-thinking things when we ruminate, to stop doing it, and to refocus our attention on what is important.

Now provide some theoretical understanding about the nature of thoughts arising in consciousness. Describe the internal causes of intrusive thoughts and their extinction. Explain and normalize distractibility during practice using the "fasting metaphor," as explained in the main text. In addition, or alternatively, you can complete your explanation of intrusive thoughts by explaining very briefly how thoughts compete for access to conscious awareness according to their *frequency*, *recency* and *depth* of activation in neural networks.

Introduce the Mindfulness of Breath Exercise

The MOB exercise is on track 6. Conduct a brief practice with your client. This enables you to check how they are practicing, including the correctness of their posture. You can also check their understanding of "mind-wandering" and intrusive thinking.

Explain Homework Exercises

- Withdraw PMR and start the practice of mindfulness of breath. The audio instructions are on track 6, and the introduction on track 5. Explain to your client that the audio track lasts 20 minutes and that they need to continue practicing on their own, in silence, for another 10 minutes to complete the 30-minute practice. Emphasize the need to practice *twice* daily and to make a strong effort to commit.
- Encourage applied practice in daily life, where your client remains aware of the breath and the type of thoughts entering their mind, lets go of unhelpful thoughts and recognizes and encourages helpful ones. Mention that long-lived reactive habits will only change if practice is sufficient; the more we practice the better.
- Read Handouts 2.1, 2.2 and 2.3.
- Fill in the Daily Record of Mindfulness Meditation Practice (Handout 2.4)

Application with Groups

Session Aim

Session 2 introduces mindfulness of breath (MOB) and the rationale for it (developing metacognitive awareness, inhibitory control over intrusive thoughts and attention shifting) and provides a detailed explanation of thought intrusion (recency, frequency and co-emergence effects).

Materials

- Whiteboard and markers.
- Audio equipment for audio instructions
- Handouts: 2.2 Practice Tips, 2.3 Homework Exercises, 2.4 Daily Record of Mindfulness Practice.

Review Homework Exercises and Progress

Group members share their experience of the practice. Welcome feedback on the home exercises set last week and clarify points as they arise. Ask participants how their week was in general. Did they notice anything different this week? Notice, value and validate small changes. This helps reinforce their practice. Encourage questions and clarify any aspect of the practice as necessary.

Deepening Motivation

Depressed and anxious clients often experience a fear of failure, which makes any new task appear difficult to achieve. Therapy-based expectations can become a new source of anxiety and a reason for dropping out. If they have struggled to commit to regular practice, you may wish to employ Socratic questioning: "If you were given the skills to change your condition, would you use them?" or "Out of a hundred, how much would you be prepared to change; zero being not at all and a hundred being completely?" If less than 100 %, clarify their reasons, which might include self-doubts, fear of failure or low motivation. Challenge their view using Socratic dialogue: "It may sound a bit strange, but could you tell me why you would like to change?" If you keep prompting with "...and what would be the purpose of that?" or a similar question, at some point, they might say, "I don't want to pass my depression (or anxiety, etc.) to my kids," or "I don't want my partner to suffer." At this point, emphasize that one reason for them to go through this program is compassion: "Did you realize how compassionate you can be? Much of what motivates you to go through all these efforts is your compassion and love for your (e.g., children or family), did you realize that?"

Ask, "What could happen if you don't change?" Emphasize the "cost" (homework), mentioning it is sometimes difficult to keep up with the practice. Emphasize the need for commitment: "When would you be prepared to spend 30 minutes in the morning and 30 minutes in the evening on your therapy? And where could you practice?"

Deliver a Rationale for Mindfulness of Breath

Present a rationale for the practice of mindfulness of breath (MOB). The following is an experiential exercise using the "finger task" and rationale for the participants' homework. It can also be used as an ad-hoc explanation for thought intrusion during practice if the information it contains has not been discussed prior to implementing MOB homework.

> Before you start your training of MOB this week, let's try it for a few minutes together here and make sure that you understand it, so you can practice confidently at home. First, sit with your neck and back straight, and rest the palms of your hands on your thighs. Now close your eyes and focus all your attention at the entrance of your nostrils whilst breathing naturally, without controlling your breath. Just feel the breath as it naturally passes through the nostrils. Try also to feel the touch of the breath on the inner walls and outer rings of the nostrils, and the small area below the

> nostrils above the upper lip, and pay attention to this part patiently and attentively for a minute, until I give you more instructions…

Wait silently for about thirty seconds allowing participants to experience some intrusive thoughts.

> Great! Keeping your eyes closed, as soon as you notice that a thought has just popped into your mind, slightly raise the index finger of your dominant hand, keeping your wrist on your thigh. Keep your finger raised until you are able to bring your attention back to your nostrils and then gently let it rest again on your knee. Do this with each thought that arises in your mind while you simply monitor your breath. You may have to do this many time in the next few minutes. This is not a problem and it is not a reflection of lack of skill. What really matters is that you catch each thought as it arises, that you calmly and patiently release attention from the thought and redirect attention to the breath as soon as possible. Do your best for the next few minutes, remembering to use your finger to help me understand what your thoughts are doing… Note also that a sound is not a thought. The sounds of birds or cars outside the building are not thoughts unless you think about them, like how beautiful they sound or how noisy they are. So, don't raise your finger if you hear something and *don't* think about it. Raise your finger only if you are actually thinking about the sounds you hear. Do this for the next few minutes.

Observe the participants' attitude, body language and frequency of thought intrusion for about one minute. Occasionally, some people show little or no thought intrusions. If you think that some participants display some social desirability (i.e., tries to impress you), especially if they have meditated or done yoga before, gently clarify what you are looking for by reframing the task in terms of looking at the "ability to catch emerging thoughts." At other times, a person might be so caught-up in a stream of thoughts that he or she is unable to realize that they are actively engaged in the thinking process. A typical example of this is a concern about their posture or appearance while practicing with closed eyes. Even though this engages an ongoing assessment of how they present in front of you, especially if they are socially anxious, people new to MOB will often assume that these kinds of thoughts don't count as intrusive thoughts. Now ask the participant to open their eyes and to discuss their experience.

> Have you noticed how agitated the mind is? We try to rest our attention peacefully and quietly on the breath and our minds don't let us. There is no rest there, only busyness and agitation. Have you noticed how this is similar when you try to relax at home? Unless we have a drink, watch TV, read a book or use other distractions it is difficult to unwind and free our mind from thoughts, especially negative ones…is that right?… Let me give you some explanations for this by looking at what happens in the brain when we process information…

Now is good time to explain how MOB is a method that trains three major executive functions.

> When we practice mindfulness of breath, we train ourselves to maintain our attention to the natural flow of breath. The first skill we develop is "metacognitive awareness,"

which enables us to detect intrusive thoughts and see them for what they are, just thoughts, just mental events. This helps us remain a more objective observer, rather than assuming that we *are* the thought. This is a very important skill because it gives us the option to respond in a way we choose, rather than reacting automatically. The second skill is to prevent the usual reaction to the thought, which is to think it. We learn not to engage with the thought. This is called "response inhibition." Basically, this means that we take control of our response. The third skill is to refocus attention on the target of attention, the breath at the entrance of the nostrils. To practice this, we disengage attention from the thought and systematically reallocate it back to the breath, gently, patiently, and without frustration. Through this continual effort of releasing and shifting attention, we develop "cognitive flexibility." These are the three main mental skills that allow us to be aware that we are over-thinking things when we ruminate, to stop doing it, and to refocus our attention on what is important and on the task at hand.

Now provide some theoretical understanding about the nature of thoughts arising in consciousness. Describe the internal causes of intrusive thoughts and their extinction. Explain and normalize distractibility during practice using the "fasting metaphor," as explained in the main text. In addition, or alternatively, you can complete your explanation of intrusive thoughts by explaining very briefly how thoughts compete for access to conscious awareness according to their *frequency*, *recency* and *depth* of activation in neural networks.

Introduce the Mindfulness of Breath Exercise

Conduct a brief practice of MOB with participants. The audio instructions are on track 6. See also the printed script in Appendix 2. This enables you to check how they are practicing, including the correctness of their posture. You can also check their understanding of "mind-wandering" and intrusive thinking.

Explain Homework Exercises

- Withdraw PMR and begin to practice MOB. The audio instructions are on track 6, and the introduction on track 5. Explain to participants that the audio track lasts 20 minutes and that they need to continue practicing on their own, in silence, for another 10 minutes to complete the 30-minute practice. Emphasize the need to practice *twice* daily and to make a strong effort to commit.
- Encourage applied practice in daily life, where participants remain aware of the breath and the type of thoughts entering their mind, let go of unhelpful thoughts and recognize and encourage helpful ones. Mention that long-lived reactive habits will only change if practice is sufficient; the more we practice the better.
- Read Handouts 2.1, 2.2 and 2.3.
- Fill in the Daily Record of Mindfulness Meditation Practice (Handout 2.4).

Frequently Asked Questions

Question: My client tells me that she loves this practice and listening to the audio instructions. She loves the French accent! She asked if she really has to do the last 10 minutes in silence as instructed. Can she just listen to the instructions again during that time?

Answer: It seems that your client is getting attached to the voice in the instructions. This is because her positive judgment about her experience creates pleasant body sensations, to which she gets attached, and then reacts with craving when these are no longer present when she is practicing in silence. This may be difficult for her to understand at first, but what your client likes so much is her own body sensations. She probably does not have these sensations when she practices without the audio instructions, so practicing in silence is less appealing. She needs to understand that attachment is a trap in day-to-day life and one of the central purposes of MiCBT is to change this. When there is no voice (and therefore no pleasant sensations), the absence of the pleasant sensations is experienced as unpleasant, which makes her react with aversion. As we become more experienced, practice needs to increasingly be in silence. This will develop the capacity to remain non-reactive to experiences of craving for pleasant sensations, and this capacity will generalize to an improved ability to handle cravings in daily life.

Question: My client said that he stopped mindfulness of breath midway because the more he tried to keep his attention on the breath, the more thoughts were intruding, so he was becoming frustrated. He decided to move on to the body-scanning technique and likes it.

Answer: Mindfulness of breath requires sustained attention, response inhibition and attention shifting. These executive functions are often depleted in clients who cannot focus due to their condition and are therefore difficult to practice. Remind your client that whenever his attention moves to thoughts, the aim of practice is to gently bring it back to the breath, *equanimously*, patiently and without frustration. This repeated effort is what develops the three executive skills. To move to body scanning at this stage seems to be an avoidance of the unpleasant body sensations co-emerging with negative judgments. Your client needs to be reminded to be kind to himself, appreciating his effort and enjoying his practice, so he can develop powerful skills that will serve him well in life. Explain that what happens during meditation is a reflection of what happens in daily life. If your client develops patience and tolerance with his meditation experience, he will notice that patience and tolerance will also increase in daily life because of the effects of neuroplasticity.

Explain to your client that another important reason for having sufficient practice in mindfulness of breath is that it prepares us for the next skillset. He needs to develop the skills that enable him to keep attention on the intended object, the breath, so that during body scanning he is sufficiently able to sustain his attention on body parts without being incessantly carried away by intrusive thoughts. If he is able to sustain his attention effectively for at least 30 seconds despite the emergence of thoughts, he will be more able to feel body sensations, which in turn will allow effective desensitization to take place. In other words, the skills developed through mindfulness of breath are pre-requisites for effective body-scanning and interoceptive desensitization.

Question: My client has strong pain in her hip and lower back during meditation. She fears that her practice might be the cause of it. She is starting to dislike the practice because the pain stays even though she adopted a better posture.

Answer: It is wonderful that your client practiced in spite of her discomfort. It takes courage and commitment and it would be good to validate her effort. Remind her that mindfulness practice is simply a way of attending to our already existing experiences. It does not *create* anything, including pain; it only allows us to feel what is already there. If the intense sensations are manageable, then suggest that she does her best to allow them to be present while remaining calm and without negative judgments, and that she continually returns attention to the breath whenever it has moved to the area of intense sensation or to thoughts. If the pain sensation is so intense that your client struggles to focus on the breath, then she needs to address it more directly. Ask her to direct attention to the area of most intense body sensation and stay focused on it for half a minute to a minute, noticing as many details of the sensation as possible with curiosity, open-mindedness and acceptance. Ask her to notice how impermanent the sensations are when she observes them objectively and doesn't try to get rid of them. She will see that the sensations stay for a while and then pass away in their own right, without her intervention. It is important that she understands what it means to observe patiently and without judging and reacting until they begin to change. Understanding intellectually and knowing how to practice it can be widely different! Note that if she perceives pain sensations as something that is a part of her, she will feel that she hates these parts of herself. Remind her that it is not *her* pain; it is just sensations.

You may also explain that mindfulness meditation was introduced in America in the late 1970s as an adjunct method to medical treatment for people with severe chronic pain, and research shows that it has been successfully used for this purpose in many countries since. We have done our own studies showing systematic pain reduction with only 30-second interoceptive exposure to pain sensations with equanimity. Also, your client may want to check with her doctor to see if there is anything that needs medical attention or treatment, just for her peace of mind.

Question: My client tells me that he can't focus well on the breath. He says his mind is either drowsy or dull, and he loses track of what he is supposed to do. He can easily be distracted for ten minutes at a time and feels that he is wasting time. He is usually a very active man.

Answer: This is usually because we are not used to being relaxed and calm while awake and alert. If your client likes to be mentally or physically stimulated, the reduction of sensory stimulation during practice will be a sharp contrast that he might not easily be able to accept. Yet, it is important to accept the experience *as it is* and not become reactive to it. All mental states are impermanent. Remind your client that maintaining a sense of genuine curiosity will help it pass more easily, but it will require effort to remain alert, patient and tolerant.

Question: My client reports that she feels tired when she practices. She starts to fall asleep after five or ten minutes, so she decided to lie down to practice. Is that okay?

Answer: Feeling tired and drowsy is very common when we start this practice. Even after a good night's sleep, we can experience laziness and drowsiness, but lying down will only add to her difficulty to stay awake. It can be a real barrier to effective practice. Ensure that your client arranges the room so that it is not too hot or too dark, and that she sits in an upright position. Practicing with a full stomach, too late in the evening or after having a glass of wine or other intoxicants will compound the problem. If all of these things have been addressed, then suggest that she breathes a little harder for a minute or so. This will make the sensations of the breath touching the skin easier to detect. She can then return to normal breathing when she is more awake. If drowsiness persists, she could practice with eyes slightly open. To prevent being visually distracted, she should open her eyes just enough to see the floor not more than 2.5 meters ahead of her knees. This will allow some light to enter her eyes and wake the brain, and give her a visual reminder of where she is and what she is trying to do without being too distracting. Suggest practicing this way for one to two minutes and then returning to the practice with closed eyes. However, if practicing with eyes open does not immediately help and she still feels very drowsy, she should try to practice standing up for a few minutes at a time. If drowsiness persists while standing up, suggest that she washes her face with cold water or walks for a minute or two to wake up. Encourage her to persist and remind her that drowsiness is impermanent too.

Question: My client reports that his mind is all over the place, even after a whole week of practicing mindfulness of breath. He reports that he is thinking of his divorce and the kids, and finds it hard to focus after just a few seconds. He prefers the PMR practice, as he was more present and less distracted with it. Should he return to PMR for some time?

Answer: While practicing mindfulness of breath, your client is no longer able to distract himself from his burden and is starting to notice how his mind is agitated and scattered. It has no stability, no calmness, which is what he is looking for with this practice; he wants things to be different to the way they currently are. This is precisely what creates our problems in life. We either don't see things as they are or don't want them to be as they are. During practice, he has the opportunity to change his habit of either resenting unpleasant experiences that are present, or expecting pleasant experiences that are absent.

Your client experiences issues related to the divorce and the well-being of his children. You could normalize his difficulty in focusing by explaining the "frequency effect," which we discussed during the course. If he has been thinking about the relationship issue regularly since the marriage problems occurred, his brain cells processing the memory of this information have been activated frequently and their connectivity remains strong. This strength of activation keeps the memory active and easily available. Because the frequent activation of these thoughts maintains them just below his threshold of awareness, they readily enter consciousness as soon as he relaxes sufficiently—this is a major problem with conditions such as PTSD, as clients often use maladaptive methods (such as intoxicants) to prevent their painful memories from crossing their awareness threshold.

Accordingly, you can reassure your client that his difficulty is normal and part of the training. You may add that one of the things that reassures children is their parents' ability to demonstrate genuine emotional stability and calmness. This can happen more easily if your client uses agitation as a training context to remain calm despite having challenging thoughts. Ask your client to continue practicing mindfulness of breath for an additional week, but this time on his own and in silence, without the recorded audio instructions. If thoughts are obsessive or otherwise overpowering, he will need to apply the "three-second rule", which consists of limiting the distraction time to three seconds. As soon as the persisting thought has been perceived, your client counts to 3 and commits to make an effort to switch his attention back to the breath within three seconds. This is usually helpful and gets easier with practice.

He needs to practice as much as possible with patience, remaining tolerant of his experience and without seeking any particular short-term result. Of equal importance, he needs to clearly distinguish the thought from the "self." The task is to just observe the way things are in the present moment, as physical sensations and mental states manifest themselves while we breathe in and out, without identifying with them. Attending to the breath and nothing else keeps the mind stable despite the underlying agitation. The sooner your client does this, the quicker his mind will settle. You may also explain the skill-transfer effect of neuroplasticity: the more he trains his brain to be objective and less reactive with his meditative experience, the easier it will be for him to experience things the way they are in daily life with more patience, acceptance and mental stability.

Question: During practice, my client is having some flashbacks of a painful memory, so she becomes anxious and it puts her off practicing. She asked me if playing soft music in the background would be a useful distraction from the memory. Any thoughts on this?

Answer: This is an opportunity to examine what this memory is made of. There is a thought and your client may have noticed accompanying sensations in the body, which may be more or less intense. The thought itself is not what your client is reacting to. Although the thought may include memories of sounds and images, the emotion associated with the memory is experienced through the co-emerging sensations in the body. The reactive part of the mind is used to reacting when body sensations become intense. This is something your client needs to observe and understand better during practice. The practice of examining an experience *as it is* helps us learn not to take it personally and prevents us to be caught up in it.

When she has a flashback, simply making her experience of co-emerging body sensations the object of her observation, with curiosity and open-mindedness, could support the arising of a calm mental state. On the other hand, playing music in the background will distract her from observing this mechanism and interfere with this important learning. Her attention would switch from breath to music, leaving little room for desensitization. While avoidance made things worse for her, exposure will "set her free."

If in the process her co-emerging sensation gets stronger, then it is best to focus on them rather than maintaining attention on the breath. Ask her to pay attention to the most intense aspect of the sensations and study it carefully looking for characteristics, such as temperature, heaviness, movement or solidity. Is it dense and solid, or diffused and radiating? Is it hot, warm, or cold? Is it heavy or light? Ask her to remain calm while staying with paying attention to the sensations for a little while. She needs to remember that the actual event is in the past, never to return, and that the only real issue is her difficulty handling the consequence of these thoughts in the body—the sensations.

Question: My client reports feeling very bored during the practice. I asked her to be patient, but patience is not her best strength. I wonder if there is a way of explaining boredom with the co-emergence model. I think she would relate to that.

Answer: Boredom is a very common experience when we start mindfulness meditation because we are not deliberately producing sensory stimulation, to which we are so attached. This can create doubt about the practice or about oneself. The practice is just an unbiased way of paying attention to whatever is taking place in our experience from moment to moment. What took place for your client was a set of experiences that she categorized as boring. This shows that just sitting calmly is something she dislikes because her expectations are unmet and she has other, unwanted, experiences instead. In her daily life, the same habit of being easily bored in the absence of stimulation is likely to be observed. Mindfulness practice can assist her in understanding this unhelpful habit. For instance, when she evaluates a situation as being boring, an unpleasant body sensation co-emerges, and this is precisely what she is reacting to, and needs to prevent. You could show her how this can be case-conceptualized through the co-emergence model of reinforcement, using the Diary of Reactive Habits [Handout 3.1].

Handout 2.1 Typical Difficulties Encountered in Practice

Too Tired to Practice

Conditions such as stress, anxiety and depression can make you feel tired, and sometimes people complain that they cannot get up early or feel too tired to practice in the evening. Mindfulness training will help you be calmer and less reactive, and therefore better at dealing with stress in your life, which reduces tiredness. Do your best to practice twice a day for a week, morning and evening, and see how energized you can feel!

Too Busy to Practice

We all have time pressures, but if you think carefully about how you use your time you will probably find that there are activities you could change or cut out from your daily routine even if just for the short term. How much time do you spend on social media or watching television? Write out a plan for your day and try to use your time wisely. Cut out the time-wasters and low-priority activities. Sometimes, we follow routines that are unhelpful or even obsessive. For example, we can be a little too rigid about when to get up or go to bed, or we may think that something bad will happen if we don't follow our usual habits or rituals. You have decided to do the MiCBT program because you want to experience change in your life. Begin by changing your daily routine and make time for what is important to you and perhaps for those you love.

Agitation

Misunderstanding the techniques of mindfulness in the early stages of practice often leads to some agitation, and sometime the desire to stop practicing. Agitation can also occur for other reasons. For example, we can experience agitation in the forms of feeling irritable because of external background noise, becoming frustrated with intrusive thoughts, experiencing the room temperature as intolerable, or thinking that we are lacking time or feeling rushed. In addition, we often interpret these unpleasant experiences as *feeling bored*, forgetting that *boredom* is just another mental state that can be observed and accepted with interest and curiosity when we meditate. We are reacting to the unpleasant body sensations that we produce when we judge situations negatively. It is reassuring that after a period of, accurate and sufficient practice (twice daily), our acceptance improves and agitation usually wanes because we train our mind to be calmer.

Lost in Thoughts

When starting mindfulness training, it is usual for our attention to keep on being distracted by thoughts. With continued and correct mindfulness practice, intrusive thoughts gradually decrease and people feel more in control of what their mind is doing. If thoughts are overpowering and you cannot focus on the breath, use the "three-second rule"—limiting the distraction time to three seconds. As soon as you are aware that a thought has entered your mind and your attention is no longer on breath sensations, count to three slowly, making a real effort to switch your attention back to the breath within the three seconds. This is usually very helpful. It is a little bit like bringing the part of your brain that deals with attentional control to the gym. It gets easier with practice.

Craving and Aversion

During the practice, we can get caught up in pleasurable memories or future expectations. For example, we might remember a sexual experience or think about our next party or exciting travel plans. Similarly, we can remember a painful experience or anticipate one that might be happening in the future. Whether your thoughts are about pleasant or unpleasant experiences, prevent reacting to the content of the thoughts with craving or aversion. Remember the task and refocus on the object of concentration instead, which in Session 2 is sensations associated with the breath.

Drowsiness

People can sometimes feel drowsy when practicing mindfulness even after a good night's sleep. Sometimes this is due to relaxing deeply after some stress. Because our nervous system is not used to the eyes being closed whilst being deeply relaxed, except during sleep, our brain sometimes acts as if it is time to sleep. Keep in mind that feeling drowsy can also be caused by sitting in a room that is too warm or too dark, having a full stomach after a meal, or after having had an alcoholic drink. Check your practice schedule and practice environment and make sensible adjustments, such as changing the room temperature and eating or drinking alcohol (if you must) only *after* your practice. You might also find it useful to sit in a less comfortable seat or modify your posture, keeping your neck and back straight, with your knees below the level of your buttocks, as this helps to support the natural curve of the lower spine. If you are still feeling drowsy, breathe slightly deeper for a minute or so, feeling the touch of the breath in the nostrils. If drowsiness persists, you can wake the brain by letting a small amount of light enter your eyes. Rather than fully opening your eyes, open your eyelids just enough to let you see the floor no further than about 2.5 meters away from your knees. If this is insufficient to counteract drowsiness, try practicing while standing up for a few minutes. If this is still insufficient, go for a short walk and splash your face with cold water before coming back and continuing the practice. What is reassuring is that drowsiness is impermanent too!

Confusion and Doubts

If there is a misunderstanding of the reason why we use mindfulness—the practice instructions, or some difficulties we may have during the practice, for example—people can experience doubt. There are three types of doubt: (1) doubt about the mindfulness technique; (2) doubt about the person who teaches it to you, and (3) self-doubt—doubt about your own ability to do the practice. Make sure you discuss any doubt that you may have with your therapist. Importantly, if you commit to practice diligently for the whole of this week, the benefits you get will help you conquer your doubts and encourage you to continue your commitment further for the rest of your training.

Handout 2.2 Practice Tips

When starting the training, it is best to choose a specific place to practice and to practice at the same times. You will begin to associate this location with your practice and this will make your daily practice easier to maintain.

It is useful to limit contact with sensory stimulation that will distract you. This means minimizing seeing, hearing, smelling, tasting, touching, moving the body *and* voluntary thinking. If you are too stimulated, your attention will go to the external stimuli, such as the sounds of waves or birds, the touch of the wind or the heat of the sun on the skin, instead of focusing on sensations associated with the breath. Indoors, in a quiet room, is the best place to start. Later on, when you become skilled, you will be able to practice anywhere without being too distracted.

When we begin to practice mindfulness meditation, we are sometimes under the impression that the whole world should stop. Although we know it is not realistic, we still think that the phone should not ring, children should be silent, the floorboards should not creak and cars should not be so noisy at this time of day. If we think like that, we react and can become tense; however, with practice we get more skilled at not reacting to sounds in the environment and maintaining attention on the breath. Noises are part of life and we can use them to increase our levels of tolerance and detachment.

Pets love it when their owner meditates. They feel safe and attracted by the calmness of their owner. They just want to snuggle against them and stay there for as long as possible. If you have a pet, meditating with a cat or a dog on your lap may be pleasant, but it can also be a great distraction from the task and is therefore not recommended. If your pet is unable to stay away from you, it is best that he or she is kept out of the room where you practice. This may sound a little harsh, but it can be done gently and it will allow you to practice effectively.

Handout 2.3 Homework Exercises

Commitment to daily practice for the whole week is very important. You don't need to commit for weeks or months. Instead, commit fully for this week and see what benefits you notice.

These are the things you need to do this week:

- Practice mindfulness of breath (MOB) *twice* a day, using tracks 5 and 6 of the audio instructions. Please fill in the practice record form (Handout 2.4) and return it to your therapist in your next session.
- Apply your practice of MOB in daily activities. This means that you need to remember to be aware of your breath and as soon as you are aware that a thought you didn't wish to have enters your mind, let it go. Try also to recognize if it is a benign or harmful thought. A harmful thought is one that makes you desire what you want and can't have, or hate what you have and don't want. See these thoughts as old habits of the mind and choose to think what *you decide* to think!
- Read the handouts given to you by your therapist.

Handout 2.4 Daily Record of Mindfulness Meditation Practice

Day	Date	Morning *(circle)*	Duration	**Efficacy rating** *Rate from 1 to 10 how well you noticed distractions and brought your attention back to the breath. 1 = not well at all; 10 = extremely well*	Evening *(circle)*	Duration	**Efficacy rating** *Rate from 1 to 10 how well you noticed distractions and brought your attention back to the breath. 1 = not well at all; 10 = extremely well*
Monday		I practiced Yes / No			I practiced Yes / No		
Tuesday		I practiced Yes / No			I practiced Yes / No		
Wednesday		I practiced Yes / No			I practiced Yes / No		
Thursday		I practiced Yes / No			I practiced Yes / No		
Friday		I practiced Yes / No			I practiced Yes / No		
Saturday		I practiced Yes / No			I practiced Yes / No		
Sunday		I practiced Yes / No			I practiced Yes / No		

References

Barnhofer, T., Chittka, T., Nightingale, H., Visser, C., & Crane, C. (2010). State effects of two forms of meditation on prefrontal EEG asymmetry in previously depressed individuals. *Mindfulness*, doi: 10.1007/s12671-010-0004-7

Cayoun, B. A. (2010). *The dynamics of bimanual coordination in ADHD: Processing speed, inhibition and cognitive flexibility*. Saarbrucken, Germany: Lambert Academic Publishing.

Cayoun, B. A. (2011). *Mindfulness-integrated CBT: Principles and practice*. Chichester, UK: Wiley.

Cayoun, B. A. (2015). *Mindfulness-integrated CBT for well-being and personal growth: Four steps to enhance inner calm, self-confidence and relationships*. Chichester, UK: Wiley.

Cayoun B.A. (2017). The purpose, mechanisms, and benefits of cultivating ethics in Mindfulness-Integrated Cognitive Behavior Therapy. In L. Monteiro, J. Compson, & F. Musten (Eds.) *Practitioner's guide to ethics and mindfulness-based interventions. Mindfulness in behavioral health*. Cham: Springer.

Cayoun, B. A., & Shires, A. (submitted for publication). Co-emergence reinforcement: A proposed transdiagnostic mechanism in emotional disorders and their remediation through mindfulness and cognitive-behavioral interventions. Manuscript submitted for publication.

Chambers, R., Lo, C., & Allen, N. B. (2008). The impact of intensive mindfulness training on executive cognition, cognitive style, and affect. *Cognitive Therapy and Research*, 32, 303–22.

Doll, A., Hölzel, B. K., Bouckard, C., Wohlschlager, A. M., & Sorg, C. (2015). Mindfulness is associated with intrinsic functional connectivity between default mode and salience networks. *Frontiers of Human Neuroscience*, 9, 461. doi:10.3389/fnhum.2015.00461

Goenka, S.N. (1987) *The discourse summaries: Talks from a ten-day course in Vipassana Meditation condensed by William Hart*. Vipashyana Vishodhan Vinyas, Bombay, India.

Hart, W. (1987). *The art of living: Vipassana Meditation as taught by S. N. Goenka*. New York: HarperCollins.

Hölzel, B. K., Lazar, S. W., Gard, T., Schuman-Olivier, Z., Vago, D. R., & Ott, U. (2011). How does mindfulness meditation work? Proposing mechanisms of action from a conceptual and neural perspective. *Perspectives on Psychological Science*, 6(6), 537–559.

Kabat-Zinn, J. (2013). *Full catastrophe living, revised edition: How to cope with stress, pain and illness using mindfulness meditation*. London, UK: Hachette.

Koster, E. H., Rassin, E., Crombez, G., & Näring, G. W. (2003). The paradoxical effects of suppressing anxious thoughts during imminent threat. *Behaviour Research and Therapy*, 41(9), 1113–1120.

La Fontaine, J. (1668). *Fables, Book 2 Fable 11*. Retrieved June 3, 2017 from http://www.gutenberg.org/ebooks/50316

Shapiro, N. (2007). *The complete fables of La Fontaine, Book III (Work from 1668)*. Chicago: University of Illinois Press.

McClelland, J. L., Rumelhart, D. E., & the PDP Research Group, (1986). *Parallel distributed processing: Explorations in the microstructure of cognition* (Vol. 2). Cambridge, MA: Bradford Books/MIT Press.

Siegel, R. D. (2009). *The mindfulness solution: Everyday practices for everyday problems*. New York: Guilford Press.

Smith, A., Zunini, R., Anderson, C., Longo, C., Cameron, I., Hogan M., and Fried, P. (2011). Impact of marijuana on response inhibition: an fMRI study in young adults. *Journal of Behavioral and Brain Science*, 3, 124–133. doi:10.4236/jbbs.2011.13017

Suchotzki, K., Crombez, G., Debey, E., van Oorsouw, K., & Verschuere, B. (2015). *In vino veritas*? Alcohol, response inhibition and lying. *Alcohol and Alcoholism*, 50, 74–81. doi:10.1093/alcalc/agu079

Teasdale, J.D., Segal, Z.V., and Williams, J.M.G. (1995) How does cognitive therapy prevent depressive relapse and why should attentional control (Mindfulness) training help? *Behaviour Research and Therapy*, 33, 25–39.

Van Dam, N. T., van Vugt, M. K., Vago, D. R., Schmalz, L., Saron, C. D., Olendzki, A., … Meyer, D. E. (2017). Mind the Hype: A critical evaluation and prescriptive agenda for research on mindfulness and meditation. *Perspectives on Psychological Science*, 1–26. doi:10.1177/1745691617709589

Xu, L., Vik, A., Groote, I, R., Lagopoulos, J., Holen, A. Ellingsen, Ø., et al. (2014). Nondirective meditation activates default mode network and areas associated with memory retrieval and emotional processing. *Frontiers in Human Neuroscience*, 8, 86. doi:10.3389/fnhum.2014.00086

Session 3: Understanding and Regulating Emotions

To live lightheartedly but not recklessly; to be gay without being boisterous; to be courageous without being bold; to show trust and cheerful resignation without fatalism—this is the art of living

—Jean de la Fontaine, 1668

Introduction

This chapter explains how the mechanisms of emotional reactivity can be understood using the co-emergence model of reinforcement (see Chapter 2), thereby providing a strong rationale for mindfulness skills training through equanimity towards body sensations. The benefits of mindfulness of body sensations (*vedanánupassaná* in Pali) are described as the core elements of emotion regulation. Up to now, your client has learned to regulate attention. It is now time to work with emotions in a way that is most congruent with the direct experience of emotions. It will become clear to your client that the transformative factor of their practice is equanimity, not awareness; awareness accompanied by catastrophic thoughts can actually make things worse. Through the practice of body scanning, you will teach your client to recognize the onset of emotions and neutralize their learned response, before emotions become too difficult to handle skillfully, leading to reactivity.

Checking Client Readiness

Your client has now completed the third week of mindfulness training. Check with them how their week was. Could they remain committed to practicing for 30 minutes twice daily? Committing is a skill in itself that is not well-developed in some clients. If your client was unable to commit to daily practice, using the

The Clinical Handbook of Mindfulness-integrated Cognitive Behavior Therapy: A Step-by-Step Guide for Therapists, First Edition. Bruno A. Cayoun, Sarah E. Francis, and Alice G. Shires.

Companion website: www.wiley.com/go/Cayoun/Mindfulness-integrated

Socratic dialogue to clarify their reason is likely to be productive. If your client was able to commit to daily practice, did they benefit from it? Can they maintain attention on their breath for at least half a minute without being caught up in thoughts? When thoughts arise, can they let them go more quickly than they did when they started a week ago? If they were able to practice regularly for half an hour twice a day, they are ready to start the practice of "body scanning," which consists of surveying sensations in the entire body systematically and with an equanimous attitude.

Delaying the Next Step

The ability to sustain attention and inhibit usual responses is very important for the technique of body scanning. If clients tend to be too stressed, anxious or agitated, it is common for them to need a little more practice of mindfulness of breath. If your client gets so caught up in thoughts that they barely last five to ten seconds focusing on the breath, then they might benefit from practicing the "3-second rule." Ask them to make a firm commitment to return to the breath within three seconds after a thought has arisen. They will find that they can notice the arising of a thought but if they wait longer than about three seconds, the mind becomes too engaged with the thought and it is harder to disengage attention from the thought and bring it back to the breath. Ask your client to continue practicing mindfulness of breath for a few more days or even a whole week, without audio instructions. This will prevent them focusing on the instructor's voice and becoming too relaxed and drowsy.

Proceeding with the Next Step

A good marker for deciding whether to move to the next step or not is the ability to maintain focus for about 30 seconds. This is because the next mindfulness exercise will require your client to be able to remain focused for up to about 30 seconds on areas of the body in which they cannot feel a sensation. Therefore, they need this particular attentional ability before moving on to the next step. If your client's mind is calmer after their week's practice and they are able to maintain focus on their breath for at least half a minute without being caught up in emerging thoughts, then proceed with teaching them the next exercise, body scanning. The rest of this chapter describes body scanning in some detail.

Mindfulness of Body Sensations

Over the years, many colleagues with an interest in Buddhist psychology, and trained in a mindfulness approach elsewhere, would ask why MiCBT emphasizes the role of developing mindfulness through body sensations. It might be useful to note that in several teachings ("*suttas*"), the Buddha clearly emphasized the importance of interoception, the capacity to feel sensations in the body, in order to understand and decrease suffering (e.g., *mahasatipatthana sutta*, *anapanasati sutta, kayagatasati sutta*, and *rohitassa sutta*; see also Hart, 1987). Interoception has also been acknowledged and clearly highlighted in modern neuroscience (Hölzel et al., 2011; Kerr, Sacchet, Lazar, Moore, & Jones, 2013).

Your client may have perceived by now that when they quieten and still the mind, they begin to notice a range of previously undetectable experiences, such as intrusive thoughts, sounds or body sensations. One of the important skills to develop during mindfulness of breath is the ability to observe the relationship between mind and body. When practitioners have their own experience of mind–body interconnectedness, they begin to understand how thoughts and emotions continuously interact. This leads them to a better ability to understand where emotions come from and how they manifest in the form of sensations in the body, co-occurring with thoughts. They begin to understand the notion of co-emergence every time they take something personally or evaluate a stimulus as being important to them.

The Four Characteristics of Body Sensations

Affective neuroscience clearly demonstrates that interoception plays a central role in the processing of emotional information (e.g., Dunn et al., 2010; Farb et al., 2015). Research from several authors supports the view of Eastern traditional schools of mindfulness that body sensations are the building blocks of emotions (Barrett, 2006; Pollatos, Gramann, & Schandry, 2007; Seth & Critchley, 2013). The conceptualization, measurement and teaching of interoceptive skills in the MiCBT approach (Cayoun, 2011) are the results of the integration of affective neuroscience with the ancient wisdom of "the four elements," described in the Buddha's Greater Discourse on the Foundations of Mindfulness (*Mahasatipatthana sutta*; Walshe, 2012). In this description, the four elements of the physical universe are earth, air, fire and water, which we experience in the body through their interoceptive concomitants as a sense of mass, motion, temperature and fluidity.

In addition, these four essential interoceptive characteristics interact to produce a multitude of internal experiences, including emotions, depending on the type of evaluative thought that we generate. Session 3, Figure 1 shows these four characteristics of body sensations placed on four measurable dimensions using visual analogue scales, which will be a convenient way of recording your client's experiences after Session 4.

The *mass* scale represents the entire continuum of mass experience, from very light sensations (typically accompanying joy) to very heavy sensations (typically accompanying sadness). The *motion* scale represents the entire continuum of oscillatory experience, from sensations that are very still (typically accompanying calmness or some pain sensations) to sensations of agitation (typically accompanying an itch or high-arousal states, such as increased heart rate and "butterflies in the stomach"). The *temperature* scale represents the entire continuum of temperature experience, from very cold sensations (typically accompanying fatigue or fear) to very hot sensations (typically accompanying anger). The *fluidity* scale represents the entire continuum of cohesiveness/ solidity experience, from very fluid, loose and diffused sensations (typically accompanying peacefulness or dissociative states) to very constricted and dense sensations (typically accompanying anxiety and fear). Body sensations often emerge in consciousness with a

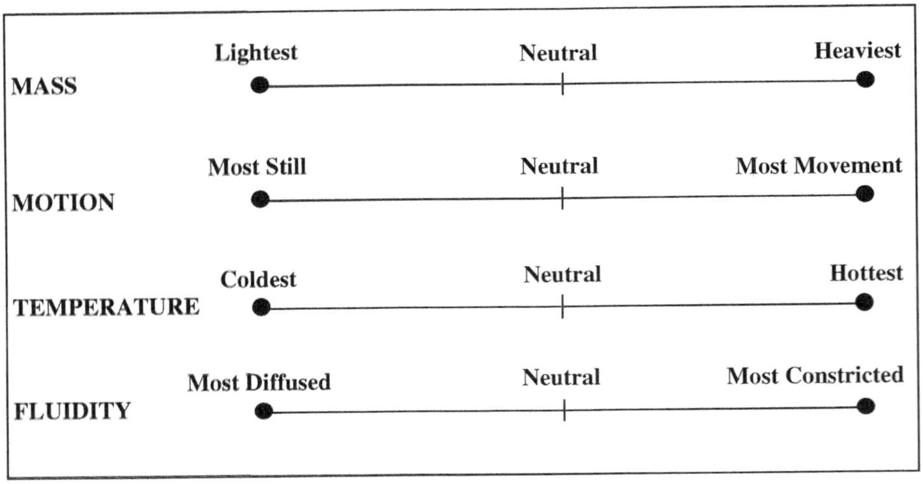

Session 3, Figure 1 The four basic characteristics of interoception.

predominance of one or two, and sometimes three of these characteristics. Each emotion is characterized by its own typical "signature" in the body. We will discuss this further in Session 4, next week, when we'll teach your client to recognize and measure their interoceptive awareness and ability to remain equanimous with the four characteristics of interoception.

The Main Purpose of Learning Body Scanning

Body Scanning as a Generalized Interoceptive Exposure Method

This week's practice involves learning to survey the body in small areas (2 to 3 inches or 5 to 8 centimeters diameter) at a time from head to toe, while noticing and accepting the experience, as per the audio instructions for part-by-part unilateral body scanning. As for the past week, practice should be twice a day for half an hour, each day. Clients learn to simply pay attention to each part of the body, feel it (or the initial lack of sensations), and then move their attention to the adjacent part, in descending and ascending order. Technically speaking, they are continually exposing to what they feel from moment to moment while preventing any response. Exposure and response prevention methods are not new in behavior therapy, especially with OCD (Abramowitz, 1996) and panic disorder (Craske & Barlow, 2007), but they tend to require directing attention to the stimulus and the behavioral response, rather than emphasizing the internal experience. When they do require focusing on interoception, for instance with panic attacks (Craske & Barlow, 1993/2008), there is no training in equanimity, which is defined as "the conscious and deliberate act of being non-reactive towards an event experienced within the framework of one's body and thoughts as a result of non-judgmental observation" (Cayoun, 2011, p. 17). Summarizing monastic and lay teachers' traditional descriptions, equanimity is also a deliberate attitude of non-attachment, non-aversion and non-deludedness coupled with clear discernment that provides emotional stability (Hart, 1987; Pradhan, 1950). When perceived objectively (in terms of interoception) and with equanimity, emotions are no longer a source of concern. As they arise, we can notice what they are actually made of, without identifying with them or interfering with them in any way. We just study them as parts of the current experience, knowing that they will change. Understanding mindfulness training accurately, as a set of exposure methods, reminds us why it is important that people who implement mindfulness-based interventions in mental health contexts need to have mental health training.

Body Sensations and Emotion Regulation

With your client, you can illustrate the role of body sensations in emotions with three basic emotions: anger, fear and sadness. Ask your client to take a moment to remember an experience of anger and ask them how they knew that they were *actually feeling* the anger. Most people will describe quite intense sensations in the body, such as agitation and a need to move, flushing in the face and some muscle tension. What we are looking for are answers that describe body sensations. When someone says, "flushing in the face" you may ask, "Yes, and how did you know your face was flushed?" Similarly, if the person says, "agitated" you may ask, "What did the agitation feel like?" You will notice that people with less emotional awareness will tend to describe their anger and other emotions in terms of behavior. For example, when you ask how they know that they are feeling angry, they may reply, "I slam the door" or "I shout." It is useful to continue using a Socratic questioning style and ask what they were patiently *feeling* without falling in the trap of leading clients' answers.

Similarly, use the same method with anxiety and fear. Ask how they know that they're *actually feeling* the experience of fear or anxiety when they are afraid. They may describe that they feel a temperature change, a tightness in the chest or other areas of the body, including the abdomen, which people sometimes call "butterflies in the stomach." It slowly becomes clearer that sensations in the body are an essential part of the emotional experience. It is the same with other emotions. For example, with the experience of sadness, many people describe heaviness in the body (the hallmark of sadness) and pressure around the eyes, tightness in the throat, and sometimes constriction in the chest. Sadness cannot be experienced without sensations in the body. The same applies to the whole range of other emotional experiences, including disgust, shame, hatred, love and so on. If we do not feel sensations in the body during an emotional experience, we cannot feel the emotion. This may be due to a dissociative state or a lack of ability to feel, as in some psychopathologies (e.g., Lackner & Fresco, 2016). This is common and sometimes useful in managing stress or immediate threats, but it can be pathological and become chronic if reinforced.

You can now explain to your client that since body sensations are essential components of emotions, training the mind to feel and accept body sensations results in an improved ability to accept emotions and be less distressed by them. As sensations become acceptable, so do emotions. It needs to make sense to them that body scanning with equanimity produces emotion-regulation by preventing habitual reactions to body sensations (Cayoun, 2011; Desbordes et al., 2015; Hölzel et al., 2011).

Implications of Co-emergence Effects

You may recall from Session 2 our explanations of intrusive thoughts through three internal mechanisms—recency, frequency, and depth of neural activation, the latter being responsible for co-emergence of cognition and interoception. As explained through the co-emergence model of reinforcement (see Chapter 2), evaluating a situation as being personally important activates the medial prefrontal cortex, which cascades into the simultaneous activation of the insular cortex, which translates into experience as a co-emerging body sensation. If the evaluation triggers a sufficiently intense sensation, we will translate this as an emotion.

In daily life, the way we think leads to how we feel, and we have stored millions of memories in this co-emergent way since early childhood. Because of the association of evaluative thoughts and body sensations, one can act as a memory cue for the other. Thinking about a painful event in our past easily triggers the associated sensations, and we feel the emotional tone of the memory. A good example of this mechanism is in PTSD, where people often do all they can to avoid feeling sensations when they re-experience a traumatic memory. The reverse is also true. Just as thoughts can act as memory cues for emotional memories, their associated body sensations can also act as memory cues (Cayoun & Shires, Manuscript submitted for publication 2018). This applies to all senses, not just interoception. Odors, sounds, images and tastes can also act as memory cues.

If you practice mindfulness meditation, it may already be obvious to you that a sensation in the body can trigger memories, whether we are conscious of it or not. If the sensation we now feel is sufficiently similar to a sensation we felt in the past, the current sensation can trigger this memory, however old it may be. In other words, the body acts as a repository of memories, some more emotional than others. We have proposed that the purpose of this configuration is to prevent the decay of memories that we have judged as important (Cayoun & Shires, Manuscript submitted for publication). These include memories of situations that either threaten or promote survival.

Clinical Relevance

When taken into account in therapy, the understanding of co-emergent encoding and retrieval in memory can explain much of the data reported by clients. For example, it can explain a lot of the intrusive thoughts that seem to appear randomly during practice, daydreaming or relaxation. It can also explain elements of reinforcement and relapse. For instance, if two different and chronologically separated events are put in memory with a similar emotion, the more recent event can trigger memories of the previous if body sensations are sufficiently similar to act as a memory cue. For example, a 32-year-old client with a dependent trait was grieving her grandmother, who had recently died from a cardiac arrest. A few days later, she was very surprised to re-experience unrelated elements of bereavement. She said, "The grief of losing my marriage three years ago is all coming back since my Nan died." On prompting, she described feeling a similar "interoceptive signature" in both loss situations. She explained that both her ex-husband and her grandmother had been the only people who had provided her with real support, and she felt similar emotions and sense of loss when they departed. She reported that her practice of mindfulness helped her cope and prevent relapse into major depression.

Relevance in Dreams

The same principles are likely to apply to dreams, especially since one of the roles of dreaming is to consolidate memories (Payne & Nadel, 2004). For example, if you feel hot while sleeping, body sensations of heat may affect the dream content in different ways. They could trigger memories of actual events during which you felt hot in the past or produce an unrealistic dream scenario associated with the current experience, such as walking under the sun in the Sahara. Although clients tend to report sleeping better at this stage of their training, we often hear that their dreams can be unusually vivid or "strange." If you recall our discussion on intrusive thoughts in Session 2, the following two examples reflect the depth of neural activation during dreams and the consequent co-emergence effect. In the case of dreams, memories often appear as symbols that differ according to the context of the emotion.

A young woman with Generalized Anxiety Disorder recently dreamed that she was paralyzed while asleep and felt great pressure on her chest and throat, and that someone had dragged her out of bed. This actually happened to her a few years earlier, when she was too anxious to get up and face the day. Her ex-boyfriend had forcefully pulled her out of bed, insisting she should get on with the day, rather than avoid it. She reported that the dream occurred after feeling very stressed and hopeless at work. The body sensations she felt in the dream were similar to those she felt when her boyfriend pulled her out of bed.

A 53-year old man with chronic depression, married with three children, reported being a lucid dreamer and having more dreams since starting body scanning. He would also dream about snakes and wake up more tired. He was wondering why his dreams were so colored by fear given that his meditation practice was going so well and was so beneficial. He was also a strong believer in the Christian faith. On prompting, he shared that the snakes in his dreams were symbols of evil. He also revealed that he was often using pornography to masturbate at night before going to sleep, but felt guilty about it, associating it as an unholy trait. He realized that the body sensations he felt during the dreams and those which he felt while sharing his guilt were very similar. His increased interoceptive sensitivity may have allowed him to feel these sensations still resonating in his sleep, which then co-emerged with evaluative thoughts that are congruent with his conceptualization of evil and guilt.

Explaining the Co-emergence Model of Reinforcement

It is useful to explain the co-emergence model of reinforcement at this stage of the training, as described in Chapter 2, because it serves as a solid theoretical rationale for scanning the body. This week, your client will start to learn how to recreate equilibrium between the four components of information processing—Sensory

Perception, Evaluation, Body Sensation and Reaction—in order to become less judgmental and less reactive, as well as more objective and present to experiences in the body. For this, they will train to become aware of, and decrease the activity in, the Evaluation and Reaction functions of the mind and increase the awareness and activity in the Sensory Perception and Body Sensation functions. Becoming more mindful of body sensations and less reactive to them helps create mental balance and prevents the usual cycle of emotional reactivity.

Here is a suggestion for a brief, simple and very conversational explanation that can be given to clients. This mechanism is explained for you in detail in Part 1 (Chapter 2). Start with the model in equilibrium state (Figure 2.2). A good way to go about it is to use the Diary of Reactive Habits (Handout 3.1) as a visual aid:

> We perceive all situations with our senses and we automatically evaluate them to make sense of them. This may be very subconscious and immediate, or we might think about it consciously and take our time. What we don't suspect is that when we judge that a situation is relatively important to us, it immediately produces some changes in the body. We can say that the evaluation or judgment "co-emerges" with body sensations; co-emergence means that two things happen at the same time. If we evaluate the situation as acceptable or pleasant for us, the body sensation will be pleasant, but if we evaluate the situation with some negativity, the sensation will be unpleasant. Some sensations can be very intense and others very faint, so we can't feel them all, especially if we are not trained for it. Have you noticed that when something is very important to you, you feel stronger sensations in the body, compared to when things are not important to you? For example, if someone you really care about calls you and says they just had a bad accident and need your help, how would you feel in the body?… The next step is the reaction. Now that's interesting because we usually believe that we react to situations either outside ourselves or because of things like pain or unhelpful thoughts. When we take training in mindfulness, we progressively realize that we react to the consequence of our thoughts in the body; we react because of the body sensations that co- emerged with judgmental thoughts. What usually predicts whether someone will react or not is the intensity of the body sensations. The more intense a sensation, the more likely it is that we will react, either by wanting to get rid of it if it is unpleasant, or by wanting to maintain it and increase it if it is pleasant. What is very important for us is the understanding that if our reaction is to get rid of an unpleasant sensation or to increase a pleasant one, then guess what we will do in the future…, we will repeat the same behavior of craving pleasant sensations and avoiding unpleasant ones. This is how we learn things instinctively, but we can also modify our habits of reacting through training. Does this make sense so far?

You can now show the model in disequilibrium state (as in Figure 2.3) and explain the following in an engaging way:

> These four components can become imbalanced if we continue to be judgmental and reactive for too long; this imbalance can define our mode of behaving and even the sense of who we are. This is how we form unhelpful habits, which in turn can make our life very unpleasant and unfulfilling. So, what we need is to decrease the amount of evaluation and reaction and reallocate attention to where it is lacking, to sensory perception and interoception, which means feeling sensations in the body. This recreates balance in the way we process information and we feel less judgmental and less

reactive as we progress. Research shows that if we train ourselves to do this for some time, our brain starts to connect itself in that way and it becomes much easier for us to let go of unhelpful thoughts and emotional reactions. Basically, it becomes easier to change bad habits. Do you think this would be helpful for you as well, given what you are wishing to change?

Experiential Explanation of the Co-Emergence Model

Understanding experientially how body sensations co-emerge with cognition helps with teaching "the rationale" for MiCBT, encouraging the client's trust, commitment and motivation for therapy. This also promotes a sense of direction in therapy, which helps clients commit to treatment despite the initial difficulties usually encountered. Below is a dialogue between a client (C) and therapist (T), that takes place in the first therapy session, immediately following the client's description of their main complaint. Explaining the rationale is useful for this situation because the client presents with high arousal (anger). The client described feeling very angry with their adolescent son who was defiant, not doing homework and not cleaning up his room.

An Example of Rationale Delivery

(T = therapist, C = client)

T: What do you feel when you think about the situation with your son?
C: Bad, very angry.
T: How do you know you feel angry?
C: I feel it! It feels horrible.
T: How do you know it feels horrible? Do you feel it now?
C: Yes, a bit.
T: Where do you feel it now?
C: In my chest.
T: So you are experiencing anger in your chest as a strong body sensation?
C: Yes, it is quite strong.
T: Close your eyes and show me how large it is?
C: It's about four inches and a long shape.
T: Is it cold, hot? Does it move or is it still? Does it have any weight, heavy or light? Observe carefully and objectively like a scientist.
C: It feels hot and heavy.
T: Are there any other sensations in your body?
C: Yes, now I feel tension in my shoulders and my face feels warm.
T: Observe the sensations in the chest area. Are they the same?
C: No, they are not so strong now.
T: So the sensation you felt in your chest is changing?
C: Yes, it doesn't feel as strong anymore.
T: How do you usually react when you feel these sensations in your body?
C: I slam doors or shout at someone.
T: How long does it usually take to calm down?
C: Normally not long if I let it out but longer if I don't.

T: So how do you feel now?
C: I feel OK now.
T: Has your anger gone?
C: Almost.
T: That's good. So, the anger has almost gone in a few minutes without letting it out?
C: Yes.

The belief that venting anger is necessary to feel relieved was successfully challenged.

Example of Use of the Diary of Reactive Habits

T: From the MiCBT perspective, these are the stages in which we process information (*pointing to the model's components on the Diary of Reactive Habits* worksheet). Earlier, you described being very angry when your son is being rebellious.
C: Yes.
T: Do you remember the last time you were angry with your son?
C: Yesterday.
T: What did your son do that led you to feel angry? Try to be specific.
C: I asked my son to help with the washing up and he ignored me and kept playing on his iPad.
T: Ok. (*showing the first component, Situation or Stimulus*). So, we can write "asked son to wash up." Then the second stage is the Perception stage; it is about the senses you use to perceive the information. This stage allows us to perceive what's happening inside or outside ourselves. In this case, it was the lack of response from your son that you observed. (*pointing to the Evaluation component*)
T: So how did you interpret what your son was doing?
C: I thought he didn't respect me or care about helping me out.
T: Ok, so we can write that down here in the Evaluation box. *(using the "downward arrow" technique)*
T: What did it mean to you that he was not respecting you?
C: It meant that he does not care about other people.
T: If it were true, what would that mean to you?
C: It means that he is not being a good person.
T: And if that were true what would that mean to you?
C: It means that I have been a bad parent. *(now move to the Interoception/ body sensations box)*
T: So, how did it make you feel when you had the thought that you are not a good parent? (*client is learning about his responsibility for feeling the way he did.)*
C: I felt very angry.
T: Ok, and how did you know it was anger?
C: I could feel it in my body.
T: So your emotion was in your body? *(this provides a good rationale for using body scanning as a form of emotional regulation method.)*
C: Yes.
T: Good…so what type of sensation was it?
C: I felt hot everywhere and I could feel my heart pumping.
T: Ok, so we can write this in the fourth box, which represents the Interoception stage. There's "temperature" for the heat and "motion" for your heart pumping.

Then we do something to make ourselves feel better, right? So how did you try to make yourself feel better in this situation?

C: I shouted at my son.

T: Did it work?

C: A little bit, but then I felt bad and I was still thinking about it during the evening.

T: So, we can write this in the last box, the Reaction stage. And if it worked even a little bit, what do you think you'll do next time it happens?

C: Just the same I suppose… that's what I do when it's too much.

T: Yes, and we call this "reinforcement." If a reaction helps you decrease some discomfort or increase pleasure, we keep on doing it and it becomes a habit, a learned response. Would you like to learn to change your habit?

C: Yes, that would be good.

T: OK, so let's see what we need to do. Can you see how your interpretation created your experience? And when you felt so bad, you reacted by shouting, you boiled in anger for ten minutes. It is important to understand that you didn't react to the situation because it is not yet an experience; you didn't react to your interpretation because it is not an experience either. Can you see how your reaction was toward the unpleasant body sensations? You reacted to the unpleasant experience in your body, and these were created by your thoughts about the event.

(On the form, draw a circle over the Evaluation box and another over the Reaction box, and a smaller circle within the Perception and within the Body Sensation boxes.)

With mindfulness training, we aim to re-establish a balance in the way we process information. You learn to be more objective. The task is to increase our objectivity and ability to feel sensations (*showing Perception and Body Sensation*) and to decrease our negative thoughts and reactions (*showing Evaluation and Reaction*). This is the first stage of MiCBT. You will need to practice each day to change habits. In Stage 2, we will look at dealing with more specific situations in detail. Now, we start by learning the skill of mindfulness to decrease your reactivity.

Mindfulness of Body Sensation Through "Body Scanning"

It is useful to explain the connection between mindfulness of breath and the body scanning practice. Through mindfulness of breath, we learn to disidentify from thoughts and let them go. We *regulate* attention. We learn to switch attention back to the breath more quickly and we are able to direct attention to where we want it to be. We call it "attention regulation." Now it is time to regulate emotion using the same principles, but applied to body sensations.

Body sensations are "just sensations" we feel in the body and the faculty of feeling them is technically called "interoception." It is our interoceptive awareness that allows us to feel sensations in the body. Body scanning involves paying careful and objective (unbiased) attention to body sensations by just noticing "how it feels." You will often hear instructions saying, "just observe," which means "just feel" rather than see or imagine.

The audio instructions for body scanning are on tracks 7 and 8. The practice starts from the top of the head, surveying the entire body, all the way down to the tips of the toes and then returning to the top of the head in the same vertical way, very patiently and equanimously. To make it easier for your client to remember the procedure, Handout 3.2 includes a figure depicting the direction of attention and approximate size of attentional fields during scanning. Clients will learn to *feel*, *accept* and *move* continuously from part to part without avoiding or clinging to any one part. If we can feel, accept and let go of body sensations, we can do the same when feeling an emotion. We move in a vertical direction, rather than from side to side, to facilitate the subsequent, more advanced, methods that require moving attention in a rapid and continuous "flow."

There are sensations throughout the entire body, but our mind is not sharp enough to feel them all. One of the reasons for this is a lack of alertness. Another is the difference in brain enervation responsible for the perception of sensations across various body parts. For example, the top of the head is much less enervated than the lower part of the face. The reason why this changes once we start the practice of body scanning is that daily practice allows those neural connections to increase in number and strength (Cebolla et al., 2017; Gotink, Meijboom, Vernooij, Smits, & Hunink, 2016). This is why it is important to practice sufficiently and accurately. When sensations cannot be felt in a particular spot, the audio instructions will ask your client to stay on the blank spot for up to about 10 seconds and then move on to the next part patiently and without any reaction. In next week's practice they can stay focused on blank spots for up to 30 seconds, before moving on.

The goal of this week's practice is to be able to develop equanimity (non-reactivity) with all body sensations, whether they are pleasant, unpleasant or neutral, so that our unbiased observation lets us perceive the impermanence and impersonality of all experiences. In traditional teachings, equanimity is the balance and neutrality of the mind that prevents us from identifying with emerging experiences. In an equanimous state, the mind holds firm in remaining non-reactive despite its contact with an intense experience. Specifically, it doesn't react with craving when the experience is pleasant or with aversion when the experience is unpleasant. It is not possible to be mindful unless we are equanimous and we cannot be equanimous unless we are mindful. Becoming equanimous means being able to be level-headed, patient, even-minded and non-reactive. Equanimity enables us to let go of judgments and emotional reactivity, neutralizing reactive habits.

Reminder on Mixing Techniques

The term "body scanning" was originally introduced by John Kabat-Zinn in the early 1980s (Kabat-Zinn, 1982) and has since been used in numerous models of mindfulness training. As a result, some people can easily assume that the body scanning method you are teaching them here is the same as the body scanning method they may have learned elsewhere, and adopt the same mode of practice. For some people, this may hinder the development of MiCBT skills, because various methods have different emphases and differ in their ability to teach equanimity and non-identification with the object of exposure. Mixing mindfulness techniques can also create confusion and even harm if the client (or indeed the therapist) does not understand that this is an exposure method and that painful experiences can arise. It is prudent to ask your client only to use the downloadable audio instructions provided with this book. Each approach to body scanning has its own purpose, and it is recommended to leave other approaches aside while engaging in this program. Clients can choose the method that benefits them most once the program is completed.

Application with Individual Clients

Session Aim

Session 3 introduces body scanning and the rationale for developing interoceptive awareness and equanimity and provides a detailed explanation of the co-emergence model using the Diary of Reactive Habits (Handout 3.1).

Review Homework and Progress

Clarify any issues raised if necessary. When homework is incomplete or not done, remain equanimous while explaining the notion of prioritizing. Explain that people tend to do first what will be most rewarding or least unpleasant and this is why we prioritize activities the way we do. Use the Socratic dialogue or other useful questioning methods if necessary. Discuss difficulties including possible pain, agitation, craving and aversion, drowsiness and doubts.

Deliver the Rationale for Body Scanning

1 Using the Diary of Reactive Habits (Handout 3.1), explain the basic co-emergence model of reinforcement to the client. Ask your client to close their eyes and recall a recent challenging situation and write this situation in the upper-left box (Situation/ Stimulus). Ask how they knew the situation was happening (heard, saw, etc.) without leading, and write it in the Sensory Perception box, modeling the script described in the main text. Now explore the personal implications in the situation using Socratic questioning and the "downward arrow" technique to elicit the Evaluation components ("If this were true, what would it mean to you?"). Then ask how this interpretation made them feel ("How does it make you feel to think this way?"). Investigate what co-emerging body sensations they are feeling as they describe their view and do a brief exposure to the predominant sensations, guiding them through the four characteristics of body sensations. Use timing sets of 30 seconds and guidance to decrease arousal through equanimity. Once the percentage of arousal (Subjective Units of Distress) has decreased through interoceptive exposure, enquire about the reaction that your client had to this situation ("What did you do to make yourself feel better?"). Show how negative reinforcement takes place when the mode of coping (written in the Reaction box) provides relief from unpleasant sensations.

2 Explain the omnipresence of change or *impermanence* in all aspects of life, and emphasize the need to remain aware of impermanence while practicing, especially with very pleasant or very unpleasant experiences: all things pass.
3 Discuss equanimity, its role in developing experiential acceptance, including acceptance of oneself. Explain that since we identify with thoughts and emotions, self-acceptance starts with acceptance of our own thoughts and body sensations.
4 Explain that training in mindfulness of sensations through daily body scanning helps regulate emotion.

Introduce the Four Characteristics of Body Sensations

Discuss the hedonic continuum with the three main ways of experiencing body sensations (pleasant, unpleasant, and neutral) and the four basic characteristics of body sensations (mass, motion, temperature and fluidity). Describe them while showing Session 3, Figure 1, or by drawing each continuum on a note pad or whiteboard.

Explain Homework Exercises

- This week, the homework is part-by-part unilateral body scanning. Explain that it will be more productive if interoceptive attention is directed vertically, rather than sideways, given that most advanced scanning methods will require a continual downward and upward "flow" of attention that does not lend itself to scanning horizontally.
- The audio instructions are found on track 8, and the brief introduction is on track 7. Ask your client to practice twice daily and record their practice every day on Handout 3.4.
- Read Handout 3.2.
- Fill out the Diary of Reactive Habits (Handout 3.1) when experiencing a stressful event.

Fill out the Interoceptive Awareness Indicator (Handout 3.3) using a highlighter or coloring pen (so you can still see the printed area) to record where they can feel sensations. Fill out the Daily Record of Mindfulness Meditation Practice (Handout 3.4).

Delaying the Next Step

Clients who cannot focus for at least 30 seconds on the breath without being carried away by thoughts should spend a little longer on the practice of mindfulness of breath, *without* using the audio instructions. Generally, two or three days of committed *effortful* practice will suffice, but some clients might need another whole week of mindfulness of breath before being able to focus elsewhere on the body with some mental stability.

Application with Groups

Session Aim

Session 3 introduces body scanning and the rationale for developing interoceptive awareness and equanimity and provides a detailed explanation of the co-emergence model using the Diary of Reactive Habits (Handout 3.1).

Materials

Whiteboard, Stage 1 CD or MP3 and CD/MP3 player, Interoceptive Awareness Indicator and Daily Record of Mindfulness Meditation Practice forms (Handouts 3.3 and 3.4).

Review Homework and Progress

Clarify any issues raised if necessary. When homework is incomplete or not done, remain equanimous while explaining the notion of prioritizing. Explain that people tend to do first what will be most rewarding or least unpleasant and this is why we prioritize activities the way we do. Use the Socratic dialogue or other useful questioning methods if necessary. Discuss difficulties including possible pain, agitation, craving and aversion, drowsiness and doubts, using the examples of group participants willing to volunteer their experience.

Deliver the Rationale for Body Scanning

1 On the whiteboard, reproduce the five components of the co-emergence model (see Diary of Reactive Habits (Handout 3.1),). Explain the principles on the board by illustrating the five components with a real-life experience one of the participants has had this week. Ask someone to volunteer a stressful event in the last week. Try to not to use an event that was too stressful, or you will end up doing individual therapy during your group session—alternatively, use one of your examples. Write their challenging situation in the upper-left box (Stimulus). Ask them to close their eyes and recall the recent challenging situation and write this situation in the upper-left box (Situation/Stimulus). Ask how they knew the situation was happening (heard, saw, etc.) without leading and write it in the Sensory Perception box, modeling the script described in the main text. Now explore the personal implications in the situation using Socratic questioning and the "downward arrow" technique to elicit the Evaluation components ("If this were true, what would it mean to you?"). Then ask how this interpretation made them feel ("How does it make you feel to think this way?"). Investigate what co-emerging body sensations they are feeling as they describe their view and do a brief exposure to the predominant sensations, guiding them through the four characteristics of body sensations. Use timing sets of 30 seconds and guidance to

decrease arousal through equanimity. Once the percentage of arousal (Subjective Units of Distress) has decreased through interoceptive exposure, enquire about the reaction that your client had to this situation ("What did you do to make yourself feel better?"). Show how negative reinforcement takes place when the mode of coping (written in the Reaction box) provides relief from unpleasant sensations.

2 Explain the omnipresence of change or *impermanence* in all aspects of life, and emphasize the need to remain aware of impermanence while practicing, especially with very pleasant or very unpleasant experiences: all things pass.
3 Discuss equanimity, its role in developing experiential acceptance, including acceptance of oneself. Explain that since we identify with thoughts and emotions, self-acceptance starts with acceptance of our own thoughts and body sensations.
4 Explain that training in mindfulness of sensations through daily body scanning helps regulate emotion.

In-session Practice

Conduct a group practice of part-by-part body scanning using track 8 on the MP3 or CD. If you prefer to use the printed script, it can be found in Appendix 2. Explain that it will be more productive if interoceptive attention is directed vertically, rather than sideways, given that most advanced scanning methods will require a continual downward and upward "flow" of attention that does not lend itself to scanning horizontally. Introduce the Interoceptive Awareness Indicator (Handout 3.3) and ask them to fill it with a highlighter or coloring pen (so you can still see the printed outline underneath the filled in sections) to record where they can feel sensations.

Explain Homework Exercises

- This week the homework is part-by-part unilateral body scanning. Explain that it will be more productive if interoceptive attention is directed vertically, rather than sideways, given that most advanced scanning methods will require a continual downward and upward "flow" of attention that will not lend itself to scanning horizontally.
- The audio instructions are found on track 8, and the brief introduction is on track 7. Ask participants to practice twice daily and record their practice daily (Handout 3.4).
- Read Handout 3.2.
- Fill out the Diary of Reactive Habits (Handout 3.1) when experiencing a stressful event.
- Fill out the Interoceptive Awareness Indicator (Handout 3.3) using a highlighter or coloring pen (so you can still see the printed area) to record where they can feel sensations.
- Fill out the Daily Record of Mindfulness Meditation Practice (Handout 3.4).

Delaying the Next Step

Clients who cannot focus for at least 30 seconds on the breath without being carried away by thoughts should spend a little longer on the practice of mindfulness of breath, but *without* using the audio instructions. Generally, two or three days of committed *effortful* practice will suffice, but some clients might need another whole week of mindfulness of breath before being able to focus elsewhere on the body with some mental stability.

Frequently Asked Questions

Question: How can I explain to my client that it's important to scan the body in a particular order?

Answer: Moving in order is important for three reasons. The first is related to procedural memory. Your client may forget some body parts if he doesn't move in a systematic order. Because the mind can be so easily distracted, the audio instructions are designed to guide people in a systematic order through each part of the body, so that they are able to maintain the order when they are ready to practice without instructions.

The second reason for scanning in a consistent order is related to unintentional neglect. Unless there is a systematic order in scanning, we may neglect some areas, avoiding body parts that are either difficult or unpleasant to feel. Our attention will instead be drawn to areas of the body where sensations are obvious and easy to feel. As a result of missing the opportunity to practice detecting subtle sensations in all areas of the body equally, we limit our ability to develop the capacity to feel the very early signs of change in the body, such as the early stages of onset of emotions. Trying to feel very subtle sensations in every area of the body produces the required effort to develop brain pathways that are not yet sufficiently connected in the insula and somatosensory cortex, where we feel body sensations.

The third reason for scanning in this systematic order is to facilitate the more advanced scanning methods that you will soon be teaching your client. Part-by-part unilateral scanning is the first and most basic body-scanning method and is used for two weeks only. The more advanced methods require us to "sweep" our attention in a single movement through the entire body very quickly, eventually at the speed of our breath. The only way to be able to do this is to have trained our attention to scan downwards and upwards systematically. Therefore, it is important that clients' scanning direction is, as much as possible, vertical and not horizontal. However, it's okay if they survey small parts of the body in a slightly different order, such as small parts of the face or other body parts that are difficult to survey vertically.

Question: My client is a little confused about the speed of scanning. How long should it take her to scan the whole body?

Answer: When using audio instructions, the time for the scanning cycle is predetermined by the length of the audio track, which is approximately 30 minutes. This week, your client needs to survey the body once, from the top of the head down to the tips of the toes, and from the tips of the toes back up to the top of the head. This constitutes a scanning cycle. Next week, she will practice without audio instructions so she will be able to move her attention through the body at her own pace, doing easily two to three cycles in each 30-minute session, without missing too many body parts.

Question: My client reports that he can't really feel any body sensation, but he doesn't appear dissociated. Is this possible? How can I best assist him?

Answer: It is common for people to believe that they can't feel body sensations because they expect sensations to be something special, and in their perception, nothing special happens, apart from some annoying itches and pains! However, this method instructs them to pay attention to common, ordinary, everyday sensations. As your client heard during the audio instructions, *anything he feels* is a body sensation. This might be a sensation of temperature, such as feeling hot or cold in some body part. It could be sensations associated with movement, such as an itch or heartbeat. There could be a sensation of heaviness or lightness, such as feeling heaviness in the neck and back due to some fatigue. Sensations could also be related to the experience of density and solidity, such as feeling constricted in some body parts. For example, he might feel tightness in the chest or stomach if he is anxious. The opposite of solidity and density would be feeling very diffuse and "fluid" sensations in some body parts, where there might be a sense of expansion rather than contraction.

All these are ordinary body sensations. The last thing we want to do is look for something special. If your client looks for something that is not there, he creates an unrealistic expectation and this is not beneficial. We practice in order to *observe* our experiences in the body *just as they are*. This means that if he cannot feel a particular body part, he just needs to *accept* that he can't feel sensations in this part at this moment, understanding that this will also change.

Where he cannot feel a sensation in a particular area, he should stay focused on that blank spot for up to about 10 seconds at this early stage, and then move on to the next part very patiently, with tolerance and equanimity, as in the audio instructions. From next week, he will be able to stay focused on blank spots easily for up to 30 seconds before moving on to the next part, because his mind will be sufficiently trained to sustain attention and not get lost in thoughts. He also needs to remember that while feeling sensations is important, his attitude to the practice is even more important, because his attitude also affects the way certain brain areas are connected. If he remains patient and tolerant when he doesn't get what he wants during practice, he will have the same attitude outside the practice. This is because the brain he uses for meditation is the brain he also uses in daily life. The way he wires it during practice is the way it becomes shaped for daily life.

Question: My client tells me that she can't feel a particular area of her body, no matter how much she tries, and then feels she is not capable. How can I assist her to overcome this?

Answer: I would first validate her hard work and then explain to her that she also needs to work with equanimity. Otherwise, her attitude will reinforce her belief that she is not good enough, even for therapy. She needs to understand how to keep her mind steady and firmly anchored in objective observation and not to take any of her experiences personally. She only needs to witness them. Ask her to simply *notice* that some parts can be felt and others cannot be felt at this stage. This has nothing to do with her, as a person. Sometimes trying too hard can worsen the problem, because it leads to the involuntary activation of emotional pathways at the cost of sensory activation, in places that let us feel body sensations. As a result, the harder we try, the less we feel. Do you think that this has been her experience? I would ask her if this also reflects her attitude in life; does she try too hard and take the failure to achieve her goals personally? This kind of reflection usually strikes a chord for people.

It is also important to know that people who are chronically stressed or anxious tend to avoid the typically unpleasant visceral sensations in the abdomen and chest areas. When this interoceptive avoidance has been established for a while, it can make the abdomen or chest areas difficult to feel. This is also common with chronic pain, where a decrease in grey matter volume has been consistently identified in up to eight brain areas, including in the insular cortex, which enables us to feel sensations. With mental health issues as well, connectivity to the insula seems to be decreased, presumably because this is the way in which we suppress painful emotions—i.e. by not feeling body sensations. Hence, feeling the front part of the torso can take a little longer for some people.

Often, people will also report that they cannot feel a body part as they are scanning through it, but they can feel it as soon as they move their attention to another body part. It is useful to normalize this common phenomenon and ask them to simply notice it equanimously. It is beneficial and a good modeling exercise for clinicians to say that they cannot explain all phenomena, including this one, but it is fine to just observe and learn from them with interest. Remind your client not to take part in the phenomenon, not identify with it, and that sooner or later things will change. An important aspect of mindfulness practice is to *just observe* patiently how change happens.

Question: My client reports feeling agitated when he practices but he does not experience agitation at other times of the day or in other current situations in his life, and he wonders if it is normal. I am not sure how to explain it either.

Answer: Agitation is very common when we start the practice, and it comes and goes even once we have some experience with meditation, depending on several factors. One is what has recently happened in daily life. Another is what we may have recently or frequently anticipated to happen in the future. Agitation can also occur due to non-conscious but stressful body sensations or the sub-conscious anticipation of feeling discomfort. The "control parameter" is equanimity.

When agitation persists and our equanimity is insufficiently developed to overcome it, it is known as one of the "five hindrances" to the practice. However, this is also an opportunity to carefully observe where sensations associated with the agitation are located in the body and practice interoceptive exposure to them.

For this, your client needs to hold his attention there while remaining calm and equanimous for a minute or two. He needs to study what he notices with curiosity and genuine interest, keeping in mind that no sensation is here to stay forever; all sensations are impermanent, just like everything else. It will help to keep in mind that the experience is *just* an experience and not one that defines who he is. As he will learn more actively next week, he could focus on the four characteristics of sensations (mass, temperature, motion and fluidity). This will help him not to take his experience personally. If he examines his experience in a detached and equanimous way, his agitation is likely to subside rapidly and allow something else to emerge, often a sense of calmness or even drowsiness.

Question: My client practiced body scanning with another therapist before and says that she prefers to lie down during the practice, as she was instructed to do before. She says it is more relaxing. Would this be OK in MiCBT as well?

Answer: We can certainly cultivate mindfulness in all physical positions and during physical activities. In fact, we will do this in MiCBT as well, as part of applying our meditative skills in daily life. However, it is important to practice sitting up because lying down is likely to contribute to a subtle dullness, even if she doesn't overtly feel drowsy. We also notice that people are often confusing relaxation and mindfulness. It is understandable that people will prefer and choose a method that is more relaxing over one that requires exposure to what is sometimes fairly unpleasant. MiCBT includes relaxation (PMR) only in the first week of training and quickly moves to exposure with the aim of desensitization. The goal is to develop equanimity, insight and resilience, not relaxation. Why not relaxation? Because we can turn to relaxation on the basis that we resent feeling discomfort. This includes fearing anxiety symptoms, which ironically can lead to full-blown panic attacks. Wanting to relax away unpleasant sensations is still an aversive response! Indeed, while intending to relax, what we are actually practicing is interoceptive avoidance. This is not to say that relaxation is not beneficial, as long as it is not based on wanting to "get rid of stress," which is an aversion toward unpleasant sensations.

If your client does not have a serious medical condition preventing her from sitting with her neck and back relatively straight and aligned, she would benefit from adopting a sitting posture. Explain that because she is not yet used to being alert and deeply relaxed at the same time, lying down will make her either insufficiently alert, and therefore not able to observe subtle events in the body, or will contribute to becoming lost in thoughts and will prevent her from refocusing on body sensations quickly. Additionally, she will feel unnecessarily drowsy to practice on days when she is feeling more tired. If she is too tired to practice sitting up, she could have a short rest before her practice. She could lie down for 5 to 10 minutes, have a rest, and then sit up for practice.

So far, there have been no studies showing that lying down yields better results than sitting up straight, nor has the sitting posture been empirically shown to be superior. All we have is our personal and clinical experience over the years, as well as the guidance of our own monastic and secular meditation teachers, who taught us in the way that mindfulness meditators have been practicing for over 2500 years. We suggest that practicing sitting up will yield the best and quickest results, even if she initially struggles.

Question: My client reports having a slight headache when he scans his body and wonders if it is because he could be trying too hard. He also says that he is scanning the body with his eyes and it tires him.

Answer: Visual tracking of where our attention goes is very common when we start this practice, and it can lead to a headache. The brain is usually more skilled at using vision than interoception, simply because we use our visual modality significantly more than our feeling modality in daily life. It is of no surprise that "seeing," or visualizing, is easier and more familiar than feeling. The brain is also very good at problem-solving. What it cannot do with one sensory modality, it will try to do with another. It automatically tries to adapt by "seeing" what it cannot feel. This is similar to a blind person using their hearing modality to compensate for the lack of sight.

Normalizing the experience is important. Reassure your client that visual tracking is not bad or dangerous, but encourage him to prevent it as soon as possible. With practice, his increased ability to feel will replace the habit of trying to see. Instruct him to rest the eyes in a fixed position and to do his best to attend to the body parts that he is scanning without using the eyes. This will improve over time.

Question: How do I best assist my client when she says that her mind is still too scattered to focus on the body and she wants to continue practicing mindfulness of breath?

Answer: Normalize your client's experience. She simply needs to make an effort to inhibit her usual response to thoughts by having firm determination to return her attention to the part of the body she is scanning within three seconds once a thought has arisen. This is called the "3-second rule." We tend to be aware of a thought intruding in consciousness as soon as it happens, and it is easy to begin to actively "think" it if we don't disengage from it immediately. Remind your client that she is more likely to be caught up in thoughts that have salient co-emerging sensations. This is because we tend to react inadvertently to the body sensations co-emerging with thoughts, rather than to the thought itself (i.e., the cognitive aspect of the thought). If a thought becomes too persistent, as in people with OCD, ask your client to detect what is the most intense sensation in the body and stay focused on it equanimously, dividing it into its four basic characteristics of mass, temperature, motion and fluidity. Once this interoceptive exposure to the emotional component of the thought has occurred for up to a minute, it is likely that the thought will be less "sticky" and less obsessive. Note also that some thoughts will emerge because we are scanning the body.

This is what co-emergence means; it is both a top-down *and* a bottom up process.

Question: My client was taught that mindfulness is simply about being in the present moment without making judgments. How would you suggest that I respond?

Answer: Mindfulness, as we consider it in MiCBT, is a mental tool for the investigation of our experience in the present moment. We don't practice just to "be mindful." We simply use it as a tool to see things the way they truly are and to decondition the mind from habits that promote suffering. By using this tool, we can discern which thoughts, emotions or actions are wholesome and which ones are not. It is not just about being in the present moment. Mindfulness involves direct observation and *thorough* experiential understanding that experiences such as pain and pleasure are only temporary. Through carefully observing our own experience, we determine that identifying with, for example, pleasure, leads to attachment, which leads to craving when pleasure is no longer present, which then gives rise to unhappiness.

Accurate mindfulness training promotes equanimity, which reduces the tendency to identify with the experience. Of course, fostering a sense of self by identifying with our experience reinforces craving and aversion, which are habits that maintain unhealthy behavior and cause suffering. Equanimity is the attitude that enables the prevention of craving and aversion, which facilitates our awareness of being in the present moment. With equanimity, joy is easy to let go of when it passes, and dissatisfaction is easy to allow when it comes. Life becomes easier when we have learned to accept it just as it presents itself, in the present moment.

Handout 3.1 Diary of Reactive Habits

Fill in the boxes each time you encounter a situation that evokes an emotional or stressful experience

SITUATION INTERNAL/EXTERNAL

What actually happened?

SENSORY PERCEPTION

How did (do) you know this was happening?

EVALUATION

What did it mean to you?...
...and if this were true, what would it mean to you?
Repeat as above until "I" increases in importance.

BODY SENSATION

How did it make you feel to think this way?

REACTION/RESPONSE

What did you do to make yourself feel better?

DATE OF EVENT: ____________________

TIME OF EVENT: ____________________

INTENSITY OF DISTRESS: Then ________%

INTENSITY OF DISTRESS: Now ________%

NAME: ____________________

IN THERAPY SINCE (Date): ____________

Handout 3.2 Body Scanning: Understanding Feelings and Equanimity

When we have thoughts about something that we think is important to us, it automatically creates some sensations inside the body, and when the sensations are intense, we perceive these as feelings or emotions. For example, if you have the thought that you are a failure, then you will notice some discomfort inside the body. Some changes happen, even small ones that we normally don't pay attention to, such as in skin temperature and heart rate, or simply some movement in the stomach. Even if you are not aware of them, they affect how you feel and react.

When we have a negative or scary thought, unpleasant sensations (feelings) arise with the thought, such as a warm, swirling movement in the stomach. We may react to these sensations by trying to avoid them. We might have an alcoholic drink, a coffee, a cigarette, food, or even go for a run. This may mask the sensations and provide some relief in the short term, but it can become a problem later. We begin to realize this connection between thoughts and feelings as we develop our mindfulness practice. We also understand that learning to pay attention to body sensations allows us to be more quickly aware of emotions and manage them more skillfully as soon as they arise.

This week, the practice involves sitting still and focusing as before, but this time focusing attention on the body instead of the breath. This will train you to identify body sensations while you scan the body. You will be aware of sensations in the body. Focus attention on your body in a systematic way from top of the head to the toes taking small areas (2 or 3 inches or 7or 8 centimeters square) at a time. The drawing in Session 3, Figure 2 shows small circles that represent the size of the spots of attention when we scan the body. On the torso area, you can see that the direction of your attention is vertical, not horizontal. Track 8 of your audio instructions will guide you with this practice.

As soon as you notice a sensation, move to the next area and do the same, from one part to the next. This is why it is called "part-by-part body scanning." If you do not notice sensations on a certain spot, then stay there for about ten seconds or so and then move on to the next spot. Make sure that you accept it when you can't feel a sensation. After all, this is also an experience. It is the *reality* that you experience at this time, on this part of the body. You will learn to accept reality as it presents itself, from moment to moment.

Body scanning helps us to become aware of the intimate relationship between thinking and feeling. We learn to survey the whole of the body part by part, noticing arising sensations without judgment, neutrally. We start to realize that sensations come and go all the time. We are learning about the connection between body sensations and subtle changes in emotion. What we call an emotion is the result of thinking and the body sensations that co-arise. For example, with anger we may think, "She shouldn't have spoken to me like that," and then notice sensations that are hot, dense, heavy, or movement and agitation in the body. We call this feeling "anger" and we may say "I am angry" and may even react by shouting or speaking forcefully.

Session 3, Figure 2 Drawing showing the size and direction of attention for part-by-part unilateral scanning.

With practice, you may notice that you want more of the pleasant sensations and less of the unpleasant ones. If we become aware that accepting body sensations is a key part of feeling relief from emotions, we can simply observe the sensations and wait for them to change without having to *do* anything. This enables us to be much more in control of our responses to emotions. As we become aware of the body, we may become more aware of sensations, emotions and responses and are able to respond differently. We are developing "equanimity." Equanimity is the ability to keep the balance of our mind by not reacting to body sensations and take our experience personally, which is the goal of our practice from here on. Remember that being aware informs you, whereas being equanimous transforms you.

Handout 3.3 Interoceptive Awareness Indicator

Name:....................................... Age:......... Sex:........ Date:............

Date when training started:........... Scanning methods this week:.............

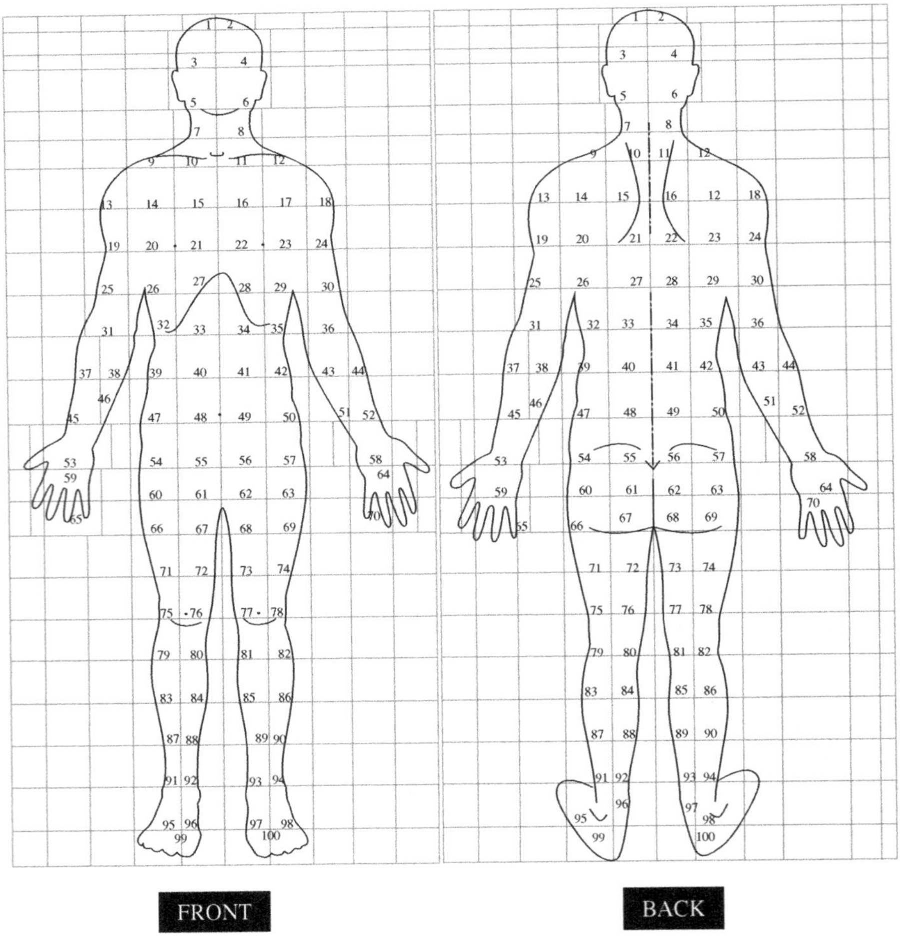

Please color the parts in the silhouette where you can feel any type of body sensations. Try not to spend too long coloring the parts. It is OK if you go slightly over the silhouette edge.

Results

There are 100 numbered boxes (square and rectangular shapes) within or crossing the outline of the silhouette. To calculate the percentage of interoceptive awareness, count the total number of colored boxes. A numbered box is counted as valid if at least half of its surface that falls within the silhouette is colored.

Total interoceptive awareness = (%back + %front / 2) = ...%

Note: This form can be downloaded in full-size format from http://clinicalhandbook.mindfulness.net.au/handouts

Handout 3.4 Daily Record of Mindfulness Meditation Practice

Day	**Date**	**Morning** *(circle)*	**Duration**	**Efficacy rating** *Rate from 1 to 10 how well you noticed distractions and brought your attention back to the breath or body. 1 = not well at all; 10 = extremely well*	**Evening** *(circle)*	**Duration**	**Efficacy rating** *Rate from 1 to 10 how well you noticed distractions and brought your attention back to the breath or body. 1 = not well at all; 10 = extremely well*
Monday		I practiced Yes / No			I practiced Yes / No		
Tuesday		I practiced Yes / No			I practiced Yes / No		
Wednesday		I practiced Yes / No			I practiced Yes / No		
Thursday		I practiced Yes / No			I practiced Yes / No		
Friday		I practiced Yes / No			I practiced Yes / No		
Saturday		I practiced Yes / No			I practiced Yes / No		
Sunday		I practiced Yes / No			I practiced Yes / No		

References

Abramowitz, J. S. (1996). Variants of exposure and response prevention in the treatment of obsessive-compulsive disorder: A meta-analysis. *Behavior Therapy*, 27, 583–600. doi: 10.1016/S0005-7894(96)80045-1

Barrett, L. F. (2006). Valence is a basic building block of emotional life. *Journal of Research in Personality*, 40, 35–55. doi:10.1016/j.jrp.2005.08.006

Cayoun, B. A. (2011). *Mindfulness-integrated CBT: Principles and practice*. Chichester, UK: Wiley-Blackwell.

Cayoun, B. A., & Shires, A. (Manuscript submitted for publication). Co-emergence reinforcement: A proposed transdiagnostic mechanism in emotional disorders and their remediation through mindfulness and cognitive-behavioral interventions. Manuscript sent for publication.

Cebolla, A., Galiana, L., Campos, D., Oliver, A., Soler, J., Demarzo, M..., Garcia-Campayo, J. (2017). How does mindfulness work? Exploring a theoretical model using samples of meditators and non-meditators. *Mindfulness*. doi:10.1007/s12671-017-0826-7

Craske, M. G., and Barlow, D. (1993/2008). Panic disorder and agoraphobia. In D. Barlow (Ed.), *Clinical handbook of psychological disorders: A step-by-step treatment manual* (pp. 1–47) (2nd ed.). New York: The Guilford Press.

Craske, M. G., & Barlow, D. H. (2007). *Mastery of your anxiety and panic* (4th ed.). New York, NY: Oxford University Press.

Desbordes, G., Gard, T., Hoge, E. A., Hölzel, B. K., Kerr, C., Lazar, S. W., Olendzki, A., & Vago, D. R. (2015). Moving beyond Mindfulness: Defining equanimity as an outcome measure in meditation and contemplative research. *Mindfulness*. doi:10.1007/s12671-013-0269-8

Dunn, B.D., Galton, H.C., Morgan, R., Evans, D., Oliver, C., Meyer, M., et al. (2010). Listening to your heart: how interoception shapes emotion experience and intuitive decision making. *Psychological Science*, 21, 1835–1844.

Farb, N., A. S., Daubenmier, J., Price, C. J., Gard, T., Kerr, C., Dunn, B. D., et al. (2015). Interoception, contemplative practice, and health. *Frontiers in Psychology*, 6, 763. doi:10.3389/fpsyg.2015.00763

Gotink, R. A., Meijboom, R., Vernooij, M., W., Smits, M., & Hunink, M. M. G. (2016). 8-week mindfulness based stress reduction induces brain changes similar to traditional long-term meditation practice – A systematic review. *Brain and Cognition*, 108, 32–41. doi:10.1016/j.bandc.2016.07.001

Hart, W. (1987). *The art of living: Vipassana meditation as taught by S.N. Goenka*. San Francisco: HarperCollins.

Hölzel, B. K., Lazar, S. W., Gard, T., Schuman-Olivier, Z., Vago, D. R., & Ott, U. (2011). How does mindfulness meditation work? Proposing mechanisms of action from a conceptual and neural perspective. *Perspectives on Psychological Science*, 6, 537–559.

Kabat-Zinn, J. (1982). An outpatient program in behavioral medicine for chronic pain clients based on the practice of mindfulness meditation: Theoretical considerations and preliminary results. *General Hospital Psychiatry*, 4, 33–42.

Kerr, C. E., Sacchet, M. D., Lazar, S. W., Moore, C. I., & Jones, S. R. (2013). Mindfulness starts with the body: somatosensory attention and top-down modulation of cortical alpha rhythms in mindfulness meditation. *Frontiers of Human Neuroscience*, 7, 12. doi:10.3389/fnhum.2013.00012

Shapiro, N. (2007). *The complete fables of La Fontaine (Work from 1668)*. Chicago: University of Illinois Press.

Lackner, R. J., & Fresco, D. M. (2016). Interaction effect of brooding rumination and interoceptive awareness on depression and anxiety symptoms. *Behaviour Research and Therapy*. doi: 10.1016/j.brat.2016.08.007.

Payne, J. D., & Nadel, L. (2004). Sleep, dreams, and memory consolidation: The role of the stress hormone cortisol. *Learning and Memory*, 11, 671–678.

Pollatos, O., Gramann, K., & Schandry, R. (2007). Neural systems connecting interoceptive awareness and feelings. *Human Brain Mapping*, 28, 9–18. doi:10.1002/hbm.20258

Pradhan, P. (1950). *Abhidharmasamuccaya*. Santiniketan, Visva Bharati.

Seth, A. K., & Critchley, H. D. (2013). Extending predictive processing to the body: emotion as interoceptive inference. *Behavioral Brain Science*, 36, 227–228.

Walshe, M. (2012). *The long discourses of the Buddha: A translation of the Digha Nikaya*. Boston: Wisdom Publications.

Session 4: Applied Practice and Skill Transfer

No emotion, any more than a wave, can long retain its own individual form.
— Henry Ward Beecher, 1871

Introduction

This chapter guides therapists in assisting clients to understand the role and practice of equanimity and developing awareness of the four characteristics of body sensations. It describes the role of focusing on these four interoceptive characteristics as an emotion-regulation strategy that prevents over-identifying and over-reacting to a distressing experience. Your client will be introduced to the applied practice of equanimity as a means of reducing distress both in and outside sitting practice. It will become clearer to them that awareness only *informs* the response, whereas equanimity *transforms* it. This week, your client will practice without any audio instructions, which will deepen their focus, understanding and skills. This week's practice requires sitting in "strong determination" (*Adhitthana* in Pali), which in this context essentially means practicing with a resolute commitment to remain equanimous, i.e., remaining non-reactive and not identifying with whatever experience arises in consciousness while remaining immobile. Doing this while passing attention systematically through the entire body, part-by-part, results in greater development of equanimity.

Checking Client Readiness

Your client has completed the first week of training in mindfulness of body sensations. It is important to check on their progress. Were they able to practice for 30 minutes twice a day? Did they feel that their practice was beneficial? Check if they can feel sensations in some parts of the body. Were they any less reactive this

The Clinical Handbook of Mindfulness-integrated Cognitive Behavior Therapy: A Step-by-Step Guide for Therapists, First Edition. Bruno A. Cayoun, Sarah E. Francis, and Alice G. Shires.

Companion website: www.wiley.com/go/Cayoun/Mindfulness-integrated

week? For example, could they notice body sensations, both pleasant and unpleasant, without reacting with craving or aversion? Could they remain equanimous if they didn't notice sensations in some areas? If they preferred to practice without audio instructions, this probably means that they could recall the instructions and manage intrusive thoughts which can be challenging when practicing in silence.

If your client has not practiced as much as required, ask them to re-commit; to start again with the practice without guilt or self-blame and with a new commitment. It is useful to remind clients that learning to be kind to themselves is important when learning these new skills. Use Socratic questioning to clarify what may have been a hindrance to their practice: not discussing it can sometimes maintain a problem that is simple to address. Remaining open, non-judgmental and empathic can bring that "aha!" moment, and a re-commitment is easier for the client to envisage.

Delaying the Next Step

If your client has practiced daily but gets caught up in thoughts or cannot feel many body sensations, then it may be useful for them to do a few more days of mindfulness of breath until their mind is calmer and a little more settled on the breath. They can then proceed with body scanning with audio instructions for a few more days, and then proceed with the practice of body scanning without audio instructions. Sometimes clients will need another whole week with mindfulness of breath (preferably without instructions) before resuming body scanning. However, it is also important to explain that it is not necessary for them to have no thoughts or feel the whole body before starting to practice in silence. Noticing some blank spots and having intrusive thoughts is a very usual and necessary experience, and we can use these experiences to develop equanimity and insight about how cognitive and interoceptive systems operate.

Ask your client to fill in the Interoceptive Awareness Indicator (Handout 3.3). If your client is able to focus attention and feel at least 20 % of the body's surface area, ask them if they can now practice without audio instructions. If they are confident that they can and clearly remember the instructions, then they are ready to proceed with the next step and increase the efficacy of their practice. If, when your client starts practicing in silence, they consistently struggle with focusing attention, it may be useful for them to start each practice with 10 minutes of mindfulness of breath before continuing with 20 minutes of body scanning. The first 10 minutes will help sharpen their mind so they can focus better when they practice body scanning. However, at this stage, time should be spent on scanning the body as much as possible, so this precaution should only be applied if their struggle with focusing attention is greater than typically expected for this task.

Increasing Practice Efficacy

It is beneficial for clients to understand how to strengthen awareness of body sensations and their equanimity toward them. It is also important for clients to be able to apply awareness and equanimity in day-to-day events and situations. The transfer of such new skills in daily life can be rapid for some people and very slow for others. If mindfulness meditation was self-implemented for the purpose of personal growth only, we would have plenty of time to meditate until neuroplasticity produces a progressive transfer of equanimity skills in daily life. In contrast, a clinical context necessitates sufficiently rapid change to produce and maintain the reinforcement of daily practice. Keeping in mind that mindfulness practice is a set of metacognitive and interoceptive exposure tasks, it is often far from being a pleasant activity. Accordingly, we need rather rapid and successive rewarding effects to keep clients engaged with the practice routine. For this reason, this week and in preparation for the next, we capitalize on more effective development of equanimity for rapid and sufficiently substantial change in daily life by practicing in silence, with strong determination.

Silent Practice

The audio instructions serve the important purpose of guiding clients as they learn the basic skills of a given task. However, if used for too long, they can be intrusive and become a source of interference. Generally, after about a week of practicing with instructions, people need silent practice. Practicing with instructions should assist in learning new information and consolidating it for about a week. If kept longer than this, listening to instructions interferes with the most productive aspect of the practice, the neutralization of the emotional component of intrusive thoughts—desensitization. This means that we actually need thoughts to intrude in consciousness at this early stage of the practice. If you recall Session 2, our memory of painful events can be neutralized and even changed by the uncoupling of the amygdala response (associated with visceral interoception) from the memory (Cayoun & Shires, manuscript submitted for publication; Hölzel et al., 2011).

Thoughts that would easily emerge in conscious awareness during silent practice can remain "masked" by the sound and meaning of the audio instructions. In cognitive science, this is called "structural interference," which involves two or more modality-congruent stimuli (e.g., two thoughts or two images processed at the same time in the same brain structure) competing for access to consciousness (McLeod, 1991, Wickens, 1984). It is also the case that if the instructions are boring to a client with ADHD or OCD, for example, then the internally generated stimulus (e.g., a thought) is likely to intrude in consciousness despite listening to audio instructions (Cayoun, 2010). However, for a person whose mind has been calmed by the previous two weeks of practice, the externally-generated stimulus (audio instruction) is likely to distract attention and prevent thoughts from emerging in consciousness. It acts a little bit as a mantra. One stimulus interferes with the other and prevents its processing. There are different theories about it, but basically, the stronger/ louder stimulus wins. With a mantra or soothing voice, the mind settles easily. This is the fundamental purpose of using a mantra in concentrative meditation techniques, such as Transcendental Meditation. This would be fine if our purpose was simply to learn to concentrate, but it doesn't serve our purpose of exposure and desensitization well. Indeed, some of your clients will ask if they can continue practicing with the audio instructions… and this has nothing to do with the French accent of Dr. Cayoun! In addition, over-learned instructions can lullaby us to sleep. Therefore, you will need to explain to your client to practice without audio instructions this week, while remaining strongly determined to develop equanimity.

Of course, clinical practice is rarely straightforward and there is often a need for flexibility and adjustment. Clients with conditions such as ADHD, OCD, hypomania and those with pervasively intrusive thoughts might struggle more than others to concentrate on the body without the interference produced by audio instructions. This is also common in older adults with early dementia because they often forget the instructions, even after having practiced 14 times in a week. In these cases, it may be helpful for clients to continue using the instructions for a few more days or a week, and occasionally a little longer depending on their progressive ability to inhibit intrusive thoughts.

Equanimity through Strong Determination

Silent practice helps us reprocess thoughts and associated body sensations that spontaneously emerge from memories. Since we prevent voluntary thinking and we are no longer distracted by instructions, thoughts arise from memory networks, even though we may not recognize them as memories. Remember that we process at least 20,000 conscious and non-conscious thoughts every day, which amounts to a conservative half a billion thoughts in a lifetime (some authors propose three time this amount), but we can only recall a few.

If you think back to the explanations for intrusive thoughts in Session 2 and Session 3, you'll recall that scanning the body is scanning through our past. This is because events that seemed important to us in the past were encoded and stored in memory with accompanying (co-emerging) body sensations, and are recalled in the same way. The body sensations felt during body scanning can become memory cues for memories encoded with a similar "feel;" i.e., a similar hedonic tone. This is why traumatic memories are so distressing and clients with PTSD are often pathologically avoidant. As their practice improves, it becomes clear to them that what they are avoiding are body sensations. By remaining equanimous, we allow these sensations to be fully felt while not buying into their associated memories. By preventing movements, such as changing posture, we minimize becoming distracted from the sensations associated with memories, and increase the chance of desensitizing from habits of avoidance.

Sitting without moving at all is also important if we are to realize how we tend to react to sensations, clinging to the pleasant and pushing away the unpleasant ones. We can notice that all experiences are impermanent, and therefore impersonal. Pure observation of the ever-changing sensations without any reaction helps to neutralize reactive habit patterns, not only reactions to the current sensations but to other similar ones that arise in day-to-day life. Accordingly, you will need to ask your client to commit to remaining equanimous as much as possible during the silent practice by sitting completely still while scanning the body—except for postural correction in context of drowsiness, burping, yawning, sneezing, coughing and swallowing saliva, which are not reactions due to craving or aversion. This is traditionally called "sitting in strong determination" (Hart, 1987). Surrendering to and accepting whatever is arising in a non-emotional way will speed the results of practice. Your client will learn to *welcome* unpleasant experiences without identifying with them.

Use of the Mindfulness-Based Interoceptive Exposure Task (MIET)

Sometimes, clients report coming across a body sensation that is quite intense and demanding of attention, preventing them from scanning other body parts. This does not only happen for people with chronic pain and does not mean that there is a problem in this part of the body which we should worry about. However, given that people's tendency is to catastrophize discomfort, you will occasionally need to explain simply that the sheer length and accuracy of practice lowers our threshold of awareness, and what would usually barely reach conscious awareness becomes conscious (Cayoun, 2011). This increased "interoceptive salience" (Uddin, 2014) gives us the impression that we are feeling an intense sensation, which occasionally can even seem unbearable. This occurs because improvements in interoceptive awareness through body scanning allow detection of very subtle sensations, such as early cues of distress. Feeling and addressing these sensations equanimously before they become unmanageable emotions is an important skill in MiCBT. It is a little bit like developing a magnifying glass that helps us perceive embryos of emotions. People are often surprised when the intensity of the sensation passes away soon after they open their eyes or become otherwise distracted.

If your client experiences very intense sensations, you may advise them to focus their attention in the center of the sensation. They should place their attention on that spot, just observing it and examining it in detail without any reaction whatsoever, with equanimity. Remind your client of the four characteristics of sensations and ask them to focus on these characteristics: mass, temperature, motion and fluidity (see Session 3 for detail). If your client can be equanimous for about 30 seconds, then the intensity of the sensation is likely to decrease significantly and allow them to continue to scan the body. If the sensations continue to demand attention, suggest that they stay longer, up to two minutes, and then resume with the systematic scanning of other parts of the body.

This task has its origins in traditional *Vipassana* meditation (Goenka, 1987; Hart, 1987) and has been specifically integrated in the MiCBT model since its inception in 2001 to train clients in distress tolerance with crisis. Recently, we have named this procedure the Mindfulness-based Interoceptive Exposure Task (MIET) for the purpose of facilitating communication in empirical research and dissemination. We have studied it as a separate method of applying equanimity in clients with chronic pain (Cayoun, Simmons, & Shires, 2017) and in experimentally-induced pain. When using mindfulness-based interoceptive exposure, your client is learning that they can face unpleasant sensations without avoidance or anxiety, remaining patiently and calmly present until the intensity is at least partly reduced. In this way, obstacles become learning opportunities.

When we experience boredom or strong discomfort during daily practice, each minute seems to take a very long time to pass. Sustaining equanimity over time helps clients to manage their sitting practice better. When we remain equanimous, peaceful and present to the experience without reacting to any sensation, time passes more quickly and clients report that the half-hour practice seems much shorter.

Pacing of the Scanning

The audio instructions are recorded in a way and at a pace that suits most people, but some develop interoceptive awareness more quickly than others. Withdrawing audio instructions lets your client move at their own pace. It is useful to explain to your clients to move attention more quickly through the body parts that they can easily feel and stay longer on those they cannot feel clearly or those that seem unpleasant to attend to. This will prevent them from dwelling on pleasant sensations and avoiding unpleasant ones. They develop the ability to simply feel the sensation, accept it and move on to the adjacent body part without attachment.

Unbound by audio instructions, the quicker pace of body scanning this week will enable your client to cycle through the body at least twice by the end of the week (see homework at the end of this chapter), thus increasing the amount exposure to body sensations and the opportunities to develop both interoceptive awareness and equanimity. When we scan faster, we are also less likely to cling to sensations and thoughts, or to become bored. By the end of this week's practice, clients are usually able to pass their descending and ascending attention through the entire body two or three times in 30 minutes. Encourage your client to scan between two and three body cycles, from the top of the head down to the toes, and back up to the top of the head.

Effects of Body Scanning on the Development of Insight

As we age, we experience how things change, including our own body, our needs, and our relationships, our level of insight develops naturally. It has been shown that people's sense of self, the way they think about themselves, changes with age (Ready et al., 2012). As we grow older, we tend to become less attached to aspects of the person we think we are, even if they were qualities that we thought were very important. Even our values change over time, especially unwholesome ones. This is reflected in statements such as, "I used to worry a lot about what other think of me, but I don't really mind it anymore," or "In the past, it was very important to me that my family went to church on Sunday, but now what matters most to me is that they are good people." As we mellow with age, we contextualize both the positive and negative aspects of ourselves with more flexibility and have less rigid rules about how we should see our sense of "self."

Nevertheless, this usually takes place with struggle, disappointment and loss over time. Emotional pain is a great teacher, and its relief a great lesson. In behavioral science, the relief from pain is called *negative reinforcement*. Eventually, we come to learn that we develop insight in areas of our life that lacked it, because where we lacked insight, we suffered.

Fortunately, such insight can be developed through mindfulness practice. We don't have to wait for the aging process and miss opportunities earlier in life. We often hear our clients say, "I wish I had learned this method earlier in my life," and "why don't they teach this at school?" Fortunately, mindfulness training at schools is slowly being implemented (Weare, 2012). Mindfulness meditation enables us to have an equanimous attitude toward both pleasant and unpleasant experiences.

It enables us to experience firsthand the ephemeral nature of our thoughts and sensations. Since we usually identify with our thoughts and sensations, it becomes possible to notice that these "micro bits of the self" come and go. Indeed, they are impermanent. When mindfulness is practiced accurately, it doesn't take long before this repeated observation results in improved cognitive flexibility in daily life. Our decisions and actions are increasingly based on the current information, rather than on past reactivity, beliefs and attachment to who we are.

If your client has already sufficient insight to understand this information, it may be beneficial to explain these mechanisms, even very simply. The use of Socratic dialogue will help you to not sound like you're trying to teach Buddhism, as this is not what we are trying to do. Of note, the understanding that everything is in a constant state of change, a continual flux, was also taught by the Greek philosopher Heraclitus (Khan, 1981), who interestingly lived at exactly the same period as the Buddha and died only three years earlier. Heraclitus is most known for his teachings on impermanence, and his and the Buddha's overlapping philosophies have been strong influences on modern therapies, such as Cognitive Behavior Therapy (Robertson, 2010) and Rational Emotive Behavior Therapy (Kwee & Ellis, 1998; Ellis, 1979).

Applying the Practice and Recording Equanimity

You introduced the four characteristics of body sensations to your client in Session 3 when describing the Diary of Reactive Habits. This week, you will ask your client to observe emotional experiences in terms of sensations using the *Mindfulness-based Interoceptive Signature Scale* (MISS; Handout 4.1; Cayoun, 2011),which is a visual analogue scale to measure an overall index of equanimity, as shown in Session 4, Figure 1). The MISS will help your client to measure how they feel in stressful situations and observe how their equanimity is developing. The four fundamental characteristics of interoception are mass, temperature, motion, and fluidity. You can use the example of a recent emotional experience that your client has had to show them how to use the MISS form to record their experience of the four characteristics of body sensations on the four scales. This will enable you to verify their understanding and troubleshoot their implementation.

Procedure

Ask your client to notice where the strongest sensation associated with the emotional experience is located in the body. Next, ask them to rate the intensity of the sensation by putting a mark on the intensity scale ("Intensity before"). Then ask them to put a mark on each of the four scales (the lines) to indicate how the sensations feel. For example, if the most salient sensation feels heavy, they put a mark toward the end of the "mass" scale. If it also feels hot, they need to put a mark on the end of the temperature scale accordingly, and so on.

When they have marked up all four scales, ask them to join each of the dots on the first four scales with a solid line; this represents the qualitative dimension

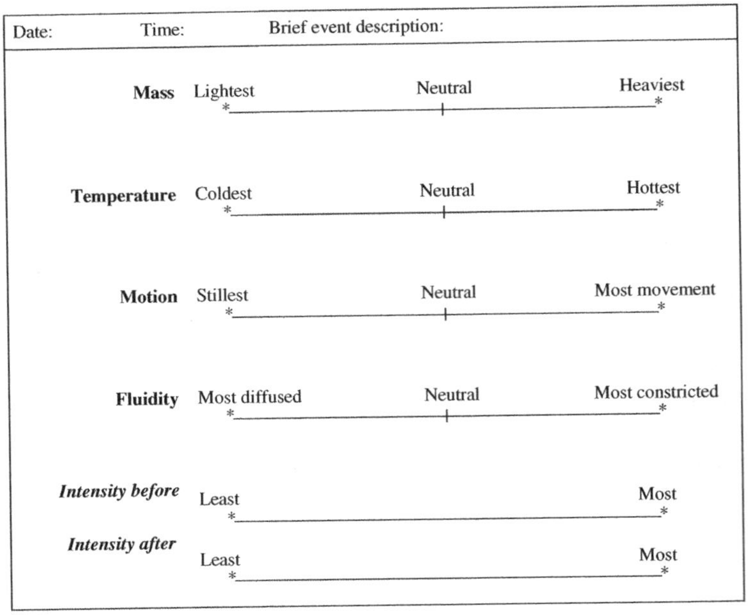

Session 4, Figure 1 Mindfulness-based Interoceptive Signature Scale (MISS). Reproduced from Cayoun (2015).

(hedonic tone) of the distress attributed to the sensation. Ask them to focus non-judgmentally and with equanimity on the sensation for 30 seconds (this is best done timed and with closed eyes within the session with you) and then to place a new set of marks on the first four scales. Ask them to join the marks with a dotted line this time; this line indicates the level of interoceptive change following the exposure task. Ask them to note the intensity of the sensation after the exposure as well, and mark the last scale ("Intensity after") accordingly. See the following examples.

Measuring the Development of Equanimity

Here is an example of how anger is represented by a middle-aged man who plotted his interoceptive experience on each of the scales. His rating of the quality of his anger experience is shown by the solid line in Session 4, Figure 2. The dotted line represents how the sensations felt after focusing on the sensations objectively and equanimously for about 30 seconds. The client was able to report a reduction of heat in the cheeks and arms, and agitation in the abdomen. He also recorded the difference in pre- and post-exposure intensity with the dots on each Intensity sub-scale (the last two lines).

Similarly, Session 4, Figure 3 shows an example of how sadness was experienced by a young woman (the event was remembering the death of her mother). After implementing this task several thousands of times over the past 18 years, we have noticed emotion-specific patterns of interoceptive experience. We have observed that anger tends to be represented by a convex shape, whereas sadness

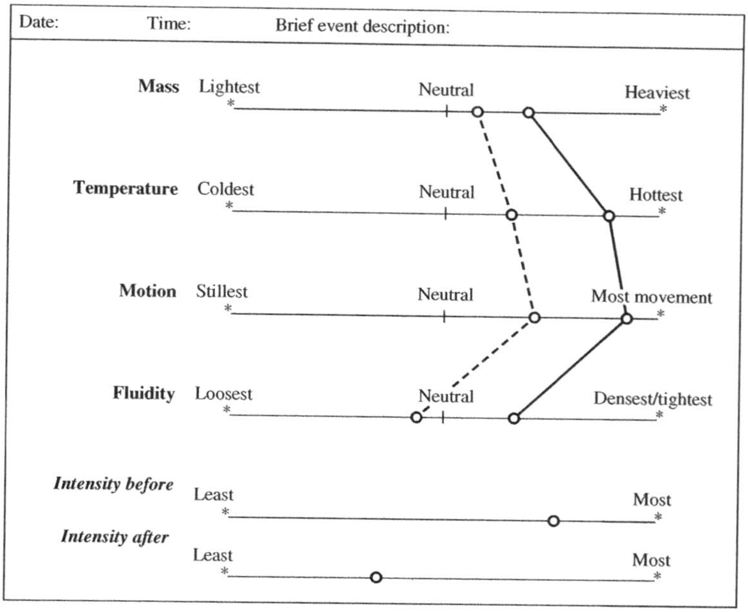

Session 4, Figure 2 Interoceptive change over 30 seconds for a person experiencing anger. Reproduced from Cayoun (2015).

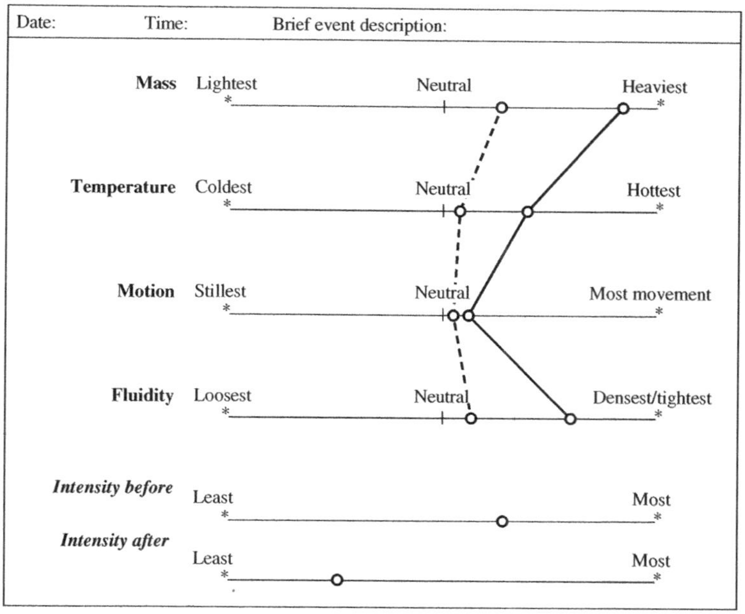

Session 4, Figure 3 Interoceptive change over 30 seconds for a person experiencing sadness.

tends to be represented by a concave shape. Anxiety tends to resemble an S shape. The change after 30 seconds of exposure is noticeable. Sometimes, usually with very intense sensations, the client may need to repeat the exposure task two or three times before they are able to experience the change clearly. If they are not reporting a change in the quality or intensity of the most intense sensation, it is often because they have engaged in thinking about the event (e.g., mother's death) or have reacted to the sensation, rather than focusing with equanimity on the actual sensations that are arising. The client needs to adopt an objective and curious attitude toward the sensations; they need to observe with interest.

The distance between the dots on each of the four lines indicates the change in intensity levels and provides an indication of progress in developing equanimity. In the midst of a stressful experience, stress hormones would normally continue to be released. As we apply equanimity toward body sensations, the impact of stress hormones dissipates, as shown by the reduction of intensity on the scale. The immediate relief that occurs is therefore likely to be the result of instantaneous release of analgesics in the brain, such as endorphins, or/and top-down inhibition of ascending nociceptive information, as happens in the MIET application with pain experience (Cayoun et al., 2017).

Application with Individual Clients

Session Aim

This session covers the development of interoceptive awareness and equanimity and the application of these skills in daily life. It discusses how to apply interoceptive awareness of the four characteristics of body sensations for the purpose of regulating emotions in stressful situations. This week, the practice is without audio instructions in order to deepen and strengthen the client's skills.

Review Homework and Progress

Ask your client to complete the Daily Record of Mindfulness Meditation Practice form in case they haven't yet done so. Use this information to provide feedback. Ask your client for feedback on the home exercises set for the previous week. Clarify points if necessary. Remain equanimous if homework is not done and remind your client of their therapy goals and that the exercises are a necessary part of the change process. Use the Socratic dialogue while keeping an empathic stance to check if they experience pain, agitation, doubts or other standard aversive experiences that may be barriers to their practice and provide a normalizing explanation. Check readiness to move to scanning without audio instructions using the Interoceptive Awareness Indicator. Delay this week's practice by a few days if your client feels sensations on less than 20 % of the body's surface area.

Introduce Silent Practice

Explain the basis for practicing in silence, i.e., without audio instructions:

- Audio instructions are useful to teach how the methods are practiced and can assist in reducing overwhelming intrusive thoughts when people are new to the practice. However, like mantras, they also interfere with the deepening of the practice by producing "structural interference" (see main text).
- Without audio instructions, the practice can also be paced according to your client's scanning skills. Suggest scanning the body two to three times by the end of this week, which will encourage your client to keep moving attention.

Introduce Immobility

Explain that from now on, your client should practice without moving at all, in complete immobility. This will increase awareness of subtle physical experiences because all sensations, including discomfort, are more readily noticed when we sit completely still. Silent practice is more likely to require effort in applying equanimity with arising discomfort, including pain, agitation or intrusive thoughts, among others. Sitting still in spite of physical discomfort teaches patience, tolerance and experiential acceptance, rather than avoidance. Equanimity will deepen and generalize across most types of body sensations. However, your client can straighten their posture if they realize that they are slouching. They can also allow autonomic reactions that are not related to interoceptive avoidance, such as coughing, sneezing, yawning, burping, and swallowing saliva.

Externalizing and Measuring Equanimity

Remind your client of the four basic characteristics of body sensations; mass, temperature, motion and fluidity. Discuss the use of the Mindfulness Interoceptive Exposure Task (MIET) as a means of applying equanimity and regulating emotions in day-to-day life. Use an example of emotion that your client experienced recently. Introduce the Mindfulness-based Interoceptive Signature Scale (MISS) as a method of recording applied equanimity.

Explain Homework Exercises

- *Sitting practice.* Daily practice of part-by-part (unilateral) scanning *without* audio instructions. Ask your client to practice with "strong determination" to not move while remaining equanimous, and to commit to practice twice daily. Clients who cannot focus enough on the body may still need the audio instructions.
- *Applied practice.* Explain that cultivating mindfulness in day-to-day life is important so that we become mindful and equanimous across all life contexts, not just during meditation. When we pay mindful attention to what we are

doing in the present moment, we experience things more clearly. This includes pre- and post-sleep awareness of body sensations, taking time to notice body sensations just before sleep and at the moment of waking. Above all, ask participants to remain continually mindful of body sensations and equanimous in day-to-day life this week.

- *Recording applied equanimity*. Implement the MIET using the MISS (Handout 4.1) at least five times during the week.
- Read Handout 4.2 and fill out the Daily Record of Mindfulness Meditation Practice (Handout 4.3).

Application with Groups

Session Aim

This session covers the development of awareness and equanimity and the application of these skills in daily life. It discusses the application of awareness of the four characteristics of body sensations for emotion regulation in stressful situations. This week the practice is without audio instructions to deepen and strengthen the clients' skills.

Materials

Whiteboard, Stage 1 CD and CD player or MP3 player if using MP3 format, a copy of the MISS, Interoceptive Awareness Indicator, and Daily Record of Mindfulness Meditation Practice forms for each participant. Outcome measures if needed.

In-session Practice

Conduct a group practice of part-by-part body scanning. Unless you are already experienced in both practicing and teaching this method, we recommend using the audio instructions of track 8. Alternatively, if you deliver the practice yourself, remember that your participants are new to scanning and you need to pace your instructions according to the script in Appendix 2.

Review Homework and Progress

Ask participants to complete the Daily Record of Mindfulness Meditation Practice form in case they haven't yet done so. Use this information to provide feedback. Ask the group for feedback on the home exercises set for the previous week. Clarify points if necessary. When home exercises are incomplete or not done, remain equanimous and remind participants of their goals and that the exercises are a necessary part of the change process. Use the Socratic dialogue while keeping an empathic stance to check if they experience pain, agitation, doubt or other standard aversive experiences that may be barriers to their practice and provide a normalizing explanation.

Check readiness to move to scanning without audio instructions using the Interoceptive Awareness Indicator. Delay this week's practice by a few days for those who feel sensations on less than 20 % of the body's surface area.

Introduce Silent Practice

Explain the rationale for practicing in silence, i.e., without audio instructions:

- Audio instructions are useful to teach how the methods are practiced and can assist in reducing overwhelming intrusive thoughts when clients are new to the practice. However, like mantras, they also interfere with the deepening of the practice by producing "structural interference" (see main text).
- Without audio instructions, the practice can also be paced according to the client's scanning skills. Suggest scanning the body two to three times by the end of this week, which will encourage them to keep moving attention.

Introduce Immobility

Explain that, from now on, participants should practice without moving at all, in complete immobility. This will increase awareness of subtle physical experiences because all sensations, including discomfort, are more readily noticed when we sit completely still. Silent practice is more likely to require effort in applying equanimity with arising discomfort, including pain, agitation or intrusive thoughts, among others. Sitting still in spite of physical discomfort teaches patience, tolerance and experiential acceptance, rather than avoidance. Equanimity will deepen and generalize across most types of body sensations. However, participants can straighten their posture if they realize that they are slouching, and allow their autonomic reactions that are not related to interoceptive avoidance, eg coughing, sneezing, yawning, burping, and swallowing saliva.

Externalizing and Measuring Equanimity

Remind the group of the four basic characteristics of body sensations; mass, temperature, motion and fluidity. Use the white board and draw each continuum and use an example of emotion. Discuss the use of the Mindfulness Interoceptive Exposure Task (MIET) as a means of applying equanimity and regulating emotions in day-to-day life. Introduce the Mindfulness-based Interoceptive Signature Scale (MISS) as a method of recording applied equanimity.

Explain Homework Exercises

- *Sitting practice*. Daily practice of part-by-part (unilateral) scanning *without* audio instructions. Ask the group to practice with "strong determination" to not move while remaining equanimous, and with commitment to practice twice daily. Clients who cannot focus enough on the body may still need the audio instructions.

- *Applied practice.* Explain that cultivating mindfulness in day-to-day life is important so that we become mindful and equanimous across all life contexts and don't limit the skills to be used during meditation. When we pay mindful attention to what we are doing in the present moment, we experience things more clearly. This includes pre- and post-sleep awareness of body sensations, taking time to notice body sensations just before sleep and at the moment of waking. Above all, ask participants to remain continually mindful of body sensations and equanimous in day-to-day life this week.
- *Recording applied equanimity.* Implement the MIET using the MISS (Handout 4.1) at least five times during the week.
- Read Handout 4.2 and fill out the Daily Record of Mindfulness Meditation Practice (Handout 4.3).

Frequently Asked Questions

Question: My client reports having an amazing out-of-body experience. How should I discuss this?

Answer: First, normalize the experience. This is a common one for more advanced practitioners. There are also several accounts of meditators having this experience in the *suttas* (teachings of the Buddha). However, suggest that they treat this experience as interesting but just as impermanent as all other experiences. Explain that wanting it again (craving it) will cause them to suffer, first because it distracts them from the actual practice, and second because it won't happen when they want it to happen. All experiences are impermanent and so clinging to them and wanting them again causes people some level of discomfort, suffering. Focusing on the past with craving means that we miss what is happening in the present moment, reinforcing the habit of craving what we don't have, which in turn keeps the brain wired for craving. Therefore, it is best to not be too elated by this single experience. If it happens again, your client needs to simply observe what happens with curiosity, but also with equanimity. If it doesn't, they need to just accept it, understanding that it was impermanent and they are not going to miss out if it never returns.

It would be prudent for your client to share this experience only with you and, eventually, very trusted friends. This is because this experience might be invalidated by people unfamiliar with advanced effects of mindfulness meditation, which could result in deep disappointment and even a sense of rejection in your client. It might also make some people want the same experience and start to practice mindfulness meditation with an unproductive motivation, out of craving.

Question: My client tells me that long-standing worries seem to emerge during practice. How does this happen at this stage in their training?

Answer: It may be that your client has been anxious for some time and the visceral sensations co-emerge with worrisome thoughts. Alternatively, it may be that they have not been anxious but some sensations have acted as memory cues that trigger memories of worrying. Reacting to the process will only reinforce their reactive habit. Remind your client that you have discussed with them the process where thoughts and body sensations co-emerge during practice, and it is useful to perceive this fundamental mechanism. This will help to normalize their experience, which they might be catastrophizing.

The next challenge for them is not to get involved in the process, not to react to it. Rather they should simply observe it as objectively as possible, without identifying with what is observed. Allow what is happening to change in its own right, without trying to change it. By practicing in a calm and detached way while scanning the body, we can notice that it goes both ways: sensations can be triggered by thoughts and thoughts by sensations. Therefore, a decrease in worrying creates a decrease in the sensations that arise with thoughts, and with less intense sensations (usually co-emerging with the worry) there are also fewer reactions. The single act of remaining equanimous eliminates the entire chain of automatic events leading to reactivity.

If it becomes too difficult to focus on scanning the body because their mind cannot settle, then it is best for them to use mindfulness of breath for a few sessions, and possibly for several days. They would also benefit from using the 3-second rule, described in Session 2, until they can focus better.

Question: My client has practiced body scanning 13 out of 14 times this week, but she reports that she is not yet able to feel many sensations in some body parts, like her abdomen and calves. She has been visualizing and imagining these parts to help with this. Is this the best approach?

Answer: It is very common to need more time to feel sensations across the whole body, and when we cannot feel some areas of the body we almost automatically visualize the part that we cannot feel. If one brain function does not fulfill our needs, another will come to the rescue, so to speak. Some groups of cells in the insular and somatosensory cortices have not yet been sufficiently trained to connect with each other, so there are parts of the body that are still difficult to feel while meditating. However, if we get into a habit of visualizing body parts, we will train our brain to connect cells that allow us to *see* rather than *feel* the body. Our purpose is to train ourselves to *feel* body sensations, inhibiting the habit of reacting to them and develop equanimity towards them, not just concentrating on them (for which visualization would be a good method).

The instruction for your client is to *just notice* the blank spots when scanning, while preventing craving or aversion from arising. Ask her to pay attention to the "blank spot" (where she cannot feel sensations) for about 30 seconds before moving to the next spot, "smilingly," patiently, and without feeling disappointed or frustrated, accepting that this is how it is right now in this part of the body, and this, too, is impermanent. With sufficient practice, it is possible to feel the entire body, except hair and the outer part of the nails. Not getting what she expects when she scans the body is an opportunity to work on her patience and equanimity. She can learn to do the same in daily life, when she cannot get what she wants.

Question: My client reported a strong pain in his knee when he is practicing. He wonders if the body scanning is making it worse. How should I advise him?

Answer: We do not create pain when scanning the body, we simply notice it. The practice only allows us to see what already exists. It is *not* what causes the problem because the pain he feels when he practices is already there. He is more aware of it during practice because he is not distracted and he is becoming more sensitive to subtle experiences in the body. It is like wearing glasses for the first time. You see things clearly, just as they are. If he was not at any risk before practicing, then he is not at any risk during practice and it is useful to normalize his experience and prevent doubt and anxiety. However, if he wonders whether there is a real problem, it is always a good idea for him to check with his doctor.

It is also useful to remind your client about the four basic characteristics of body sensations and implement the MIET after practicing a few minutes together during your next session with him. He needs to understand that since what we call "pain" is simply an intense sensation, it can be addressed with equanimity. Ask him to focus his attention at the center of this intense sensation, patiently and equanimously for about 30 seconds (approximately seven to ten breaths). While paying attention, identify which of the four basic characteristics are predominant. He needs to pay attention without reacting and notice what happens if he genuinely allows the experience to be just as it is, rather than resenting it and wishing that it goes away. Remind your client to *observe and welcome* the four basic characteristics (mass, motion, temperature and fluidity) that compose the intense sensation and let those characteristics just be, accepting them unconditionally. As we have shown in our studies and consistent with routine observations, these sensations will change due to the immediate inhibition of the nociceptive signal and possibly the secretion of natural opiates in the brain, such as endorphins. If the pain is extreme, then suggest having a rest by moving the leg a little or have a small break from the practice and return to it a little later.

If he thinks that this experience is personal and it affects who he is, then it will be difficult for him to handle and he will become reactive. If he hates the pain in his knee, then his lack of equanimity will only produce stress hormones, increasing stress and intolerance of pain. Equanimity needs to be applied to all reactive habits, including to those that seem justified. Simply recognizing that "this is *just* a thought" or "this is *just* a sensation" (e.g., pain) helps to minimize identification with the experience without having to avoid it. If he can learn to apply a degree of equanimity and realize that the pain sensations are not a part of him, they arise to eventually pass away, he will be putting painful sensations to good use and not "wasting" his suffering.

Question: My client is reporting drowsiness and falling asleep during body scanning and that she is having strange dreams and daydreaming. How should I best advise her?

Answer: People who start meditating with this method often report changes in sleep habits, and having more intense or vivid dreams is a common occurrence. Because your client has been scanning the body for a whole week, she has become more conscious of body sensations, including those associated with emotions that she may have tried to suppress. Memories associated with some of the sensations felt recently in daily life and detected during sleep are more available for processing during both meditation and sleep. This is because accurate mindfulness practice and sleep are situations where the mind is not busy with voluntary cognitive activities and where we least control (e.g., suppress) the spontaneous emergence of thoughts.

Sudden changes in the way we dream are often signs of memory stimulation or increased access to current emotions, and the emotional tone of the dream often reflects what was felt during the day. It can also reflect what was felt and suppressed over the previous weeks. It can be useful to ask your client if she recently felt the same type of emotions in her daily life as she felt in her dream. In fact, much insight and therapeutic benefit can be achieved simply by asking this once you have explained the co-emergence effect in dreams (see Session 2).

Start by normalizing the experience—explaining that sensations emerging during sleep can co-emerge with thoughts, many of which may be interpreted in very strange ways in dreams. Then exemplify this mechanism to make it easy to understand. Here is a common example of how this can be briefly presented: "If you have been worried all day about speaking at tomorrow's work meeting, scanning the body would allow you to feel body sensations associated with that anxiety. If the sensations are still activated when you go to bed, then once you are asleep, you may dream about anything stored in memory during your lifetime that involves feeling these types of sensations, including childlike or symbolic scenarios. Your dream could be about finding yourself naked in the street, being humiliated at school, or even sitting an exam which you are frightened to fail. This depends a lot on your beliefs, or schemas, as we often call them." It is always best to use one of your own experiences if you can recall one. After presenting the mechanism in this way, you can then prompt your client and discuss possible issues that need attention.

Question: One of my clients with generalized anxiety worries about not falling asleep as easily this week. Is this just a coincidence or could it be the effect of the meditation? What should I advise him to do about it?

Answer: There seems to be a clear relationship between how much we practice and the amount of sleep needed. When you have a lot of energy, you do not need to sleep as much. Most people who train through this program report feeling more relaxed in daily life and having more energy, although this is more likely to be the case for people who have committed to practicing twice daily. Often people need less sleep also because sleep quality has improved. By this stage of the program, many whose sleep was disrupted can sleep through the night and are less tired in the evening, which may mildly delay sleep onset. However, more practice can have the opposite effect for some people. These people will sleep longer if they usually do not get enough sleep. In general, mindfulness practice tends to regulate sleep.

However, anxious people will often look at the clock and catastrophize the situation. Worry about not having enough sleep will arouse stress hormones instead of calming the mind, aggravating the situation. They also need to reduce cognitive activity because thinking on purpose keeps the mind awake. With disrupted sleep,

I would not advise that you suggest nocturnal physical activity either, as is sometimes recommended in sleep hygiene manuals. Although physical activity is a better option than ruminating and worrying in bed, it remains a poor solution compared to staying in bed and settling the mind on the breath.

It would be helpful for him to turn his alarm clock away so he cannot see the time. This would make checking and worrying more difficult to do. Then, he could practice what we call "subtlest breathing." This requires focusing attention with closed eyes on the small spot below the nostrils above the upper lip, a spot no wider than the size of a fingertip, and breathing very softly so that we can barely feel the faint touch of breath on that small spot. We call this finding the threshold of interoceptive awareness. Once aware of the very subtle sensations, the mind tends to settle. We believe there are two main reasons for this: First, the inhibitory control applied on a very small area helps prevent the activation of just about anything other than the activation of limited sensory networks, resulting in less activity in cognitive areas of the brain responsible for worrisome thoughts (i.e., default mode network and amygdala). Second, the very subtle breath decreases heart rate, which facilitates the suppression of amygdala activity by the ventromedial prefrontal cortex. This technique works more often than not, when it is well-practiced.

Question: My client is still not very clear about the reasons for scanning the body. She appears to have benefited from mindfulness of breath and understands why it is beneficial to keep her mind in the present moment, but she is not keen on body scanning. I actually don't think that she can feel that much. How should she proceed?

Answer: There is what appears to be just a small difference between being attentive in the present and being mindful, but the consequence of missing this difference can be enormous when it comes to clinical outcomes. Being alert and attentive in the present is just the beginning. Attentiveness and mindfulness have very different aims, mechanisms and outcomes. Being mindful requires being present, whereas being present does not require being mindful. If mindfulness was just about being in the present, then you could be completely and continually absorbed in an obsessive behavior, remaining very concentrated and in the present moment. This kind of situation can occur with autistic clients and those with OCD. Without mindfulness, just being in the present moment can also be used as a context for harming oneself or others. Think of someone waiting behind a bush or around a street corner to attack someone. The person is purposefully attentive, in the present moment, but full of judgments and craving or aversion. Think also of a traumatized soldier experiencing hypervigilance, where attention is in the present, but it is accompanied by fear.

Mindfulness is much more than being present in other ways as well. While it is the ability to be present that allows us to develop the skills necessary to be mindful, we need to develop other skills. Once our attention is in the present moment, *then* we can perceive our mental, emotional and physical states more clearly. Because we remain equanimous, we can look at what is happening with a degree of objectivity and interest, and notice the impermanent nature of our experience. When we apply mindfulness in daily life, we can be aware of our motivations and intentions, and change them if they are likely to contribute to our own or someone else's suffering.

In particular, your client needs to understand the important role of interoceptive awareness, both in mindfulness training and in daily life. Feeling body sensations enables us to detect early cues of distress, before emotional reactivity starts. Because body sensations act as memory cues, scanning the body is also scanning through the storehouse of our memories. Many memories have decayed to the extent that we can only experience them through their corresponding body sensations, without realizing that what is being felt during body scanning may be part of a memory. Most sensations we feel are already conditioned because of past experiences. Accordingly, every time we prevent a habitual reaction to a particular sensation, we neutralize the conditioned response. As reactions are prevented across the whole body during scanning, past habits are being neutralized. This means liberation from emotional reactivity and the unhelpful views and values that promote it. Mindfulness of breath alone cannot easily help us achieve this. It is probably an overkill to explain the processes of *memory reconsolidation* to your client, but you might benefit from having a look at the literature, especially the pioneering and continuing work of Karim Nader at McGill University (e.g., Nader & Hardt, 2009; Nader, Schafe, & Le Doux, 2000). The more you know, the more confident you will be in simplifying your explanation to clients, while knowing that you are not omitting what is important.

However, if your client's ability to feel sensations is low, it might be useful to slow down the pace of delivery. One thing to ensure first is that your client is actually practicing; try to prompt gently. Another is that her practice is accurate. Keeping in mind that practice frequency, duration and accuracy are the condition for success with this approach, they are the first thing to check before deciding to alter the delivery. We also recommend that you measure her interoceptive awareness using the Interoceptive Awareness Indicator form (see Session 3). If she feels less than 20 % of the body, it is preferable that she continues to practice mindfulness of breath for a few more days (up to a week), ensuring that she commits to practicing *twice daily* and using the 3-second rule if needed, before resuming with scanning without audio instructions.

Question: I want to be able to explain more clearly to my clients the importance of not identifying with their experience. Can you help?

Answer: This is ultimately something that people learn best during their practice and as a result of it. They progressively notice that when they identify with a thought, a co-emerging body sensation arises. If they identify with the sensation, reaction arises. If they also identify with the reaction, new thoughts in the form of judgment arise, and the cycle of self-reinforcement continues. Our sense of self, of who we are, the so-called ego, is being maintained through this "cycle of becoming." As we develop mindfulness and equanimity, it becomes clearer that *we* create and maintain a sense of self moment by moment, through our attachment to different aspects of our body and mind.

More specifically, we identify with, and remain attached to, the four components of the mind that we call Sensory Perception, Evaluation, Body Sensation and Reaction, and to the component of matter, the physical world, including our body.

These five components were discussed through the co-emergence model of reinforcement in Part 1 of the book. We construct, reinforce and eventually modify our sense of self every moment by identifying with our experiences of the body, such as the five senses through certain tastes, smells, images, sounds and tactile sensations. We identify with thoughts, including our beliefs, imagination, and memories of events that shaped our lives. We identify with emotions through the sensations we feel in the body. We also identify with our actions. These become further associated with worldly things, such as a house or a car that we identify as being "mine," a part of "me." The same applies to relationships and career. We give them a special value and are attached to them. The more we need to feel important, especially if our sense of self-worth depends on it, the more this "I" needs to be strengthened through more associations. Accordingly, our need for identification with the aforementioned five components increases. We feel the need for more or better "things," more sensations, more thoughts, and more reactions. This is what constitutes the essence of a materialistic life.

Problems arise when the association between these things and our sense of self becomes disassociated, or when there is an involuntary separation between the two. As nothing is permanent, we tend to believe that a part of "me" is lost, which leads to grief and depression, and on occasions to extreme distress and reactivity, including suicide. To illustrate this, here is an example of an exchange between one of the authors and one of his clients, whose high-flying career eventually faded away, leading to Adjustment Disorder with typical existential ruminations, and eventually major depression (the client's description has been de-identified):

> [...] I really hope that you are fabulously well. I am seeking your thoughts as a wise man on the wonderful emotion of passion. How is it gained and moreover what can destroy it? Can negative people associated with the subject about which someone is or was passionate cause a person to lose their passion? Do we build up passion knowingly or is it a quietly naturally forming state of mind? Do we naturally lose a level of passion? Are there answers to the above or held views? How can I access the learning as I feel somewhat bereft of what once was a significant level of professional passion? Or am I simply asking too much to know more? [...]

> **Answer:**
> [...] As we age, passion typically gives place to reason. I believe this is partly because of natural brain changes (decrease in grey matter and increase in white matter volume in several areas) and partly because of our ability to learn what works and what doesn't, what hurts and what soothes. The first belief to adjust is that passion is an emotion; it is not. It is an aggregate of components that include a thought (often a memory), immediately followed by a very pleasant body sensation, which leads simultaneously to a craving response. Accordingly, passion may be experienced for, or about, anything or anyone. The second belief to adjust is the belief that we are "a passionate person" or we are not. What gives this impression is only our habit of identifying with who we are. We develop a tremendous amount of attachment to this "I" which makes it very difficult to change over time despite nature's call for adjustments (e.g., family members expecting us to change, job opportunities changing, the body itself not responding in the way it used to, etc.).

> What you are experiencing is a wonderful opportunity to let natural forces guide you through the inevitable journey of change. Even passion gets you stuck... and it did. From what I understand about life, so far, is that the best, reliable and rewarding passion one can ever entertain in the long term is passion for change. By this, I don't mean change in the environment; I mean change in our mind and heart. When you become passionate about discovering "who" you become next, you can't cling to, and mourn, who you thought you were. Embracing change is remaining young. It is a little bit like a new birth that we can get excited about. There is no more grief in that. I am hoping that this is how I will continue to perceive life at the moment of death, preparing for the next exciting episode. This, indeed, is a wholesome passion, as it does not lead to suffering.

It is likely that the fundamental reason why your clients are seeking your assistance has also something to do with this principle. If so, they would benefit from understanding how attachment to an illusory sense of self creates suffering. However, if this concept seems difficult for them to understand at this stage, you can come back to it later as their understanding progressively deepens through mindfulness practice. They need to start with dis-identifying from their experience one thought at a time, one sensation at a time, and one reaction at a time. The benefit derived from this practice will be the best teacher.

Question: When I ask my client to use the Mindfulness-based Interoceptive Signature Scale, how do I instruct them to fill it in if there is an issue in a work meeting or a situation in which they are in public. Should they fill it in afterwards?

Answer: Many situations will not easily permit clients to complete the form in the middle of a distressing situation. Common examples are distressing experiences while driving a vehicle or interacting with people. However, it is important for clients to always have a MISS form and a pen available to use. Ask your client to make a mental note of how the sensations feel in the body during distress in terms of the four interoceptive characteristics both before and after applying equanimity for 30 seconds and record their experience on the form as soon as possible afterward.

Handout 4.1 Mindfulness-based Interoceptive Signature Scale (MISS)

Instructions

Use one of the blank forms below to identify your experience of body sensations on each of the four categories (*Mass, Temperature, Motion, Fluidity*). When you experience a distressing event, notice the body sensations associated with it. Then, as soon as you can (either during or soon after), represent the strongest sensation in your body by placing a small dot on each of the four lines representing a category of body sensation. Then join each of the dots with a solid line. After focusing on the sensation neutrally and with acceptance for half a minute, place another dot on each of the four categories to represent how you are now experiencing body sensations. Then join those dots with another line (a ***dotted line***) to show any change. Record also the change in intensity before and after this 30-second exposure by placing a small dot on the last two lines.

Date:	Time:	Brief event description:		
Mass	Lightest *	Neutral	Heaviest *	
Temperature	Coldest *	Neutral	Hottest *	
Motion	Stillest *	Neutral	Most movement *	
Fluidity	Loosest *	Neutral	Densest/tightest *	
Intensity before	Least *		Most *	
Intensity after	Least *		Most *	

Date:	Time:	Brief event description:		
Mass	Lightest *	Neutral	Heaviest *	
Temperature	Coldest *	Neutral	Hottest *	
Motion	Stillest *	Neutral	Most movement *	
Fluidity	Loosest *	Neutral	Densest/tightest *	
Intensity before	Least *		Most *	
Intensity after	Least *		Most *	

Date:	Time:	Brief event description:		
Mass	Lightest *	Neutral	Heaviest *	
Temperature	Coldest *	Neutral	Hottest *	
Motion	Stillest *	Neutral	Most movement *	
Fluidity	Loosest *	Neutral	Densest/tightest *	
Intensity before	Least *		Most *	
Intensity after	Least *		Most *	

Note: This form can be downloaded in full-size format from http://clinicalhandbook.mindfulness.net.au/handouts

Handout 4.2 Applied Practice

Extending your skills and feeling more in control of emotions

It is time to put your new skills into practice so that it benefits you and others in daily life. This week, you will train yourself to remain mindful of your body sensations in all day-to-day situations. You will apply your equanimity in as many stressful situations as possible, so that your brain learns to reconnect itself in a less reactive way when you are faced with challenging situations in the future. This is an important skill to develop now so that you can move on to the next set of skills in Stage 2 of this program.

Practice in silence and immobility

Here is a point-form summary of this week's exercises:

- Practice your 30-minute meditation as you did last week, but in silence, without any audio instructions, using a timer. Most smart phone and tablets have a timer.
- Scan the body at your pace. This means faster where you can easily feel sensations and slower where you cannot. Where you cannot feel a sensation in a particular area, remember to stay focused on that blank spot for up to about 30 seconds (roughly seven breaths), and then move on to the next part very patiently, with equanimity. Try to do at least two body cycles during each 30-minute practice by the end of this week. As a general guide, surveying the body (down and up) between two and three times is a good pace. If you cannot do at least two cycles in a week from now, it may be because you are too drowsy or still getting caught up in thoughts for too long. This is not a problem. Just revise the handouts you were given for Session 2 and apply the instructions until you can discuss it with your therapist.
- From now on, meditate with strong determination to remain equanimous and to not move your body, except for coughing, sneezing, yawning, burping, swallowing saliva and straightening your posture. Remember that because you use the same brain during and outside meditation practice, what you do during meditation will reflect in daily life. The less reactive you become in one context, the less reactive you will be in the other. Therefore, every discomfort you smile at during your practice is a little bit of freedom from distress in your daily life.

Applied practice

- In your day-to-day life, notice the details of your experiences, including taking time to notice body sensations in bed while falling asleep and at the moment of waking.

  Maintain awareness of body sensations and equanimity throughout the day.

- When you feel stressed or otherwise emotional, use the "Mindfulness-based Interoceptive Signature Scale" (Handout 4.1) to record your experience of body sensations before and after 30 seconds of focusing on them with equanimity. The detailed instructions are on Handout 4.1. If you feel sensations in detail but you don't resent it and remain "personally detached." the intensity of the sensation is likely to decrease within the first 30 seconds, especially if you fully accept the feeling you get from the four characteristics. You will need at least two copies of Handout 4.1.
- To ensure that you have enough practice, find at least five situations that you know will be moderately stressful, and practice equanimity towards your body sensations while you are in those situations, as explained by your therapist and on Handout 4.1.
- Ensure that it is not you who creates the stressful situation, as this would not be appropriate. Use situations that are unpleasant but manageable, except now it will be with equanimity and an understanding that all experiences are impermanent.

Handout 4.3 Daily Record of Mindfulness Meditation Practice

Day	**Date**	**Morning** *(circle)*	**Duration**	**Efficacy rating** *Rate from 1 to 10 how well you noticed distractions and brought your attention back to the body. 1=not well at all; 10=extremely well*	**Evening** *(circle)*	**Duration**	**Efficacy rating** *Rate from 1 to 10 how well you noticed distractions and brought your attention back to the body. 1=not well at all; 10=extremely well*
Monday		I practiced Yes / No			I practiced Yes / No		
Tuesday		I practiced Yes / No			I practiced Yes / No		
Wednesday		I practiced Yes / No			I practiced Yes / No		
Thursday		I practiced Yes / No			I practiced Yes / No		
Friday		I practiced Yes / No			I practiced Yes / No		
Saturday		I practiced Yes / No			I practiced Yes / No		
Sunday		I practiced Yes / No			I practiced Yes / No		

References

Beecher, H. W. (1871). *The Sermons of Henry Ward Beecher in Plymouth Church*. Brooklyn: J. B. Ford.

Cayoun, B. A. (2010). *The dynamics of bimanual coordination in ADHD: Processing speed, inhibition and cognitive flexibility*. Saarbrücken, Germany: Lambert Academic Publishing.

Cayoun, B. A. (2011). *Mindfulness-integrated CBT: Principles and practice*. Chichester, UK: Wiley.

Cayoun, B., Simmons, A., & Shires, A. (2017). Immediate and lasting chronic pain reduction following a brief self-implemented mindfulness-based interoceptive exposure task: A pilot study. *Mindfulness*, 1–13.

Ellis, A. (1979) The practice of rational-emotive therapy. In A. Ellis and J. M. Whiteley (Eds.) (1982), *Theoretical and empirical foundations of rational-emotive therapy*. Brooks/Cole, Monterey, California, pp. 61–100.

Goenka, S. N. (1987). *The discourse summaries: Talks from a ten-day course in Vipassana Meditation condensed by William Hart*. Vipashyana Vishodhan Vinyas, Bombay, India.

Hart, W. (1987) *The art of living: Vipassana meditation as taught by S.N. Goenka*. San Francisco, CA: Harper and Row.

Hölzel, B. K., Lazar, S. W., Gard, T., Schuman-Olivier, Z., Vago, D. R., & Ött, U. (2011). How does mindfulness meditation work? Proposing mechanisms of action from a conceptual and neural perspective. *Perspectives on Psychological Science*, 6, 537–559.

Khan, C. H. (1981). *Heraclitus: The art and thought of Heraclitus*. Cambridge, UK: Cambridge University Press.

Kwee, M. & Ellis, A. (1998). The Interface between Rational Emotive Behavior Therapy (REBT) and Zen. *Journal of Rational-Emotive & Cognitive-Behavior Therapy*, 16, 5–43. doi:10.1023/A:1024946306870

Lazar, S. W., Kerr, C. E., Wasserman, R. H., Gray, J. R., Greve, D. N., Treadway M. T., et al. (2005). Meditation experience is associated with increased cortical thickness. *Neuroreport*, 16, 1893–1897.

Nader, K., & Hardt, O. (2009). A single standard for memory: the case for reconsolidation. *Nature Reviews Neuroscience*, 10, 224–234.

Nader, K., Schafe, G. E., & Le Doux, J. E. (2000). Fear memories require protein synthesis in the amygdala for reconsolidation after retrieval. *Nature*, 406, 722–726.

MacLeod, C. M. (1991). Half a century of research on the Stroop effect: An integrative review. *Psychological Bulletin*, 109, 163–203.

Ready, R. E., Carvalho, J. O., & Akerstedt, A. M. (2012). Evaluative organization of the self-concept in younger, midlife, and older adults. *Research on Aging*, 34, 56–79.

Robertson, D. (2010). *The philosophy of Cognitive-Behavioural Therapy (CBT): Stoic philosophy as rational and cognitive psychotherapy*. London: Karnac.

Shires, A., Sharpe, L. Samson, J., Colagiuri, B., & Newton-John, T. (2017). The relative efficacy of mindfulness versus distraction: the moderating role of attentional bias. Manuscript submitted for publication.

Uddin, L. Q. (2014). Salience processing and insular cortical function and dysfunction. *Nature Reviews Neuroscience*. doi:10.1038/nrn3857

Weare, K. (2012). Evidence for the impact of mindfulness on children and young people. *The Mindfulness in Schools Project*. Retrieved April 28, 2014 from https://mindfulnessinschools.org/wp-content/uploads/2013/02/MiSP-Research-Summary-2012.pdf

Wickens, C.D. (1984). Processing resources in attention. In R. Parasuraman and D.R. Davies (Eds.), *Varieties of Attention*. London: Academic Press.

Session 5: Integrating Mindfulness and Behavioral Methods

Action seems to follow feeling, but really action and feeling go together; and by regulating the action, which is under the more direct control of the will, we can indirectly regulate the feeling, which is not.

—William James, 1890

Introduction

This chapter is designed to guide you in the application of Stage 2 of MiCBT, the "exposure stage," on the assumption that your client has practiced regularly and their equanimity during practice and in daily life is growing. This week, you will teach them the first advanced body scanning technique, "symmetrical scanning." So far, with Stage 1 of MiCBT, you have been teaching your client to develop the skills of metacognitive and interoceptive awareness, as well as equanimity, both during meditation practice and in daily life. You have assisted your client to learn about regulating emotions by becoming aware of body sensations in a non-reactive manner. The body scanning practice taught your client how to extinguish their conditioned response to internal triggers; they learned to inhibit their responses to thoughts and the accompanying body sensations as they scanned the body. Thus, they have been learning to desensitize to unhelpful emotions. Having invested time in focusing initially on their internal environment from Session 1 to Session 3, they started to apply their emotion-regulating skills externally in Session 4. They are now ready to apply their skills in external contexts for the purpose of regulating behavior in challenging situations where avoidance may be a habitual behavior. In Stage 2, your client begins to use mindfulness skills to manage their fears and build self-confidence.

The Clinical Handbook of Mindfulness-integrated Cognitive Behavior Therapy: A Step-by-Step Guide for Therapists, First Edition. Bruno A. Cayoun, Sarah E. Francis, and Alice G. Shires.

Companion website: www.wiley.com/go/Cayoun/Mindfulness-integrated

Checking Client Readiness

Check your client's practice during the last week. Have they practiced regularly? Have they avoided any aspects of the practice, such as the applied practice with the mindfulness-based interoceptive exposure task (MIET)? If this is the case, you will need to discuss this with them and assist them to move on to the next step, which still requires a commitment to practicing twice daily. Try to use Socratic dialogue as much as possible while remaining kind and empathic, and validate whatever effort they made so far, as we discussed earlier in the book. Sometimes, people feel insecure if they feel that things are changing a little too quickly. Remember that clients are deconstructing parts of their reactive identity and therefore their experiential avoidance; although this is exciting and empowering for most, it can appear unfamiliar and unsafe to others.

Has there been a crisis for your client? Sometimes a crisis emerges in daily life and it may be better to postpone Stage 2 for a week or so, until the crisis has sufficiently subsided and a degree of equanimity is regained. Is your client still improving their equanimity in daily life? Is your client more able to apply equanimity during distressing experiences within 30 seconds? If so, one of the two following observations on the Mindfulness-based Interoceptive Signature Scale (MISS) should be apparent: (1) the "recovery line" (dotted line) is progressively closer to the neutral point in the middle of each scale. This progressive trend towards the neutral (center) point of the scales is usually a reflection of increased equanimity; (2) additionally, or alternatively, the recovery line is further away from the "distress line" (solid line) towards the neutral point after 30 seconds. Provided the distress is significant in the first place and the distance between the two lines increases over time, then they are increasingly able to recover from distress within 30 seconds. The best way of quantifying equanimity with the MISS is to combine both patterns of change and take into account the difference between pre- and post-intensity to derive an overall impression.

Some clients do well with the daily formal meditative practice but find reasons not to use the MISS to record their emotion-regulation data during last week's potential distressing experiences. In this case, there is no need to delay the next step. They can still apply their practice in daily life using the MISS while commencing Stage 2. Nonetheless, it is important to check why they didn't practice using the MISS and ensure that the client understands that interoceptive exposure in daily life will assist their exposure in Stage 2.

In short, since the central skills needed for exposure in Stage 2 are interoceptive awareness and equanimity, we need to ensure that clients are developing them. If your client can feel sensations in approximately 80 % of the body even if they experience intrusive thoughts, they can move on to this week's body-scanning method, symmetrical scanning, using the audio instructions. Alternatively, we may need to delay the next step for a short period.

Delaying the Next Step

If your client cannot feel much in the body or continues to react emotionally to triggers, we need to delay Stage 2 for a week or so and work committedly a little longer to developing interoceptive awareness and equanimity. Should this be necessary, we need to ensure that clients do not feel like a failure, which is most likely for those whose sense of self-worth is already low. Normalizing the process and remaining equanimous ourselves is central to prevent shaming the client. However, this does not mean being passive, and a frank discussion will be necessary.

It is possible that your client has practiced regularly but remains unable to feel much in the body. In this case, use the Interoceptive Awareness Indicator form (Handout 3.3) to estimate the percentage of interoceptive awareness during practice. If the client's interoceptive awareness remains significantly below 80 %, it is important to delay the next step and discuss the accuracy of their practice, especially reducing the duration of being lost in thoughts. Since this is usually due to poor inhibitory control, explaining to the client how to use the "3-second rule" can be very helpful in resisting distractibility and increasing focus. However, poor response inhibition and difficulty sustaining attention can be caused by fatigue and other barriers to practice. Accordingly, a useful approach is to discuss "the five hindrances" common to all meditation techniques (agitation, aversion, craving, drowsiness/fatigue and doubt) and their solutions, as discussed in Chapter 2. This helps both the client and the therapist to normalize the common challenges that we all encounter at some point.

You need to ensure that none of these hindrances becomes a habit and assist your client to re-commit and repeat last week's practice of unilateral part-by-part scanning for at least a few more days before moving on to bilateral scanning, as explained next. Ask your client to continue practicing part-by-part unilateral scanning without audio instructions and to practice the MIET with the MISS (Handout 4.1), as described in the previous chapter. When they can notice sensations in approximately 80 % of the body, they can move on to this week's method using the audio instructions for symmetrical scanning.

Advanced Scanning: Symmetrical Scanning

Purpose of Advanced Scanning in MiCBT

Advanced scanning methods have been traditionally taught in the Burmese *Vipassana* tradition of mindfulness training. Within this tradition, the purpose is to become aware of the constant and impersonal flow of vibrating energy: the subtlest reality of our mind and body and their impermanence and insubstantiality. This fosters a gentle detachment from what we typically identify as the sense of self. In MiCBT, the main purpose of advanced scanning is to deepen interoceptive awareness sufficiently to detect subtle changes in the body, especially subtle cues of distress, early in the sequence of an emotion while they are still manageable. Becoming aware of sensations before they intensify to become an emotion allows us to respond much earlier, prior to being swept away by the increasing intensity of the interoceptive experience, thus preventing the habitual emotional reaction.

Because of daily practice, neurons processing interoceptive information in the insula and somatosensory cortex are now sufficiently connected to allow conscious access to subtle body sensations. Studies examining brain reorganization after mindfulness training show evidence of neuroplasticity in these brain areas (Craig, 2003; Farb, Segal, & Anderson, 2013; Lazar et al., 2005; see also Tang, Hölzel, & Posner, 2015, for a review). Brain reorganization explains why we can maintain the ability to feel body sensations outside the meditative context without having to scan the body. This can also be a little strange to some clients and it needs to be normalized and validated—it is useful to explain it as an achievement that could not have taken place without the client's commitment to frequent and accurate practice.

The Method

The first advanced scanning method is symmetrical scanning, which is a training in bilateral interoceptive attention. Your client will still train to survey the entire body part-by-part, from head to toe and toe to head, but will focus simultaneously on both sides of the body's midline, symmetrically. With symmetrical scanning, insula areas in both hemispheres are trained to work together with equal strength, allowing us to feel what happens on both sides of the body simultaneously. Surveying both sides of the body at the same time requires less time than surveying one side at a time for each scanning cycle. This enables us to pass our unbiased attention through the same areas of the body more often and train the mind to become aware of more parts at the same time while preventing reactivity. As a result, brain pathways for interoceptive awareness are more rapidly connected due to the greater scanning frequency, increasing sensitivity to small changes in sensation both during and outside the meditative context.

During practice, clients will need to remain equanimous when they cannot feel both sides at the same time and there is usually a "lead–lag" between the sides they scan. Normalize this in terms of a habitual "stronger wiring in the brain" for some body parts than for others, mentioning also that this will change with practice. It usually takes three to four days for people to feel both sides of the body symmetrically in most places. Ensure that clients don't catastrophize their initial difficulties. They need to know that this is a training and they are not supposed to know how to practice it before they learn it, which takes time.

The audio instructions for this practice are on track 10 and the introduction is on track 9. Symmetrical scanning will require your client to continue scanning the body, part by part, scanning spots of attention 2 to 3 inches (5 to 8 cm) in diameter at a time, starting from the top of the head, but attending to both sides of the body at the same time. The advanced scanning tracks are about 15 minutes long and your clients will need to practice for another 15 minutes in silence, without instructions. Remind your client that each session needs to last 30 minutes. To keep their timing simple, they can set a timer (e.g., on their smart phone or tablet if they have one) to 30 minutes and then start playing the audio instructions until the end, and continue to practice in silence until their timer lets them know that 30 minutes have passed. Ask them to record their daily practice for the week as usual, using Handout 5.7.

Integrating Mindfulness with Exposure Skills

Addressing Avoidance

Whereas avoidant behavior is a natural survival mechanism in human life, dysfunctional avoidance impairs life. Naturally, we tend to welcome pleasant and safe experiences and avoid the unsafe and unpleasant ones. Avoiding situations because they may be distressing is occasionally necessary, but learning to avoid unpleasant experiences turns into a problem itself. Ultimately, learned avoidance leads to a sense of missing out, failure and depressed mood. Avoidance habits are common in most disorders and can have a negative effect on people and on those with whom they live and work. Since avoidance also tends to be a reinforcing or maintaining factor for most mental health conditions, it is vital that clients learn skills to minimize avoidant behavior.

Avoidance can range from simple to extremely impairing behavior. We may simply avoid chores and other common activities because we don't find them to be interesting, even though they may be necessary. Avoidant behavior can also be severe and based on intense fears. However, this does not mean that it is maladaptive. For instance, a soldier avoiding bullets while in the trenches might save his or her life and this is therefore adaptive. In contrast, maladaptive avoidance impairs normal functioning. When these fears are sustained over time, severe avoidance becomes chronic and sometimes so much part of one's personality that the person has difficulty realizing that their habits are avoidant. They live according to their avoidant habits, and short and long-term decisions are often dictated by them. This can be compounded by the dysfunctional use of alcohol and other drugs, which is more often than not an attempt to avoid some experiences.

Interestingly, avoidant habits can also permeate mindfulness training if clients don't receive accurate guidance by a trainer familiar with what constitutes avoidance. For example, when distressed in daily life, clients may decrease their discomfort by focusing on their breath. At first glance, this sounds like a good idea; indeed, it is better than overreacting. However, informed by learning theory and the co-emergence model of reinforcement, it becomes clear that the client is distracting themselves from feeling the unpleasant body sensations associated with the distressing situation. They are using *awareness* of breath (not *mindfulness*) as means of interoceptive avoidance. This may be a useful strategy when distress levels are overwhelming, given that awareness of co-emerging sensations is depleted during distressing events (as per the model in disequilibrium state in Chapter 2; see also Friedman & Forster, 2010; Harshaw, 2015), but it remains a coping strategy that is based on distraction. In MiCBT, we ask people to detect the sensation and use it as means of exposure and desensitization, as your client did last week.

Moreover, meditation on its own can maintain or even reinforce avoidant behavior, such as social avoidance. If you already have had the opportunity to use a mindfulness-based approach with clients who present with social anxiety and/or avoidant trait, meditation as a homework exercise is heaven for them! Even after meditating for months in retreats or the solitude of a cave, they often remain socially anxious. Unless exposure is included, most anxiety-based problems remain unresolved. This does not only apply to anxiety disorders. Depressed clients can also be avoidant, especially of social interactions.

It is now time to teach clients how to apply the techniques they've learned so far to assist them in regulating behavior in daily life by decreasing avoidance. This will improve their confidence and sense of self-efficacy. During the next two weeks, you will be teaching them how to apply their mindfulness skills to challenge external situations that they normally avoid, using a combination of imaginal and in-vivo exposure techniques. First, they will learn to combine mindfulness skills with imaginal and interoceptive exposure through a method called "bipolar exposure." Second, they will learn to combine mindfulness skills with exposure and cognitive reappraisal to reverse avoidant behavior and increase self-confidence. These are the exposure skills that constitute Stage 2 of MiCBT.

After about two weeks, clients typically find that situations they have avoided for years are much easier to address. Applying exposure skills in daily life will increase their confidence to make effective change in behavior and build a sense of self-efficacy. It will assist them to decrease avoidance, freeing them to act and decreasing the probability of relapse.

Introducing the Hierarchy of Avoided Behaviors

After explaining the rationale for exposure in Stage 2 of the program, you will need to assist your client to develop a hierarchical exposure record. You can use the form provided in this chapter (Handout 5.4) and create a list of stressful situations that your client tends to avoid. First, ask your client to write down ten to twelve events or situations that they are likely to avoid because they appear distressing to them. Some clients will struggle with this task, either because avoidance is not in their character or because avoidance is so established that they cannot perceive it as such. In this case, use Socratic questioning to assist the client so they can find at least two situations. If they cannot find enough situations during the therapy session, they can add more on their list at home as part of their homework this week. It would be useful for them to ask people closest to them (parents, partner, friends, children) what *they* think that the client tends to avoid. It is sometimes surprising what clients can learn just from asking.

Now ask your client to assign a percentage of distress to each situation or "item" listed. They need to sincerely imagine the distress that they would experience if they were really in that situation today. Ideally, some should be rated low and others high. Make sure the client chooses a range of situations with varying levels of expected distress.

Then the client needs to choose five situations of varying distress levels from their initial selection. They should not list five situations of similarly high distress levels because this would require them to approach situations that create high anxiety without having learned the skills to handle them. Similarly, ask your client to try not to list five situations that would cause them only 15 % or less distress, as this would not help with the most challenging issues and is not distressing enough to justify its avoidance. Although a situation with a low score may be frustrating and we may tend to avoid it when we can, it does not produce much anxiety when we carry through with it. We have noticed over the past 17 years that people begin to avoid situations that they rate at about 20% or 25% distress, so encourage your client to begin with an item that doesn't cause much more distress than this. The five items should also be situations that they think would be beneficial to address, and that they are able to organize exposure to within the next two weeks.

Then ask the client to write them down with a pencil on the Exposure Record Sheet (Handout 5.4), in ascending order of difficulty, from least distressing at the top to most distressing at the bottom, and to write their baseline ("pre-exposure") amount of distress from 1 to 100 in the "%" space. Session 5, Figure 1 shows an example of items and their SUDS.

Exposure Record Sheet—Subjective Units of Distress (SUDs)

Situation 1: *Doing small talk when friends are visiting*
Initial rating date: *July 10* What percentage of distress would this situation cause you? *25* %
2nd rating date: ______ Percentage of distress that this situation now causes you: ____ %
3rd rating date: ______ Percentage of distress that this situation now causes you: ____ %
4th rating date: ______ Percentage of distress that this situation now causes you: ____ %

Situation 2: *Socializing at work*
Initial rating date: *July 10* What percentage of distress would this situation cause you? *40* %
2nd rating date: ______ Percentage of distress that this situation now causes you: ____ %
3rd rating date: ______ Percentage of distress that this situation now causes you: ____ %
4th rating date: ______ Percentage of distress that this situation now causes you: ____ %

Situation 3: *Going to the gym*
Initial rating date: *July 10* What percentage of distress would this situation cause you? *65* %
2nd rating date: ______ Percentage of distress that this situation now causes you: ____ %
3rd rating date: ______ Percentage of distress that this situation now causes you: ____ %
4th rating date: ______ Percentage of distress that this situation now causes you: ____ %

Situation 4: *Talking to someone at work about being bullied*
Initial rating date: *July 10* What percentage of distress would this situation cause you? *80* %
2nd rating date: ______ Percentage of distress that this situation now causes you: ____ %
3rd rating date: ______ Percentage of distress that this situation now causes you: ____ %
4th rating date: ______ Percentage of distress that this situation now causes you: ____ %

Situation 5: *Going in my basement because of spiders*
Initial rating date: *July 10* What percentage of distress would this situation cause you? *95* %
2nd rating date: ______ Percentage of distress that this situation now causes you: ____ %
3rd rating date: ______ Percentage of distress that this situation now causes you: ____ %
4th rating date: ______ Percentage of distress that this situation now causes you: ____ %

Session 5, Figure 1 Example of pre-exposure targets and corresponding baseline subjective units of distress (%).

Since we need to start small to develop the necessary skills and then progressively address more challenging situations, ranking the situations is important. It would be best if Situation 1 is expected to cause your client between 20 % and 35 % distress; Situation 2, between 30 % and 50 % distress; Situation 3, between 50 % and 70 % distress; Situation 4, between 70 % and 80 % distress; and Situation 5, between 80 % and 100 % distress. Of course, this is only a rough guideline. Note also that the "date" on the form is the date on which you rate each situation. The pre-exposure date is the date on which the item and its related percentage of distress are recorded on the form, *before* the exposure starts. The subsequent dates are the dates on which reviews are done. Usually, the therapist reviews all ratings on the list during each subsequent therapy session, but reviews can also be done on a weekly basis by the client if there is a long gap between this and the next therapy session.

The Bipolar Exposure Method

Once your client's form is filled in with situations that they would find distressing, they are ready to start using bipolar exposure. Bipolar exposure combines mindfulness and behavior-therapy skills into a single desensitization method. This is an integrative method specifically developed for MiCBT, and is called "bipolar" because it uses imagery of extreme opposites (two poles) on a distress continuum—imagining the worst and the best possible scenarios that may occur in an avoided situation while remaining equanimous.

You may wonder what is the advantage of preceding standard (*in vivo*) exposure with imaginal exposure, since in-vivo exposure is also efficacious. Given that there is experiential equivalence between imagery and in-vivo stimulation, both produce body sensations with the same type of hedonic (feeling) tone, even though their intensity may differ—real-life situations are usually experienced more intensely. Given the degree of experiential equivalence between the two contexts, decreasing avoidance of a fear signature in one context (imagery) decreases our avoidance of the same fear signature in other contexts (*in vivo*). This offers direct access to the generalization of desensitization, as will be discussed and exemplified later in this chapter.

Implementing Bipolar Exposure

Bipolar exposure consists of a three-step exercise that lasts about eleven minutes, and is to be performed immediately after every 30-minute mindfulness meditation practice. It requires using imagination to simulate various scenarios that we could come across in each listed situation, in four successive sessions over two days, before facing the situation in real life. Explain to your client that they need to keep their eyes closed throughout the procedure. Here is what you specifically need to do to assist your client with each situation that they have listed on the form. Session 5, Figure 2 is a pictorial representation of the exercise.

1 Ask your client to start with the first situation on their list. They need to be sitting with eyes closed. Instruct your client that for the first five minutes to visualize one or several *worst*-case scenarios that could occur if they were not

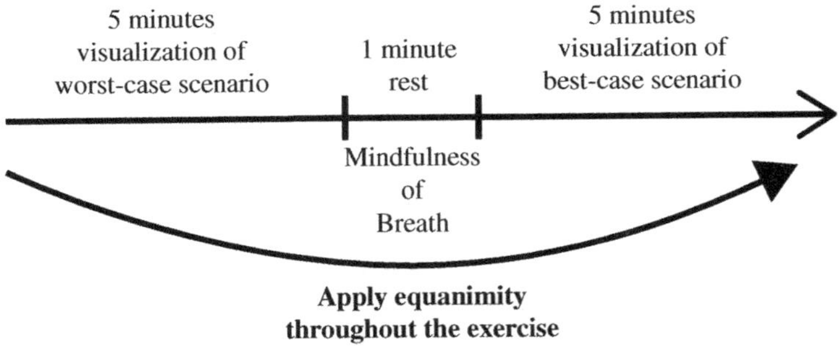

Session 5, Figure 2 Representation of the bipolar exposure procedure. Adapted from Cayoun (2011).

avoiding the situation. While visualizing and catastrophizing the event, they do their best to remain equanimous. As they imagine the very worst that could happen when they enter the situation two days from now, they monitor the sensations that these negative thoughts create in their body and do their best to not react to them, to not identify with them, and perceive them for what they are: just impermanent sensations in the body. Remind the client that sensations are made of four characteristics: mass, temperature, motion and fluidity. As they combine an unpleasant experience with equanimity, the emotional aspect of their anticipated distress is being neutralized. With practice, their usual response is being unconditioned and extinguished, which allows the client to reappraise their self-efficacy.

2 After five minutes, ask your client to switch their attention to the entrance of their nostrils for a whole minute, resting their attention on the breath while keeping their eyes closed, letting their mind calm down and relax as their breath settles. Note that later on, with highly distressing items on their list, they may need a slightly longer break than one minute to regain a sufficiently relaxed state before proceeding with the next task. The one-minute duration is only a rough guide for less distressing items. However, longer than three minutes may alter the momentum of exposure.

3 For the last five minutes, ask your client to switch their attention to the situation, again while keeping their eyes closed, but this time visualizing one or more *best*-case scenarios that could realistically occur when they will be in this situation in real life two days from now. While visualizing and embellishing the situation, ask them to do their best to remain equanimous. While they imagine the very best scenarios, some pleasant body sensations are likely to co-emerge. Ask your client to do their best to not react to these sensations, even though they may be pleasant. Some people can be surprised by this procedure, sometimes wondering why it wouldn't be useful to want and "attract" pleasant scenarios. This problem with this view is that we produce a preference for a chosen outcome. We may become attached to it. As soon as we do so, inadvertently, we automatically decide that another type of outcome is not preferred or even acceptable. We may resent it. Consequently, if the outcome is not what we preferred, we repeat the habit of resenting what we have and craving what we don't have. With bipolar exposure, we also extinguish the

craving to avoid disappointment if the outcome is not according to our wishes. Hence, pleasant or unpleasant, clients remain equanimous and unattached to the experience. Again, encourage your client to apply mindfulness to the experience by removing any personal judgment regarding the sensations in the body, remembering to observe them in terms of their four basic characteristics (mass, motion, temperature, fluidity). Here we are neutralizing the craving response, rather than the aversive response.

It is worth noting that since people who are distressed generally tend to have more negative thoughts than positive ones, it is much easier for them to feel unpleasant sensations in the first five minutes of this exercise, than it is to feel pleasant sensations in the last five minutes. The brain has been used to producing connectivity among structures that now facilitate certain types of experiences more than others. Consequently, your client might find it more complex to switch from the unpleasant scenarios to the pleasant ones during their first attempts. This is common, and it is useful to normalize their experience—without missing the opportunity to remind them of the consequences of negative thoughts and of the unique opportunity they now have to change them. Just ask your client to lengthen the resting period to about two minutes instead of one. This will give your client a little more time to let go of the emotional load attached to the unpleasant scenarios while remaining with the breath. They will have more time to switch emotions and will feel pleasant sensations more easily in the last five minutes; this is usually possible by the third session. In any case, whether the sensations are pleasant or unpleasant, your client needs to simply observe the sensations and their impermanent nature while remaining equanimous.

Using bipolar exposure at the end of four consecutive sessions of body scanning will train your client's inhibitory pathways in the prefrontal cortex to neutralize emotional reactivity, which will serve them well during the actual situation. Your client will be ready for what is known as "in-vivo exposure." In vivo is Latin for "in the living," meaning in a real-life situation. With bipolar exposure, your client will have trained their nervous system to remain equanimous towards the emotional tone attached to fearful expectations. They will also gain a sense of predictability and safety.

Implementing in-vivo Exposure

Your client should practice mindfulness meditation for 30 minutes, immediately followed by bipolar exposure with "Situation 1" for 11 minutes, twice-daily for two days. After the fourth practice, ask your client to engage in "Situation 1" in real life, being aware of the four characteristics of body sensations while equanimous, just as they did during their bipolar exposure. Provided it is ethically acceptable and logistically possible, ask your client to continue to put themselves in Situation 1 as often as possible after that, but without the use of bipolar exposure, until their distress rating reaches 5 % distress or less. For example, if Situation 1 on their list is avoiding going to the supermarket, then ask them to go to the supermarket as often as possible, until it is no longer an issue. If Situation 1 is avoiding the presence of a work colleague, then suggest that your client does their best to be in the presence of that colleague daily if possible, even briefly, until the presence of this colleague stops producing unpleasant body sensations to which the client usually reacts.

After applying bipolar exposure to Situation 1 for two days, and while starting in-vivo exposure to Situation 1, your client can start bipolar exposure to Situation 2 after each meditation practice. You can also ask your client to re-rate the percentage of distress that each of the situations now creates. Hence, one situation is being addressed with imagery while the previous one on your client's list is being experienced in real life. Instruct your client to proceed with this method until all the listed situations have been addressed and none of them remains a source of avoidance. Tell your client to take the time they need, but try to keep up the momentum, as this will help maintain their progress. Clients can usually complete bipolar and in-vivo exposure for two to three items per week. Accordingly, the standard duration of Stage 2 is two weeks, though there should some flexibility.

Generalization of Fear Extinction

The SUDS ratings are expected to decrease at each review. It might surprise you or your client, but this decrease includes the ratings of items which haven't yet been subjected to exposure. This is because the items listed on the sheet are only the situations that trigger avoidance. What clients are actually avoiding is the body sensations that have become associated with those triggers. Remember that the co-emergence model of reinforcement shows that we react to co-emerging interoception, not stimuli.

During bipolar exposure, as explained earlier, the exposure is to body sensations triggered by the visualization of expected aversive events while remaining equanimous. After a few trials of associating equanimity with the interoceptive signature of fear following the imagination of the aversive stimulus, the experience of the four characteristics of body sensations ("interoceptive signature") becomes deconditioned. In other words, we are less afraid and avoidant of fear itself. This deepening of insight into operant conditioning allows us to understand that what we avoid is the sensation of fear, not the trigger. The only thing that differs is the intensity of the sensations, but the signature is essentially the same across most avoided situations. Since we avoid situations that evoke the same (fear) signature, a decrease of rating for even just the first two items on the list is likely to have a beneficial consequence on the items that have not yet been subjected to exposure. Session 5, Figures 3 and 4 show the ratings of actual clients demonstrating this effect. Session 5, Figure 3 shows the SUDS form of a client diagnosed with Major Depressive Disorder and Generalized Anxiety Disorder, and Session 5, Figure 4 was filled in by a client diagnosed with Avoidant Personality Disorder. As you can see, the generalization of fear extinction is not dependent upon the disorder or the nature of the fear.

Given that we are essentially decreasing our fear of feeling fear-related sensations, *all* fears should decrease, including those that are not mentioned on the form. We simply become less fearful and avoidant in general. Just as anxiety can generalize to multiple contexts (as in GAD), so can its extinction. You may call this "generalization of fear extinction." Accordingly, when you review your client's

Patient with Major Depressive Disorder and Generalized Anxiety Disorder

Situation 1: *Saturday night drinks*

Initial rating date:	*March 16*	Percentage of distress:	*30* %	
2nd rating date:	*March 22*	Percentage of distress:	*20* %	Exposure done
3rd rating date:	*April 3*	Percentage of distress:	*15* %	Exposure done
4th rating date:	*April 12*	Percentage of distress:	*5* %	Exposure done

Situation 2: *Driving other people*

Initial rating date:	*March 16*	Percentage of distress:	*40* %	
2nd rating date:	*March 22*	Percentage of distress:	*30* %	Exposure done
3rd rating date:	*April 3*	Percentage of distress:	*15* %	Exposure done
4th rating date:	*April 12*	Percentage of distress:	*10* %	Exposure done

Situation 3: *Family gatherings*

Initial rating date:	*March 16*	Percentage of distress:	*70* %	
2nd rating date:	*March 22*	Percentage of distress:	*60* %	*No exposure yet*
3rd rating date:	*April 3*	Percentage of distress:	*50* %	Exposure done
4th rating date:	*April 12*	Percentage of distress:	*25* %	Exposure done

Situation 4: *Asking to work reduced hours*

Initial rating date:	*March 16*	Percentage of distress:	*80* %	
2nd rating date:	*March 22*	Percentage of distress:	*60* %	*No exposure yet*
3rd rating date:	*April 3*	Percentage of distress:	*30* %	Exposure done
4th rating date:	*April 12*	Percentage of distress:	*10* %	Exposure done

Situation 5: *Providing training to groups of staff at work*

Initial rating date:	*March 16*	Percentage of distress:	*100* %	
2nd rating date:	*March 22*	Percentage of distress:	*100* %	*No exposure yet*
3rd rating date:	*April 3*	Percentage of distress:	*75* %	*No exposure yet*
4th rating date:	*April 12*	Percentage of distress:	*45* %	*No exposure yet*

Session 5, Figure 3 Example of exposure targets and corresponding subjective units of distress (%) ratings with and without exposure over time. Note that the client did not have the opportunity to organize Situation 5.

scores of the first few items next week, ensure that you review all five items, rating both those that received exposure and those that did not.

Note that although clients are likely to become more confident each week, those with Avoidant Personality Disorder and other symptom clusters that include pronounced avoidance will be tempted to drop out of therapy at this stage. It is useful to simply speak about it openly with clients. Let them know that they can slow down the pace of the program when necessary, but they need to hold firm on their commitment. The most important is for them to know that they will not be judged, whatever the outcome may be.

Patient with Avoidant Personality Disorder

Situation 1: *Social chats with people I know*

Initial rating date:	*June 9*	Percentage of distress:	*40*	%	
2nd rating date:	*June 17*	Percentage of distress:	*30*	%	Exposure done
3rd rating date:	*June 25*	Percentage of distress:	*10*	%	Exposure done
4th rating date:	*July 19*	Percentage of distress:	*2*	%	Exposure done

Situation 2: *Kissing my partner*

Initial rating date:	*June 9*	Percentage of distress:	*50*	%	
2nd rating date:	*June 17*	Percentage of distress:	*20*	%	Exposure done
3rd rating date:	*June 25*	Percentage of distress:	*10*	%	Exposure done
4th rating date:	*July 19*	Percentage of distress:	*0*	%	Exposure done

Situation 3: *Phone conversations*

Initial rating date:	*June 9*	Percentage of distress:	*70*	%	
2nd rating date:	*June 17*	Percentage of distress:	*60*	%	Exposure done
3rd rating date:	*June 25*	Percentage of distress:	*50*	%	Exposure done
4th rating date:	*July 19*	Percentage of distress:	*25*	%	Exposure done

Situation 4: *Asking a friend or my partner for help*

Initial rating date:	*June 9*	Percentage of distress:	*80*	%	
2nd rating date:	*June 17*	Percentage of distress:	*50*	%	*No exposure yet*
3rd rating date:	*June 25*	Percentage of distress:	*20*	%	Exposure done
4th rating date:	*July 19*	Percentage of distress:	*5*	%	Exposure done

Situation 5: *Conversation with a stranger at social events*

Initial rating date:	*June 9*	Percentage of distress:	*90*	%	
2nd rating date:	*June 17*	Percentage of distress:	*65*	%	*No exposure yet*
3rd rating date:	*June 25*	Percentage of distress:	*45*	%	*No exposure yet*
4th rating date:	*July 19*	Percentage of distress:	*25*	%	Exposure done

Session 5, Figure 4 Example of exposure targets and corresponding subjective units of distress (%) ratings with and without exposure over time.

Application with Individual Clients

Session Aim

The aim of this session is to introduce the second stage of the MiCBT program, including advanced scanning methods to increase awareness of early distress cues and the integration of exposure therapy. Clients learn that avoidant behavior relies on avoidance of unpleasant body sensations, and training themselves to remain equanimous with these sensations while exposed to external triggers helps in the process of desensitization and reduces avoidance. While continuing to develop interoceptive awareness, clients learn to understand and manage avoidance and increase self-confidence.

Review Homework and Progress

Check with your client in the usual way: "did you practice twice a day?" etc. Facilitate feedback on the homework set last week. Have the client fill in the Interoceptive Awareness Indicator, which you introduced during Session 3 to give you an idea of how much their interoceptive awareness has improved. Ask to see the Mindfulness-based Interoceptive Signature Scale (MISS) given to them in the last session. Point to the best measure of progress: decreased distress latency (the reduction in the usual duration of reactivity following a stressor), visible on the MISS as the amount of qualitative and quantitative changes within about 30 seconds. Check for other improvements that may be occurring (better sleep, etc.). Bringing these improvements to their attention is validating and helps them to see that their practice is paying off. Discuss possible difficulties with the practice.

Introduce Symmetrical Scanning

Explain the rationale for advanced scanning: these methods increase awareness of early distress cues and emotion regulation. Describe symmetrical scanning and explain that in this exercise we are learning to attend to larger areas and training both hemispheres to work together (Handout 5.1), thereby increasing the rate of brain reorganization.

Introduce Bipolar Exposure

1 Briefly remind the client of the co-emergence model, as a rationale for the way in which Stage 2 is designed. Explain that since the locus of reinforcement is interoception: we only react to body sensations, not to triggers. Desensitizing from fear-related body sensations through bipolar exposure helps in-vivo exposure and minimizes its discomfort.
2 Discuss what sort of situations your client tends to avoid (see explanation on Handout 5.2). Ask how beneficial it would be if they no longer avoided these situations. Explain that the new exercise for this week will help them deal with avoidance and greatly increase their self-confidence. Ask your client to think of several situations that they find distressing and as a result may avoid. On a piece of paper, ask them to brainstorm a list of ten to twelve situations that they usually avoid in order to decrease their anxiety.
3 Distribute the Exposure Record Sheet (Handout 5.4). Once they have chosen five situations, as explained in Handout 5.3, ask your client to write them down on the form in order of difficulty, with the least distressing first (top of page) and the most distressing last. Offer some help where necessary. A good source of inspiration and motivation is to share your own past avoidant behavior, something that you have resolved using this method. If you choose

to do so, we suggest that you limit your self-disclosure to what you are no longer avoiding.

4 Explain the "experiential equivalence" between imagery and in-vivo stimulation. Explain that both produce the same type of emotional tone (body sensations), so becoming less reactive with a type of interoceptive signature in a specific situation results in being less reactive to it in other situations—i.e. we simply desensitize from fear altogether.

5 Explain bipolar exposure (Handout 5.5). To facilitate the understanding of the task, it is also useful to draw the graph of Session 5, Figure 2 on the whiteboard while explaining the principles of the exercise. You may also give the client a paper copy of the figure, copied from the main text. Ask the client to choose the first two or three distressing items on their SUDS list for this week's exposure tasks. They will use bipolar exposure to the first item for the first four sessions (two days) and then expose to the item *in vivo*. They start to work with the second item on the third or fourth day and repeat the task with the same schedule. Reiterate the central role of equanimity towards body sensations in achieving full desensitization.

Explain Homework Exercises

- Symmetrical scanning for 30 minutes twice-daily (note that the audio instructions last only 20 minutes and clients need to continue practicing in silence for another 10 minutes). An explanation for your client is in Handout 5.1.
- Explain the problems associated with avoidance (Handout 5.2).
- Applied practice of equanimity in daily life.
- Bipolar and in-vivo exposure to at least two SUDS targets (Handouts 5.3, 5.4 and 5.5).
- Read the handouts.
- Fill in the forms for this week, including the Daily Record of Mindfulness Meditation Practice (Handout 5.7).

Delaying the Next Step

If the client cannot feel sensations in about 80 % of the body, as reflected by the Interoceptive Awareness Indicator, they may have difficulties feeling both sides of the body at the same time and should delay symmetrical scanning by a few days. They should focus on the breath for about ten minutes before scanning the body in a unilateral manner (as per last week), *without* using the audio instructions.

Application with Groups

Session Aim

The aim of this session is to introduce the second stage of the MiCBT program, including advanced scanning methods to increase awareness of early distress cues and the integration of exposure therapy. While continuing to develop interoceptive awareness, clients learn to understand and manage avoidance and increase self-confidence.

Materials

Whiteboard and markers, MP3 recording of symmetrical scanning (also available in audio CD format) MP3 player or CD player, Daily Record of Mindfulness Practice, SUDS form (Exposure Record Sheet), and the Interoceptive Awareness Indicator form. Outcome measure forms, as needed.

In-Session Practice

Conduct a 10-minute group practice of unilateral part-by-part body scanning, which they would have practiced in the previous week. This time, do not guide clients through the body parts. Rather, give brief and assertive instructions such as "start scanning the entire body part by part, remaining alert, attentive, and equanimous no matter what you experience..." Provide intermittent reminders: "Remain aware, attentive and keep moving through the entire body..."

Review Homework and Progress

Check in with participants in the usual way: "how was your week?" Ask clients to fill in the Daily Record of Mindfulness Meditation Practice form in case they haven't yet done so. Use this information to provide feedback. Ask clients to fill in the Interoceptive Awareness Indicator, which you introduced during Session 3 to have an idea of how much their interoceptive awareness is improving. Ask to see the Mindfulness-based Interoceptive Signature Scale (MISS) given to them in the last session. Point to the best measure of progress: decreased distress latency (the reduction in the usual duration of reactivity following a stressor), visible on the MISS as the amount of qualitative and quantitative changes within about 30 seconds. Check for other improvements that may be occurring (better sleep, etc.). Bringing these improvements to their attention is validating and helps them to see that their practice is paying off. Discuss possible difficulties with practice.

Introduce Symmetrical Scanning

Explain the rationale for advanced scanning. Explain that these methods increase awareness of early distress cues and emotion regulation. Describe symmetrical scanning and explain that in this exercise we are learning to attend to larger areas and training both hemispheres to work together (Handout 5.1), thereby increasing the rate of brain reorganization. Offer a 15- to 20-minute group practice using the audio instructions on track 10 or using the script in Appendix 2.

Introduce Bipolar Exposure

1 Briefly remind your group participants of the co-emergence model as a rationale for the way in which Stage 2 is designed. Explain that since the locus of reinforcement is interoception (we only react to body sensations, not to triggers), desensitizing from fear-related body sensations through bipolar exposure helps in-vivo exposure and minimizes its discomfort.

2 Discuss what sort of situations your clients tend to avoid (see explanation on Handout 5.2). Ask how beneficial it would be if they no longer avoided these situations. Explain that the new exercise for this week will help them deal with avoidance and greatly increase their self-confidence. Ask clients to think of several situations that they find distressing and as a result may avoid. On a piece of paper, ask them to brainstorm a list of ten to twelve situations that they usually avoid in order to decrease their anxiety.

3 Distribute the Exposure Record Sheet (Handout 5.4). Once they have chosen five situations, as explained in Handout 5.3, ask clients to write them down on the form in order of difficulty, with the least distressing first (top of page) and the most distressing last. Offer some help where necessary. A good source of inspiration and motivation is to share your own past avoidant behavior with the group; something that you have resolved using this method. If you choose to do so, we suggest that you limit your self-disclosure to what you are no longer avoiding. A useful way to encourage participants is to ask: "Ok everyone, I need an example of an avoided situation that would create between 20 % and 30 % distress." Invite suggestions and write one down on your whiteboard. This also serves to show how to fill-in Handout 5.4. Thank the participant(s) who volunteered self-disclosure and move on to the other items in the same way: "Great, now who can offer a situation that would produce between 35 % and 50 % distress?" and so on.

4 Explain the "experiential equivalence" between imagery and in-vivo stimulation. Explain that both produce the same type of emotional tone (body sensations), so becoming less reactive with a type of interoceptive signature in a specific situation results in being less reactive to it in other situations—i.e., we simply desensitize from fear altogether.

5 Explain bipolar exposure (Handout 5.5). To facilitate the understanding of the task, it is useful to draw the graph from Session 5, Figure 2 on the whiteboard while explaining the principles of the exercise. You may also give participants a paper copy of this figure, copied from the main text. Ask participants to use the first two or three distressing items on their SUDS list for this week's exposure tasks. They will use bipolar exposure to the first item for the first four sessions (2 days) and then expose *in vivo* to the item. They start to work with the second item on the third or fourth day and repeat the task with the same schedule. Reiterate the central role of equanimity towards body sensations in achieving full desensitization.

Explain Homework Exercises

- Symmetrical scanning for 30 minutes twice-daily (note that the audio instructions last only 20 minutes and clients need to continue practicing in silence for another 10 minutes). An explanation for your client is on Handout 5.1.
- Explain the problems associated with avoidance (Handout 5.2).
- Applied practice of equanimity in daily life.
- Bipolar and in-vivo exposure to at least two SUDS targets (Handouts 5.3, 5.4 and 5.5).
- Read the handouts.
- Fill in the forms for this week, including the Daily Record of Mindfulness Meditation Practice (Handout 5.7).

Delaying the Next Step

Participants who cannot feel sensations in about 80 % of the body, as reflected by the Interoceptive Awareness Indicator, may have difficulties feeling both sides of the body at the same time and should delay symmetrical scanning by a few days. They should focus on the breath for about ten minutes before scanning the body in a unilateral manner (as per last week), but *without* using the audio instructions.

Frequently Asked Questions

Question: I am not sure how fast my client should scan his body with symmetrical scanning. Some clients can go faster than others and I am not sure if they should keep the pace from last week.

Answer: Just as they did last week, clients should move at their own pace, but ensure that they understand the need for effort. Some still confuse meditation with relaxation and therefore don't get the benefits that awareness and equanimity procure in the longer term. If there is any area of the body where they can't feel sensations, they should continue scanning the whole body symmetrically to complete the cycle. After that, they go back to survey the blank spots one at a time, remaining equanimous for about 30 seconds (up to a minute). If their concentration is poor, about 15 seconds would be a good start.

Question: At least one-third of my group can't feel some body parts symmetrically, but most can feel most of their body with unilateral scanning. What I should I advise them to do?

Answer: This usually represents a small delay in some people's skill development, and is very common. You simply need to normalize this challenge by explaining that this skill takes time to develop because the brain usually switches very rapidly between the two hemispheres and now we are training it to feel both sides at once instead. It takes time for the insula (where we feel most body sensations) in both cortices to fire in the same place and at the same time while training the corpus callosum to pass that information between the hemispheres without confusion, or "neural crosstalk" as we call it. Encourage clients to continue with symmetrical scanning a few more days, but without audio instructions so they can improve their concentration.

Question: My client cannot feel sensations in some parts of her body in spite of practicing twice daily. It is not yet clear to me, but there are some indications of past trauma. Is it possible that she has developed some level of dissociation to sensations because this has been an effective way of coping with trauma of some kind?

Answer: Indeed, dissociation is more common than we realize, and is sometimes reported by clients only at this stage—although we would normally notice this earlier in the program when measuring interoceptive awareness in the previous two sessions. I would first verify that the client is practicing enough and accurately. This means practicing for 30 minutes twice-daily, with equanimity, and certainly not mixing other techniques. If the client has become too caught-up in thoughts, it is possible that she has resorted to an easier method that she used in the past. Some insufficiently informed teachers sometimes modify the original teachings to make things easier for clients, but at the cost of efficacy. Some even introduce methods that are not related to mindfulness (e.g., mantras, visualization or even background music).

Once this is verified, I would first investigate the nature of the limitation. If it is related to being too caught up in thoughts (poor inhibition), I would emphasize that effort is necessary. I would also ask them to practice the 3-second rule (mentioned earlier in the book). If it is not a distractibility issue, I would examine with them if there is any apprehension about feeling certain areas of the body, and if there are any significant memories associated with these areas. I would practice a short period with the client while in the session, ensuring that the blank spots are not being avoided, and then simply normalize the experience—not feeling is actually normal until sufficient neuroplasticity is produced.

If scanning the body results in an abreaction or a painful memory, it is important to assist the client in staying on this area, focusing on the four basic characteristics of sensations, equanimously, until the intensity subsides, which should take between 30 and 60 seconds if well conducted. In other words, they practice exposure to neutralize their response and consequently reappraise their self-efficacy in regulating emotions. At this point, should traumatic memories emerge, it is most important to (1) discuss them without leading or contributing to falsely constructed memories, (2) discuss the client's usual possible habitual strategies for avoiding the memory or the related emotions, and (3) discuss the importance of addressing the issue and the current ideal opportunity to do so by using bipolar and in-vivo exposure methods.

Question: I have a client with generalized anxiety, although he still shows some OCD symptoms, who says he still gets caught up in his thoughts when he scans the body and can only do mindfulness of breath. What do you do when this happens?

Answer: Many people, especially those with a habit of worrying frequently, struggle with their thoughts during mindfulness meditation. One can also be attached to thinking in some ways. It may initially seem counterintuitive when we are not very experienced with mindfulness meditation, but the most useful way of letting go of a persisting thought is to focus on its co-emerging body sensation. If you remember the co-emergence model of reinforcement, thoughts related to matters that we evaluate as being important are encoded and stored in memory in a co-emergent way. We tend not to remember the rest of our memories easily. This means that thoughts that emerge in consciousness during practice are accompanied by body sensations. If we are able to feel these rather salient sensations associated with an intrusive thought and remain equanimous, we can neutralize its emotionality. When repeated, this has a desensitizing effect that modifies, or even prevents, the "reconsolidation" of the memory. This "weakens" the thought's capacity to compete against other thoughts with a more salient co-emergence and reduces its intrusiveness. This applies to using exposure with obsessions in OCD.

It is also useful to consider how progress is measured in this case, because avoidance can lead clients to report feeling better, but it won't allow them to develop the skills and move forward with the program. Just as progress with equanimity toward emotions is determined by the *duration* of reactivity, progress with equanimity toward thoughts is determined by the *duration* of intrusive thoughts. Progress is neither reflected by the type nor by the frequency of emotions and thoughts. What matters is how long it takes before we start smiling again!

Question: My client really couldn't find anything that she avoids. She is socially active and doesn't seem to avoid challenges in her life. She is just anxious.

Answer: Avoidant behavior can be found in many of the things we do and is not limited to the things we don't do. If your clients can't find situations that they avoid, ask them to ask their partner, siblings, son or daughter, or their best friends. One of them is likely to let them know what they think they avoid. A typical example is needing to have a level of intoxication (e.g., with alcohol) to be able to socialize. In this case, the client avoids social anxiety and would most probably avoid the social context if drinking was not possible. Sometimes, simple justifications can mask low-level avoidance—a student procrastinating because of a fear of failure while thinking that they have plenty of time to finish their assignment, or a parent picking up his or her child from school, waiting in the car while other parents are happily talking to each other nearby, assuming that he or she is not interested in these people, as a way of masking their social awkwardness. Detecting a habit of avoiding intimacy with one's partner can also be difficult for some people. It is therefore important to explain that avoidant behavior is also reflected by the things we do, not just the things we don't do.

Sometimes, a client disappointed in a family member will avoid speaking to them for fear of conflict. In this case, it is better to reserve exposure to this kind of avoidance until we reach Stage 3 of MiCBT, the interpersonal stage, which is specifically designed to address this more complicated form of avoidance. Whether at Stage 2 or Stage 3, discussing potential avoidance openly, using the Socratic method with empathy, can reveal a great deal to our clients—even if it is simply the avoidance of making time for practicing mindfulness meditation twice daily. However, there may be very unusual cases where unhelpful situational avoidance cannot be found. In this case, we simply accept it and limit the homework to symmetrical scanning. We will attempt to use exposure again at Stage 3.

Question: My client reports that he avoids lots of things from a particular category of experience. Should he write a hierarchy of intensity within that particular category of avoided situations, or should I try to help them find different categories of situations for their hierarchy?

Answer: It's OK to have several items related to the same family of problems, such as three increasingly intense OCD-related situations, but it is also important to have a variety of situations. The reason for this is that it is more productive for developing self-confidence to experience relief across a variety of fears. As long as clients learn that all sensations are acceptable and manageable, and they remain equanimous, whatever they use for exposure in the outside world will help them. Even people with Avoidant Personality Disorder are only avoiding the co-emergent body sensations. They do not actually avoid the external situations but believe that they do because they are not yet sufficiently aware of body sensations systematically associated with their evaluation. This is because of the extremely rapid co-emergence of these two functions. They simply assume that visceral sensations are the result of sensory contact with the stimulus, instead of witnessing them to be body sensations co-emerging with fearful thoughts, and consequently avoid the stimulus to prevent feeling the discomfort. This applies to all categories of experiences and across all disorders. Your client needs to learn this from you, and then verify it through their own experience of meditation and exposure.

Handout 5.1 Symmetrical Scanning

Congratulations! Your commitment prepared you enough for the practice of advanced scanning methods. This is an important achievement. The main purpose of advanced scanning is to train your mind to notice very subtle changes in the body so you gain deep levels of awareness, and in more places at the same time. The aim is to become aware of sensations as soon as they come up and while they are still faint, and make a decision about how to deal with them before they become an emotion. You will be more able to cope if you deal with sensations *before* they get so strong that you are swept away by the discomfort. The longer it takes you to detect body sensations related to emotions, the more intense they become and the harder it is to prevent your usual reaction. This is the main reason for starting to learn how to detect early signs of distress this week, by learning more advanced methods of surveying the body.

The first advanced method is called "symmetrical scanning." You will need to survey the body part by part, as you have been doing until now, but surveying *both sides of the body* at the same time. The audio instructions for this exercise are on track 10 and the introduction is on track 9. The advanced scanning tracks last on average 15 minutes only and you will need to practice for another 15 minutes in silence without instructions. Remember that each session needs to last 30 minutes. To keep your timing simple, you can set a timer to 30 minutes, play the audio instructions until the end and then continue in silence until your timer lets you know that 30 minutes have passed. Use the Daily Record of Mindfulness Meditation Practice (Handout 5.7) form to record this week's practice.

Scan the entire body symmetrically downward, from the top of the head to the tip of the toes. Once you reach the toes, return to the top of the head in the same way, symmetrically, and remaining equanimous (i.e. not concerned) if whether you do not yet feel both sides at the same time.

With symmetrical scanning, both hemispheres of the brain are trained to work together with equal strength, allowing us to feel what happens on both sides of the body at the same time. You will be quicker at scanning the body when you scan both sides together, because you will be passing your attention on the same areas more often. The brain pathways for sensations will get more connected, which will make you more sensitive to small changes. You will also be more aware of your body in everyday life and notice sensations arising *before* you need to react. For example, you may be able to notice the sensations of heat and agitation as you are becoming angry and *before* you behave in ways that are unhelpful or damaging.

Remain equanimous when you cannot feel both sides of the body at the same time in some parts. Remember that when we start to learn this scanning method, it is often difficult to feel both sides of the body at the same time in some body parts. For example, both armpits are initially difficult to feel at the same time. This creates a small delay in feeling some parts and our attention wants to switch quickly from side to side. It is perfectly OK to allow this to happen, but watch that you keep making effort to feel both sides more and more at the same time. This is because our "feeling brain" (called the insula) is currently better connected for some body parts than for others, but this will soon change with practice. It usually takes three to four days for people to feel both sides of the body symmetrically in most places. Avoid worrying about the normal initial difficulties, or your worry will actually prevent you to feel both sides, especially the subtle sensations. Remember that this is a training and you are not supposed to know how to practice it before you learn it, which takes time. Always remain equanimous, patient and tolerant with yourself.

Handout 5.2 The Nature of Avoidance

Avoidance is part of human life. We welcome pleasant and safe experiences and avoid the unsafe and unpleasant ones. This is a feature of survival found in all animals. Avoiding situations because they may be distressing is occasionally necessary, like seeing a horror movie with your friends if it makes you anxious, or avoiding some friends who binge on alcohol because they become reckless, but much of our avoidance is unhelpful. It often makes a problem worse, or creates a whole new set of problems.

Avoidant behavior is very common. It can include avoiding going to the shops because we hate to be in crowded places, putting off a task at work because of fear of making a mistake, and avoiding breaking up a relationship for fear of being alone again. We might tell a lie to avoid feeling embarrassed or we might use alcohol as a way of avoiding feeling awkward in social situations. We might be very conscious of our appearance because we want to avoid being criticized. Sometimes avoidant behavior can be more severe and result in being afraid to leave the house or telling others that we are in trouble and need help. This type of avoidance can lead to mental health issues.

Avoiding situations because we think they will cause us to feel uncomfortable can also make us feel that we are missing out on life experiences and opportunities. Avoiding socializing with people can isolate us and make us feel depressed. Unless we challenge our behavior skillfully, most habits of avoidance tend to become stronger and harder to change. We learn to live according to them and we feel dictated by them. They may become part of our personality so that we say to ourselves "this is how I am" and stop trying to change.

This week, you will learn a way of reducing your habitual avoidance by decreasing the anxiety associated with it. This is an "exposure" approach that uses the skills of noticing body sensations and accepting them that you have already learned to do during your meditation. This method helps us desensitize from fear itself. We learn not to avoid sensations of fear because fear is just made of body sensations that arise and pass away. These sensations will no longer be threatening and you won't need to avoid the situations in which you feel them. This will increase your self-confidence. Of course, you will need to maintain your commitment to your practice of mindfulness twice-daily, and continue to develop your equanimity while scanning.

Handout 5.3 Instructions for Bipolar Exposure

Part 1: Preparation (you will need a pen and paper)

Now that you have become more equanimous to body sensations, let's use your new skills to reduce your habit of avoiding certain important situations.

- First, write down a list of ten to twelve events or situations that you definitely avoid or that you would avoid if you could because they appear distressing to you.
- Next, score how distressing each situation would feel if you were in it today. Score the distressing feeling and body sensations on a scale from 5 % (barely distressing at all) to 100 % (your maximum distress).
- Next, choose five situations from your list that you think would really benefit you or others if they could change. Choose situations with a range of levels of distress; so not all with an 80 % distress level or with a 20 % distress level. Avoidance of everyday chores might cause about 15 % to 20 % distress (e.g. cleaning the toilet!). We usually start to avoid situations because of anxiety when they cause us 20 % to 25 % distress, so start with a situation that causes at least this level of distress. A situation that causes you between 20 % and 35 % distress would be fine because you are definitely trying to avoid it if you can, but it is not too distressing to begin with and you won't find the task too difficult to do. You will learn to deal with more challenging situations when you have gained some skills with the easier ones. As a rough guide, it would be best if Situation 1 caused you between 20 % and 35 % distress; Situation 2 between 30 % and 50 % distress; Situation 3 between 50 % and 70 % distress; Situation 4 between 70 % and 80 % distress; and Situation 5 between 80 % and 100 % distress. Remember, this is only a rough guide.
- Now write them down on the horizontal line of the Exposure Record Sheet (Handout 5.4). For example, "Going out of the house." Start with the least distressing situation under the heading Situation 1. Write down today's date in the "Initial rating date" section and write down the corresponding percentage of distress in the "%" area, according to how distressing this situation would be for you to do now. As we discussed, this should be between 20 % and 35 %. Do the same for Situation 2, where your distress level should be a little higher. Then write down the other three situations, with their associated distress levels.
- Don't write anything on the three other lines below Situation 1 (2nd, 3rd and 4th ratings), because you will record your progress here over the following three sessions with your therapist. However, if you cannot see your therapist for several weeks, then you can score your progress weekly, by yourself, by writing the date of your reviews and your new percentage of distress. Do this for all the five situations every time you review progress, even if you haven't done the exposure to some of them yet.

Now you are ready to train yourself to develop equanimity with your first avoided situation, at the end of your daily mindfulness practices. After 30 minutes of mindfulness meditation, practice "bipolar exposure" as explained below. Do that procedure for Situation 1 after each meditation practice, four times in a row; this means twice a day on two consecutive days.

Part 2: "Bipolar Exposure"

1 Complete your 30-minute practice of mindfulness meditation (symmetrical scanning).
2 Start the bipolar exposure exercise with Situation 1. For the first five minutes, close your eyes and visualize (also imagine the sound, taste or smell) the *worst* that could happen if you were in this situation now. Imagine different unpleasant scenarios for this situation. You need to do this while not reacting to co-emergent sensations, remaining equanimous.
3 After five minutes, rest your mind for about one minute by practicing mindfulness of breath. Let go of the story and just focus on the breath.
4 After about a minute, for the following five minutes, visualize the very *best* that could happen in this situation, again while *remaining equanimous.* This time, try not to react with attachment to the pleasant sensations that can co-emerge with the pleasant scenarios. This can be hard because we are not used to desiring pleasant experiences.
5 After five minutes, again, rest your mind for a minute by practicing mindfulness of breath and abandon the scenarios, even if they are pleasant to imagine.
6 Do this for four sessions (two sessions per day if you committed to meditating twice daily), and then follow the instructions of Part 3, below.

Part 3: "In-vivo Exposure": Doing It In Real Life

7 You are now ready to confront Situation 1 in real life ("*in vivo*"). Try to stay non-reactive (equanimous) when you are doing the task for real in the manner that you intend to, without avoiding, while doing your best to remain equanimous to the co-emerging body sensations. Please read carefully and follow the instructions on Handout 5.5 ("Practice of in-vivo Exposure").

Handout 5.4 Exposure Record Sheet: Subjective Units of Distress (SUDS)

Write down on a sheet of paper ten events or situations that are distressing and that you are likely to avoid. Then, in the space below, list five of them in ascending order of difficulty, the most distressing and least manageable last. Write the date in "Initial rating date" only, and the amount of distress each situation causes you, on a scale from 1 % to 100 %. Other dates and distress scores will be used after the issues have been targeted. The reviews will be done each session with your therapist.

Remember to brainstorm a list of ten to twelve situations before making your five selections to go into the forms below.

Situation 1: ____________________

Initial rating date: ________ What percentage of distress would this situation cause you?___%
2nd rating date: ________ Percentage of distress that this situation now causes you: _____%
3rd rating date: ________ Percentage of distress that this situation now causes you: _____%
4th rating date: ________ Percentage of distress that this situation now causes you: _____%

Situation 2: ____________________

Initial rating date: ________ What percentage of distress would this situation cause you?___%
2nd rating date: ________ Percentage of distress that this situation now causes you: _____%
3rd rating date: ________ Percentage of distress that this situation now causes you: _____%
4th rating date: ________ Percentage of distress that this situation now causes you: _____%

Situation 3: ____________________

Initial rating date: ________ What percentage of distress would this situation cause you?___%
2nd rating date: ________ Percentage of distress that this situation now causes you: _____%
3rd rating date: ________ Percentage of distress that this situation now causes you: _____%
4th rating date: ________ Percentage of distress that this situation now causes you: _____%

Situation 4: ____________________

Initial rating date: ________ What percentage of distress would this situation cause you?___%
2nd rating date: ________ Percentage of distress that this situation now causes you: _____%
3rd rating date: ________ Percentage of distress that this situation now causes you: _____%
4th rating date: ________ Percentage of distress that this situation now causes you: _____%

Situation 5: ____________________

Initial rating date: ________ What percentage of distress would this situation cause you?___%
2nd rating date: ________ Percentage of distress that this situation now causes you: _____%
3rd rating date: ________ Percentage of distress that this situation now causes you: _____%
4th rating date: ________ Percentage of distress that this situation now causes you: _____%

Handout 5.5 Practice of in-vivo Exposure

After four sessions of the bipolar exposure exercise, you will be ready for exposure to a real-life situation. Now that you have prepared your nervous system to remain equanimous towards the emotions attached to your expected fear, you have started to manage and neutralize your reactivity and you will be more equipped to face the situation in real life. Your practice of bipolar exposure has trained inhibition pathways in your prefrontal cortex to be activated in the context of avoidance and will serve you well in the actual situation.

If practical and ethical, continue to find times when you can be in Situation 1 as often as possible. If Situation 1 on your form is "avoiding the supermarket," then try to go to the supermarket as often as possible, until it is no longer an issue. If Situation 1 is avoiding meeting a certain colleague at work in the morning, then after your first real life exposure, do your best to meet that colleague every morning thereafter, even briefly, until meeting this colleague stops producing body sensations to which you react.

After doing bipolar exposure to Situation 1 for two days, start real life exposure to Situation 1 on Day 3, while also starting bipolar exposure to Situation 2 after each meditation practice. Continue bipolar exposure with Situation 2 on Days 3 and 4, (total of 4 bipolar exposure practices with Situation 2), before proceeding with exposure to it in real life on Day 5. To illustrate this next step, let's use the example of fear of socializing with friends. If this were your Situation 2, then you would practice bipolar exposure (imagining only) with this situation for four sessions. Also, you would be practicing Situation 1 in real life (going to the supermarket) every day or as often as possible. As you can see, one situation is being addressed in your imagination while the previous one on your list is being experienced in real life. Continue like this until your listed situations have all been addressed, and none of them remain a source of avoidance for you.

Handout 5.6 Homework Exercises

1 Symmetrical body scanning practice twice daily
2 Use bipolar exposure for two days only for Situation 1 on your Exposure Record Sheet.

Following bipolar exposure to Situation 1 for two days, start facing that situation in real life as often as possible—every day if appropriate and start to practice bipolar exposure (in imagination) with Situation 2 after your 30-minute meditation practice for the following two days.

3 After four sessions of using bipolar exposure with Situation 2, start facing that situation in real life as often as possible too.
4 Meanwhile, start using bipolar exposure with Situation 3 for another two days. During that time, you are still facing Situations 1 and 2 in daily life. This week you should be able to work on your first two or three situations.

Handout 5.7 Daily Record of Mindfulness Meditation Practice

Day	**Date**	**Morning** *(circle)*	**Duration**	**Efficacy rating** *Rate from 1 to 10 how well you noticed distractions and brought your attention back to the body. 1 = not well at all; 10 = extremely well*	**Evening** *(circle)*	**Duration**	**Efficacy rating** *Rate from 1 to 10 how well you noticed distractions and brought your attention back to the body. 1 = not well at all; 10 = extremely well*
Monday		I practiced Yes / No			I practiced Yes / No		
Tuesday		I practiced Yes / No			I practiced Yes / No		
Wednesday		I practiced Yes / No			I practiced Yes / No		
Thursday		I practiced Yes / No			I practiced Yes / No		
Friday		I practiced Yes / No			I practiced Yes / No		
Saturday		I practiced Yes / No			I practiced Yes / No		
Sunday		I practiced Yes / No			I practiced Yes / No		

References

Craig, A. D. (2003). Interoception: the sense of the physiological condition of the body. *Current Opinion in Neurobiology*, 13, 500–505.

Harshaw, C. (2015). Interoceptive dysfunction: Toward an integrated framework for understanding somatic and affective disturbance in depression. *Psychological Bulletin*, 141, 311–363. doi:10.1037/a0038101

Friedman, R. S., & Forster, J. (2010). Implicit affective cues and attentional tuning: An integrative review. *Psychological Bulletin*, 136, 875–893. doi:10.1037/a0020495

Farb, N. A. S, Segal, Z. V., & Anderson, A. K. (2013). Attentional modulation of primary interoceptive and exteroceptive cortices. *Cerebral Cortex*, 23, 114–126.

Lazar, S. W., Kerr, C. E., Wasserman, R. H., Gray, J. R., Greve, D. N., Treadway M. T., … et al. (2005). Meditation experience is associated with increased cortical thickness. *Neuroreport*, 16, 1893–1897.

Tang, Y., Hölzel, B. K., & Posner, M. I. (2015). The neuroscience of mindfulness meditation. *Nature Reviews Neuroscience*, 16, 213–225. doi:10.1038/nrn3916

Session 6: Generalizing Self-Confidence and Self-Efficacy

As is our confidence, so is our capacity.

—William Hazlitt, 1837

Introduction

This chapter is designed to guide you in delivering the second part of Stage 2 of MiCBT. It introduces the next advanced method of scanning, "partial sweeping," in which the body is scanned more quickly so that awareness of subtle and fluid sensations can be acquired. The chapter also consolidates the use of the exposure skills that your client started using last week to increase and generalize their confidence and self-efficacy in dealing with habits of avoidance. Scanning practice has enabled the detection of more subtle sensations and now faster scanning techniques will further increase connectivity in the somatosensory and insula cortices. With faster scanning often comes the experience of deeply pleasant sensations and there is the strong possibility of attachment to these and craving for more. This session provides a good opportunity to discuss these matters and support your client's understanding of equanimity. Being equanimous to both pleasant and unpleasant sensations is equally important. Faster scanning techniques enable larger neural networks to activate together and the subtle waves of sensations may give rise to memories that are not normally accessible. Accordingly, this chapter will also make recommendations for addressing the possible emergence of traumatic memories in some clients.

Checking Client Readiness

Check with your client that they have been able to maintain commitment to their twice-daily 30-minute practice. Check also how their week was in general, remaining patient and empathic, as it is important that clients don't feel unheard or

The Clinical Handbook of Mindfulness-integrated Cognitive Behavior Therapy: A Step-by-Step Guide for Therapists, First Edition. Bruno A. Cayoun, Sarah E. Francis, and Alice G. Shires.

Companion website: www.wiley.com/go/Cayoun/Mindfulness-integrated

unable to share any personal concerns that may have arisen since their last session with you. This will also maintain good rapport. Those who have managed to commit to the practice may report feeling calmer due to a decrease in emotional reactivity. If practice has been insufficient this week, discuss this with your client and ask how they plan to increase their practice in the coming week. They may need to continue for a few more days or the whole week with symmetrical scanning. Check if they were able to practice bipolar and in-vivo exposure methods with some of their exposure targets last week. First discuss their experience, validating their effort and clarifying possible ambiguous matters, and then discuss the items for the coming week a little later in the session.

Delaying the Next Step

Your client will be ready to move on to the next step ("partial sweeping") when they are able to feel approximately 80 % of the body more often than not. If this is not yet the case, then suggest that they continue with symmetrical scanning for a few more days and that they drop the audio instructions as this will help them to focus on the sensations without any distractions. As with all the practices in MiCBT, ask your client to adopt a non-judgmental approach to arising sensations, simply noticing, accepting and then moving to the next part of the body.

Regarding the exposure tasks, if your client has not done their exposure to low-rated items on their subjective units of distress (SUDS) list, they will need to address these less distressing items before moving on to more distressing ones. It is common that clients include exposure targets that are logistically difficult to address. For example, an acrophobic farmer who lives on flat land far away from the city may not have had the opportunity to come to town for in-vivo exposure to heights (e.g. using bridges, buildings, etc.). In this case, they could use a more logistically realistic exposure target that has a similar distress rating.

Moreover, it is common that clients rate their listed items with an inaccurate level of distress. They will often try to fit in some exposure items on their list according to the instruction of following a hierarchy of distress levels, which can make their rating inaccurate. For example, a client whose initial ratings on their draft list of 10 to 12 items range between 50 % and 95 % distress will struggle to fill in the first two items on their Exposure Record Sheet, because we tell them to start with a 20 % to 30 % item. Accordingly, clients will list a 50 % SUD item as a 20 % item, just to meet the form's requirement. As a result, consciously or not, some clients will be avoidant of starting the procedure. This needs to be discussed with the client so that easier items may be added to facilitate the task.

Sometimes it is the opposite. Clients will occasionally include situations that used to be a source of avoidance before they started MiCBT, but which have been largely neutralized by the level of equanimity that they developed during Stage 1. Accordingly, they may assign a percentage that is no longer relevant, which results in difficulties visualizing the worst-case scenarios and lack of arousal. In this situation, clients often start exposure with initially highly rated items, which should realistically be scaled down. There is no need to delay the procedure, but additional items will be needed in order to develop the skills to generalize the client's sense of self-efficacy and to prepare for Stage 3, discussed in the next session.

Advanced Scanning: Partial Sweeping

The next advanced scanning method is "partial sweeping." This requires surveying both sides of the body at the same time, but in a continuous flow of attention, rather than attending to separate spots part by part. They may already be able to feel more subtle sensations when scanning the body. This is partly because the somatosensory cortex and insular cortex (the brain areas that are associated with feeling body sensations) have started to be more densely connected. They may report feeling some pleasant tingling sensations through entire parts of the body. This is quite normal and an indication that they are working effectively. As the practice proceeds, there is an experience of fluidity of sensations which means that large networks of brain cells are activated simultaneously with little effort. Even if your client does not feel this type of sensation yet, this will change, provided they are practicing sufficiently and accurately.

Note that sweeping can trigger craving reactions, because sweeping through very subtle, fluid and diffused sensations can be very pleasant. Sweeping attention can also imitate wave-like emotions, such as sadness, anger or pleasure. Emotions stored in memory that feel like waves of sensations are more easily recalled by sweeping techniques. However, such memories may not be retrieved consciously. They manifest as body sensations, such as feeling a little hot or agitated for a few seconds or minutes without understanding why. Some people may continue to experience them in daily life for some time if they lack equanimity during their practice, although this is more likely to occur in people with a tendency to avoid emotions.

This needs to be understood as an integral part of the practice. Traditionally, these and other manifestations have been parts of what is known as "stages of insight" (see Grabovac, 2015, for a comprehensive discussion). They provide the ideal means of spontaneous desensitization because their arising is organic, not forced, and is sufficiently close to the "surface" (our awareness threshold) to mean that they are emotions that we frequently experience or suppress. These can be more intense when people attend an intensive *Vipassana* meditation retreat, where meditators practice about 12 hours a day for 10 days or longer, but not with the soft approach of MiCBT.

It is important that your client understands and remains aware that all experiences are impermanent and not to become attached to any experience that arises during the practice. They need to simply notice without expectations and without identifying with the experience. Sweeping attention through the body with objectivity and equanimity allows us to notice pleasant and unpleasant sensations equally. Early cues of craving and distress can then be easily addressed with equanimity, and their learned response can be rapidly neutralized. This practice can bring about a decrease in the frequency and duration of emotions in daily life, because of the neuroplasticity associated with equanimity.

Sometimes, it can be a little surprising for people to find it more difficult to remain equanimous with pleasant sensations than with unpleasant ones. Remind your client to remain even-minded towards all experiences regardless of their pleasant or unpleasant nature. Remind them not to identify with the experience even though it may evoke an autobiographical memory. This means that however pleasant or unpleasant a sensation may be, it is not theirs or a part of them; it is just an impermanent experience that is happening in the body and is bound to pass away. Remembering this will help your client to let go of craving and aversion.

The Method

The scanning method is clearly described in the audio instructions on track 12. Ask your client to listen to the introduction on track 11 before proceeding to track 12. With partial sweeping, we start as usual from the top of the head and pass our attention in a continuous "sweeping" fashion through the entire head down to the beginning of the neck and throat, feeling as many parts of the face as we can at the same time while moving attention downward. If feeling the entire head is not yet possible, we sweep whatever smaller parts are possible to sweep (e.g. the scalp first, then the face), and then pass our attention to the other areas part by part. We can then proceed in the same way with the neck and throat, then shoulders, arms and hands symmetrically, down to the fingertips. We then proceed with the torso, the buttocks and lower limbs, both legs and feet symmetrically—or one at a time to begin with if sweeping symmetrically is not yet possible.

Because the torso is such a large area, we usually take it in steps. For the first two days, we sweep the front part of the torso first, starting at the base of the throat. In a single movement of attention, we try to feel the entire chest and areas of the abdomen as we move downward toward the groin. Next, we start from the base of the neck and in a single movement of attention, surveying the entire upper and lower back areas as we move downward toward the buttocks. Once the entire back has been scanned, we start from the armpits and in a single movement of attention, feel both sides of the torso simultaneously, as attention moves downward toward the hips. Most people can do this fairly well after two days of practice (i.e., four sessions). For the following four sessions (day 3 and day 4), we can combine the front and back parts of the torso. This means sweeping the chest and upper back, then abdomen and lower back, simultaneously. Then, for the last three days of the week, we can combine front, back and both sides of the torso in a single flow of attention.

When sweeping through the legs, we start from the top of the thighs and sweep slowly and progressively down to the tips of the toes in one single movement of attention, feeling as many parts as possible on the way. Once we reach the tip of the toes, we scan the body back up toward the top of the head in the same way, by sweeping attention through the entire body. We do as many cycles as possible during each 30-minute practice. As we learn to sweep, we may initially miss several parts because we move attention through very large areas. That is to be expected. Nonetheless, we try not to interrupt the flow of attention, but note which parts have been missed and survey them separately, part by part, after two or three sweeping cycles. Once these parts have been surveyed separately, we can resume with sweeping for a few cycles again, and so on.

Craving and Aversion

By now, your client has become increasingly aware of craving and aversion in their formal practice, as well as in daily life. One of the reasons why craving is difficult to resist is that we assume that a desirable consequence will result from it, so we give a special value to the things we desire. We initially liked and got attached to what we come to crave (and don't have), believing that it is, or should be, a necessary part of who we are, and that we should absolutely have it. Once we eventually have it, we want it to be permanent. Not surprisingly, this becomes a great cause of suffering because everything changes, even the things we want most, such as love and pleasure. This is a reality that affects everyone and is not limited to the clinical population. A person who craves an intimate relationship and believes that he or she is not a worthwhile person without a partner, may then have difficulty leaving the relationship even if it becomes destructive.

Managing craving becomes more possible for your client as their equanimity develops. As they sweep through body parts, pleasant sensations become memory cues for pleasures of the past. Just as unpleasant memories can be recalled, very pleasurable past events can re-emerge spontaneously, including past romantic and sexual experiences. If your client is equanimous to a type of sensation, this sensation may become a memory cue for similar sensations felt in the past. With very pleasant sensations, old cravings continue to arise. After a few days of partial sweeping, many clients notice the emergence of cravings and report that they are now enjoying their practice. Of course, this is a double-edged sword, as it could also mean that they have "succumbed to temptation," so to speak. Although we don't expect clients to dislike their practice, we need to ensure that they are aware that clinging to pleasant sensations leads to craving these sensations when they are absent. Not having the pleasant experience in each subsequent practice can also lead clients to being disappointed or to the believe that they are regressing. It is helpful to remind clients that this is not about regressing but that like thoughts, sensations come and go.

Clients also need to understand that the way they behave during meditation is how they will behave in daily life. Craving the pleasant and resenting the unpleasant during meditation will only increase their reactivity in daily life. With this in mind, assist your clients to be unattached to the pleasant flow of subtle tingling sensations that they encounter during sweeping techniques, explaining that they also arise and pass away, and are just as impermanent as unpleasant sensations. This is a simple but profound insight that can change a person's life.

A Drop of Wisdom

Aside from the method itself, it is also useful to briefly explain the over-arching psychoeducational rationale for addressing craving and not aversion only. Clients benefit from learning that aversion and craving are two sides of the same coin, so to speak. As we desire what we want and don't have, we become resentful. Once we have become resentful, our desire is to get rid of resentment. So, craving is the true culprit in the drama of our lives. This is not to say that we shouldn't desire wholesome changes. What we are referring to here is the mental action of craving in order to experience either a surge of pleasant sensations or as a relief from unpleasant ones (i.e., positive or negative reinforcement). The less we crave, the less likely we are to be disappointed and resentful when we don't obtain the object of craving. Therefore, decreasing the propensity to crave what we don't have will at the same time decrease the propensity to resent. To a clinician, this may seem like a drop of wisdom in an ocean of ignorance for some clients, but it usually resonates well if explained in a way that matches the client's mindset. Using Socratic dialogue will help with this and stop you from sounding as though you are trying to preach.

Extending the Integration of Mindfulness and Exposure: Bipolar and in-vivo Exposure

Checking Progress with Exposure Tasks

Check with your client on how they managed with the easier (first two or three) avoided situations listed on their Exposure Record Sheet. Ask them if they were able to stay equanimous with the sensations that arose when they imagined the worst- and best-case scenarios for five-minute periods. Ask if they were able to confront the situation in real life and how that went. If the exposure went well, then ask your client to start addressing the SUDS items that they rated as being more challenging.

Before moving forward, it is important to verify that clients really understand what we are trying to do with bipolar exposure and overcome any possible confusion. A common confusion is related to the choice of scenarios for each item listed on the Exposure Record Sheet. For example, a colleague's client, whose social anxiety precluded her from socializing, complained about feeling lonely. On her Exposure Record Sheet, she listed the item as "feeling lonely when I'm alone at home." She then proceeded to visualize the worst- and best-case scenarios when being alone at home. One may argue that no longer being lonely in one's own company is a great outcome, but this was not the issue that the client needed to address. In addition, being alone at home *was* the avoidant behavior that prevented her from being anxious and should not be reinforced. She was avoiding socializing and connecting with people for fear of rejection. Since the exposure in Stage 2 is to address avoidant behavior, exposure to being at home alone was not an item congruent with the task. Instead, the therapist redirected her focus accurately and she eventually performed the exposure tasks that enabled her to socialize. As you can see, writing items accurately on the form is important, as it can prevent unproductive exercises.

Another possible confusion is related to omitting interoceptive desensitization during visualization. Some clients can waste a whole week following the pictorial representation of bipolar exposure (Session 5, Figure 2), experiencing stress by visualizing the worst-case scenarios, followed by a feeling of relief when visualizing the best-case scenarios, and concluding that the point of exercise was to think positively and feel reassured! It is central to this method that clients understand the purpose of visualization. If it is not clear to them, explain that visualization only serves as a trigger for visceral sensations, and that the desensitization component is the consequence of applying equanimity to these body sensations. The consequence is an acceptance of arousal and its resulting decrease in intensity, which allows the progressive ability to reappraise one's capacity to cope.

Moreover, some people struggle with visualizing scenarios. There are individual differences that cannot be ignored, but experts in imagery procedures have argued that if a situation in imagination is sufficiently personalized and realistic, then anybody is able to use imagery. The way in which these criteria can be met in MiCBT is twofold. First, we need to ensure that the avoided situation has a strong enough effect on the client and that the client is genuinely anxious about facing it. This means ensuring that the client didn't rate the corresponding item higher than it actually is, for example by assigning to it 30 % distress when it only causes 10 % distress. This would lead to strong imagery and would translate as next to no arousal. Second, we need to ensure that the emphasis is on visualizing body sensations associated with the situation, as these readily personalizes the event that the client is trying to elicit. Because more sensory modalities (both mind and body) are involved in the imagery procedure, the client can easily overcome their possible lack of imagery capacity.

Avoidance and Desensitization Can Affect Personality

Any event that causes some level of pain or discomfort can lead to avoidance, which is usually negatively reinforced through reducing discomfort with further avoidance. We can readily generalize avoidance to other stressful or uncomfortable situations because the qualitative nature (hedonic tone) of the interoceptive signature that underlies fear is similar across avoided situations; it mostly changes in intensity. If you ask your client about the nature of feelings of embarrassment or stress, for example, they will point to unpleasant body sensations. When they continue to avoid situations to prevent their discomfort, clients start to identify with this avoidant behavior and make life choices accordingly. They may maintain their avoidance by justifying it through beliefs such as, "I'm not a morning person" or "I don't socialize because I'm not a party animal." Avoidance may have become part of the client's sense of self.

As we discussed in Session 5, it makes sense that as we can generalize unhelpful behavior, so we can also generalize helpful behavior. If the fear of feeling a particular type of interoceptive signature decreases because of equanimity, then the fear of similar types of sensations also decreases in other fear-provoking situations. As the exposure process in Stage 2 progressively demonstrates, interoceptive exposure desensitizes from reacting with fear, anger and other emotions, and is not limited to particular situations. Equanimity works at the core of what maintains one's personality and enables one to change as a person. As your client proceeds with Stage 2, they progressively *become* a less avoidant and more confident individual.

Measuring Progress with Desensitization

It is important for clients to measure progress by recording how much the distress has decreased. In itself, this is a powerful reinforcer of their sense of self-efficacy. It also gives an idea of how equanimity is being applied in avoided situations. Using the Exposure Record Sheet that your client filled in last week, ask them to write down today's date in the "2nd rating date" for each of the five situations. Then ask your client to re-rate the level of distress they would expect to experience today in each of the five situations, even though they have practiced exposure with only two or three of them on the list. Ask them to write their new percentage of distress on the same line as today's date and see whether there has been a change.

The new expected distress rating is usually lower than that of last week, partly because of their reappraisal of self-efficacy. As they notice that they manage unpleasant sensations better with some situations, they begin to reevaluate their overall coping ability with sensations in other situations. Here, the cognitive reappraisal is a "bottom-up," rather than "top-down," process. However, occasionally, clients will rate some items higher than at baseline. This is usually because they were a little too optimistic to begin with and assumed that the situation was much easier to address than they had realized. This should not be a concern. We can explain this to clients and re-order the item on the form according to this more realistic baseline level of distress. This will enable the client to use exposure to this situation only when they are ready for this level of intensity.

Addressing Traumatic Memories

In trauma, we know that memories are sometimes suppressed and that body sensations are a significant component of a traumatic memory whether or not the memory is available to conscious awareness (Van Der Kolk, 2014). If arising sensations trigger painful memories, then being able to remain calm and unperturbed allows desensitization. If (or rather when) this occurs, use the *Example of Rationale Delivery* discussed in Session 3, and then use the Diary of Reactive Habits (Handout 3.1) as exemplified in Session 3 to conceptualize trauma-related behavior.

In the event that a client is tormented by intrusive traumatic memories that their level of equanimity could not extinguish during the week, we recommend that they stop scanning the body altogether and simply practice PMR (see Session 1) followed by loving-kindness meditation, which is recorded on track 18 of the MP3 list and lasts 8 minutes (11 minutes with the introduction on track 17). This is because scanning is an exposure to internal cues, some of which could possibly maintain the memory in consciousness. The client needs to be soothed for a week or two, according to the level of distress severity, before feeling confident that they can restart gently (perhaps once daily) with mindfulness of breath for about a week, before returning to scanning. Of course, we always need to proceed slowly and with caution, especially with clients with complex trauma and dysregulated emotions, but most clients generally can reduce their distress within a week or two. Remember that the evidence shows that exposure is generally the best approach to addressing trauma (Courtois & Ford, 2009; Foa, Keane, Friedman, & Cohen, 2009) and the last thing we want is to become avoidant ourselves. Ultimately, these are only generic recommendations. Since there is no "one size-fits-all" procedure, even for transdiagnostic models, your clinical judgment will be the best guide for how you choose to schedule the procedures.

Application with Individual Clients

Session Aim

The aim of this session is to introduce the next method of advanced body scanning, called "partial sweeping." Your client will learn to survey their body more quickly and learn to neutralize deep-seated emotions. This session also reviews and consolidates exposure skills to decrease more pervasive and established avoidance, resulting in increased self-confidence and self-efficacy. Clients gain a better understanding of craving and aversion.

Review Homework and Progress

Check if your client was able to keep a commitment to practicing 30 minutes twice-daily again. If they practiced committedly and with the correct understanding, they are likely to be less reactive in day-to-day life. When your client is able to feel approximately 80 % of the body more often than not when scanning the body symmetrically, they can move on to the next step, partial sweeping, using the audio instructions. If they practiced daily but cannot feel as much, they should continue practicing with symmetrical scanning practice for a few more days, without audio instructions, before starting partial sweeping. You will also need to assess whether your client was able to do the exposure tasks and provide clarifications if needed. Ask your client to re-rate each item on the Exposure Record Sheet following exposure. Check if the expected subjective units of distress (SUDS) decreased since last week. If so, they are now ready to address more significant situations.

Introduce Partial Sweeping

Explain the rationale for partial sweeping: (1) accelerating interoceptive neuroplasticity, (2) increasing equanimity with craving and deep-seated patterns of emotional reactivity, and (3) preparing for the next advanced scanning method. The audio instructions for partial sweeping are on track 12 of the MP3 list, and your client should listen to the brief introduction on track 11 before their first practice. As in previous weeks, each practice session needs to last 30 minutes. The advanced scanning tracks last about 15 minutes so they will practice for another 15 minutes in silence. Ask your client to record their practice times as usual.

Understanding Avoidance and How It Becomes Generalized

Explain that when we continue to avoid situations, we start to identify with this avoidant behavior and make life choices accordingly. We then begin to justify the avoidance and develop schemas about who we are and who we are not ("I'm not a morning person" or "I'm not a party animal").

Craving and Aversion

Explain the role of attachment or craving to certain ideas (e.g. I must get a promotion at work). In this case, I am attached to the idea that I need a better job or more money and now I believe that my sense of self, my worthiness, will be impacted if I am not offered the job. Explain how craving and aversion reinforce each other and maintain suffering. Equanimity helps us manage craving and aversion. Explain that during sweeping techniques we are likely to experience sensations that may be pleasant, and the mind has the tendency to want more. Being equanimous to all sensations allows us to perceive our experience more objectively and with detachment, knowing that however pleasant it may be, it will also pass.

Exposure Tasks with New SUDS Items

Provide encouragement and promote commitment by asking your client how they would feel if their last two or three avoided situations were no longer a problem for them. Ask them to imagine the amount of confidence they are likely to feel if they no longer needed to avoid these situations. Ask your client to do the exposure tasks for the last items on their list, exactly as they did last week with the first few situations following on from their 30-minute body scanning practice. They also need to continue to put themselves (*in vivo*) in the situations they already started addressing last week, until these are no longer creating anxiety. For the remaining items on their list, they should apply the same technique as follows:

1. Day 1 and Day 2: Use bipolar exposure (i.e., in imagination) for the next situation (e.g. situation 3) on the Exposure Record Sheet (Handout 6.4)
2. Day 3: Start facing that situation in real life as often as possible; every day if appropriate.
3. Day 3 and Day 4: Meanwhile, start using bipolar exposure for Situation 4 for another two days, while still facing Situation 3 in real life.
4. From Day 5: After two days (4 sessions) of using bipolar exposure with Situation 4, start facing that situation in real life as often as possible.
5. The client can add another situation and further decrease avoidance habits this week.

It is not always possible to work so quickly with the avoided situations because your client may not have the opportunity to practice exposure in real life within the week (e.g. fear of flying). In this case, ask your client to work on it when the opportunity arises and use another item with a similar level of expected distress in the meantime.

Explain Homework Exercises

- Partial sweeping (tracks 11 and 12).
- Continue applying equanimity in daily life.
- Bipolar and in-vivo exposure to the next situations on the SUDS form.
- Read Handouts 6.1, 6.2, 6.3 and 6.5.
- Fill in the Daily Record of Mindfulness Meditation Practice (Handout 6.6).

Application with Groups

Session Aim

The aim of this session is to introduce the next method of advanced body scanning, called "partial sweeping." Participants will learn to survey their body more quickly and learn to neutralize deep-seated emotions. This session also reviews and consolidates exposure skills to decrease more pervasive and established avoidance, resulting in increased self-confidence and self-efficacy. Clients will gain a better understanding of craving and aversion.

Materials

Whiteboard and markers, MP3 recording of partial sweeping (also available in audio CD format) MP3 player or CD player, Daily Record of Mindfulness Practice, Exposure Record Sheet, and the Interoceptive Awareness Indicator form. Outcome measure forms, as needed.

In-session Practice

Conduct a 15-minute group practice of symmetrical part-by-part body scanning, which they would have practiced in the previous week. Do not guide participants through the body parts. Rather, give brief and assertive instructions such as "start surveying the entire body part by part and symmetrically, remaining alert, attentive and equanimous with each experience…" Provide intermittent reminders: "Remain aware, attentive and keep your attention moving through the entire body symmetrically…"

Review Homework and Progress

Check with group members in the usual way – "How was your week?" Ask them to fill in the Daily Record of Mindfulness Meditation Practice form in case they haven't yet done so. Use this information to provide feedback. Ask participants to fill in the Interoceptive Awareness Indicator, which you introduced during Session 3, as it offers you an idea of how much their interoceptive awareness has improved. Briefly provide feedback on the home exercises. If some participants practiced daily but cannot feel sensations in about 80 % of the body, they should continue practicing with the symmetrical scanning for a few more days, without audio instructions, before starting partial sweeping. You will also need to assess whether everyone was able to do the exposure tasks, and provide clarifications if needed. Ask participants to re-rate each item on the Exposure Record Sheet following exposure. Check if their expected subjective units of distress (SUDS) decreased since last week. If so, they are now ready to address more significant situations.

Introduce Partial Sweeping

Explain the rationale for partial sweeping: (1) accelerating interoceptive neuroplasticity, (2) increasing equanimity with craving and deep-seated patterns of emotional reactivity, and (3) preparing for the next advanced scanning method. The audio instructions for partial sweeping are on track 12 of the MP3 list, and participants should listen to the brief introduction on track 11 before their first practice. As in previous weeks, each practice session needs to last 30 minutes. The advanced scanning tracks last about 15 minutes, so they will practice for another 15 minutes in silence. Ask participants to record their practice times as usual.

Understanding Avoidance and How It Becomes Generalized

Explain that when we continue to avoid situations, we start to identify with this avoidant behavior and make life choices accordingly. We then begin to justify the avoidance and develop schemas about who we are and who we are not ("I'm not a morning person" or "I'm not a party animal").

Craving and Aversion

Explain the role of attachment or craving to certain ideas (e.g. I must get a promotion at work). In this case I am attached to the idea that I need a better job or more money and now I believe that my sense of self, my worthiness, will be impacted if I am not offered the job. Explain how craving and aversion reinforce each other and maintain suffering. Equanimity helps us manage craving and aversion. Explain that during sweeping techniques we are likely to experience sensations that may be pleasant, and the mind has a tendency to want more. Being equanimous to all sensations allows us to perceive our experience more objectively and with detachment, knowing that however pleasant it may be, it will also pass.

Exposure Tasks with New SUDS Items

Provide encouragement and promote commitment by asking participants how they would feel if their last two or three avoided situations were no longer a problem for them. Ask them to imagine the amount of confidence they are likely to feel if they no longer needed to avoid these situations. Ask them to do the exposure tasks for the last items on their list, exactly as they did last week with the first few situations following on from their 30-minute body-scanning practice. They also need to continue to put themselves (*in vivo*) in the situations they already started addressing last week, until these are no longer creating anxiety. For the remaining items on their list, they should apply the same technique as follows:

1 Day 1 and Day 2: Use bipolar exposure (i.e., in imagination) for the next situation (e.g. situation 3) on the Exposure Record Sheet.
2 Day 3: Start facing that situation in real life as often as possible; every day if appropriate.
3 Day 3 and Day 4: Meanwhile, start using bipolar exposure for Situation 4 for another two days, while still facing Situation 3 in real life.
4 From Day 5: After two days (4 sessions) of using bipolar exposure with Situation 4, start facing that situation in real life as often as possible.
5 Participants can add another situation and further decrease avoidance habits this week.

It is not always possible to work so quickly with the avoided situations because some participants may not have the opportunity to practice exposure in real life within the week (e.g. fear of flying). In this case, ask them to work on it when the opportunity arises and use another item with a similar level of expected distress in the meantime.

Explain Homework Exercises

- Partial sweeping (tracks 11 and 12).
- Continue applying equanimity in daily life.
- Bipolar and in-vivo exposure to the next situations on the SUDS form.
- Read Handouts 6.1, 6.2, 6.3 and 6.5.
- Fill in the Daily Record of Mindfulness Meditation Practice (Handout 6.6).

Frequently Asked Questions

Question: One of my clients is getting frustrated because he still cannot feel many sensations in the body. He is quite avoidant, and I wonder if the issue is just avoidance or a real problem feeling the body. Should he move ahead anyway?

Answer: Although we advise to adhere to the MiCBT protocol as much as possible and to cover all the tasks in the order presented, we need to remain flexible in the delivery of the program. This may mean allowing for small delays in moving on to the next skillset. Sometimes clients practice enough but struggle to feel body sensations. This typically happens with anxious clients who dissociate. This needs to be discussed in terms of practice accuracy, especially with regards to difficulties disengaging from thoughts. Discussing the "five hindrances" to all meditative practices is usually the first port of call. Using Socratic dialogue is always a good tool. Here is an example of how one of us (BC) used it recently with an avoidant middle-aged male who had had some difficulty committing to the practice since the start of the program (T = therapist, P = client):

T: How did you go with your practice this week?
P: I haven't been very good this week.
T: Do you think that the amount of practice really determines how good you are as a person?
P: Maybe not, but I made a commitment and I didn't keep it.
T: Why did you make that commitment?
P: To get better.
T: Why is it so important for you to get better?
P: Because I don't want to be so depressed and so scared of doing new things.
T: This sounds like a good reason. But you have been avoidant most of your life, so why are you so eager to change now?
P: Well, I guess I don't want to pass that on to my children; I can see that my younger son is becoming a bit like me already.
T: Are you saying that you are trying to change for your children's well-being?
P: Yes, I feel terrible about them seeing me always like this.
T: Did you realize that you are making all these efforts out of love and compassion for your children?
P: I didn't see it this way before. I thought it was more out of guilt and duty.
T: Well, in this case, it is no wonder that guilt and duty are not very motivating reasons to practice, but can you see how beneath your guilt and fear there is a deeper motivation, the love you have for your children?
P: Yes, now I can see it, and this is very true; I love them so much.
T: So, could I propose that from now on you keep in mind your deeper and truer motivation for this training, your own well-being and the well-being of your children?
P: Sure, I can do that.
T: Great, so from now on, please keep in mind that every time you are going to practice, you do this for you, of course, but you do it also for others; for people you love, out of compassion for them. Would spending this time on you be more acceptable if you knew it was out of compassion for others around you?
P: Yes, definitely because that's my problem, I feel bad about spending all this time on me when I could do more things at home.
T: Do you mean more of your time to serve others?
P: Yes...
T: Could practicing daily and getting better serve others as well?
P: Well, that's what my wife is saying. What bothers her most is my depression.
T: So, what would you like to do about it?
P: Ok, now I get the point; I'll talk to her and will definitely commit!

Question: I have a client who asked why we have to practice scanning through the whole body. If we know that we tend to carry stress and tension in the stomach, chest and throat, for example, why don't we just scan those parts?

Answer: If the practice was only to relax, then decreasing tension only in the tense areas would make sense, but this is not the purpose of this approach. We are using an interoceptive exposure (not relaxation) method for the purpose of cultivating equanimity and "egolessness," which is the ability to prevent identification with our experience. This the is essence of a mindfulness approach.

Note also that not all mindfulness teachers teach students to scan in the same way. Some suggest focusing primarily on a sensation wherever we can feel it in the body, stay with it, accept it and then move to another. It certainly is easier to feel strong sensations than subtle ones, but it limits us. Our mind does not become subtle, as our *Vipassana* teacher (S. N. Goenka) would say.

In contrast, surveying parts that are too subtle to be felt yet creates a greater demand on the brain's insular cortex, which produces new or stronger connections as a result. Although this has yet to be empirically demonstrated, we have observed the experiential differences between these methods. It is commonly reported that scanning the body in the way described in MiCBT enables the rapid ability to sweep the surface of the body at the speed of a single breath. Therapists training in MiCBT who have previously learned to focus randomly on strong sensations throughout the body have not yet reported achieving this profound level of interoceptive awareness prior to learning these scanning methods. These methods, in the *Vipassana* tradition, enable us to detect very early cues of distress and achieve deeper stages of insight into our impermanent nature.

Question: Some clients are asking about how deeply they should feel in the body when they practice partial sweeping. Should they be feeling deep inside the body, as well as at the surface?

Answer: At this stage, we are still focusing on the surface of the body, but if they feel anything deeper, then feeling these sensations is fine, although they must make an effort to apply equanimity with these deeper sensations. In a few weeks, we will use a scanning technique called "transversal scanning" to specifically teach them to feel sensations deep inside the body.

Question: How can I explain to my client that she should not block negative thoughts when they come up?

Answer: It is very difficult to not think a thought that has just arisen, especially when it is accompanied by a degree of emotion. You can help her by instructing her that as an unwanted thought arises, she can focus all her attention on the body sensations associated with it and remain there quietly, peacefully and equanimously. Once the emotionality of the thought (body sensations) has subsided, she will find the thought subsiding too. This is because evaluative thoughts and body sensations co-emerge and are interdependent for their respective longevity. When we are aware of body sensations associated with a thought while remaining equanimous, the associated thoughts are easier to let go.

Question: One of my clients started partial sweeping and almost immediately started to experience old cravings for tobacco and alcohol. Is this just a coincidence?

Answer: It is not likely to be a coincidence because many people experience some cravings when they practice sweeping techniques: some early and others later. Craving when sweeping is common because when we sweep through very subtle body sensations, the pleasurable experience that it creates can resemble past experiences of pleasure. Because these sensations co-emerged with thoughts and other senses when we experienced those pleasures, they can later act as a memory cue for these and other pleasurable events.

Question: Since she started using the sweeping technique, my client reports having more intrusive thoughts than before. She worries that she is no longer making progress. I wonder if she has lost her motivation because things are going very well for her now. Any tips?

Answer: It could be a motivational issue, but this is very common when we start this scanning practice, even with motivated people. Thoughts intrude more easily now because scanning in this way stimulates more of them. This is because when we encode and then store a memory, the thought and other sensory percepts are encoded and stored in a co-emergent way, i.e., with some body sensations. This is the brain's efficient way of remembering what is important to remember in life, such as ways of surviving—the more strongly a sensation is associated with a memory, the less likely we are to forget it. As you can imagine, we have made countless associations between thoughts and body sensations. Understood in this way, body sensations are often parts of memories we can't recall cognitively. Now, let's link this to your question. When your client started scanning the body with the slow, part-by-part unilateral scanning method, she focused on a narrow area at a time and thoughts that co-emerged were associated only with that small area. In contrast, sweeping across large areas and much more rapidly allows many more co-emerging thoughts to arise in consciousness. Some will be clear memories, while others will appear random.

Question: I am not sure what to instruct my client to do during the one-minute rest in the bipolar exposure task. Are there specific instructions?

Answer: Ask your client to simply attend to the breath as he or she did in mindfulness of breath meditation. The idea is to calm and rest the mind, so that when we start the last five-minute exposure on pleasant scenarios, we are able to focus without the arousal effects felt during the previous distressing scenarios. It acts as a circuit breaker. Keep in mind that clients should rest a little longer on the breath with the more distressing items on their SUDS list. They can stay focused on the breath up to three minutes between the two five-minute exposures if necessary.

Question: What if my client does not undertake the last situation on the hierarchy. Should I just move on and tell him not to worry about this one?

Answer: This would depend on his reason for not addressing this situation. We need to know whether this was due to difficult logistics or avoidance. If there were logistical issues, it would be useful to help your client to find another situation that has a near-equivalent level of distress, and continue exposure with this new one. If it is avoidance, discussing the matter patiently and empathically with your client could be very fruitful. Ultimately, you can only offer to teach him the skills and it is his choice to learn them.

Question: I have a client who wants me to help him stop smoking tobacco. Can I use this exposure for addictions?

Answer: Certainly, but there are useful preparations that will increase the probability of success. He first needs to change the contexts of smoking, because addiction is also context-specific. Context helps us identify with our habit, which is why meditation teachers suggest practicing in the same place and at the same time. Using this notion to our advantage, your client could start this week by using bipolar exposure, followed by in-vivo exposure, to stop smoking the same tobacco or type of cigarettes, using the other hand to smoke, smoking in places other than the usual ones (e.g. not smoking inside the home), not smoking while drinking coffee or alcohol, not smoking while driving, and not smoking around people. Essentially, the idea is to make the basic context less habitual and less pleasant.

It would be best for him to divide these changes into two situations on his SUDS form and practice the easier changes first. In the second part of the week, break down attachment to the remaining and more important contexts, such as not having cigarettes at the usual times or at home. The changes will be more acceptable following four sessions of bipolar exposure, and he will not be expected to decrease the amount or frequency of smoking yet. However, from the second week, he could start using bipolar and in-vivo exposure to reduce his consumption. For the first half of the week, he could delay smoking until the craving "signature" in the body has changed and the unpleasant sensations associated with the unfulfilled craving have subsided due to his equanimity. He can allow himself to smoke a cigarette only then. Basically, he can only smoke when he stops feeling like it!

In the second part of the second week, it will be very feasible to use exposure to decrease the number of cigarettes by about 50 %. In his third week, he could do exposure to smoking a maximum of two cigarettes at the most addictive times (usually morning and night) and for the whole week. In the last two days of the third week, he can start bipolar exposure to not having any in the following (fourth) week. He needs to clearly accept that those cigarettes in the third week will be his last. People benefit from reframing their effort in terms of "renunciation skills" rather than "abstinence skills." We refuse, rather than feel deprived by the process. Since people are only addicted to body sensations, not to substances, this method can be applied to most addictive habits. The manner in which this approach is altered is more a function of the severity of the addiction, rather than its type.

Handout 6.1 Partial Sweeping

Congratulations for reaching this stage of your training. So far, you have worked hard at learning to cope with various sorts of challenges, mostly those that create unpleasant sensations. It is time for you to become more aware and skillful with the pleasant ones. This is because they are responsible for our habit of craving the things we want and cannot have. As you may have noticed over the years, this is a great source of suffering. Partial sweeping is the second type of the advanced method of scanning the body and will train you to resist the usual habit of craving. It will also help you in dealing with emotions in general. This time you will survey both sides of the body at the same time with a continual movement or flow of attention, in a "sweeping" fashion. The audio instructions on tracks 11 and 12 will guide you through this practice.

Start from the top of the head and "sweep" the entire head down to the beginning of the neck and throat, feeling as many parts of the head and face as you can at the same time while moving attention downward. It is normal to struggle a little when we start. Often, people can only sweep through the scalp or the face separately. If this is your experience too, that's not a problem; just sweep your attention through the scalp first, then the front of the face, and then the sides, including the ears. After a few attempts, you will be more able to feel the entire head in one go. Remember to move your attention downward.

Once you have passed your attention through the entire head, continue with the neck and throat, then both shoulders, arms and hands symmetrically, down to the fingertips. Then continue with the torso, the buttocks and lower limbs, both legs and feet preferably symmetrically, but one at a time to begin with if sweeping symmetrically is not yet possible. Because the torso is such a large area, we usually take it in steps. For the first two days, survey the front part of the torso first, starting at the base of the throat. In a single movement of attention, try to feel the entire chest and areas of the abdomen as you move downward toward the groin. Next, start from the base of the neck and in a single movement of attention, survey the entire upper and lower back areas as you move downwards toward the buttocks. Once the entire back has been scanned, start from the armpits and in a single movement of attention, feel both sides of the torso at the same time, as attention moves downward toward your hips. You might be able to do this fairly well after two days of practice (i.e., four sessions). For the following four sessions (day 3 and day 4 this week), you can combine the front and back parts of the torso. This means sweeping the chest and upper back at the same time, then abdomen and lower back at the same time. Then, for the last three days of the week, you can combine front, back and both sides of the torso in a single flow of attention.

When sweeping through the legs, start from the top of the thighs and sweep slowly and progressively down to the tips of the toes in one single movement of attention, feeling as many parts as possible on the way. Once you reach the tip of the toes, scan the body back up toward the top of the head in the same way, by sweeping attention through the entire body. Do as many cycles as possible during each 30-minute practice. You may initially miss several parts as you move your attention through very large parts of the body. This is quite normal. Just note where you are missing parts without interrupting your flow and go back after two or three body cycles to survey the blank spots separately, part by part. Once these parts have been surveyed separately, continue with sweeping for a few cycles again, and so on. If your sweeping speed is very slow, then survey the blank spots part by part after the first sweeping cycle, then resume with the sweeping practice. Always remember the main skill with all scanning practices: *feel*, *accept* and *move*.

Handout 6.2 Measuring Progress with Desensitization

Sometimes, people can't see their therapist weekly. If this is the case for you, or if for whatever reason you have not yet done so with your therapist, please measure last week's progress using the Exposure Record Sheet that you filled out last week.

On the form, write down today's date below last week's date in the "2nd rating date" space. Do this for each of the five situations, even though you have practiced exposure to only two or three of them. Write your new percentage of distress on the same line as today's date, under the one that you recorded previously. Is there any change due to your exposure practice?

Although it may seem a little strange to re-rate the situations that you haven't yet addressed, we have seen for many years that when we feel more at ease with unpleasant body sensations in the first few situations, we also begin to feel more at ease with these sensations when they occur in other situations. Are you ready for more progress? Imagine how life would be and how you would feel if your last two or three avoided situations were no longer a problem. Imagine the amount of confidence you are likely to feel with other situations not listed here. This week, following your 30-minute meditation practices, take the challenge and practice the exposure tasks for the last items on your list, exactly as you did last week with the first few situations.

Handout 6.3 The Generalizing Effects of Avoidance and Desensitization

Painful events in our life can often lead to habits of avoidance. When our habits are prolonged, our brain learns to connects itself in way that makes avoidance easier to do, and avoidance to one specific area of life can lead to a generalization of avoidance to other stressful situations. It can also lead to an avoidance of stress itself and, importantly, the sensations in the body that make up stress. Unfortunately, avoiding things that are unpleasant can lead to a whole host of problems and restrictions in our lives.

In particular, prolonged avoidance leads to identification with the avoidant behavior. Very soon, it becomes part of who we are and we begin to make choices accordingly; *we* become avoidant. We progressively forget the initial reasons for our avoidance and begin to justify it in unhelpful ways. For example, we may justify our refusal of invitations to social events by telling people that we are not a social person, even if we become socially isolated and depressed as a result.

If we can generalize an unhelpful behavior, then we can generalize a helpful one. If something is learned, it can be unlearned. You will find that if you have decreased your avoidance in one situation, you become less avoidant of other similar situations. For example, if your exposure skills lead you to be less uncomfortable asking for help from a family member, then you are also likely to be less anxious asking for help from a work colleague. If the discomfort that you had experienced has a certain pattern or "signature" of sensations (i.e., if it feels similar in terms of its temperature, heaviness, movement and denseness), then you will probably find that you don't need to avoid other situations that cause similar sensations.

Fear is at the root of most avoidant habits and has its own signature in the body. Exposure desensitizes us from reacting with fear, anger and other reactive emotions, and not just from the situations that we avoid. This is because equanimity works at the core. It is the most powerful strategy for making rapid and reliable change and needs to be practiced daily. Therefore, you will be using an exposure method that uses your body sensations to desensitize you.

Handout 6.4 Exposure Record Sheet: Subjective Units of Distress (SUDS)

Write down on a sheet of paper ten events or situations that are distressing and that you are likely to avoid. Then, in the space below, list five of them in ascending order of difficulty, the most distressing and least manageable last. Write the date in "Initial rating date" only, and the amount of distress each situation causes you, on a scale from 1 % to 100 %. Other dates and distress scores will be used after the issues have been targeted. The reviews will be done each session with your therapist.

Remember to brainstorm a list of ten to twelve situations before making your five selections to go into the forms below.

Situation 1: ______________________________

Initial rating date:________ What percentage of distress would this situation cause you?___%
2nd rating date: ________ Percentage of distress that this situation now causes you:_____ %
3rd rating date: ________ Percentage of distress that this situation now causes you:_____ %
4th rating date: ________ Percentage of distress that this situation now causes you:_____ %

Situation 2: ______________________________

Initial rating date:________ What percentage of distress would this situation cause you?___%
2nd rating date: ________ Percentage of distress that this situation now causes you:_____ %
3rd rating date: ________ Percentage of distress that this situation now causes you:_____ %
4th rating date: ________ Percentage of distress that this situation now causes you:_____ %

Situation 3: ______________________________

Initial rating date:________ What percentage of distress would this situation cause you?___%
2nd rating date: ________ Percentage of distress that this situation now causes you:_____ %
3rd rating date: ________ Percentage of distress that this situation now causes you:_____ %
4th rating date: ________ Percentage of distress that this situation now causes you:_____ %

Situation 4: ______________________________

Initial rating date:________ What percentage of distress would this situation cause you?___%
2nd rating date: ________ Percentage of distress that this situation now causes you:_____ %
3rd rating date: ________ Percentage of distress that this situation now causes you:_____ %
4th rating date: ________ Percentage of distress that this situation now causes you:_____ %

Situation 5: ______________________________

Initial rating date:________ What percentage of distress would this situation cause you?___%
2nd rating date:________ Percentage of distress that this situation now causes you:_____ %
3rd rating date: ________ Percentage of distress that this situation now causes you:_____ %
4th rating date: ________ Percentage of distress that this situation now causes you:_____ %

Handout 6.5 Homework Exercises

Exposure Tasks

Follow the instructions from last week and apply them to the situations that you haven't yet addressed. Here is a point-form summary of the task, assuming that you have already practiced exposure to two avoided situations listed on your Exposure Record Sheet. Do your best to address the remaining items this week.

1. Day 1 and Day 2: Use bipolar exposure (i.e., in imagination) for the next situation (e.g. situation 3) on your Exposure Record Sheet.
2. Day 3: Start facing that situation in real life as often as possible; every day if appropriate.
3. Day 3 and Day 4: Meanwhile, start using bipolar exposure for Situation 4 for another two days, while still facing Situation 3 in real life.
4. From Day 5: After two days (4 sessions) of using bipolar exposure with Situation 4, start facing that situation in real life as often as possible.

You are also welcome to add another situation if you can and further decrease avoidance habits this week.

Implementing Partial Sweeping Techniques Track 11 and 12

The audio instructions for the partial sweeping technique are found on track 12 of your audio instructions. You may also listen to the brief introduction on track 11 before your first practice. Remember that each session needs to last 30 minutes; given that advanced scanning tracks last on average 15 minutes, you will need to practice for another 15 minutes of partial sweeping in silence, by yourself. Use Handout 6.6 to record your daily practice for the entire week. Remember also to maintain your awareness of body sensations while remaining equanimous throughout the day. The more training, the better.

Handout 6.6 Daily Record of Mindfulness Meditation Practice

Day	**Date**	**Morning** *(circle)*	**Duration**	**Efficacy rating** *Rate from 1 to 10 how well you noticed distractions and brought your attention back to the body. 1 = not well at all; 10 = extremely well*	**Evening** *(circle)*	**Duration**	**Efficacy rating** *Rate from 1 to 10 how well you noticed distractions and brought your attention back to the body. 1 = not well at all; 10 = extremely well*
Monday		I practiced Yes / No			I practiced Yes / No		
Tuesday		I practiced Yes / No			I practiced Yes / No		
Wednesday		I practiced Yes / No			I practiced Yes / No		
Thursday		I practiced Yes / No			I practiced Yes / No		
Friday		I practiced Yes / No			I practiced Yes / No		
Saturday		I practiced Yes / No			I practiced Yes / No		
Sunday		I practiced Yes / No			I practiced Yes / No		

References

Courtois, C. A., & Ford, J. D. (2009). *Treating complex traumatic stress disorders: Scientific foundations and therapeutic models*. New York: Guilford Press.

Foa, E. B., Keane, T. M., Friedman, M. J., & Cohen, J. A. (2009). *Effective treatments of PTSD: Practice guidelines from the International Society for Traumatic Stress Studies* (2nd ed). New York: Guilford Press.

Grabovac, A. (2015). The stages of insight: Clinical relevance for mindfulness-based interventions. *Mindfulness*, 6, 589–600. doi:10.1007/s12671-014-0294-2

Hazlitt, W. (1837). *Characteristics, in the manner of Rochefoucauld's maxims*. London: Templeman.

Van Der Kolk, B. (2014). *The body keeps the score*. New York: Viking Penguin.

Session 7: Developing Interpersonal Insight

The true wisdom is to be always seasonable, and to change with a good grace in changing circumstances.

—Robert Louis Stevenson, 1907

Introduction

This chapter will guide you in the implementation of Stage 3 of the MiCBT program, the "interpersonal stage," which usually takes two weeks to complete. The purpose of Stage 3 is to extend the use of mindfulness to interpersonal situations and develop interpersonal insight and efficacy. Whereas Stage 1 taught not to react to one's own experience, Stage 3 teaches not to react to another person's reactivity. This week, clients learn to externalize their mindful attention and equanimity toward others. They will also learn non-verbal interpersonal skills and will recognize where responsibility lies when people are agitated or upset and learn to set healthy interpersonal boundaries. In the second week of Stage 3, they will make use of these skills to handle complex and conflictual communication with others and to develop a mindful and assertive way of communicating their experiences and needs. This week's meditation practice is the next advanced body scanning technique, "sweeping en masse." It requires surveying the whole body in a single and increasingly rapid flow of attention while remaining equanimous. This method teaches us not to become attached to pleasant sensations, as we experience firsthand that, subtle or strong, all sensations are impermanent and impersonal by nature.

Checking Client Readiness

Last week, your client was asked to use partial sweeping. Check with them how this went. Were they able to maintain commitment to their twice daily 30-minute practice? Can they scan whole body parts with a single flow of attention? Check

The Clinical Handbook of Mindfulness-integrated Cognitive Behavior Therapy: A Step-by-Step Guide for Therapists, First Edition. Bruno A. Cayoun, Sarah E. Francis, and Alice G. Shires.

Companion website: www.wiley.com/go/Cayoun/Mindfulness-integrated

if they sometimes feel subtle vibrations throughout some parts of the body. Were they able to address the more challenging issues on their SUDS form? Check also how their week was in general, ensuring that they are able to share possible personal concerns that may have arisen during the week. At this stage of the program, they often just want to share their enthusiasm and gratitude for learning these skills, and it is good for us to share their joy.

Delaying the Next Step

If your client cannot feel about 80 % of the body with partial sweeping, then they should continue practicing with partial sweeping for a few more days before starting sweeping en masse. Suggest that they work a little more on the torso if that area needs more work. Although they may not feel a free flow of very subtle tingling sensations across the whole body yet, most people will feel it in separate parts of the body. People tend to feel their face, hands, feet and then limbs more easily than the torso. This is partly because the enervation in interoceptive brain areas of the face, hands and feet is greater, and partly because of a habit of avoiding viscerosomatic sensations during distress, which for some people is a daily occurrence.

If clients have not been able to use exposure with any of the challenges, then it is best to postpone the next step of the program for a few days or a whole week and work with them on finding more realistic exposure targets. This will also give them more time to address the remaining avoided situation(s). The reason for which it is best to be patient is that exposure to interpersonal contexts in Stage 3 is more complex than exposure to situational contexts in Stage 2. Stage 3 exposure will be smoother if they have already gained a sufficient amount of confidence and self-efficacy during Stage 2.

Advanced Scanning: Sweeping en masse

The main purpose of sweeping en masse is to further develop intrapersonal insight and equanimity. As they started to do last week, your client will continue to develop skills in detecting very subtle cues of potential emotions whilst inhibiting their usual reactions. This enables them to accept unsatisfied cravings, which of course arise in the form of body sensations to which they react.

However, we should not underestimate the powerful effects of chasing pleasure. As we discussed in the last session, most people, clients or not, struggle more with remaining equanimous with pleasant sensations than with unpleasant ones. This is perhaps because most people are more accustomed to experiencing discomfort than pleasure. It is usually difficult to be equanimous with the free flow of pleasurable body sensations, and it is tempting to identify with the experience and get carried away with it. We value pleasure greatly, believing that it adds something enriching to our life because of the pleasant sensations we experience. When we are not yet experienced with sweeping en masse and our equanimity is still in its infancy, we easily give in to the craving for fear of missing out. This is the micro level of information processing underlying common cravings in daily life.

When this is associated with fear and poor insight into impermanence, it serves to develop greed. This approach is not a campaign against experiencing pleasant sensations or pleasure in general. However, understanding the mechanisms of the arising of craving for sustained pleasant experiences is important. It can assist clients in identifying the shift from experiencing pleasant sensations to craving more of them, which enables clients to recognize behavioral manifestations of craving more effectively.

Clients also develop a better ability to allow older emotional memories to emerge in consciousness and be defused. Sweeping en masse neutralizes the effects that past emotional reactions, including those related to past traumas, may continue to have in our current life. It allows us to experience the profound reality of mind and body, thoughts and body sensations co-emerging and passing away continuously and very rapidly. The more clients can become aware of impermanence through experiencing change occurring in every moment, the more they are able to see that the change is not personal. The progressive realization that there is no "I" in this profound and continual process of change cultivates in us a sense of "egolessness." This realization is more aligned to the ever-changing nature of our life and encourages detachment from unhelpful beliefs and habits with which we identify. Among these are core schemas maintaining anxiogenic and depressogenic thoughts associated with autobiographical memories. The more detached clients become from these, the freer they are from their past and the less likely it is that they will relapse.

The Method

Sweeping en masse requires your client to survey the entire body in a single and uninterrupted movement of attention, from the top of the head to the tip of the toes, and then from the toes, back to the top of the head. Sometimes, people can be a little confused by the terminology used for this method. As with our own meditation teachers, we find it useful to use metaphors. We can explain that "sweeping en masse means passing our attention without interruption from head to toe, just as water poured on the head flows down the body without interruption," but that the pace of scanning is more like that of honey than that of water when we start.

Your client will probably experience blank spots for the first few days. This provides an opportunity for them to practice equanimity when they can't feel specific parts of the body. Advise them to sweep their attention through the body two or three times simply noticing blank spots as they sweep without interrupting their flow of attention. They can then survey each blank spot separately and equanimously, one at a time. They should patiently keep their attention on the blank spot, equanimously, for up to half a minute and then move to the next blank spot. Sensations might be too subtle to feel during sweeping but be more easily felt when scanning part by part. Once they have surveyed all blank spots separately, they can resume with sweeping en masse for a further two or three body cycles.

Remind your client that it is very important to be committed and determined when practicing, committed to keeping attention moving through the body, while sitting very still and equanimously. It is also useful to reiterate the explanation of co-emergence discussed in the last session: while sweeping through many parts rapidly, we are far more likely to encounter numerous sensations associated with memories.

Chain Extinction

One of the great advantages of the *Vipassana* (insight) approach to mindfulness meditation is its emphasis on "exposure and response prevention" to body sensations, which gives us access to deep-rooted schemas via co-emergence dynamics. When concentration on body sensations and equanimity is maintained while sweeping, and we are "in the zone" so to speak, it is possible to experience a series of memories associated with the same interoceptive signature and hedonic tone. Some of our past events, and the way in which we reacted to them, are called for processing due to their co-emergence with the sensations that we are currently feeling. If we have the wisdom and strength (inhibitory control) to remain equanimous and resist the learned reactions, the emotional load of all these memories will be neutralized. We call this "chain extinction" (Cayoun, 2011) because the typical need to react to a chain of seemingly linked past events is being extinguished. This usually leads to sudden insight into how schemas are maintained and abandoned. Although chain extinction is far more common during intensive meditation retreats because of the associated deeper level of concentration and equanimity, some clients do report experiencing it during the program, especially those who have practiced meditation regularly in the past.

Nonetheless, when it comes to desensitization, there is always a chance that people reinforce a habit instead of extinguishing it. If we experience such a chain of events emerging from memory and we react in the same way that we did in the past, our reactivity, along with the associated schema, is reinforced. Accordingly, clients need to understand the importance and practice of equanimity in order to benefit. A degree of reinforcement is common when people begin to develop the skills in the first few days. So long as the frequency of extinguishment outweighs the frequency of reinforcement, the effort remains worthwhile. As practice becomes more accurate, the frequency of extinguishing responses becomes increasingly greater than that of reinforcing them. As a therapist, it is also important that you are aware of the potential harm that ill-informed or confused clients can do to themselves (Grabovac, 2015; see also Van Gordon, Shonin, & Garcia-Campayo, 2017, for a brief review).

Blissful Experiences

The free flow of sensations can be perceived as a blissful experience and it may be difficult to remain equanimous with it. Bliss is part of human life and can be felt at any age. It is useful, therefore, to discuss it with clients. However, this needs to be discussed without creating expectations that they will definitely experience it, otherwise they begin to crave and the practice becomes a bliss-chasing operation that is bound to disappoint. Your client will not experience bliss if they are not practicing meditation sufficiently and accurately, i.e., with equanimity. If their skills develop sufficiently, however, they may have an experience in which they cannot feel solidity anywhere in the body and thoughts are no longer intrusive. They may feel pleasant warmth and soft tingling throughout the body; sometimes it's just a sense of profound calm and peacefulness while not feeling anything at all in the body. In terms of the four characteristics of sensations discussed in Sessions 3 and 4, the predominant ones are mass (lightness) and fluidity (looseness).

This experience is called "dissolution," or "*bhanga*" in Pali, which was the popular language of the time of the Buddha (Goenka, 2000). It is the fifth out of the 16 "stages of insight" (in Pali *nanas*, pronounced "nyanas"), found in traditional Buddhist psychology records (Namto, 1989). This sense of dissolution can last a few seconds, minutes or even hours if we don't interfere with it by moving, opening our eyes or interrupting the practice. However long it lasts, this experience provides a tangible sense of "egolessness," a sense that there is no permanent "I" that we can associate with our body and fleeting mind. We experience a much deeper sense of what we call "reality" and, if inclined toward personal growth, we reappraise some of our attachments to superficial value. Some people report having a sense that their life is "flowing."

Note that when they are insufficiently informed, some people tend to become attached to the pleasant sensations and others fear the experience of not feeling the body as they are used to. Accordingly, bliss is only context-specific, based on a person's appraisal. Some might crave the bliss that doesn't seem to come back, and soon resent their imagined lack of progress because blank spots or discomfort have returned. Others might worry about losing control and find the fragile onset of blissful dissolution quickly replaced by the experience of fear (moving/ stirring and dense/ constricting sensations). When explaining to clients the well-documented "five hindrances" to mindfulness meditation, craving and aversion clearly apply here (e.g., Brahm, 2006; hart, 1987). Desiring what is pleasant and being averse to what is unpleasant lies at the core of human discomfort and suffering, in life and in meditation practice. It is useful to remind clients that they are learning to develop equanimity with *all* experiences and that attachment to *any* experience during practice will slow their progress. Not wanting what we have and wanting what we don't have during meditation, thinking that things *should* be different, is only a reflection of how we conduct ourselves in daily life. Cultivating egolessness promotes acceptance and alleviates tension.

At this stage of their training, it is more easily understood by clients that the sense of who we are changes moment by moment. It is a dynamic process determined by our current mental state, whether we are conscious of this process or not. It will be helpful for them to understand that accurate mindfulness practice helps us reduce our attachment to a fixed sense of self. If understood, relating to people with egolessness in mind will improve interpersonal communication. If clients can be mindful that others also have an illusory sense of self, then they can integrate the notion that people's emotional reactivity is based on their lack of awareness. Establishing this understanding progressively leads to more interpersonal acceptance and paves the way to the cultivation of empathy, which we will focus on in Stage 4.

Integrating Mindfulness with Interpersonal Skills

A Rationale for Cultivating Interpersonal Mindfulness

The way we affect, and are affected by, our relationships is important for mental health and well-being. Our sense of worthiness is largely dependent on our relationships with others. It is well-established that a healthy social life is important to survival (Dunbar, 1998) and interpersonal issues impact people's levels of anxiety and depression, including suicidality, and promote relapse (Hames, Hagan, & Joiner, 2013). Clients need to understand that their emotions continually affect others. Without interpersonal insight and equanimity, they may maintain unhelpful interpersonal habits. Since people voluntarily or involuntarily share what they feel, being unmotivated or depressed will most likely affect their relationships. Their social network progressively breaks down, as friends and family feel drained in that person's company. Several studies have shown clear beneficial effects of mindfulness in interpersonal communication (Burgoon, Berger, & Waldron, 2000; Huston, Garland, & Farb, 2011; Kramer, 2007). Social neuroscience also shows some of the neural correlates of impoverished social skills (e.g., Lupien et al., 2011; Tottenham et al., 2010), and how mindfulness skills can produce rapid change in these areas through neuroplasticity (Davidson & McEwen, 2012; Holzel et al., 2010).

Stage 3 improves interpersonal insight and reduces interpersonal avoidance, the avoidance of communicating with others when unpleasant emotions are involved. Explain to your client that having learned how reactivity is taking place in themselves during Stage 1 can help their understanding of others' reactivity. In turn, this can make a marked difference in the way they understand their relationships and how they behave with others. For those who have been clinically depressed or anxious, this is an important factor in preventing relapse, because clinical depression and anxiety often damage people's social life and isolate them. This isolation makes depression and anxiety more likely to re-occur.

For most clients, moving from Stage 2 to Stage 3 will only require a simple explanation and validating statement such as, "you worked hard at doing the exposure exercises; congratulations, you're ready for Stage 3...," and then an explanation of why it would be beneficial to increase interpersonal effectiveness. However, with clients whose social or communication skills are poor because of avoidance, it is useful to provide a rationale using the Socratic dialogue approach discussed in previous sessions. This allows the client to be more personally engaged in the process of learning, rather than limit engagement to devotional compliance. Here is a brief example with a socially anxious and depressed client (T = therapist, C = Client:

T: Can you remember situations when you were happy in your life?
C: Not really. I used to be pretty depressed most days.
T: Most days? This means that you were not depressed every single day, right?
C: Yes, I suppose.
T: Try to remember at least one situation when you were actually happy or at least having some fun and you were not alone.
C: Ok, I remember being happier when I was with my previous partner.

T: Can you actually recall a specific time or situation when you were happy then?

C: Yes, I remember being on holiday in the north of the State with the whole family; everyone was having great fun.

T: Did you keep your happiness to yourself, or did you share it with the family?

C: Oh no, I shared it with them... well, I was happy anyway, so they could see that.

T: Do you think they cared as to whether you were happy or not?

C: I think they did.

T: Do you think it affected them?

C: Yeah, we were having fun together.

T: Great. Can you now remember being in a social situation where you were unhappy?

C: Oh yeah, plenty of those! That's why I prefer staying at home.

T: OK, can you remember any situation where people who really cared about you were having fun even though they saw you being unhappy?

C: ...No, I can't remember them not caring about it.

T: Do you mean that your unhappiness affected them too?

C: Yes, it did, for sure. In fact, Jane said she wanted to leave me *because* I looked miserable all the time.

T: So, you're saying that the more unhappy you were, the more it affected people around you?

C: Yeah, big time!

T: Can you see that just as our joy and happiness affect others, our unhappiness does too?

C: Yep, that's pretty right!

T: Do you think that the way we deal with people and the way they deal with us is important for our well-being?

C: Yes, that's why I was staying at home so much before I started this therapy, because being around people affected me too much, but it's not so bad anymore.

T: If I told you that you can use the mindfulness and exposure skills that you have already learned in the past weeks to improve your social and communication skills with people and feel better around them, would you be interested?

C: Yeah, that would be awesome!

T: Great, let me explain how we can start...

Experiential Ownership

Main Purpose

The rationale for Stage 3 of MiCBT is supported by several studies. Research shows that the ability to accurately estimate another person's mental state relies on the capacity to suppress the self-referential activity of the default mode network (DMN), specifically the ventromedial prefrontal cortex (Kang, Lee, Sul, & Kim, 2013). A successful social life is important for the maintenance of mental health (Siegle, 2012). During the first step of Stage 3, we teach a technique called "experiential ownership" to increase the client's awareness of other people's internal experiences and the nature of their reactivity. Based on the clients' deepened interpersonal insight, they learn to apply equanimity to their own experience and prevent reacting to others reactivity.

They also learn to take responsibility for how they feel and relinquish illegitimate responsibility for how others feel, understanding that every person's emotions are made of body sensations produced by that individual's own judgmental thoughts. In other words, clients learn to "own" their experience (though they know that it is impermanent) and "disown" that of others. Although others are responsible for their own feelings, it doesn't mean that clients become heartless and careless. They simply apply equanimity when other people react emotionally and recognize that feeling guilty or fearful of someone else's emotionality may cause unhelpful behaviors in themselves, such as avoidance. They learn to handle complex and conflictual communication by recognizing where responsibility lies when people are agitated or upset and setting healthy interpersonal boundaries. This helps decrease the probability of transference effects and minimize conflicts. Of course, this is a very useful method for therapists too, especially to prevent countertransference with some clients.

Empowerment through Insight and Reappraisal

Importantly, clients also train themselves to observe others' emotional reactivity as a form of suffering, rather than malice, on the basis that suffering is the product of unawareness. They make use of the experiential knowledge developed in Stage 1, when they realized that we react with craving when we feel pleasant sensations and with aversion when sensations are unpleasant; we don't react directly to external triggers. Their mindfulness training is now used to understand the mechanisms underlying others' reactivity as well. Remembering why their life was more difficult before starting this program (at least two months ago), clients understand that if a reactive person received the training that they had, that person might not be as reactive. This helpful reappraisal is empowering and helps prevent taking others' reactivity personally. As will be described a little later, taking full responsibility for what we feel is also a great source of empowerment. The next section explains how these skills are acquired.

Choosing Appropriate Situations for Exposure

For this part of the training, ask your client to think of situations where there is at least the potential for interpersonal tension. Help your client choose situations in which both your client and the other person are likely to feel uncomfortable—this will ensure that your client will be able to practice experiential ownership, as explained below. For example, some tension may occur because of a past conflict, a past habit of avoiding someone, or perhaps because we know that an issue that makes us feel awkward will be raised. Conflictual, or at least uncomfortable, situations could occur when we remind our children that it is bedtime, or when we say "no" to someone we love or otherwise respect, or to someone who is not used to being refused. Of course, we are only referring to pre-existing tensions, as it would be inappropriate to ask clients to *create* tension with someone.

Other possible situations may be events like attending a meeting where two colleagues are in conflict, or eating in the staff area with people who feel tense in each other's company. These situations would be OK to use but those directly involving your client will be best. In any case, the situations that they choose must be ones where they will feel discomfort (unpleasant body sensations) around someone else.

Using Bipolar and in-vivo Exposure

Once they have selected situations for exposure, ask your client to use bipolar exposure and begin to desensitize for two to four sessions by imagining the situation and visualizing worst-case and best-case scenarios while remaining equanimous, as they have learned to do in previous sessions. After the imaginal exposures, they are ready to face the situation in real life (*in vivo*). If they feel confident and don't need to use bipolar exposure before doing the task, then they may face the situation in real life directly. The four steps of Experiential Ownership are outlined below. Ask your client to practice them as often as possible during the coming week, with a minimum of two attempts to ensure that they don't interpret a single and successful attempt as the result of good luck.

The Method

Step 1—Taking responsibility for one's experience.

Instruct your client to scan their body very quickly while being in the tense situation. They will use their sweeping skills to sweep their whole body rapidly, within two or three seconds (hence the relevance and congruence between the scanning skills and interpersonal dynamics in Stage 3). Up to this stage, your client has probably been thinking what most people do when they are not trained in this technique, which is that someone else made them feel uncomfortable. Instead, they need to take note of the sensations they feel while remaining equanimous, and take *full responsibility* for their experience, *owning* the experience but not identifying with the sensations. Again, *their* mind produces the experience; *their* mind is responsible for their experience.

Remind them that body sensations arise because of their thoughts. If your client notices heat in their face, explain that this is produced by their mind as it evaluates the situation. If they experience "butterflies" in the stomach, explain that these are not put there by anyone. This empowers them because they stop believing that someone else is *making them* angry, anxious or sad, and therefore that someone else has such power over them. The ability to "own" their experience, instead of feeling victimized, is also empowering because they realize that they can do something about it. Of course, all this happens within seconds.

Step 2—Recognizing the other's experience.

After they have equanimously scanned their own body, ask your client to focus their attention on "scanning" the other person's body, noticing the other person's body language, including physical movements and posture, the pace, pitch and loudness of their speech, the type of words they use, their skin coloring (they may be flushed in the face), etc. This is still a mindfulness-based technique, so your client's observation must be as much as possible free from value-based judgment (such as "she is so stressed out!"). Though they cannot know another's experience for certain, this careful observation will allow your client to consider the type of body sensations that the other person may be experiencing at that moment. For example, blushing may mean there is heat in the cheeks, stretching of the neck or shoulders may indicate constriction/ denseness in those areas, and slouching or holding their head in their hands may represent a feeling of heaviness. Knowing what these experiences feel like in their own body, your client is able to perceive the other's discomfort. They "scan" the other's body just as they scan their own when they meditate—without judging and reacting, remaining equanimous. The approach to their mindfulness practice remains the same; the only thing that changes is the object of their attention.

Unless they have a clear impairment (e.g., autism spectrum disorder), most people are able to detect the emotions of others because the brain is already equipped with mirror neurons that give us the ability to recognize facial expressions and body language, and imitate the type of sensations that others may be experiencing. Clients learn to focus on the *experience* of the other person, not on the other person's reactivity. They need to perceive the other person's reaction as the manifestation of suffering. The other person is suffering because of four main reasons: (1) they experience body sensations that they resent, (2) they don't have the ability to perceive their own evaluative thoughts that create the co-emerging sensations, (3) they don't have the insight into the mechanisms of interoceptive reinforcement to understand that reacting reinforces their current and future response, and (4) they are unable to take responsibility for their own experience and therefore are unable to feel relieved by the understanding that no-one else is powerful enough to create the emotions they feel. If we summarize this, your client simply witnesses the other person's suffering that is caused by fruitless reactivity and maintained by unawareness.

Step 3—Relinquishing responsibility for the other's experience.

Once your client has understood that we are all responsible for what we feel, they are able to compassionately apply this to the other person without feeling guilty or otherwise emotionally reactive. Having paid attention to the other person's experience with more objectivity, they can accept it and "disown" it at the same time, understanding that others are responsible for the sensations produced in *their* body by *their* own thoughts. Unless there is physical contact, or your client otherwise deliberately contributes to the other person's upset, your client cannot be responsible for it and for the sensations the other person feels. Your client will need to reappraise their usual judgmental view. This reappraisal will enable them to maintain equanimity and clarity of mind and see the problem underlying the tension from different perspectives. This may enable the other person to feel more at ease, or feel heard and respected if a verbal exchange takes place.

Note here that cognitive reappraisal and mindfulness are not mutually exclusive, as is sometimes believed. On the contrary, internally generated cognitive reappraisal, one that emerges from one's own experience, is what we are hoping for in our clients. Unless unwholesome views about themselves, others and the future are replaced with helpful ones, the client will continue to feel and act bound by their conditioned habits.

Step 4—Offering a helpful response.
The ability to feel emotionally safe, owning our experience and disowning (but caring about) that of others, enables us to not take the issue personally and react emotionally. Without fear, anger or guilt, we are more able to look for solutions with clarity, creativity and a willingness to assert our understanding and needs, which your client will learn to do next week. Since clients are not asked to learn and apply assertive communication this week, their response can remain either non-verbal or minimal, using simple respectful and appropriate statements. For example, if your client made a mistake at work and the manager consequently expresses his or her anger, your client would apply the three steps above and then could say: "I am sorry you're feeling angry; I clearly made a mistake and I learned from it, so I can assure you that I will pay more attention and it won't happen again." In the context of a friend or family interaction, an example of a Step 4 response could be: "When I asked you what had happened, I didn't mean for you to become irritated about it; you don't have to answer me now if you don't want to." Of course, this is only an admission of task responsibility and work ethics while remaining equanimous, and does not mean that the client is feeling guilty or submissive. In other situations, your client will be able to respond to an issue in a more comprehensive way, especially once they complete next week's training, combining experiential ownership with assertive communication. Using this approach will assist your client to relate to the reactivity of others mindfully and equanimously.

The Investigator and the Inmate

In a rather uncommon context, the experience of a past client put these skills in perspective. Some time ago, a senior police investigator undertook the MiCBT program to address his PTSD symptoms. Toward the end of the program, he shared the following story (de-identified and reported here with permission). As he needed additional information for an investigation, he went to the local high-security prison to question an incarcerated witness, hoping to clarify his understanding of the case. He knew that the inmate was an angry man and would not easily cooperate, but he didn't expect to be immediately greeted with a tirade of insults. The inmate told the investigator "You're a f...king blue-eyed dog!" and was shocked at the investigator's reply: "But Mr. Smith, I don't have blue eyes." It was a sincere response and he didn't mean to "act smart." He simply practiced experiential ownership and saw the inmate's suffering instead of taking the insult personally. The inmate calmed down for a short while, and the investigator asked the guards to let him calm down in a more comfortable room for about 15 minutes, before resuming the interview. The guards were surprised with this interaction, expecting a more dramatic outcome.

His objectivity about the inmate's experience led to a compassionate act because he *saw* suffering, unaffected by his own sense of self. In case Buddhist psychology interests you, the Buddha explained in his teaching of the "Four Noble Truths" (*Dhammacakkappavattana Sutta*) that when a person realizes that suffering is a universal condition, this realization becomes a "noble truth"—the first noble truth (Bodhi, 2005). This is because this insight allows us to assign people's reactivity to the universal experience of suffering, rather than limiting our perception to a person's ego-based suffering; i.e., a dissatisfaction due to the person's unique personality. Here, the investigator saw "distress as distress," not "Mr. Smith's distress." The realization that everyone suffers because of our attachment to phenomena that are conditional is a great relief and leads to a better ability to accept things the way they are. Consequently, it reduces the amount of "should" in our thoughts, as in "This inmate *should* be more respectful" and allows empathy to grow.

Application with Individual Clients

Session Aim

The aim of this session is to introduce the third stage of the MiCBT program, including the next advanced body scanning method (sweeping en masse) and the first set of mindfulness-based interpersonal skills. Your client will learn to use mindful exposure to selected interpersonal situations and establish sensible interpersonal boundaries through equanimity combined with cognitive reappraisal.

Review Homework and Progress

Your client will have practiced partial sweeping last week. Check on their ability to adhere to a 30-minute practice twice daily and to scan in a sweeping, flowing manner through whole body parts. Is the level of equanimity improving? When your client can feel approximately 80 % of the body, they are ready to proceed with sweeping en masse this week. If they cannot yet feel sensations sufficiently, they should spend a few more days on partial sweeping before proceeding. You will also need to assess whether your client was able to do the exposure tasks using the last of the SUDS items, and provide clarifications if needed. Ask them to re-rate each SUDS item on the Exposure Record Sheet following exposure. Check if the expected subjective units of distress decreased further since last week. If so, they are now ready to learn how to address tense interpersonal situations with equanimity.

Introduce Sweeping en masse

Explain the procedure and rationale for sweeping en masse: (1) further accelerating interoceptive neuroplasticity, (2) further increasing equanimity towards craving and deep-seated patterns of emotional reactivity, and (3) assisting in the experiential ownership method. Discuss the possibility of very pleasant sensations arising and the need for equanimity (see the section on bliss earlier in this chapter). The audio instructions for sweeping en masse are on track 14 and the introduction is on track 13. As in previous weeks, each practice session needs to last 30 minutes. The advanced scanning tracks last about 15 minutes, so they need to practice for another 15 minutes in silence. Ask your client to record their practice times as usual.

Cultivating Interpersonal Mindfulness

Discuss the importance of relationships and effective interpersonal boundaries for psychological well-being. Explain that Stage 3 improves interpersonal insight and reduces awkwardness and avoidance, paving the way to empathy and better relationships.

Introduce Experiential Ownership

Ask your client to select a minimum of two suitable situations to practice experiential ownership. Discuss the four steps of the technique:

1. Sweeping through their body and taking full responsibility for their own experience.
2. Scanning the other person's body and recognizing the other person's experience.
3. Relinquishing responsibility for the other's experience while remaining empathic.
4. Where appropriate, initiating a clear and empathic response.

Ask your client to use bipolar exposure with the chosen interpersonal situation two to four times, and then to face the situation in real life.

Explain Homework Exercises

- Sweeping en masse (tracks 13 and 14).
- Experiential ownership in at least two situations, preceded by bipolar exposure.
- Read Handouts 7.1, 7.2 and 7.3.
- Fill in the Daily Record of Mindfulness Meditation Practice (Handout 7.5).

Application with Groups

Session Aim

The aim of this session is to introduce the third stage of the MiCBT program, including the next advanced body scanning method (sweeping en masse) and the first set of mindfulness-based interpersonal skills. Group participants will learn to use mindful exposure to selected interpersonal situations and establish sensible interpersonal boundaries through equanimity combined with cognitive reappraisal.

Review Homework and Progress

The group will have practiced partial sweeping last week. Check on their ability to adhere to a 30-minute practice twice-daily and to scan in a sweeping, flowing manner through whole body parts. Is their level of equanimity improving? If some are not adhering to regular practice, use Socratic questioning to help them re-commit. When participants can feel approximately 80 % of the body, they are ready to proceed with sweeping en masse this week. If they cannot yet feel sensations sufficiently, they should spend a few more days on partial sweeping before proceeding. You will also need to assess whether all participants were able to do the exposure tasks using the last of the SUDS items, and provide clarifications if needed. Ask them to re-rate each SUDS item on the Exposure Record Sheet following exposure. Check with each participant if their SUDS decreased further since last week. If so, they are now ready to learn how to address tense interpersonal situations with equanimity.

Introduce Sweeping en masse

Explain the procedure and rationale for sweeping en masse: (1) further accelerating interoceptive neuroplasticity, (2) further increasing equanimity towards craving and deep-seated patterns of emotional reactivity, and (3) assisting in the experiential ownership method. Discuss the possibility of very pleasant sensations arising and the need for equanimity (see the section earlier in this chapter). The audio instructions for sweeping en masse are on tracks 13 and 14. As in previous weeks, each practice session needs to last 30 minutes. The advanced scanning tracks last about 15 minutes, so they need to practice for another 15 minutes in silence. Ask participants to record their practice times as usual.

Cultivating Interpersonal Mindfulness

Discuss the importance of relationships and effective interpersonal boundaries for psychological well-being. Explain that Stage 3 improves interpersonal insight and reduces awkwardness and avoidance, paving the way to empathy and better relationships.

Introduce Experiential Ownership

Ask participants to select a minimum of two suitable situations to practice experiential ownership. Discuss the four steps of the technique:

1 Sweeping through their body and taking full responsibility for their own experience.
2 Scanning the other person's body and recognizing the other person's experience.
3 Relinquishing responsibility for the other's experience while remaining empathic.
4 Where appropriate, initiating a clear and empathic response.

Ask participants to use bipolar exposure with the chosen interpersonal situation two to four times, and then to face the situation in real life.

Explain Homework Exercises

- Sweeping en masse (tracks 13 and 14).
- Experiential ownership in at least two situations, preceded by bipolar exposure.
- Read Handouts 7.1, 7.2 and 7.3.
- Fill in the Daily Record of Mindfulness Meditation Practice (Handout 7.5).

Frequently Asked Questions

Question: I advised my client to sweep the whole body two or three times and then scan the body part by part, as for partial sweeping. What I am not sure about is if he should scan part-by-part through the whole body or only where he cannot feel during the sweeping.

Answer: After sweeping the body two or three times, your client needs to pass his attention part by part to survey only the blank spots, separately. The reason for this is to allow the places that we don't feel well to become more obvious. By focusing separately on the spots that are vague or unclear, we give more time for the interoceptive areas of the brain to connect neurons more efficiently to allow greater salience. He needs to stay longer, up to about one minute, on areas where he can't feel anything at all, then sweep again through the whole body two or three times, and again survey any blank spots separately.

Question: This week, one of my clients said that she noticed some sad memories when she was practicing. One of my group participants reported the same thing. Is that common?

Answer: Yes, this is quite common. When we scan rapidly through the body, we feel waves of body sensations. Sometimes, the free flow of sensations we feel can be a memory trigger for a past event when we felt similar sensations. These flashbacks can appear completely random and at other times they can be surprisingly meaningful. Depending on the sensations we feel, we can recall pleasant experiences or moments of fear, sadness or anger. Remember that what is occurring is simply the interaction between thoughts and sensations that she becomes aware of through moving her attention through the body. Tell her to do her best not to identify with these thoughts and sensations and not to react to them. Remind her that she is *not* her thoughts or sensations. Much sadness can be reduced in her current daily life if she remains equanimous with sad memories during meditation.

Question: How do we get out of obsessions during the practice? I have a client who says he is getting stuck with sexual memories with women and sometimes this leads to future fantasies. He is also a little too specific and as a female therapist, I am not sure how much I should allow him to disclose.

Answer: Sexual fantasies are very common, especially when people start with the sweeping methods. This is a "co-emergence effect," where body sensations become a memory cue. If the free flow of pleasant tingling sensations that your client feels while sweeping the body is sufficiently similar to sensations he felt when he was sexually aroused in the past, he can have a flashback associated with the event, however long ago this may have happened. There is a similar effect with drug-related memories. Sometimes, the ecstatic flow of tiny wavelets oscillating throughout the body can be sufficiently similar to a prior drug-induced blissful experience that a memory is triggered.

It would be sensible to first explain this to your client, and then ask him to withdraw his attention from the images and only focus on the sensation that co-emerged in the body during his practice. This needs to become an exposure task in itself in order to prevent the reinforcement of craving. He needs to fixate his attention on the initially pleasurable sensations, equanimously and objectively (with the four interoceptive characteristics in mind—mass, temperature, motion and fluidity). This interoceptive exposure will lead to a change within the first 60 seconds, and will show him how impermanent sensations are, even the most pleasant ones. In your next session with him, you can then use this evidence to help him reappraise other areas of craving that hinder his progress in life.

Question: A client in my group said she was practicing sweeping en masse and her fingers, and sometimes both her hands, lifted up from her lap on their own. She said she found it very weird, but she just continued her practice, and it stopped happening after a few days. She described this as a sort of levitation. Is this normal?

Answer: These experiences are often reported and they usually stop after a while during this program, but in any case, there is no harm in them. Some people report that their feet are trying to lift up on their own. Actually, there are even more remarkable phenomena that happen when our practice is deepened, including changes in mental abilities, but it is important not to make a big deal out of them or clients will start to crave them and practice meditation with unwholesome motivations. Doing so would be futile because we can't develop wholesome skills using unwholesome means. In case it happens again later, ask your client to simply notice her experience with curiosity, equanimity and detachment, keeping in mind that it is impermanent too.

Question: My client did not do any SUDS items for the past 2 weeks. She said she did not have time, but when we discussed what she may work on, there were some important issues; she has been avoiding her friends because she put on weight in the past six months, she can't cope with the unrealistic workload, and she avoids intimacy with her partner.

Answer: It sounds like your client is good at avoiding! Once you have ascertained that the problem was avoidance and not simply logistical challenges, you can gently use some Socratic questioning to encourage her to try this week. You might ask her, "So, what do think stopped you from doing the exposure tasks this week?... In what ways did this stop you?... Looking back, what do you think you could have done differently to overcome this and do the exposure?... How do you think you would feel if you were able to do it and overcome your avoidance...?" If this approach in not fruitful, refer back to the therapy contract and ask if she is still interested in achieving her list of success indicators. Chances are that if she is avoidant, some success indicators are related to avoidance issues, such as "I want to be able to socialize without worrying about how people judge me." Reminding your client why she is undertaking the program is often effective in re-stimulating their motivation.

Question: My client wanted to use a situation with her new boyfriend because she needs him to understand that she wants to get to know him better before they move in together. She has been putting it off and she wants to use the bipolar exposure before doing the experiential ownership technique. Is this OK?

Answer: Yes, she can use bipolar exposure first if she needs to. Next week, she will add some mindful communication skills to improve assertiveness and that may be helpful too.

Question: I have a client who says that one of the interpersonal situations he chose to work on with bipolar exposure did not seem to be so real when he imagined it; it did not bring up the same emotions. He asked if he is doing it right.

Answer: This could be happening for a few reasons. He may have overrated the difficulty of the task and therefore doesn't feel as uncomfortable as he expected when he imagines it. From a brain functionality perspective, he may have developed enough equanimity to easily inhibit the activation of the amygdala. This is what usually happens with this type of meditation. This can neutralize the arousal usually associated with these or other images that produce the same interoceptive signature, so imagining the situation no longer creates sufficient anxiety for the task. If this is the case for him, he can probably practice experiential ownership in this situation without completing bipolar exposure first.

Another possibility is that he may be having trouble really imagining and "getting into" the scenario. This may need more effort as your client could be avoiding feeling the sensations. Alternatively, he could choose another situation with a similar level of distress. He can then undertake this initially avoided item later, with more confidence. It may also be that when your client visualizes the situation, this causes a lot of distress. He may have avoided these distressing sensations regularly in the past by dissociating. If this is the case, then he may not be able to easily feel sensations because he has learned to suppress them. This is likely to change if he continues to practice accurately.

Handout 7.1 Sweeping en masse

Congratulations for making it to Stage 3 of this program, which takes a lot of courage! Stage 3 consists of social skills straining and more advanced meditation practice. This handout discusses only the meditation aspect. You have started sweeping your attention across large areas of your body and have felt some soft tingling or vibrating sensations. You are now ready to learn the third type of advanced scanning method, called sweeping en masse. "En masse" is a French term that means "in the mass" or "whole." We use this term simply because it was translated from old texts in that way and our own teachers use this term too. This technique will train you to let go of unhelpful attachments and cravings. It can also help you deal with strong emotions that come suddenly, like sadness, anger and fear.

The audio instructions for sweeping en masse are on track 14 of the MP3 list. Listen to the brief introductions on track 13 before your first practice. Remember to practice for another 15 minutes of sweeping en masse by yourself after the track finishes, so that each session lasts 30 minutes. As usual, please use the Daily Record of Mindfulness Meditation Practice (Handout 7.5) to record your daily practice for the week.

Sweeping en masse means passing your attention in a continuous way through the whole body without interrupting the "flow" of attention. As usual, you need to scan the body downward, from the top of the head to the tips of the toes and then upward in the same way, from toes to head. Keep surveying the body in this way without interruption two or three times, and then pass your attention separately, part by part, to blank spots or areas that are vague or very faint. It is normal to find blank spots, so keep sweeping and work on those unclear spots later, focusing on them for about half a minute and then to the next blank area. When you have worked on each of the blank spots, go back to passing your attention through the body in a sweeping fashion. As usual, thoughts may interrupt your flow. This is to be expected. Just refocus your attention on the body part that you were scanning, remaining very patient, tolerant and equanimous, and keep strong in your determination to attend to the task!

Developing your Equanimity with Craving

This practice helps you to develop "equanimity," which is the ability to stay calm and cool in any situation. Remember to stay equanimous even when you feel very subtle and pleasant sensations. Because feeling a flow of very pleasant (sometimes blissful) sensations reminds us of past events when we felt the same sensations, our reflex is to have the same attitude. We want more of it; we crave! Unfortunately, this trains your mind to crave the things you cannot have, and this creates dissatisfaction in life. Examples can be a job we used to enjoy and no longer have, a partner we loved and no longer see, successes or pleasures we enjoyed that are now gone, or a lifestyle we can no longer have since we started a family.

After training yourself for a while to not crave for pleasant sensations during your practice, your brain will get the message! It will begin to connect itself according to how you train it during your meditation practice and you will start noticing that you can easily apply this skill in all sorts of life situations. You will be able to notice your cravings as just sensations. For example, if you think, "I really need a coffee (or cigarette, drink, or snack) right now," you will be able to feel the sensations in your body, remain equanimous, and prevent the behavior you don't really want to perform. You will become more familiar with noticing that all sensations change, even the pleasant ones, and so you don't need to take them so seriously or so personally. Wait a while and they will change, like the weather!

It is possible that you feel extremely pleasant sensations during some of your practice sessions. If you are not feeling these yet, it may come with ongoing regular practice. If you are noticing these very pleasant sensations, don't get hooked on them because they are impermanent as well; they will pass away, just as the other sensations do. The nature of all sensations is to arise and pass away.

Handout 7.2 Experiential Ownership

The second aspect of Stage 3 of this program teaches you to apply your mindfulness skills when you are in the company of other people and to interact with them more harmoniously. As you noticed, when you are stressed or someone else is tense, it is not easy to communicate in a fruitful way because everyone is reacting; there is a lack of equanimity in our interactions. In Stage 1 of the program, you learned to not react to your own unpleasant experience. Now, in Stage 3, you are ready to apply your new wisdom in interactions with other people by not to reacting to *their* reactivity. This skill is not only very useful on its own; it will also form a very important foundation for developing assertive communication in our next session. So, the skills you will learn this week are needed for learning the next set of skills.

When you feel an emotion this week, you will continue to notice the thought that may have created it and prevent your own reactivity, but you will also observe other people's reactivity and remain equanimous with it. You will train yourself to see people's reactivity, even toward you, as the expression of their own suffering. Remember your own experiences of reacting emotionally when you are upset; is it pleasant? Are you happy? Nobody is sad, fearful, ashamed or angry, and happy at the same time. We simply suffer and express our dissatisfaction through our reactivity. This is because deep inside, these emotions are made of very unpleasant body sensations, and people who are not trained in mindfulness are reacting to the outside situation in an attempt to feel better. Therefore, if someone reacts emotionally with you, they are actually reacting because of their own sensations, and are assuming that it is your fault that they feel this way. You did that too… we all did! But they are just suffering.

Our reactions often include some habits of avoidance. Unfortunately, avoidance of speaking up, saying no, or avoidance of people altogether is just as destructive as the type of avoidance you have been working with in recent weeks. Research shows that the way we relate to each other matters a lot for our mental health. When it is unskillful, it contributes to depression and anxiety. Adding to this is the fact that people are not aware of what is really happening within themselves when they react to each other. They are not able to look in the right place to increase their awareness and change their habits. That's where the new skills you will learn this week can make a huge difference for you and others.

You will learn to apply your equanimity in moderately challenging situations with people, using a method called "experiential ownership." This will assist you in recognizing where your and their responsibility lies when people are agitated or upset, instead of feeling guilty, fearful or a need to avoid a discussion. You will learn to set healthy boundaries with people's emotions, taking into account that people are responsible for their emotions. So, if we think "she *made* me upset," this is not actually true. As you have learned in your past training, it is the way we *interpret* a situation that causes the sensations in our body, and when the sensations are very unpleasant, we usually react to feel better.

Experiential ownership teaches you to take responsibility for what you feel, and prevent taking responsibility for what others feel, in a kind and sensible way. This means "owning" your experience and "disowning" the experience of others while remaining equanimous. This week, you are invited to practice "experiential ownership" as often as possible, but in at least two different situations, as practicing it only once could lead you to believe that your success was only due to "being lucky this time." Handout 7.3 explains how to practice this method and prepare for it.

Handout 7.3 The Practice of Experiential Ownership

Choosing Appropriate Situations

Now that you know how to use exposure as a technique to learn how to deal differently with situations, you can apply the same approach to dealing differently with people where there may be some tension. Think of some tense situations that you could use. For example, meeting a friend who has said or did something that upset you in the past, having tea or coffee with work colleagues whom you have been avoiding in the staff area, allowing your mother-in-law to visit despite her habit of telling you how to manage your children, or asking your children to get off the computer, tablet or phone, and come to dinner. These must be situations where you and someone else are both likely to feel uncomfortable. It is useful to list some of these on a piece of paper and rate each situation with a percentage of expected distress, just as you did it with other issues in Session 5 when you learned bipolar exposure.

Practicing the Technique

Step 1—Take responsibility for your experience.

While being in the tense situation, scan your body very quickly by sweeping the entire body in two or three seconds – just as you are now practicing sweeping en masse but faster. Notice the sensations while remaining equanimous and take *full responsibility* for your experience. This means taking "ownership" of the experience without assuming that the sensations are you or yours. Keep in mind that nobody gives you "butterflies in your stomach" or makes you feel hot when you feel angry or embarrassed. Fortunately, no one has the power to do that. Even if someone is being rude to you, only your mind can create these experiences, and therefore nothing else but your mind is responsible for them. This alone is reassuring and reduces our reactivity.

Step 2—Recognizing the other's experience.

Now turn your attention to the other person and "scan *their* body," so to speak. Discreetly notice what the person may be feeling. For this, observe things like their posture, breathing, eye contact, level and tone of their voice, speed and choice of words, possible reddening in the face, fidgeting, or a stretching neck or shoulders. Be discreet or it will look a bit strange and they might get irritated. Try very hard not to judge what you see (e.g., "she is so stressed out!"). Instead, just notice it as their brain automatically reacting to the body sensations that they are now feeling. You can guess what kind of body sensations this person is feeling if you observe carefully and do not judge. After all, we generally feel the same when we are reacting. The brain is actually wired to help us with this. There are nerve cells called "mirror neurons" at the center-top frontal part of the brain that let us know what is going on with others. We couldn't have survived socially without being able to recognize when someone is happy or angry. As we become less caught up in our own emotions, we become better at noticing what's going on with others and we can see that they are very uncomfortable when they are emotional; they are suffering. Once you have recognized the suffering of that person, accept it for what it is. See it as a reflection of what we all experience out of unawareness of how things work within ourselves. See it as part of the human condition, rather than "malice" of that person. Indeed, you will be practicing "*the art of seeing suffering*," not evil.

Step 3—Let go of responsibility for the other's experience.
Quickly note that just as nobody gives you "butterflies in your stomach" or makes you feel hot when you feel angry or embarrassed, you cannot do this to that person either. Unless there is physical contact or you otherwise deliberately contribute to that person's upset, you cannot be responsible for it and for the sensations they feel. They alone are responsible for the sensations in their body and you are responsible for yours. Try not to feel upset or guilty because of how they feel.

Step 4—Offer a helpful response.
Of course, not taking responsibility for the other's experience doesn't mean not caring. On the contrary, when you are not affected by strong emotions and remain equanimous, you can stay clear-headed and calm, and there is place in your heart for some compassion. It is difficult to be compassionate if we experience negative emotions. It is your ability to see how others create their own suffering and not identify with their experience and react to their sensations that will lead you to remain kind in the situation, managing it more effectively. This can mean offering simple empathic statements, such as "I just wanted to know what had happened and didn't mean for you to become irritated about it, but you don't have to answer me now if you don't want to" or "I am sorry that you feel this way, I just asked you to go to bed because I care about you." We will work on assertive communication next week, so keep your responses simple this week.

Summary of the Steps

1 Scan your body quickly; notice and accept (own) whatever sensations you are feeling.
2 "Scan" the other person's body and guess the type of sensations they may be having. (If you feel that the other person is so angry that they might become very aggressive then it may be wise to remove yourself from the situation and let them calm down.)
3 Remind yourself that you are not responsible for the other person's feelings; only they can create body sensations in their body. Accept that they are

having a difficult experience and that their unpleasant sensations are the consequence of their thoughts.

4 Make a simple comment if you think that it is appropriate. It may be better to say nothing while the other person's sensations begin to settle.

Using Bipolar Exposure as Preparation

Now use the same bipolar exposure method that we used before: imagining the situation and think of the worst-case scenarios first, take a short break and then the best-case scenarios. Remain equanimous throughout the exercise. Do at least two sessions of bipolar exposure (you may need more for more intense issues) and then face the situation in real life, as explained earlier. See if you can address several situations during the week. You may find that you can tackle some situations without the exposure beforehand.

Handout 7.4 Homework Exercises

1 Sweeping en masse practice twice daily.
2 List a number of situations where you could feel tense around a person. Choose some that you could use for your exposure this week and list them in order of distress levels.
3 Practice experiential ownership in a minimum of two situations this week.
4 Use bipolar exposure two to four times before facing the most difficult situation in real life. You may not need bipolar exposure with the gentler situations.
5 Fill in the Daily Record of Mindfulness Meditation practice (Handout 7.5).

Handout 7.5 Daily Record of Mindfulness Meditation Practice

Day	Date	Morning *(circle)*	Duration	**Efficacy rating** *Rate from 1 to 10 how well you noticed distractions and brought your attention back to the body. 1 = not well at all; 10 = extremely well*	Evening *(circle)*	Duration	**Efficacy rating** *Rate from 1 to 10 how well you noticed distractions and brought your attention back to the body. 1 = not well at all; 10 = extremely well*
Monday		I practiced Yes / No			I practiced Yes / No		
Tuesday		I practiced Yes / No			I practiced Yes / No		
Wednesday		I practiced Yes / No			I practiced Yes / No		
Thursday		I practiced Yes / No			I practiced Yes / No		
Friday		I practiced Yes / No			I practiced Yes / No		
Saturday		I practiced Yes / No			I practiced Yes / No		
Sunday		I practiced Yes / No			I practiced Yes / No		

References

Bodhi, B. (2005). *In the Buddha's words: An anthology of discourses from the Pali Canon.* Boston, MA: Wisdom Publications.

Brahm, A. (2006). *Mindfulness, bliss, and beyond: A meditator's handbook.* Boston, MA: Wisdom Publications.

Burgoon, J. K., Berger, C. R., & Waldron, V. R. (2000). Mindfulness and interpersonal communication. *Journal of Social Issues*, 56, 105–127.

Cayoun, B. A. (2011). *Mindfulness-integrated CBT: Principles and practice.* Chichester, UK: Wiley.

Davidson, R. J. & McEwen, B. S. (2012). Social influences on neuroplasticity: Stress and interventions to promote well-being. *Nature Neuroscience*, 15, 689–695.

Dunbar, R. I. M. (1998). The social brain hypothesis. *Evolutionary Anthropology*, 6, 178–190.

Goenka, S. N. (2000). *The discourse summaries.* Onalaska, WA: Vipassana Research Publications.

Grabovac, A. (2015). The stages of insight: Clinical relevance for mindfulness-based interventions. *Mindfulness*, 6, 589–600. doi:10.1007/s12671-014-0294-2

Hames, J. L., Hagan, C. R., & Joiner, T. E. (2013). Interpersonal processes in depression. *Annual Review of Clinical Psychology*, 9, 355–377.

Hart, W. (1987). *The art of living: Vipassana meditation as taught by S. N. Goenka.* New York: Harper Collins.

Holzel, B. K., Carmody, J., Evans, K., et al. (2011). Stress reduction correlates with structural changes in the amygdala. *Social Cognitive and Affective Neuroscience*, 5, 11–17.

Huston, D., Garland, E. L., & Farb, N. A. S. (2011). Mechanisms of mindfulness in communication training. *Journal of Applied Communication Research*, 39, 406–421.

Kang, P., Lee, J., Sul, S., & Kim, H. (2013). Dorsomedial prefrontal cortex activity predicts the accuracy in estimating others' preferences. *Frontiers in Human Neuroscience*, 7, 686. doi:10.3389/fnhum.2013.00686

Kramer, G. (2007). *Insight Dialogue: The interpersonal path to freedom.* Boston, MA: Shambhala.

Lacoboni, M. (2009). Imitation, empathy, and mirror neurons. *Annual Review of Psychology*, 60, 653–670.

Lupien, S. J., Parent, S., Evans, A. C., et al. (2011). Larger amygdala but no change in hippocampal volume in 10-year-old children exposed to maternal depressive symptomatology since birth. *Proceedings of the National Academy of Sciences of the USA*, 108, 14324–14329.

Namto, S. S. (1989). *Insight meditation: Practical steps to ultimate truth.* Aurora, CO: Vipassana Dhura Meditation Society. See also a 2011 revised edition at http://www.vipassanadhura.com/PDF/practicalsteps.pdf

Siegel, D. J. (2012). *The developing mind: How relationships and the brain interact to shape who we are* (2nd ed.). New York: Guilford Press.

Stevenson, R. L. (1907). *Crabbed Age and Youth: And other essays.* Maine: Thomas Mosher.

Van Gordon, W., Shonin, E., & Garcia-Campayo, J. (2017). Are there adverse effects associated with mindfulness? *Australian and New Zealand Journal of Psychiatry*, 51, 977–979. doi:10.1177/0004867417716309

Session 8: Mindful Communication Skills

The most important single ingredient in the formula of success is knowing how to get along with people.

—Theodore Roosevelt

Introduction

This chapter provides guidance to implement the second part of Stage 3, during which you will teach your client to apply their mindfulness skills to improve interpersonal communication. Last week, your client learned to take responsibility for their own experience while being mindful of the experiences of others; their nonverbal signals. This week, your client will enhance their verbal communication skills. They will learn to overlay their new ability to "see others' suffering" with a tolerant and assertive verbal approach to help address challenging issues that cause mutual discomfort. Clients learn to be confident enough to express their point of view and needs, while feeling less anxious, guilty, ashamed or otherwise uncomfortable. Developing mindful communication skills will enable your client to learn that the message must be louder than the messenger, and not the other way around. This week, they also learn a deeper way of scanning the body, "transversal scanning," which provides a means of neutralizing and extinguishing more established emotional complexes and unhelpful habits.

Checking Client Readiness

Your client has now completed a week of practicing sweeping en masse. Check how their practice went. Check if your client can attend to sensations across the whole body in a single flow, feeling subtle sensations, like tingling vibrations, through the whole body. If this is the case, are they able to be equanimous to this

The Clinical Handbook of Mindfulness-integrated Cognitive Behavior Therapy: A Step-by-Step Guide for Therapists, First Edition. Bruno A. Cayoun, Sarah E. Francis, and Alice G. Shires.

Companion website: www.wiley.com/go/Cayoun/Mindfulness-integrated

pleasant experience? Perhaps they have started to notice that life appears to be a little easier. It is useful to remind them that the brain that meditates is also the brain that functions in daily life, and therefore our experience of meditation either reflects or determines our experience in daily life; one context predicts the other, due to neuroplasticity. If their meditative practice is running more smoothly, their experience of daily life will also seem smoother, and vice-versa. Check also if they were able to practice the experiential ownership task and ask how this went. Were they better able to withstand tense situations with others? Did they remain equanimous despite the temptation to escape or argue?

Most importantly, could they perceive others' suffering (arousal, withdrawal, etc.) for what it is—just suffering? In other words, could they perceive someone's reactivity as a reflection of *universal* suffering due to unawareness, rather than judging it and attributing it to the person with whom they interacted? To the extent that they could, they practiced "egolessness," which in turn promotes acceptance and empathy. Do your best to validate even "little drops" of such mental qualities. These drops are like seeds that your validation nourishes; it is often the only nourishment they receive.

Delaying the Next Step

If your client has not been able to do enough practice using the sweeping method, they will need to continue practicing it for a few more days, or even for a week if necessary. It is not expected that your client will feel a free flow of sensations each time they practice; feeling it only some of the time would be quite common. These experiences, like all others, are impermanent and should be observed with equanimity. This is worth discussing with clients. If sweeping en masse has been practiced and they can occasionally feel the entire body in a single flow of attention, they can proceed with the next step and begin practicing transversal scanning.

Regarding the experiential ownership task, sometimes clients get a little stuck with the logistics and report having had no opportunity to find tense situations. This can be genuine, but it can also be motivated by avoidance, especially if they initially presented with social anxiety or an avoidant trait. We need to combine our patience and tolerance with an assertive stance about the task, or we may unintentionally encourage their avoidance. Remember that the way we teach these skills also serves as modeling and influences clients; our intervention is not limited to task performance, so that if we avoid tackling their avoidance, *we* model avoidance.

If your client has not yet been able to practice experiential ownership, then it may be preferable to postpone the next exercise, which involves assertive communication. The reason for this is that it is preferable that they first contextualize their equanimity in tense interpersonal situations before adding assertive communication, which would not be effective if they lack equanimity.

Advanced Scanning: Transversal Scanning

The scanning techniques that are taught in MiCBT are sequenced in such a way that as brain plasticity develops and new connections are established, clients naturally begin to feel more subtle sensations and can move on to practice the next advanced method. When clients have learned a particular scanning method, they often find it quite natural to proceed to the next method without being aware of it. As we ask them to start the practice of a more advanced method, they often report having already started doing it "intuitively" or "naturally." Ask your client to think back to the start of the program when they began part-by-part body scanning. Perhaps they observed that they could notice sensations bilaterally even before they moved on to symmetrical scanning. Perhaps they were able to notice flowing, tingling sensations before they had moved to sweeping methods. They may also have been able to feel sensations internally before they started transversal scanning. It is a very "organic" process. We tell the brain what to do and wait till it tells us when it is ready to move on. Mind and brain work harmoniously, just as in a good teacher–student relationship.

Transversal scanning enables deeper levels of awareness of more subtle sensations and associated thoughts while equanimity continues to increase. This gives access to all sorts of pleasant and unpleasant memories, and to schemas that may have been unhelpful for some time. With this practice, over time, no stone should remain unturned; the emotional load attached to accumulated schemas becomes progressively neutralized. The deeper levels of equanimity that develop with transversal scanning enable us to face interpersonal difficulties calmly and mindfully, and address them with clear comprehension and assertive communication.

The Method

This scanning method requires passing our attention transversally "through" the body, beginning horizontally from the front to the back of the body, and then from back to front, focusing on a small area of about 8 centimeters in diameter at a time, starting with the head and moving systematically down the body. We start at the forehead and scan slowly through the interior of the head toward the back of the head, feeling (not imagining or visualizing) as many sensations as possible on the way. Once we reach the back of the head, we do the same with an adjacent area of the face of about 8 centimeters diameter and move attention from the front through to the back of the head in the same way, feeling as many sensations as possible on the way. We survey the entire head area in this way.

Once the whole face has been surveyed from front to back, we scan the *same area* from the back of the head through to the face, in the same way. When the entire head has been surveyed (front to back and back to front), we continue to the next area, the neck, first moving attention carefully from the throat through to the back of the neck, and then returning from the back of the neck to the throat, noticing all the sensations on the way while remaining equanimous. The whole body is scanned in the same way down toward the toes, continuing with the shoulders, arms and hands, the torso and then the legs, feet and toes. Once the whole body has been surveyed transversally we scan back up the body, from the toes to the head to complete the cycle.

Remind your client to adopt a non-judgmental and equanimous attitude while scanning, remaining aware that each sensation is an indication of change. They need to understand that change is continual and impersonal, and not something to possess or identify with; what is changing is not "theirs." It is worth remembering that we are not scanning through muscles and organs, we are activating neural pathways in the somatosensory and insular cortices, areas where the body is represented, allowing body sensations to be felt. This is exemplified in amputees who can still feel pain "in" an amputated limb. This is described in the literature as "phantom limb syndrome" (Ramachandran & Blakeslee, 1998). Even though the limb has been removed (e.g., after an accident), the brain cells associated with feeling this part of the body are still functioning, producing nociceptive (pain) signals although the body part is no longer there. The sensations are felt as our attention to a body part activates somatosensory and insular brain areas (see Menon & Uddin, 2010 and Uddin, 2014, for more information on this topic).

Assertive Communication

Purpose of Integrating Assertiveness

According to *Dorland's Medical Dictionary* (Dorland, 2011), assertiveness is "a form of behavior characterized by a confident declaration or affirmation of a statement without need of proof; this affirms the person's rights or point of view without either aggressively threatening the rights of another (assuming a position of dominance) or submissively permitting another to ignore or deny one's rights or point of view." There is a clear relationship between poor assertiveness and depression—the less assertive a person is, the more depressed they are likely to be—and it has been shown that someone's level of assertiveness is a better predictor of depression than their history of depressive episodes (Ball et al. 1994). It appears that those with depression tend to fear rejection and are more likely to be non-assertive and submissive (Pearson et al. 2010). Assertiveness training is used to reduce avoidance, as well as aggression in anger management programs (Huey & Rank 1984). There is a significant body of evidence that assertiveness decreases distress in a range of situations (McFall & Twentyman, 1973, Lee & Swanston Crockett, 1994).

The influence of mindfulness skills in supporting effective communication has also been well documented (Alkoby, Halperin, Tarrasch, & Levit-Binnun, 2017; Jones & Hansen, 2015), but meditation alone does not teach verbal communication. If your client lacks assertiveness (i.e., is overly passive, aggressive, pleasing, and insufficiently truthful with others) and is a poor verbal communicator, the probability of relapse into depression and related anxiety increases. Here is another example of why the integration of mindfulness and CBT is more advantageous than mindfulness meditation alone in mental health contexts. It also reminds us that a transdiagnostic method ought to address both the micro (thoughts and emotions) and macro (interpersonal) factors that precipitate, reinforce and maintain a disorder.

At this stage of the program, your client has already learned to accept and take full responsibility for how they feel and to not react to others' reactions. They are now more able to understand how others are feeling and respect their discomfort, but they have not yet integrated skillful verbal communication. Assertiveness involves being able to say what we believe, need or want, clearly and non-reactively. Someone who is assertive behaves confidently and is not frightened to express what they need to say. They ensure that others don't ignore their need or point of view. They tend to focus on the problem being discussed, rather than on the person with whom they discuss it. Before discussing why assertiveness is important for psychological well-being with your client, it is useful to explain why it can be difficult to be assertive.

Reasons for Lack of Assertiveness

One reason for poor assertiveness is a lack of verbal and emotion-regulation skills. Many people we see in therapy have not had the opportunity to learn to communicate skillfully. They are likely to struggle to be assertive without awareness and equanimity because they tend to react in order to manage their discomfort. Another reason for lacking assertiveness is overidentification with our views. This creates attitudes and emotional states that are dissonant with assertiveness; we may be conceited and forceful, defeated and fearful, or unworthy and unvalued. For example, we may hold onto the belief that if someone had committed to do something, they *should* do it, and if they don't, then we are entitled to be angry. Clients benefit from understanding that the more they think they are right (and therefore someone else is wrong), the worse they feel when their view is invalidated by others, even if they are actually "right" about an issue. It is uncommon to come across people who are aware that *being right doesn't make us happy*. It is useful to discuss this with your client, in terms of attachment to our sense of self. Most people, even those with a passive style, tend to internally assume "I" am right, this is "my" view, and therefore this view is part of "me." Over-identifying with *any* view ("right" or "wrong") leads to the following subconscious assumption: "Since this view is *mine*, and therefore a part of *me*, whoever invalidates this view also invalidates me." As you can imagine, a child growing up in an invalidating or dismissive environment is likely to accumulate exposure to such assumptions and develop schemas of worthlessness.

When it comes to communication styles and associated personality traits, we cannot overlook the importance of psychodynamic issues and the schemas that people have adopted during childhood (e.g., "a worthy father and husband should be an alpha male and a worthy mother and wife should be docile and submissive"). While this is acknowledged and considered in MiCBT, MiCBT therapists don't limit their intervention to a mere understanding of cognitive schemas and are most interested in the dynamics of the present moment. Such focus is congruent with the MiCBT theoretical framework, i.e., the co-emergence model of reinforcement (see Chapter 2).

The co-emergence model that you covered with your client in Session 3 makes it clear: the more we think that our view about an issue is *personally* important, the more intense the body sensations that co-emerge with this view will be. When we apply this to assertiveness, someone's belief that they should not be assertive because it might upset people is only held by its co-emerging unpleasant body sensations, which are perceived as a threat. By association, being assertive becomes the threat, because of how it appears to create visceral sensations. Recent behavioral and brain studies provide supportive evidence for this conceptualization, showing that the experience of body sensations activates approach-avoidance behavior independently of what we may be thinking consciously (Krieglmeyer, Deutch, De Houwer, & De Raedt, 2010; Rogers-Carter et al., 2018). By not asserting their needs, this person avoids discomfort. However entrenched this avoidance may be, it is still reliant on a learned reaction to body sensations, and *all things learned can be unlearned.*

Case-conceptualizing Communication Experience

It is useful to case-conceptualize one of your client's anticipated or past instances of poor assertive communication using the Diary of Reactive Habits (see Handout 3.1). You can insert the trigger (the situation), their perceptual experience of the trigger (how they sensed the situation), their appraisal of it (their evaluation and derived meaning/schema), how it made or makes them feel to think that way (what kind of co-emerging sensations arose and where), and what they did to feel relieved (their aversive reaction, such as venting or avoiding). This helps to bring their attention to the present and to feel empowered by the possibility of developing skills, rather than blaming their woes on their past or personality.

For example, imagine that you have a female client with low sense of self-worth, low self-confidence, a passive style of communication and a tendency to feel victimized. Instead of assuming that she cannot stand up to her forceful partner on the basis that she had a forceful and intimidating father whom she feared all her life, case conceptualization through the co-emergence model could show her that the only thing she truly fears is the configuration of body sensations (the "fear signature"). This would allow her to understand that this can be resolved through training (desensitization), to take responsibility for change, and to feel empowered by the process.

For a message to be effectively communicated, it needs to carry as little emotional tone as possible because people will focus on the emotion and may not focus clearly on the message. If a message is being communicated in an angry or otherwise forceful manner, the listener may react to the anger and not respond to the actual message. If "the messenger is louder than the message," so to speak, the listener can't hear the message. They experience more intense and unpleasant body sensations and focus on the person who appears to trigger them (unaware that they are triggered by their own evaluation), and neglect or miss the message because their evaluation of the message produces weaker sensations. Body sensations that are felt more strongly will attract most attention (see Uddin, 2014, for a review of the brain's "salience network"). The message is more likely to be heard and understood if it is delivered in a non-reactive and more rational way. In other words, *the message must be louder than the messenger.*

When we take time to objectively understand the other's situation or point of view, we can appraise the situation *as it is*, rather than how we *think* it is. Your client has been developing this insight since the last session, with the practice of experiential ownership skills. Whilst realizing the "rightness" or "wrongness" of a situation, they will now be more able to discuss it calmly, equanimously and with clarity. Mindful assertiveness will assist your client to change their avoidant or forceful communication and preserve or enhance social interactions. Just a note on terminology here: by "mindful assertiveness," we mean an assertive stance that not only involves keeping our attention in the present moment during communication, but *also* involves equanimity and egolessness.

Mindful Assertiveness

Basic Principles

This week, your client will be combining the experiential ownership exercise (Session 7) with assertive verbal communication. There are three elements that your client will be integrating:

(1) awareness of, and equanimity toward, their inner experience while taking full responsibility for it, (2) noticing *and accepting* signs of distress and reactivity in the other person without blaming the person or feeling guilty about it, and (3) using short, clear statements that are not judgmental or emotional about their own experience and needs, *without reacting to the other person's reactivity*. This can be thought of as "interpersonal equanimity." This session focuses on this third element for which we teach seven key assertive statements.

Seven Key Assertive Statements

Your client needs to consider an appropriate time and conducive context to engage in an assertive conversation. It may be best to simply ask the other person when would be a good time to have a talk, or, in a work situation, to make an appointment. It will be helpful if the other person is not rushed, distracted or irritated because your client interrupted them. It is important that your client requests and gains the other's attention and can choose to reward it upfront to engage the other person.

Introduce this structured approach to your client:

1 State the *fact*.
2 State how you *feel* (using an "I" statement).
3 State how/what you *think* (using an "I" statement).
4 State your possible error in judgment.
5 State what you *want*.
6 Provide reward.
7 Negotiate a win–win solution if there is no cooperation.

1. Stating the facts.

A fact is what *actually* happened or is happening; it is not a judgmental statement. For example, "You never do the washing up," is only a fact if the other person *never* does the washing up. Therefore, it is best to avoid using *never* and *always*, as they are absolute and are often exaggerations of something that happens *rarely* or *often*. Misinterpretations also lead the listener to feel judged, and the messenger is bound to overshadow the message, if it is heard at all. A more accurate statement may be, "Although we agreed that you would do the washing up if I cooked, this week you have only washed up once." This may help with communication, as the other person can't argue with facts. Remind your client that facts are facts!

2. Stating how we feel.

We need to discern our *personal* experience from the other's intention and behavior. The other person may then gain some sense of our felt experience (their mirror neurons may be activated) and they may be able to understand our experience better. We need to verbally *describe our emotional experience non-emotionally*, using "I" statements. For example, "I feel angry when I have to do the washing up while I'm so exhausted and you are watching TV" instead of "It's not fair that you expect me to do all the work." Such accusatory language will make the other person feel either guilty or angry, instead of allowing them to think about the impact of their behavior on others. By remaining equanimous, we can manage the conversation more productively. Remind your client that they have the right to feel what they do!

3. Stating the meaning/belief.

The next step is to say why we feel the way we do. The co-emergence model of reinforcement shows that it is our thoughts and beliefs (the way we interpret a situation) that cause body sensations to co-emerge and eventually become emotions; it is *not* the situation or a person. So, the statements we use need to explain to the other person *what belief* leads us to feel the way we do. This clearly states our responsibility in feeling what we do, which is more accurate and prevents the other person from feeling judged and blamed. For example, note the difference between, "I am angry *because you ask me to do the washing* up late at night and you don't care that I am exhausted," and "When you ask me to do the washing up late at night, I feel angry *because it means to me* that you don't care that I am exhausted." We are explaining how we are feeling because of what we believe (i.e., co-emergence), instead of attributing our feeling to the other person's behavior. This gives us the opportunity to take responsibility for our error in judgment in the next step. Remind your client that they have the right to think the way they do!

4. Acknowledging our errors.

We make sense of situations based on many filters such as beliefs, culture, values and past experiences. However, the other person does not have the same filters and therefore may interpret the situation very differently to us. Therefore, it is important to acknowledge that our evaluation of the situation may be biased and inaccurate. For example, we may say "This is my understanding, but I may be wrong and you might care a lot," or "…Look, that's what I think, but this could be incorrect because I don't really know your motivation." In this case, we are equanimous about being possibly mistaken. Nonetheless, we immediately move on to Step 5 to state what we want. Remind your client that they have the right to misunderstand things and make mistakes!

5. Stating what we want.

At this point, we can safely state what we reasonably need and want. We might not get what we want, especially when it is as unrealistic as wanting to be loved by everyone, or wanting our meat-loving partner to be vegetarian. It doesn't harm others or infringe on their rights to simply want something we value and express it respectfully. Note that it is more productive to ask for what we *do want* than what we *don't want*, simply because saying what we don't like or want does not always say what we actually want. For example, in "I don't want you to watch TV after dinner while I am washing up," the statement could be interpreted in several ways, none of which may yield the desired response by the listener. In contrast, the statement, "I want you to help me wash up after dinner before going to watch TV" clearly states our need. Even though they might not get it, remind your client that they have the right to express what they want.

6. Providing reward.
At this point, we are ready to thank the other person for their cooperation. A reward may be a thank you statement, a smile or a hug if the person is someone close. In this way, we are expressing gratitude and positively reinforcing future cooperation. If the person refuses to cooperate, we don't reward their response, but we can still thank them for making time to listen and for allowing us to say what we needed without interfering. For example, we may say "I was hoping that this would be acceptable to you, but thank you at least for listening; I hope you now understand how I feel and what I'd like."

7. Win–win solutions.
It is a reality that assertive negotiations do not always work. People will not always be prepared to change and meet the needs of others. It is important not to become passive and give in, especially if the matter is important to us. Accordingly, we need to find a "win–win solution." It will be most successful if your client can remain equanimous during this stage. The aim is to find a solution that is a compromise; for example, "That's unfortunate, but I am confident that if we both make an effort, we can find a good compromise; what do you think?" or "Thanks for listening darling, but this is not going to work for me. I care about you and me equally, so we need to be a little creative and make sure that neither of us feels more disadvantaged than the other. Can you help me with this?"

Putting it Together

It useful to go over each statement using one of your client's examples of an interaction in which their assertiveness was poor, and role-playing (swapping roles) a more assertive interaction.

Here is an example with the scenario that we have been using above: John and Sue live together and both work long hours. When they moved in together, they agreed that John would do all the cooking because he enjoys it and Sue would do the washing up after the meal. But recently, Sue has been working even longer hours and is exhausted, and she has not been washing up. This means that in the morning the kitchen is messy when they are trying to make breakfast and prepare lunches.

1 *Fact*: Sue, I know you've been working really hard and you're tired in the evenings but I noticed that in the last ten days you have washed up only twice.
2 *Feeling*: I feel angry when I have to do the washing up while I am so exhausted and you are watching TV.

3 *Meaning*: When you ask me to do the washing up late at night, I feel angry because it means to me that you don't care that I am exhausted.
4 *Error*: This is what my understanding is, but I may be wrong and you might care a lot.
5 *Want*: I want you to help me wash up after dinner before watching TV.
6 *Reward*: I was hoping that this would be acceptable to you, but thank you at least for listening; I hope you now understand how I feel and what I'd like.
7 *Negotiate*: That's unfortunate but I am confident that if we both make an effort, we can find a good compromise; what do you think?

Mindful Assertiveness and the Co-emergence Model

Being mindfully assertive in MiCBT means that the skillset used is congruent with the principles of the co-emergence model, discussed in Chapter 2, and which we explained to clients during Session 3.

Session 8, Figure 1 demonstrates the good fit between the procedure mentioned above and the underpinning theoretical framework.

Note that we follow a slightly different order when we use the seven statements of assertiveness, as indicated by the arrows of the diagram indicating a different sequence between components. Co-emergent Interoception is evoked in Step 3, and Evaluation in Step 4, because we express *how* we feel before expressing *why* we feel the way we do.

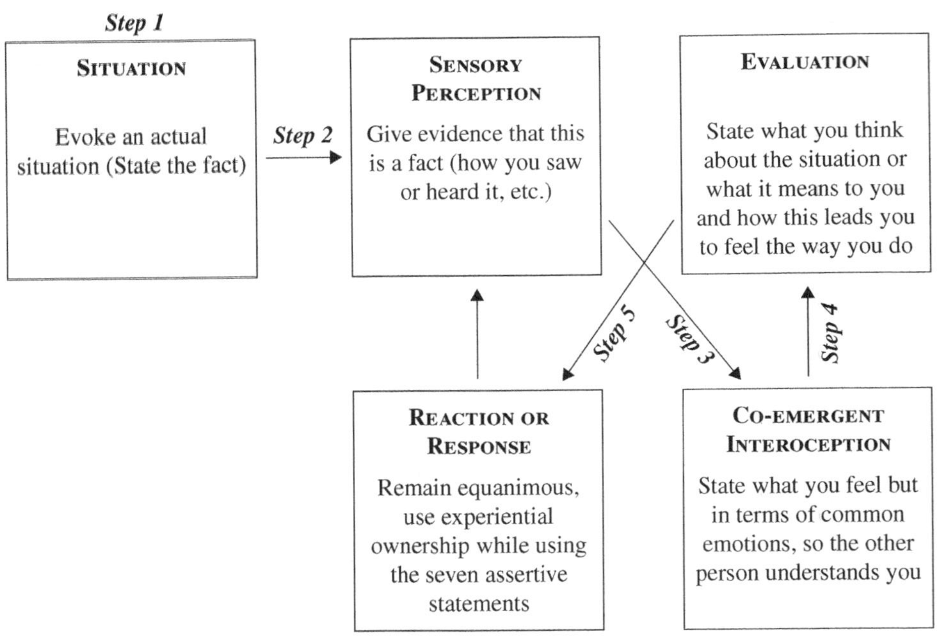

Session 8, Figure 1 Congruence between steps of assertive communication and the co-emergence model of reinforcement.

Application with Individual Clients

Session Aim

The aim of this session is to introduce the next method of advanced body scanning, (transversal scanning) and the second part of Stage 3, in which your client will enhance their verbal communication skills. They will learn to use mindful assertiveness to help address challenging interpersonal issues and become confident enough to express their point of view and needs effectively, while preserving good relationships with others.

Review Homework and Progress

Check on how your client's sweeping en masse went last week. Could they feel the flow of subtle sensations? Did they remain equanimous while feeling pleasant sensations? Discuss how exposure went and review (and re-rate) their SUDS scores on their Exposure Record Sheet. Have their scores further decreased? Validate the client's effort and successes. Was your client able to address the interpersonal issues they identified after the last session? Were they able to perform the experiential ownership task? Could they notice how others appeared to be feeling during tense interactions and could they remain non-judgmental and equanimous? Could they "see suffering" as a universal mechanism maintained by unawareness? If your client has completed all the tasks set last week and can occasionally feel free-flowing sensations in most body parts, they are ready to start transversal scanning.

Introduce Transversal Scanning

Explain the procedure and rationale for transversal scanning: feeling sensations internally and increasing equanimity with deeper levels of awareness of thoughts and sensations to neutralize enduring schema-related emotions in contexts of interpersonal conflicts, where psychodynamic issues are likely to be triggered. Explain that this scanning method requires passing attention "through" the body horizontally, focusing on small (8 centimeter in diameter) areas at a time and moving attention from the front to the back of the body, and returning from the back to the front, starting with the head, the neck, etc., moving down toward the toes systematically, and then back up toward the top of the head. The audio instructions are on tracks 15 and 16. The practice should last 30 minutes in total. Ask your client to record their practice times, as usual.

Developing Mindful Assertiveness

Assertiveness involves being able to express what we believe or want, confidently without passivity or hostility. Ask your client to select at least two situations in which to practice. Discuss the seven steps:

1. State the fact.
2. State how you feel (using an "I" statement).
3. State what you believe (using an "I" statement).
4. State your possible error in judgment.
5. State what you want.
6. Provide reward.
7. Negotiate a win–win solution if there is no cooperation.

Explain Homework Exercises

- Twice daily practice of transversal scanning (audio tracks 15 and 16).
- Choose a minimum of two situations to practice mindful assertiveness; expressing needs assertively, in a considerate, respectful and equanimous way. Participants may already have items listed on their Exposure Record Sheet that they can use.
- Bipolar exposure may be used prior to in-vivo exposure with more challenging situations.
- Read Handouts 8.1 and 8.2.
- Fill in the Daily Record of Mindfulness Meditation Practice (Handout 8.3).

Applications with Groups

Session Aim

The aim of this session is to introduce the next method of advanced body scanning, (transversal scanning) and the second part of Stage 3, in which participants will enhance their verbal communication skills. They will learn to use mindful assertiveness to help address challenging interpersonal issues and become confident enough to express their point of view and needs effectively, while preserving good relationships with others.

Review Homework and Progress

Check how the participants' practice of sweeping en masse went last week. Could they feel a flow of subtle sensations while remaining equanimous? Discuss how exposure went and review (and ask them to re-rate) their SUDS scores on their Exposure Record Sheet. Have their scores further decreased? Validate effort and successes. Were they able to address the interpersonal issues that they identified after the last session? Check if they were able to perform the experiential ownership task. Could they notice how others appeared to be feeling during tense interactions while remaining non-judgmental and equanimous? Could they "see suffering" as a universal mechanism maintained by unawareness? Participants who completed all the tasks set last week, and who can occasionally feel a free flow of sensations in most parts, are ready for transversal scanning.

Introduce Transversal Scanning

Explain the procedure and rationale for transversal scanning: feeling sensations internally and increasing equanimity with deeper levels of awareness of thoughts and sensations to neutralize enduring schema-related emotions in contexts of interpersonal conflicts, where psychodynamic issues are likely to be triggered. Explain that this scanning method requires passing attention "through" the body horizontally, focusing on small (7 to 8 centimeter in diameter) areas at a time and moving attention from the front to the back of the body, and returning from the back to the front, starting with the head, the neck, etc., moving down toward the toes systematically, and then back up toward the top of the head. The audio instructions are on tracks 15 and 16. The practice should last 30 minutes in total. Ask participants to record their practice times, as usual.

Developing Mindful Assertiveness

Assertiveness involves being able to express what we believe or want, confidently without passivity or hostility, saying what we want or believe. Ask participants to select at least two situations in which to practice. Discuss the seven steps:

1 State the fact.
2 State how you feel (using an "I" statement).
3 State what you believe (using an "I" statement).
4 State your possible error in judgment.
5 State what you want.
6 Provide reward.
7 Negotiate a win–win solution if there is no cooperation.

Explain Homework Exercises

- Twice daily practice of transversal scanning (audio tracks 15 and 16).
- Choose a minimum of two situations to practice mindful assertiveness; expressing needs assertively, in a considerate, respectful and equanimous way. Participants may already have items listed on their Exposure Record Sheet that they can use.
- Bipolar exposure may be used prior to in-vivo exposure with more challenging situations.
- Read Handouts 8.1 and 8.2.
- Fill in the Daily Record of Mindfulness Meditation Practice (Handout 8.3).

Frequently Asked Questions

Question: One of my clients reacted to the word "piercingly" in the audio instructions for transversal scanning. She is imagining that she is piecing her body. Have you come across people who disliked these words?

Answer: You can reassure your client that she is not piercing anything physically. This word simply describes how we need to be directing attention; *piercingly*. It is only our *sharp* attention that traverses the interior of the body. She needs to know that she is just feeling energy in the parts of the body that she is surveying. In fact, we don't really feel the body either, though this is a little more difficult to understand for some clients. We are merely activating neural connections in the parts of the brain that let us feel sensations in the body. These are the somatosensory cortex and the insular cortex. You can explain to her that when we scan the body transversally, we are merely activating interoceptive neurons in various networks of these brain areas. You can illustrate this by evoking brain injury examples; while damage to these brain areas will prevent people from feeling an intact limb, for example, someone whose limb has been amputated may still be able to feel it if these brain areas are intact (which is known as phantom-limb syndrome).

If she overreacts to these words and still needs the audio instructions next time you meet, you might consider doing some desensitization using the MIET (as you explained to your client when she went through the skills taught in Session 4). It could be that the words are triggering some old fears, which creates an opportunity for immediate desensitization. During the session with her, if she agrees, play the audio instructions in the room and ask her to listen to it as usual. As soon as these words are spoken, pause the recording and ask her to focus all her attention non-judgmentally on the four basic characteristics (mass, temperature, motion and fluidity) of the most intense sensation in her body while remaining equanimous. Applying this task for 30 seconds twice in a row should suffice to significantly decrease arousal—emphasize unconditional acceptance in the second trial. Then ask her to hear the words again and repeat the exposure for 30 seconds. Once the association between the words and the unpleasant sensation has been neutralized, they will no longer affect her.

Question: I have a client who finds transversal scanning more difficult than sweeping, which he likes a lot. Can he continue with sweeping en masse?

Answer: Transversal scanning is slower, requiring a part-by-part approach, so we don't feel the pleasant radiating flow of sensations as easily. It feels like harder work, and your client is experiencing separation from an experience he enjoyed, and got attached to, which can create dissatisfaction, insecurity or physical discomfort. He started to enjoy his practice with sweeping en masse, but he was asked to let it go. This reflects what commonly happens in our lives. Attachment to ease and comfort leads to disappointment when it changes. Learning to let go of the things we get attached to and crave is a useful and important lesson to be learned through meditation.

From a technical point of view, your client needs to survey the body internally with patience and tolerance with the places he cannot yet feel. Just as he did when he started with part-by-part scanning, he needs to pause for up to 30 seconds on blank spots after, even if there are many. Reassure him that skill acquisition is just a matter of time if we work at it, whether this is about the sensory areas of the brain or other functions of the body. However, he also needs to know that if he entertains judgment and reactivity about (and during) his practice, then these will be reinforced both during his practice and in daily life. Remind the client that the very purpose of this practice is to decrease, *not increase*, reactivity, as this also generalizes daily life. From a clinical point of view, this is also an opportunity for you to identify his general tendencies in daily life: avoidance of the difficult and unpleasant and clinging to the pleasant, which may be constructive to discuss with him.

Question: My client has a partner who can be verbally aggressive and rude to her. Although she would like to use assertiveness in that relationship, I am concerned that it could put her in a difficult position. How could I manage this?

Answer: Your client will need to consider this carefully, but implementing the task should be useful if her partner is not intoxicated and/or physically violent, and she is safe from physical abuse. Explore with her whether she thinks her partner would respond reasonably if he is addressed in a calm, but not passive, way without expecting any particular outcome. By following the seven-statement structure for mindful assertiveness, she might be pleasantly surprised by how well the conversation goes. You need to ensure that she understands and implements experiential ownership, which will buffer much of the expected reactivity from both sides. Some clients forget about it and try to be assertive while too affected by fear or other emotions. Focusing on another's suffering and accepting it genuinely rarely attracts an aggressive response. It would be good if you could role play the task with her during the session, ensuring that you are swapping roles and providing honest feedback after each attempt. Ask her permission to genuinely imitate her partner's attitude first, so that the simulation is authentic and helpful. You need to be honest about your impression of her approach and skills, or she will either distrust your judgment or avoid going through with the task. Remind her to train her skills with people who are easier to speak with first.

Handout 8.1 Transversal Scanning

The audio instructions for the transversal scanning technique are found on track 16 and the introduction is on Track 15. As with the other exercises, your practice sessions should last 30 minutes, so practice for an additional 14 minutes in silence after the 16-minute track finishes. Record your daily practice as you have been doing in previous weeks.

Transversal Scanning

In this method, scanning is "through" the body horizontally focusing on small areas (2–3 inches or 5–8 centimeters in diameter) at a time and moving attention from the front to the back of the body, starting with the head and moving systematically down the body. Start at the forehead and scan slowly through to the back of the head and then return your attention to the front and scan the next area from front to back. When the whole face has been scanned from front to back, scan from the back of the head to the face in the same way. This is why we call it "transversal scanning."

When the head has been scanned, continue to the next area; the neck and throat. Again, move your attention carefully from the front to the back first, and then from the back to the front, noticing all sensations equanimously, which means without reacting or taking your experience personally. The whole body is scanned in the same way: the shoulders, arms and hands, the torso and then the legs, feet and toes. Once the whole body has been scanned transversally head to toes, scan transversally back up the body. Once you get to your forehead again, you have completed a full cycle.

As you are scanning the body transversally, try not to judge what you are noticing; do your best to stay equanimous. Each sensation is a fresh new experience and shows that things change all the time. Every moment your body is changing in subtle ways; you may be experiencing the sensations that arise when there is a change in the room temperature or when you have just eaten something. Some of the changes are very subtle and you are learning to be able to notice more and more subtle sensations as you practice.

Of course, it is also possible that you are feeling sensations that are related to recent or old emotions. It is even possible to have some memories pop up at the same time. If you have this kind of experience, it can be pleasant or unpleasant, but it is absolutely normal. Let's take the example of washing the dishes. If your detergent is good, do you expect that the water where you wash the dishes will stay clean? Usually, the better your detergent, the more the dirt goes into the water, so we expect dirt in the water. If your water stays clean, you bought the wrong detergent! Well, when you scan the body while staying equanimous, your *pure* attention (your equanimous attention) works as an excellent detergent that cleans up all past negativity and unhelpful desires. Remember that these changes are not personal. Try not to control them when they happen; they happen when the moment is right. In case you are noticing that you are reacting with likes and dislikes, just notice it, *accept* that you are reacting and prevent yourself from judging it, and continue to scan the body with equanimity.

Please, keep in mind that we are *not* scanning through our muscles, our organs or our bones when we scan in a transversal way. We are only activating parts of the brain in an area that deals with receiving information about body sensations (somatosensory cortex) and an area that appears to help in "translation" of sensations (insular cortex). This means that when you pay attention to a body part, you are activating areas of the brain that create the experience of a sensation. Transversal scanning does not at all involve "piercing" any physical part of your body.

Handout 8.2 Assertiveness Training Task

The homework this week includes a mindful assertiveness task. This involves practicing the "experiential ownership" technique that you learned in the last session and combining it with communicating what your needs and opinions are, clearly and respectfully to yourself and to others. Choose two situations in which to practice. Perhaps you have listed some on your Exposure Record Sheet. The situations should be ones that you have avoided up to now or that you simply intend to address but haven't yet done so. Be aware that you're only learning how to do this, so if it doesn't go as well as you had hoped, then think about what you could do differently next time. Mistakes are not a sign of failure; they are a necessary part of all learning. Below is a description of the procedure.

Mindful Assertiveness

Choose an appropriate time and place to engage in an assertive conversation. It may be best to simply ask the other person when would be a good time to have a talk, or in a work situation to make an appointment with the person. It will be helpful if the other person is not rushed, distracted or irritated because you have interrupted them. You will need to use these main aspects of assertiveness; here are the main points:

1 State the fact.
2 State how you feel (using an "I" statement).
3 State what you believe/the meaning (using an "I" statement).
4 State your possible error in judgment.
5 State what you want.
6 Provide reward.
7 Negotiate a win–win solution if there is no cooperation.

1. State the Fact

A fact is what *actually* happened or is happening; it is not a judgment, an exaggeration or blame. For example, "You never do the washing up." is only a fact if the other person really *never* does the washing up. Similarly, "It's always me who does the washing up" is only a fact if it really is *always* you who does the washing up; it is not a fact if the other person did the washing up even once in the past ten years! So, it is best to avoid using *never* or *always* as they are often exaggerations of something that happens *rarely* or *often*. It may be better to say, "Although we agreed that you would do the washing up if I cooked, this week you have only washed up once." This may help with the communication because it is true and the other person can't argue with facts; facts are facts!

2. State How You Feel

Be clear about your *personal* experience instead of judging the other person's experience. Describe your experience verbally using "I" statements. For example, "I feel angry when I have to do the washing up when I am so exhausted, and you are watching TV." instead of "It's not fair that you expect me to do all the work." You may make the other person feel guilty instead of being able to think about how their behavior affects you. If you are not emotionally reactive, the other person will be able to manage the conversation more productively and perhaps calmly.

3. State What You Believe/What It Means To You

Say why you feel as you do. The co-emergence model shows that it is *our thoughts* and *beliefs* (the way we interpret a situation) that cause body sensations to co-emerge and become emotions. Our body sensations are not caused by a situation or a person outside ourselves. So, what we say needs to tell the other person *why* we feel the way we do. For example, "I feel angry because it seems to me (or "I believe") that you are not respecting our agreement and that you don't care that I am exhausted." You are explaining *what makes you feel angry*, instead of blaming the other person for what you are feeling. You are taking responsibility for your own feelings.

4. Stating Your Possible Error In Judgment ("I may be wrong")

We tend to assume that we know what people feel or think, or what their intentions are, especially if we think that we know this person well. Many a time, the other person does not think and feel in the way you think that they do. They might not have the intention or motivation that you think they have either. Therefore, you and the other person may interpret the same situation in a very different way, but neither of you knows it. So, when using assertive communication, it is best to acknowledge that you may be wrong. For example, you may say "I may be wrong, but it seems to me that you are not respecting our agreement or my needs." In this case you are showing that you are not afraid of admitting that you may have made an error of judgment, while allowing the other person to state their view.

5. Stating What You Want

At this point, it is time to state what you want. You have the right to want anything and say it, so long as you prepared not to get it. You still have the right to ask. It is more useful to ask for what you *do want* than what you *don't want*. For example, "I want you to help me wash up after dinner instead of going straight to the TV," rather than "I don't want you to watch TV after dinner while I wash up."

6. Providing Reward

Thank the other person for their cooperation, as this will encourage them to cooperate more in the future—they'll feel good about themselves and about "doing good." A reward may be a smile or a hug if it's someone close to you. If they have not agreed to cooperate, then you can still thank them for listening, but without rewarding them for not cooperating. For example, you could say "Thank you for listening; I hope you now understand how I feel and what I'd like." Saying this can motivate cooperation in the future.

7. Win–Win Solutions

It is a reality that assertive negotiations do not always work. People will not always be prepared to change and meet the needs of others. It is important that you don't feel that you have given in, and so you may need to find a win–win solution. It will be most successful if you can remain equanimous and creative during this stage. The aim is to find a solution that is a compromise. For example, "That's unfortunate, but I am sure if we both make an effort and stay creative, we can find a solution where neither of us feels taken advantage of. What do you think?"

Putting It Together

Here is an example using the scenario mentioned earlier: John and Sue live together, and both work long hours. When they moved in together, they agreed that John would do all the cooking because he enjoys it and Sue would do the washing up after meals. But recently Sue has been working very hard and is exhausted and she has not been washing up. This means that in the morning, the kitchen is messy when they are trying to make breakfast and prepare lunches. John is speaking to Sue:

1 *Fact*: Sue, I know you've been working really hard and you're tired in the evening, but I noticed that in the last ten days you have washed up only twice.
2 *I feel*: I feel angry when I have to do the washing up when I am so exhausted and you are watching TV.
3 *I think*: I feel angry because it seems to me that you are not respecting our agreement and that you don't care that I am exhausted.
4 *Error*: I may be wrong, and you might actually care about how I feel, but…
5 *I want*: I want you to help me wash up after dinner as we agreed, instead of going straight to watch TV.
6 *Reward*: Thank you for listening; I hope you now understand how I feel and what I'd like.
7 *Win–win solution*. If we both make an effort, I am sure that we can find a good compromise; what do you think?

Handout 8.3 Daily Record of Mindfulness Meditation Practice

Day	**Date**	**Morning** *(circle)*	**Duration**	**Efficacy rating** *Rate from 1 to 10 how well you noticed distractions and brought your attention back to the body. 1 = not well at all; 10 = extremely well*	**Evening** *(circle)*	**Duration**	**Efficacy rating** *Rate from 1 to 10 how well you noticed distractions and brought your attention back to the body. 1 = not well at all; 10 = extremely well*
Monday		I practiced Yes / No			I practiced Yes / No		
Tuesday		I practiced Yes / No			I practiced Yes / No		
Wednesday		I practiced Yes / No			I practiced Yes / No		
Thursday		I practiced Yes / No			I practiced Yes / No		
Friday		I practiced Yes / No			I practiced Yes / No		
Saturday		I practiced Yes / No			I practiced Yes / No		
Sunday		I practiced Yes / No			I practiced Yes / No		

References

Alkoby, A., Halperin, E., Tarrasch, R., & Levit-Binnun, N. (2017). Increased support for political compromise in the Israeli-Palestinian conflict following an 8-week mindfulness workshop. *Mindfulness*. doi:10.1007/s12671-017-0710-5

Ball, S. G., Otto, M. W., Pollack, M. H., & Rosenbaum, J. F. (1994). Predicting prospective episodes of depression in clients with panic disorder: A longitudinal study. *Journal of Consulting and Clinical Psychology*, 62, 359–365.

Dorland. (2011). *Dorland's Illustrated Medical Dictionary* (32nd ed.). Philadelphia, PA: Elsevier-Saunders.

Huey, W. C., & Rank, R. C. (1984). Effects of counselor and peer-led group assertive training on Black adolescent aggression. *Journal of Counseling Psychology*, 31, 95–98.

Jones, S. M., & Hansen, W. (2015). The impact of mindfulness on supportive communication skills: three exploratory studies. *Mindfulness*, 6, 1115–1128. doi:10.1007/s12671-014-0362-7

Krieglmeyer, R., Deutch, R., De Houwer, J., & De Raedt, R., (2010). Being moved: Valence activates approach-avoidance behavior independent of evaluation and approach-avoidance intentions. *Psychological Science*, 21, 607–613. doi:10.1177/0956797610365131

Lee, S., & Swanson Crockett, M. (1994). Effect of assertiveness training on levels of stress and assertiveness experienced by nurses in Taiwan, Republic of China. *Issues in Mental Health Nursing*, 15, 419–432.

McFall, R. M., & Twentyman, C. T. (1973). Four experiments on the relative contributions of rehearsal, modeling, and coaching to assertion training. *Journal of Abnormal Psychology*, 81, 199–218.

Menon, V., & Uddin, L. Q. (2010). Saliency, switching, attention and control: a network model of insula function. *Brain Structure and Function*, 214, 655–667. doi:10.1007/s00429-010-0262-0

Pearson, K. A., Watkins, E. R., Mulla, E. G., & Moberly, N. J. (2010). Psychosocial correlates of depressive rumination. *Behaviour Research and Therapy*, 48, 784–791.

Ramachandran, V. S., & Blakeslee, S. (1998). *Phantoms in the brain: Human nature and the architecture of the mind*. London, UK: Fourth Estate.

Rogers-Carter, M. M., Varela, J. A., Gribbons, K. B., Pierce, A. F., McGoey, M. T., Ritchey, M., & Christianson, J. P. (2018). Insular cortex mediates approach and avoidance responses to social affective stimuli. *Nature Neuroscience*. doi:10.1038/s41593-018-0071-y

Uddin, L. Q. (2014). Salience processing and insular cortical function and dysfunction. *Nature Reviews Neuroscience*. doi:10.1038/nrn3857

Session 9: Cultivating Compassion and Connectedness

Boundless compassion for all living beings is the surest and most certain guarantee of pure moral conduct, and needs no casuistry. Whoever is filled with it will assuredly injure no one, do harm to no one, encroach on no man's rights; he will rather have regard for everyone, forgive everyone, help everyone as far as he can, and all his actions will bear the stamp of justice and loving-kindness.

—Arthur Schopenhauer, 1903

Introduction

This chapter guides you in delivering Stage 4, the last skillset of MiCBT. It will introduce three central elements, starting with the next and most advanced body-scanning method, "sweeping in depth." This method integrates transversal scanning and sweeping en masse, and involves sweeping attention on the surface and the interior of the body together, so that the whole body can be felt simultaneously as attention moves continually in a vertical direction. The second element is the combining of advanced mindfulness skills with empathy training through the daily practice of loving-kindness meditation. The third element is to apply mindfulness skills to enhance ethical behavior and increase a sense of worth in ourselves and of others, and an overall sense of connectedness. The chapter will assist you in explaining the importance of relapse prevention to your client. You will be able to accurately describe the main purpose of dedicating a whole MiCBT stage to the development of compassion, grounded in loving-kindness meditation and ethical living: *the prevention of relapse*, resulting from the cultivation of compassion, meaning, equanimity and well-being.

The Clinical Handbook of Mindfulness-integrated Cognitive Behavior Therapy: A Step-by-Step Guide for Therapists, First Edition. Bruno A. Cayoun, Sarah E. Francis, and Alice G. Shires.

Companion website: www.wiley.com/go/Cayoun/Mindfulness-integrated

Checking Client Readiness

Last week your client worked on transversal scanning. Check if they can now feel sensations inside the body as they survey the whole body by passing attention transversally. Ask if they can notice and accept the blank spots with equanimity, despite their possible expectation to feel sensations everywhere. This can feel like re-starting part-by-part scanning all over again and trigger some impatience and frustration. It is now more likely that your client notices that they are able to be more equanimous when life disappoints because of their increased equanimity, both during their practice and in daily life.

Also check if your client managed to use the seven statements of assertiveness to conduct a conversation in which they were able to express their needs. How many times did they practice it? Could they diversify the context of practice or was it with the same person? Ask if they had cooperation from the other person in the dialogue. Even if they did not get exactly what they wanted, did they feel some sense of achievement? If not, reassure your client that this is not an easy task and it takes practice; a lot of practice. If they can feel at least 20 % of the body transversally, they can start practicing the sweeping in depth method and compassion training while continuing to practice assertive communication as often as necessary. For this practice, they should follow the written instructions described in this chapter.

Delaying the Next Step

If your client struggles to feel sensations inside the body, they should continue with transversal scanning for at least a few more days, but without the audio instructions. If one of the reasons they struggled is high distractibility, ask them to start each practice with 10 minutes of mindfulness of breath without instructions, and resume with 20 minutes of transversal scanning, until they start sweeping in depth. Similarly, if your client was not able to practice assertive communication last week, they should postpone the next stage of the program until they have done so.

It is prudent to take into account the effects of culture on interpersonal dynamics. For instance, the way in which we express ourselves harmoniously in Western and Asian countries can vary greatly. If you have been in Japan, for example, the expectation of interpersonal hierarchy and the resulting appearance of submissiveness in people's expression is not necessarily dysfunctional. Therefore, cautious evaluation is required when working with people from different cultures.

Of course, there could also be genuine logistical hindrances that would justify why we would move on to Stage 4 bypassing the assertive communication task. For instance, imagine that your client is an anxious first-year student from overseas who just arrived in this country and knows absolutely nobody in the area, and can barely speak the language. In the unlikely, but possible, situation where they get along extremely well with all members of the family in their country of origin and cannot see reasons to apply assertiveness, then you might consider skipping assertiveness of Stage 3 and moving on to Stage 4. If your client is not ready to proceed immediately with the next scanning method, they can start compassion training this week while practicing transversal scanning for a few more days.

Advanced Scanning: Sweeping in Depth

Sweeping in depth is the most advanced body scanning technique used in MiCBT. The purpose of sweeping in depth is threefold: (1) becoming more aware of emotional experience and related schemas that operate more deeply and less consciously, (2) improving equanimity in a wider range of experiences, and (3) increasing insight into the impermanence and insubstantiality of body and mind to decrease identification with experiences and help prevent relapse. As such, "in depth" means both depth of the body and depth of consciousness. The more we are able to feel the entirety of the body while meditating, the easier it is to feel it in daily life without meditating. Eventually, we are able to feel the entire body without even trying. This skill is extremely beneficial because it enables us to be in touch with what we think and feel at all times, and be comfortable with it. This equanimous state of experiential presence is the best antidote to relapse, as relapse into an emotional disorder requires emotional reactivity.

The Method

Sweeping in depth combines transversal scanning and sweeping en masse. This scanning method helps to continue the development of awareness and equanimity. Equanimity develops more as your client is able to stop identifying with the experiences in the body. Instead, they simply notice them and let them go. With practice, they will learn to feel the whole body (inside and outside) in one breath. It is useful to explain this to your client.

Sweeping in depth is a vertical interior sweep of the whole body, so that there is a single sweep of attention within the body from the top of the head to the toes. Once they have scanned from head to toe they will scan back up again to the head in the same sweeping manner, feeling as much as possible. Explain to your client to sweep with a continuous flow of attention without interruption. If, after sweeping the body two or three times, there are blank spots, they can attend to these separately. Until your client can feel internal sensations across the whole body, they can alternate practices conducting one cycle of transversal scanning (moving down and then up the whole body) and then two or three cycles of sweeping in depth and so on for the 30-minute practice.

A common analogy for scanning in depth through the whole body is to think about dye being dropped into a bottle of water, permeating all of the water. Attention is like the dye, permeating through the body (Goenka, 2000). The scanning speed will be slow at first and will speed up as your client is able to feel more sensations, and eventually they will be able to feel body sensations as they arise during their day while remaining equanimous. In this way, they will be able to connect with their emerging experience and manage the way that they respond skillfully: with wisdom, compassion and detachment from a false sense of self.

Cultivating Interpersonal Connectedness and Compassion

Purpose

As we discussed in Session 7, a lack of connectedness leads to a sense of being emotionally isolated and lonely, which contributes to depressogenic and anxiogenic modes of thinking. In turn, activating these schemas eventually leads to relapse. Note that internal disconnectedness also occurs through dissociative experience, which can lead to deliberate self-harm in anxious clients. The purpose of increasing clients' sense of connectedness is to decrease the probability of relapse. On the one hand, clients with emotional disorders have an impaired ability to feel common body sensations, as shown by impaired insula activation (Khalsa et al., 2018), and therefore have a reduced capacity to activate the secretion of oxytocin hormone in the insular cortex; on the other hand, people who learn to increase their sense of connectedness with others through loving-kindness meditation and ethical training trigger the secretion of insular oxytocin each time they feel sensations related to kindness and compassion (Lutz, Brefczynski-Lewis, Johnstone, & Davidson, 2008; Rogers-Carter et al., 2018).

Oxytocin is also called the "bonding hormone" because it is secreted when we feel a sense of connection—including during breast-feeding, socializing, sex, patting a pet dog and singing in a choir—and is a protective factor against one's sense of isolation. Experientially, oxytocin secretion seems to manifest itself predominantly through the experience of the interaction of body sensations related to fluidity, lightness and motion (rapid oscillation), all interacting to give a sense of pleasant flow of warm tingling sensations (see Session 4). Interestingly, it has been found that the brain regions that produce this experience are markedly more developed in experienced meditators than in non-meditators (Lutz et al., 2008). One of the reasons for this is that mindfulness meditators tend to also practice loving-kindness meditation, but it could also be that their ability to feel a free flow of sensations enables them to feel more connected to their bodily experience, which in turn could activate insular oxytocin—though we are not aware of existing empirical evidence for this.

Compassion can be enhanced with training, which affects areas of the brain that increase our understanding of others, including our ability to give and receive compassion and to be self-compassionate (Jazaieri, et al., 2013). Scientific exploration of mindfulness has shown that compassion can emerge spontaneously with increased mindfulness (Bradbury, 2014). Attendees of an eight-week mindfulness program showed enhanced compassion and were five times more likely to help someone in pain that those who did not attend the program (Condon, Desbordes, Miller, & De Steno, 2013).

Rationale Delivery

At this stage of the program, your client's mindfulness practice and the interpersonal insight developed during Stage 3 have created the ideal psychological substrate for them to understand how kindness and compassion impact their psychological well-being. Their increased ability to value their needs has started to increase their sense of self-worth. It has also enabled some reappraisal of the importance of understanding others, connecting with them and not passing judgment. If your client practiced experiential ownership accurately, they have started to perceive the true nature of universal suffering and understand that people's reactivity is more a matter of unawareness than a matter of "ego." This includes suffering perpetuated by greed, hatred and conceit.

Your client now needs to realize that *they are the first recipients of the emotions they generate* and learn to choose carefully what emotions to nurture and what emotions to abandon. Help your client to accept that it is their own thinking that has caused the sensations. For instance, anger-related thoughts produce co-emerging unpleasant sensations, which we would like to avoid by reacting to the situation. On the other hand, kind thoughts produce co-emerging pleasant sensations and contentment. Ask your client to close their eyes and bring to mind being angry, and then being kind and loving, and compare the sensations that arise. This helps experiential learning. Whether your client is right or wrong within their narrative, what is the most wholesome type of experience for them? We tend to be angry with others because of an unfulfilled expectation, and are usually attached to the idea that things *should* be different. This non-acceptance of current reality is causing agitation and discomfort. In contrast, accepting the situation as it is and generating love and compassion produces pleasant sensations. When explained this way, your client will be able to see that they have choice in how they feel.

It may be useful to describe the notion of "wholesomeness" at this point. In Buddhist psychology, a thought, intention, emotion or behavior is unwholesome to the extent that it creates or maintains the propensity to react with craving or aversion, or to promote the illusion of permanence (often called "delusion"). Since craving, aversion and assumption of permanence create or maintain suffering, they are deemed unwholesome. On the other hand, anything that decreases the probability or maintenance of suffering by preventing craving, aversion and assumption of permanence is said to be wholesome.

Using Socratic questioning for this is invaluable. We often ask clients questions such as, "When you felt angry because he disputed the custody of the children, you felt that your anger was justified and he deserved it, right?... But who was actually feeling it?... How did anger feel?... And did he feel any of this?... So, are you saying that even though he was in the wrong and you were victimized by his attitude, *you* were the one who suffered because of it?... This means that you felt not only a sense of powerlessness because of his decision, but also the unpleasant consequence of your anger (the experience of heat, agitation and constriction in the body) on top of it... What would it have felt like if you had kinder thoughts instead, what kind of sensations would you have felt?"

You may explain to your client that we cannot feel connected to others unless we feel connected within ourselves. Our ability to feel love and compassion is reduced if we are depressed and have a low sense of self-worth and self-loathing. In contrast, the more we feel connected to ourselves, the more we can feel connected to others, which then allows us to exhibit kindness and compassion. Explain that this can be achieved through training. Your client does not have to be born with compassion; they "don't have to have the gene."

Everyone can become compassionate, including incarcerated psychopaths (Domes, Hollerbach, Vohs, Mokros, & Habermeyer, 2013), irrespective of their past or present, provided that they connect the correct brain pathways through training.

Effects of Insight and Egolessness on Empathy

This may be a little philosophical for some, but clients benefit greatly from understanding that *only the ego attributes suffering to another's ego*. Our ability to not take things personally also allows us to not assign the cause of others' reactivity to them as a person. After all, we were once "in the same boat," so to speak, but our wisdom changed us. We learned to perceive the deeper phenomenological reality of how suffering is triggered, reinforced and maintained. This is a universal reality; it is not limited to the "nasty neighbor," the "controlling mother-in-law," or the "avoidant office manager who allows bullying in the service." Our growing understanding of the *universality of suffering* enables us to accept that it is a person's lack of mindfulness and intrapersonal insight that is the sole maintaining factor for their mental and emotional suffering.

During this stage of their training, clients learn through reappraisal to greatly reduce their habit of taking things personally and evaluating people's attitudes according to idiosyncratic values and beliefs. This allows them to widen the scope of their insight and understand and accept others' suffering for what it is and become more empathic. This is illustrated in a recent study from a team of Israeli social psychologists (Alkoby, Halperin, Tarrasch, & Levit-Binnun, 2017) who examined the effect of an intervention that combines mindfulness with cognitive reappraisal to enhance emotion regulation in the context of intergroup conflict. The results showed that participants in the mindfulness group, the reappraisal group and the combined group were more willing to support a compromise after being presented with anger-inducing information related to the Israeli–Palestinian conflict than participants who received neither mindfulness nor reappraisal training. The increased support for peacemaking policies was mediated by a decrease in negative emotions in all three groups that had received an intervention. In addition, the mindfulness group's support for peaceful solutions (win–win solutions) was also mediated by reduction in negative perceptions.

The combined impact of mindfulness and reappraisal in people's daily life during Stage 4 of MiCBT is quite remarkable. We often observe clients making life-changing decisions, such as engaging in a major health-related lifestyle change, deciding to divorce or get married, deciding to start a family, change job, buy a house, or quit all use of addictive substances. This is best explained through clients' decreased anxiety and realization and acceptance of their values. As clients have learned to be less avoidant and now learn to abstain from judging themselves harshly and to be kinder to themselves and others, they make decisions that are congruent with what they value. Although not all values are "wholesome," the clients' significant decisions during Stage 4 are usually driven by insight, good will and compassion for themselves and/or others.

Definition of Compassion

We can only be compassionate when we *see* suffering, and seeing suffering for what it truly is brings compassion. Compassion has been defined as "*the will to extend oneself for the purpose of minimizing one's own or another's suffering*" (Cayoun, 2017, p. 177; italics in the original). This is in contrast with empathy, in which, while there is an understanding and acceptance of another's experience, there is not necessarily an action motivated by the desire to decrease suffering. When we feel compassionate towards someone, there arises a desire to respond with action. The more intense the sensations are the more likely we are to act; to do something about the other person's situation (as per the co-emergence model). Compassion transcends culture, and compassionate communities create a sense of safety and connectedness. Darwin also recognized that compassion is an important aspect of successful societies, as it includes caring for our children, family and friends, and facilitates a cooperative attitude for conflict resolution (Darwin, 1871/2004). It therefore also makes sense to actively promote compassion in societies.

Loving-Kindness Meditation

One of the two methods of developing compassion in MiCBT is through the practice of loving-kindness meditation. Loving-kindness meditation (*metta bhavana* in Pali) is originally based on the Buddha's teaching of kindness, and has been taught as part of Buddhist teachings for over 2500 years (Hart, 1987; Rahula, 1974). There have been various adaptations across teachers (e.g., Cayoun, 2015; Germer, 2009; Gilbert, 2005; Monteiro & Musten, 2013; Neff, 2011), mostly to better match their student population, but the central elements remain similar with both monastic and lay teachers (Neal, 2015). In MiCBT, loving-kindness is taught as derived from the style of S. N. Goenka (Goenka, 2000) and is further informed by other influential Theravada teachers such as Ajahn Jayasaro (Jayasaro, 2010).

This week, your client will learn this method in addition to sweeping in depth. Explain to your client that loving-kindness is a short meditation practice in which they choose to engage feelings of universal love, caring, peace and harmony for themselves and others. It is essentially composed of compassion-related affirmations combined with a congruent emotional state. In MiCBT, we add a focus on body sensations. Loving-kindness meditation has been shown to improve the ability to be present-centered and less self-centered (Garrison, Scheinost, Constable, & Brewer, 2014). Your client will enhance their capacity to accept people without needing them to change, learning to connect with others and themselves in a compassionate and kind-hearted way. Since this experience of "oneness" is diametrically opposite to our clients' mental states of emotional distress, it can act as a buffer against relapse tendencies. In other words, symptoms of emotional disorders and kindness/compassion (for self and others) are mutually exclusive.

The Practice

Your client will use the audio instructions to guide them in creating loving and friendly thoughts and feelings firstly towards themselves for the first two or three minutes. Next, they will create similar aspirations for other people. They start with people close to them and then for the final two or three minutes, they begin to systematically expand out to others, including people they have had difficulties with, and finally toward all beings. These thoughts create co-emerging pleasant subtle body sensations, producing a sense of connectedness and well-being—we presume oxytocin secretion. Note that since your client learns to pair kind thoughts and pleasant sensations with the memories of people who may have displeased them or who could create future conflicts, the procedure also acts as counterconditioning. For this practice, visualization is OK so long as *body sensations* are a key focus. Loving-kindness meditation will last about 9 minutes and is added to the end of the usual 30-minute practice. The usual script may include affirmations such as "may I be safe," "may I be kind to myself," or "may I share my equanimity and peace of mind with everyone." The audio instructions are on track 18, with an introduction on track 17.

Common Difficulties with Loving-kindness Meditation

Underestimation.

Occasionally, some clients struggle switching from an interoceptive awareness practice to an affirmation exercise and underestimate the power of their thoughts. Many people don't realize that loving-kindness meditation has been taught and practiced for over 2500 years. It may be good to clarify this with some clients. The use of affirmations may also sound a little like prayer, especially for clients who either resent spirituality and religions or for those who have an affinity with them. Whereas the former can be occasionally a little reticent, the latter will usually feel "at home," so to speak. Each person has a mental representation of such processes and interprets the procedure accordingly. Your client needs to understand that thoughts such as "I am useless," "everyone is so stupid," or "no one cares about me" are also affirmations, except that these maintain or lead to depression when they are repeated, even subconsciously. The co-emerging sensations associated with an affirmation also become part of daily life because of the brain's habit of wiring the corresponding networks. Thus, negative affirmations can be very automatic and subconscious. The question is not whether to use affirmations or not in daily life; it is *which* affirmations do we want to use.

Artificiality.

Some clients find it strange to try to manufacture friendliness and compassion through training. You need to explain that their capacity to feel love and compassion in the past might have been dependent upon who was the recipient of their kindness, whether they were tired or not, in a good or bad mood, or whether the recipient had been kind to them or not. Basically, your client may not have been the real agent of their kindness, love and compassion. Through training, as demonstrated through research, they now have the opportunity to *choose* to be kind and compassionate at any time, in any place and with anybody in whom they see signs of suffering. Their compassion will become worthwhile and beneficial to them because it will no longer be mediated by their sense of self, or dependent on how their judgment dictates whether or not a person deserves their compassion.

Forgiving.

As your client develops understanding of how body sensations co-emerge with thoughts, they can see that other people operate in the same way. We all react because of our own internal discomfort; we seek out and crave pleasant sensations and try to avoid unpleasant ones. This realization makes it easier to have compassion towards others, knowing that they may not have this wisdom and their lack of awareness has consequently led to their harmful actions. Forgiveness becomes much easier with this insight. This is synonymous with forgiving a child's behavior on the basis that their understanding is limited.

Another hindrance to forgiveness is to see suffering as being something different in different people, which leads to further evaluations and schema-based comparisons. We may think, "My pain is much greater than hers." or "Well, that's my boss's problem if he is depressed now, but that's nothing compared to what I went through when he was stressing me out." Forgiveness of others is easier when we realize that they operate in the same way as we would. Being compassionate to ourselves is the important first step in being able to forgive others. As we link emotions to sensations, it also becomes easier for clients to see that "self-compassion helps to engender and is engendered by mindfulness" (Neff, 2004, p. 29). With this understanding, we are able to be compassionate *to ourselves* and we are less dependent on others' apologies or approval to be kind to ourselves.

Whatever the psychological or physical pain, it can be reappraised and normalized. Just as your client has learned to perceive a thought as *just* a thought and a sensation as *just* a sensation, they can perceive suffering as *just* suffering. Furthermore, mindfulness training has helped your client to realize and accept that all mental states pass; both happiness and unhappiness are transitory states of mind. As we develop a calm and peaceful mind, we are more able to understand suffering and frame it in terms of a human condition (Jayasaro, 2008). With a calm and equanimous mind, it is possible to realize how craving and aversion operate in other people. A calm state of mind enables us to understand that everyone struggles and suffers in very similar ways; *my* suffering is not unique to *me* nor is it worse than others. It becomes possible to understand that I am not singled out for pain and discomfort; this is universal and an inevitability for everyone. Without this realization, we feel like a victim, a victim of our own weaknesses and deficiencies of others' actions.

Forgiving those who have harmed us is, not surprisingly, a challenge, and it can be just as difficult to forgive oneself. If your client has been the subject of some abuse in the past, they may struggle to include their abuser in their loving-kindness meditation. In this case, they may leave this person out of the practice for now or they may choose to wish that the person realizes the harm they have caused, that they do not repeat it and that they be kind. Whatever your client chooses to do, it should be done in a genuine way; pretending will cause internal discomfort and disharmony between thoughts and sensations which undermines the ability to let go of the past.

Grounding Compassion in Ethical Conduct

It is important to differentiate empathy from compassion, which are terms that are sometimes used interchangeably in the literature. Whereas expressing empathy and goodwill during loving-kindness meditation is not necessarily grounded in daily action, compassion is either a genuine intention and propensity for action or a fully fledged action if the intention is sufficiently intense. However, being compassionate with one's best friends and others who are likely to return the favor or reward us with praise is not likely to be a transcending process; it might even inflate our sense of self and social persona. Helping someone can certainly be a compassionate act at times, while at other times it may be motivated by personal needs, such as validation and social desirability.

Help clients to consider whether it is possible to be compassionate and at the same time cause harm. Wishing all beings to be well during loving-kindness meditation is inconsistent with causing harm knowingly. Loving-kindness practice needs to be applied in daily life. Indeed, for compassion training to be grounded in congruent daily actions, it ought to be anchored in ethical behavior. Other authors and mindfulness program developers suggest that retaining ethics as part of a mindfulness training is of central importance (e.g., Grossman, 2015; Kramer, 2007; Monteiro, 2016; Monteiro & Musten, 2013; Shonin, van Gordon, & Griffiths, 2015). For example, Kabat-Zinn (2005, pp. 102-103) noted:

> The foundation of mindfulness practice, for all meditative enquiry and exploration, lies in ethics and morality, and above all, the motivation of non-harming. Why? Because you cannot possibly hope to know stillness and calmness within your own mind and body [...] if your actions are continually clouding, agitating, and destabilizing the very instrument through which you are looking, namely, your own mind [...] If we are continuously creating agitation in our lives, and causing harm to others and to ourselves, it is that agitation and harm that we will encounter in our meditation practice, because that is what we are feeding.

Intentional ethical actions are not necessarily obvious to others, but they emanate from a sense of connectedness, care and compassion. They also eliminate the cognitive dissonance apparent in our inconsistency between intentions and actions. The intentions we generate need to be translated into real actions. Without this, loving-kindness practice will not serve your client as much as they may need in order to prevent relapse, because good intentions are only a start. It may not prevent harmful actions. Don't they say, "The road to hell is paved with good intentions"? It is important to discuss with your client that this practice is not about nurturing a desire to be "a good person," as this only over-emphasizes one's sense of self. This is about genuinely committing to minimizing harm in all actions, engaging in self-care as well as care for others out of compassion (Jayasaro, 2011). A comprehensive analysis of ethics in mindfulness-based interventions is discussed in Monteiro, Compson, and Musten (2017), which includes a thorough account of the purpose, mechanisms, and benefits of ethics in MiCBT (Cayoun, 2017).

Rationale for Ethical Training

Understandably, doing harm to oneself or to others is likely to increase distress caused by the act itself, by subsequent guilt and self-blame, and by the possible interpersonal conflicts caused by the action (e.g., driving under the influence of alcohol or other drugs, abusing children, etc.). As therapists, we are frequently faced with this type of presentation. Once we succeed in assisting clients with their predicaments, we hope that they won't fall into the same traps, but they often do and relapse. This is partly because they fail to internalize a personal sense of ethics that is rooted in genuine compassion. As a result, "ethics" are perceived as *just rules*. Unless they are educated in mindfulness practice, they continue to react with craving for what promotes the experience of pleasure, and avoidance (including venting) of what promotes the experience of aversion.

In contrast, preventing harm out of ethical awareness requires the effort to inhibit our actions when they are deemed harmful. This kind of inhibitory control is not motivated by self-focused craving and aversion. It arises from learning and emotional intelligence; an awareness of how suffering had been increased in the past and what to do to prevent it. In other words, the effort to respect ethical boundaries emanates from one's growing compassion and wisdom. This typically promotes a sense of self-efficacy and well-being.

However, given the lack of empirical studies comparing mindfulness training with and without ethical training, not all clinicians and researchers adhere to the view that teaching explicit ethics in therapy is important. Yet, whether we agree or not, relate to it or not, argue for or against it, we are all bound by some form of ethics, without which society cannot survive. Ethics are an integral part of evolution. Individuals who are less compassionate and interpersonally aware tend to adhere to ethical guidelines because they are externally imposed rules, often based on fear or obedience, whereas more compassionate and interpersonally aware individuals tend to respect ethics-based rules in order to prevent harm—the very reason for which rules were established.

A large number of clients who seek assistance through therapy are trapped in unethical behavior, which is by definition harmful to themselves or to others. Seasoned clinicians will relate to the importance of clients' ethics. In order to engage in wholesome behavior (avoiding harmful actions), clients need to be clear about their own ethical standards, so that their actions are consistent with their standards. Discuss your client's understanding of the sorts of behavior that they recognize can cause harm to themselves or others. This will help your client to act from a sincere wish to prevent harm, rather than operating from a sense of guilt or fear of consequences. As they do, they will appreciate how their behavior (ethical or unethical) affects their social connectedness.

Practicing the Five Ethical Challenges

As mentioned earlier, there are two aspects to your client's compassion training this week. Firstly, they will develop their empathic skills with loving-kindness meditation, experiencing how it feels in the body when they generate good will towards themselves and to others. Secondly, they will learn to remain mindful of both their intentions and actions, noticing which actions increase or decrease the likelihood of feeling either calm and peaceful (characterized by soft and pleasant body sensations), or agitated and tense (characterized by intense and unpleasant body sensations). With this task, clients are asked to monitor the sensations co-emerging with both harmful and compassionate intentions before performing a verbal or physical action.

It is useful to explain to your client why we include a focus on ethical behavior in MiCBT. Capitalizing on the understanding already acquired, your client will understand that being able to remain equanimous means that their actions are generated by a clear and rational mind. Our emotional reactivity is only a reflection of our craving and aversion toward body sensations based on their salience (intensity) and hedonic tone (see Chapter 2). Emotionally-reactive states of mind are more likely to generate harmful behaviors. The five means of doing harm addressed in traditional mindfulness teachings are: harmful speech, taking what is not given, taking lives, inappropriate sexual behavior and taking intoxicants (substances that alter normal response inhibition, such as alcohol and illicit drugs).

However, it is useful to mention that people can also harm themselves and each other in many other ways. For example, neglecting children and pets, such as forgetting to feed them or give them attention, is not mentioned in the list of five basic actions, but they are certainly harmful. Our modern technology adds to the range of harmful possibilities. For instance, behavior such as road rage can easily harm by causing an accident. The list is long. However, since considering ethics in a therapy context can be very new for some clients, we limit the scope of effort to a few traditionally used guidelines. Your client's challenge this week will be to avoid engaging in all of the five types harmful behaviors. Suggest that they record on the Record of Ethical Challenges (Handout 9.4) how they felt while either preventing or engaging in harmful behavior. Help your client to take a beginner's stance to this task rather than expecting themselves to be perfect at it. This will stop them from feeling that they failed and will instead encourage them to perceive this task as a behavioral experiment, requiring an "objective" and accepting attitude.

Harmful Speech

Your client is invited to attend carefully to what they say from the perspective of the following: what I am about to say, a) is this true? b) is this a good time to talk about this? c) is this kind? d) is this respectful? e) is this useful? Harmful speech is the result of an automatic evaluation process and co-emerging body sensations to which we react by speaking inappropriately. This includes, but is not limited to, divisive speech, using harsh speech, backbiting, misleading others, wasting people's time with useless speech, etc. Can you see the benefit of preventing this? Suggest that your client should not expect to be perfect but should do their best. If they can be equanimous while paying attention to what they are saying, they are most likely engaging in constructive communication.

Taking Lives

When we discuss this aspect of ethical behavior with clients, they often say that they don't engage in killing. They don't identify as "killers," but this does not mean that they don't take lives. On closer reflection, as you discuss this with your client, they might realize that they probably kill small living things, such as insects. In any case, we are implicitly complicit in the killing of animals if we eat meat or fish, and in their daily suffering if we consume dairy products. However, they are not expected to have a vegetarian or vegan diet this week, unless this is something they already value and wish to try. MiCBT has its own boundaries; compassion will do the rest! This week, should they decide to kill something, ask your client to pay close attention to their body sensations, remaining equanimous, and do their best to prevent reacting (killing) because of the sensations. If they succeed in that instance, our working hypothesis is that their "need" to kill will become redundant and easily prevented.

Taking the Non-given

In a similar way, your clients will probably say that they are not thieves and don't steal. But we are not just evoking robbing a bank or money laundering. Invite your clients to consider stealing as "taking what is not freely given." This may allow them to realize that there are times when they do this. For example, leaving work early or taking a long lunch break, being paid for work that is not being done, using the office photocopier to copy personal documents, using the work landline without permission for long-distance personal calls, or taking credit for someone else's work (including plagiarism). Let's not get into issues of divorce-related settlement! If we stay kind to ourselves and remain objective and equanimous, we can more easily perceive aspects of our greed, however subtle it may be.

Inappropriate Sexual Behavior

Here again, clients might say that they are not rapists or don't force themselves on others, but "the devil is in the detail," as they say. Ask your client to use their mindfulness skills to honestly and equanimously notice if they might engage in inappropriate sexual behavior or if they invite someone else to do so. Ask them to notice the sensations associated with craving. For example, if they are feeling neglected in their relationship and have not addressed this with their partner, they may engage in flirtatious behavior. Eventually, the pleasant sensations that arise are interoceptively reinforced and may lead to craving for more flirtatious attention. Unfortunately, this is often how relationships get into trouble; feeling reassured and rewarded elsewhere may prevent us from trying to address the initial relationship problems. Sexual inappropriateness can also break a circle of friends or work harmony at the office.

Taking Intoxicants

Becoming intoxicated by taking mind-altering substances impacts on the mind's alertness and is likely to impact our ability to act according to our own ethical standards. When we are not able to monitor what we say or do, it is very difficult to remain equanimous and mindful of our intentions. When intoxicated, it is much harder to maintain the effort and adhere to other four ethical commitments. In addition, using drugs and alcohol can also trigger depressive, anxious, delusional or psychotic states, especially if the client experienced them prior to treatment. Because alcohol use is an accepted societal ritual, it may be valued among family members and friends. Bringing an expensive bottle of wine to a party will attract praise and even gratitude. Accordingly, avoiding alcohol can be difficult on the basis that it is a social reinforcer. The same applies to other recreational drugs.

Application with Individual Clients

Session Aim

The aim of this session is to introduce Stage 4 of the program: the empathic stage. There are three teaching elements this week, (1) the sweeping in depth method of body scanning, (2) compassion training through loving-kindness meditation, and (3) compassion training through the five ethical practices, in the context of discussing the impact of preventing harm on psychological well-being. Sweeping in depth will provide greater opportunities to develop equanimity with deeply rooted emotional reactive habits. The study, respect and consequence of ethical boundaries will assist clients to increase their sense of connectedness and compassion.

Review Homework and Progress

Review how your client progressed with transversal scanning. Check if they can remain equanimous with blank spots. Check if your client has successfully used the assertiveness statements in conversations. If not, encourage them to do so this week. If they can feel at least 20 % of the body transversally, they can start practicing sweeping in depth method and compassion training while continuing to practice assertive communication as often as necessary.

Introduce Sweeping in Depth

Explain the procedure and rationale for sweeping in depth, which is an integration of transversal scanning and sweeping en masse. Explain that sweeping in depth requires sweeping the interior of the body vertically, from the top of the head to the toes and back to the head continually. There are no audio instructions this week; the written description for clients is in Handout 9.1, so ensure that your client is provided with this handout. Remind them that each session needs to last 30 minutes.

Rationale for Compassion Training

Explain why feeling disconnected "within" and from others creates unhappiness and mental health difficulties, which in turn promotes relapse. Explain that compassion is the most conducive and rewarding way of developing a sense of connectedness, joy and well-being. Discuss also how these mental states buffer against relapse.

Introduce Loving-kindness Meditation

Introduce the practice of loving-kindness and the rationale for using it. The audio instructions are on tracks 17 (introduction) and 18 (the practice). Explain to your client that loving-kindness meditation is to be practiced following their sweeping in depth practice.

Introduce the Five Ethical Challenges

Describe the purpose of practicing personal ethics in terms of harm-minimization motivated by compassion, rather than duty or guilt. Introduce and discuss the five areas of harm (using harmful speech, taking lives, taking what is not given, becoming intoxicated and inappropriate sexual behavior) and the challenge of preventing them *out of compassion* for oneself and others. Ask your client to keep a record of their experiences when faced with preventing or engaging in harmful behavior.

Explain Homework Exercises

- The practice of sweeping in depth.
- Practicing loving-kindness: the introduction on track 17 and track 18 for instructions.
- Pay attention to the ethical nature of all actions and intentions, and try to prevent behavior that may cause harm to themselves or to other people.
- Read Handouts 9.1, 9.2 and 9.3.
- Fill in the Record of Ethical Challenges (Handout 9.4).
- Fill in the Daily Record of Mindfulness Meditation Practice (Handout 9.5).

Application with Groups

Session Aim

The aim of this session is to introduce Stage 4 of the program: the empathic stage. There are three teaching elements this week, (1) the sweeping in depth method of body scanning, (2) compassion training through loving-kindness meditation, and (3) compassion training through the five ethical practices, in the context of discussing the impact of preventing harm on psychological well-being. Sweeping in depth will provide greater opportunities to develop equanimity with deeply rooted emotional reactive habits. The study, respect and consequence of ethical boundaries will assist clients to increase their sense of connectedness and compassion.

Review Homework and Progress

Review how participants progressed with transversal scanning. Check if they can remain equanimous with blank spots. Check if they have successfully used the assertiveness steps in a conversation. If not, encourage them to do so this week. If they can feel at least 20 % of the body transversally, they can start practicing sweeping in depth and compassion training while continuing to practice assertive communication as often as necessary.

Introduce Sweeping in Depth

Explain the procedure and rationale for sweeping in depth, which is an integration of transversal scanning and sweeping en masse. Explain that sweeping in depth requires sweeping the interior of the body vertically, from the top of the head to the toes and back to the head continually. There are no audio instructions this week; the written description for clients is on Handout 9.1, so ensure that participants are provided with this handout. Remind them that each session needs to last 30 minutes.

Rationale for Compassion Training

Explain why feeling disconnected "within" and from others creates unhappiness and mental health difficulties, which in turn promotes relapse. Explain that compassion is the most conducive and rewarding way of developing a sense of connectedness, joy and well-being. Discuss also how these mental states buffer against relapse.

Introduce Loving-kindness Meditation

Introduce the practice of loving-kindness and the rationale for using it. The audio instructions are on tracks 17 (introduction) and 18 (the practice). Explain to participants that loving-kindness meditation is to be practiced following sweeping in depth.

In-session Loving-kindness Practice

Conduct in-session practice using track 18. This practice has three parts, each lasting approximately three minutes. Below is a description, which is also listed in Handout 9.2.

1 Self-compassion is developed by focusing on the center of the chest, at the level of the heart area. Notice the sensations in this area as you breathe in. As you breathe out, let these sensations spread out through the whole body, as if your heart is expanding with each exhalation. At the same time, start to create kind thoughts for and about yourself.
2 Compassion for those we love is the next focus of practice. Continue feeling the flow of tingling sensations that you may feel in the chest area as you breathe in, and as you breathe out, let these sensations and your compassion be directed towards people you love and care about for them to receive your loving vibrations. At the same time, create kind thoughts for these people who are close to you; you may also be grateful to these people for their contribution to your or someone else's well-being.
3 The third stage of the practice is to continue to focus on the tingling sensations while this time sending kindness and compassion to all beings, to everyone. This includes acquaintances, workmates, as well as people you do not know at all. Try to include people that you have had difficulties with. If this is too hard at the moment, you may leave them out for now or send a wish for them to become more aware of their deeds and that they prevent causing harm to themselves or others.

Introduce the Five Ethical Challenges

Describe the purpose of practicing personal ethics in terms of harm-minimization motivated by compassion, rather than duty or guilt. Introduce and discuss the five areas of harm (using harmful speech, taking lives, taking what is not given, becoming intoxicated and inappropriate sexual behavior) and the challenge to prevent them *out of compassion* for oneself and others. Ask participants to keep a record of their experiences when faced with preventing or engaging in harmful behavior.

Explain Homework Exercises

- The practice of sweeping in depth.
- Practicing loving-kindness: the introduction on track 17 and track 18 for instructions.
- Pay attention to the ethical nature of all actions and intentions, and try to prevent behavior that may cause harm to themselves or to other people.
- Read Handouts 9.1, 9.2 and 9.3.
- Fill in the Record of ethical challenges (Handout 9.4).
- Fill in the Daily Record of Mindfulness Meditation Practice (Handout 9.5).

Frequently Asked Questions

Question: My client tells me that when sweeping in depth he sometimes experiences very strong emotions. He worries that his practice is going backward and he will relapse into depression again.

Answer: This needs to be normalized, as experiencing emotions during practice is not a sign of relapse. It is expected, and it may actually be the case that he is preventing a relapse through the benefits of this practice. Sweeping through the body very deeply can give rise to deeply buried emotions and applying equanimity towards them neutralizes them. Explain to him not to identify with these experiences or react to them as he would have done in the past and instead stay in the present moment. If he does react, he needs to realize that he has reacted and be equanimous about it. If he doesn't react, then his overarching equanimity will quickly neutralize the reaction to both, the initial emotion and his subsequent reaction to it. Just as we call awareness of our current thinking "metacognitive awareness," we call awareness of our current state of equanimity "meta-equanimity." Applying this skill in meditation will also help your client decrease their worry-about-worry or perhaps performance anxiety in daily life.

Question: My client likes the idea of *self*-compassion, but this sounds so indulgent to her and she can't easily reconcile this concept with the idea that there is no real permanent self. How do you explain this to clients in a simple way?

Answer: Being compassionate towards ourselves helps us develop a more compassionate mind and therefore a better ability to be compassionate to others—we use the same brain in both contexts. The confusion comes from what is meant by self. Buddhist psychology identifies three types of views about the self; the nihilistic view, the materialist view and the so-called "middle way." Nihilism asserts that since everything is impermanent and there is no substantial self, there is no point in valuing and caring for anything that we call "I" "my" or "me." Materialism asserts that the self exists, and is evidenced by the independence of our body, mind, feelings and free will. Modern medical science contributes to this view, since dementia, for example, damages autobiographical memory and the related sense of self. In contrast, the "middle way," advocated by the Buddha, suggests that there cannot be a substantial, intrinsic self or "ego" because everything changes, but there is a human being. There is a person but the identity, specialness and sense of separateness from others are impermanent; they only exist based on conditions which are always in a state of change too. Therefore, while the assumption that the self exists in its own right is illusory, there is an actual human being that breathes, that feels and that needs love and comfort. The middle way is so called because it doesn't fall into the two extremes ways of conceptualizing the self, and the extreme consequences that these can have on our way of life. The middle way uses a utilitarian approach to deal with the self. We refer to ourselves by saying "I" for the convenience of communicating with each other (or we would call each other "mass of subatomic particles!") while not assuming that this "I" should stay the way it is. Consequently, it allows more flexibility to change because there is less attachment. Changing our views, habits, tastes, and decisions is made possible while preserving a fulfilling way of life.

Question: My client says that he understands about acting in an ethical way, but he thinks that the five ethical challenges are dogmatic, and they sound a bit prohibitive. He can't see how this relates to mindfulness or his problematic divorce problems. He asked if this stage is really necessary.

Answer: You can explore with him how it makes him feel if he acts unethically. You can also ask how those with whom he acts unethically may feel about his actions. Usually people will agree that the behavior caused some harm or discomfort to either themselves or to someone else. Remaining mindful of the inner experience of impulses to behave unethically, he has a chance to think things through and make choices more consciously, with genuine care and compassion in mind. Do you think he really understood this and yet still thinks it is dogmatic and prohibitive? Could you perhaps use elements of his problematic divorce, or the issues motivating the divorce, to exemplify the skills (or lack thereof) to learn at Stage 4?

Question: Sometimes, lying seems to be the most useful action and I'm not sure how flexible we can be with lies. Sometimes, in my opinion it is not useful for a client to say what they truly think. For example, one of my clients has a boyfriend who is a cruel man with symptoms of antisocial personality and psychopathy, and she is currently preparing to leave him and relocate to a friend's place on the other side of the country, where he won't be able to find her easily. He knows she wants to leave and asked her where she would go if she left him. She said she didn't know.

Answer: Wonderful! Wisdom is not a dogmatic and rigid path. On the contrary, it is about the right action at the right time, in the right place, in order to reduce suffering. While lying is usually not recommended because it harms by misleading people, sometimes we have to judge if there is potential harm in telling the truth, in both the short term and long term. Ethics is a complex subject and often there are no black and white solutions if you keep in mind the well-being of all parties.

Question: My client has told me that she doesn't think it is very realistic for her to commit to abstaining from alcohol for a whole week. She doesn't drink heavily but she shares about half a bottle of wine with her husband while cooking dinner, and says, "that's our relaxing time." In fact, I believe that she self-medicates, but how would you respond to her?

Answer: Ask her to use her mindfulness skills and note that *thinking* it is unrealistic to abstain from using alcohol is also *just a thought*. Also, the discomfort of abstaining is itself only a set of body sensations that she can now handle easily if she honestly tries. I would validate her commitment to creating a harmonious atmosphere with her partner and her desire for peace. I would then use Socratic questioning to bring her to the realization that she would prefer being genuinely at peace, rather than intoxicated. I would carefully ask her what would happen if she didn't drink for a whole week. Would they fight? Why? Would she be unable to sleep? Why? Does she need to address some anxiety? Can sex happen without alcohol or does she depend on alcohol for it? It is also possible that one expects the other to drink with them, which needs to be clarified in case her attachment to her habit is reinforced by a sense of pleasing her partner by drinking with him.

Question: My client struggles to be compassionate towards himself after the many years of behaving in a mean way to his wife.

Answer: Guilt is not a useful or wholesome way of being because it usually means that we feel anxious or bad about *ourselves*. Healthy remorse, on the other hand, means that we understand the impact of our actions on *others* and have therefore the capacity to change. So, it is more compassionate for your client to feel remorse and to commit to not repeating the harmful behavior or to blaming others who make the same mistakes. Instead of blaming himself, could he generate gratitude toward his partner for having been tolerant all these years and staying in the relationship? This would certainly be more productive, and it may give her some comfort that he now genuinely cares about her. In turn, promoting his partner's happiness is likely to assist him in forgiving himself. Loving-kindness meditation will help your client to look for the good in himself as well as in others.

Handout 9.1 The Practice of Sweeping in Depth

This scanning method combines transversal scanning and sweeping en masse. Sweeping in depth helps you to continue to develop your awareness and equanimity with old habits of reacting emotionally. Equanimity develops further as we learn not to take experiences in the body personally. We simply notice them and let them go. With practice, you will learn to feel the whole body (inside and outside) in a single breath. Of course, this takes time and practice, but anyone can learn.

Sweeping in depth means that you pass your attention vertically through the interior parts of the body in a single flow of attention from the top of the head to the toes. It is the same as sweeping en masse, but on the inside. Once you have scanned from head to toe you will scan back up again from the toes to the head in the same sweeping manner, feeling as many parts as possible. Sweep with a continuous flow of attention without interruption. When you have swept the body two or three times, go to any blank spots you may have noticed. Until you can feel internal sensations across the whole body, you can alternate two or three cycles of sweeping in depth and then one cycle of transversal scanning, and so on for 30 minutes.

A way to think about scanning in depth through the whole body is to think about dye being dropped into a bottle of water, spreading through all of the water. Attention is like the dye, spreading through the body. Your scanning speed will be slow at first and will speed up as you are able to feel more sensations. Eventually you will be able to feel body sensations as they arise during the day and remain calm and non-reactive (equanimous) about them. In this way, you will be able to be connected to what is taking place in your mind in the present moment and manage the way you respond skillfully, with wisdom, compassion and detachment. Please record your practice on the form (Handout 9.5) and return it to your therapist in your next session.

Handout 9.2 Loving-kindness Meditation

Use the audio instructions to guide yourself in creating kind and friendly thoughts about and for yourself. This takes about three minutes. Then create similar kind thoughts and well-wishes for other people. Start with people closest to you for about three3 minutes, and then other people, such as acquaintances and workmates, for the final two or three minutes. Try to include people you have had difficulties within the past or may have difficulties with in the future (you may find this hard initially, but this changes, too). Finally, send your friendly and loving thoughts toward all beings, including people you don't know. When you think in this way, you will notice pleasant subtle co-emerging body sensations, and these help us feel connected to other people. For this practice, visualization is OK so long as you keep your main focus on body sensations. This loving kindness-meditation will last about nine minutes and is added at the end of the usual 30-minute practice. After some time practicing with the audio instructions, you may like to create your own words; the usual wording includes "May I be safe," "May I be kind to myself," and "May I share my equanimity and peace of mind with everyone."

Forgiving

Now that you understand how sensations co-emerge with thoughts, you can see that other people operate in the same way. We all react because of our internal discomfort; we seek out and crave pleasant sensations and try to avoid unpleasant ones. When we realize this, it is easier to have compassion towards others because they may not have this wisdom; their lack of awareness has led to their actions. Forgiveness becomes much easier with this insight. It's a bit like forgiving a child's behavior because they are too young to understand what they do.

If you are mindful, you can see that everyone struggles and suffers in very similar ways; we all react to body sensations thinking we react to situations outside ourselves, and we are not aware of this unless we train in being mindful. We realize that *my* suffering is not unique to *me*, nor is my pain worse than the pain of other people. You will be able to notice that you are not singled out for pain and discomfort. This is a universal situation that happens to everyone: young or old, rich or poor, single or in a relationship, healthy or ill, absolutely everyone. Without this realization we feel like a victim, whether a victim of our own weaknesses or deficiencies or a victim of others' actions. You have learned to see a thought as *just* a thought and a sensation as *just* a sensation and you can now learn to see suffering as *just* suffering—not *your* suffering. You can now see that all mental states pass away; both happiness and unhappiness are short-lived states of mind.

With this understanding we are able to be compassionate *to ourselves* and we are less dependent on others' apology or approval to be kind to ourselves. Being compassionate to ourselves is the important first step in being able to be compassionate towards others.

Forgiving those who have harmed us is understandably challenging, and it can be just as difficult to forgive ourselves at times. If you have been abused in the past, you may struggle to include the person who hurt you in your loving kindness meditation. In this case you may leave this person out of the practice for now or wish that the person realizes the harm they have caused, that they do not repeat it and that they be kind to others and themselves. Whatever you choose to do, it should be done in a genuine way; pretending will only cause internal discomfort, disharmony between thoughts and sensations, and it will be harder to let go of the past.

Handout 9.3 Five Ethical Challenges

Our emotional reactivity is a reflection of our craving and aversion toward body sensations. When we react emotionally, we are more likely to perform harmful behaviors.

This week, do your best to ground the compassion you develop through loving-kindness meditation in your daily life by preventing harm to yourself and others. The five most common means of doing harm are harmful speech, taking lives, taking what is not given, inappropriate sexual behavior and taking intoxicants that prevent your normal self-control (such as alcohol and recreational drugs).

Practice five ethical challenges this week by paying attention to both your intentions and actions, and prevent doing harm. You can think of it as an experiment for the week. During this experiment, you will learn from your observations and notice how you feel after preventing these five harmful actions. Notice also the difference in your body when you can't avoid performing a harmful action, but do so without judging yourself, or you will lose your objectivity. You need to keep in mind that you are just a beginner, and you should not expect to be perfect at it. This will prevent you to feel that you failed if things don't go your way, and help you accept your experience just as it is. Please use Handout 9.4 to record your practice of ethical challenges for the week.

Handout 9.4 Record of Ethical Challenges

Date **Time**	**Situation** *(place, context time)*	**Behavior or desire** *(stealing, killing, lying, intoxication, inappropriate sex)*	**Type of response** *Were you able to prevent or stop the action? Rate intensity of resistance (%)*	**How long did your effort last?**	**How do you now feel about your response to the experience?**
Monday Time:					
Tuesday Time:					
Wednesday Time:					
Thursday Time:					
Friday Time:					
Saturday Time:					
Sunday Time:					

Handout 9.5 Daily Record of Mindfulness Meditation Practice

Day	**Date**	**Morning** *(circle)*	**Duration**	**Efficacy rating** *Rate from 1 to 10 how well you noticed distractions and brought your attention back to the body. 1 = not well at all; 10 = extremely well*	**Evening** *(circle)*	**Duration**	**Efficacy rating** *Rate from 1 to 10 how well you noticed distractions and brought your attention back to the body. 1 = not well at all; 10 = extremely well*
Monday		I practiced Yes / No			I practiced Yes / No		
Tuesday		I practiced Yes / No			I practiced Yes / No		
Wednesday		I practiced Yes / No			I practiced Yes / No		
Thursday		I practiced Yes / No			I practiced Yes / No		
Friday		I practiced Yes / No			I practiced Yes / No		
Saturday		I practiced Yes / No			I practiced Yes / No		
Sunday		I practiced Yes / No			I practiced Yes / No		

References

Alkoby, A., Halperin, E., Tarrasch, R., & Levit-Binnun, N. (2017). Increased support for political compromise in the Israeli–Palestinian conflict following an 8-week mindfulness workshop. *Mindfulness*. doi:10.1007/s12671-017-0710-5

Bradbury, H. (2014). Collaborative selflessness: Toward an experiential understanding of the emergent "responsive self" in caregiving context. *The Journal of Applied Behavioral Science*, 50, 55–79.

Cayoun, B. A. (2015). *Mindfulness-integrated CBT for wellbeing and personal growth: Four steps to enhance inner calm, self-confidence and relationships*. Chichester, UK: Wiley.

Cayoun, B. A. (2017). The purpose, mechanisms, and benefits of cultivating ethics in Mindfulness-integrated Cognitive Behavior Therapy. In L. M. Monteiro, J. Compson, & F. Musten (Eds.) *Practitioner's guide to ethics and Mindfulness-Based Interventions*, pp. 163–192. Cham: Springer. doi:10.1007/978-3-319-64924-5_7

Condon, P., Desbordes, G., Miller, W. B., & De Steno, D. (2013). Meditation Increases Compassionate Responses to Suffering. *Psychological Science*, 24, 2125–2127.

Darwin, C. (2004). *The descent of man and selection in relation to sex*. London, England: Penguin. (Original work published 1871)

Domes, G., Hollerbach, P., Vohs, K., Mokros, A., & Habermeyer, E. (2013). Emotional empathy and psychopathy in offenders: An experimental study. *Journal of Personality Disorders*, 27, 67–84.

Garrison, K. A., Scheinost, D., Constable, T., & Brewer, J. A. (2014). BOLD signal and functional connectivity associated with loving kindness meditation. *Brain and Behavior*, DOI: 10.1002/brb3.219

Germer, C. K. (2009). *The mindful path to self-compassion: Freeing yourself from destructive thoughts and emotions*. New York: Guilford Press.

Gilbert, P. (Ed.). (2005). *Compassion: Conceptualisations, research and use in psychotherapy* New York: Routledge.

Goenka, S. N. (2000). *The discourse summaries*. Onalaska, WA: Vipassana Research Publications.

Grossman, P. (2015). Mindfulness: Awareness informed by an embodied ethic. *Mindfulness*, 6, 17–22. doi:10.1007/s12671-014-0372-5

Hart, W. (1987). *The art of living: Vipassana meditation as taught by S.N. Goenka*. New York, NY: Harper Collins.

Jayasaro, A. (2008). Framing. Bahn Boon retreat discourse. Free MP3 downloadable at http://ratanagiri.files.birken.ca/dt/T09-04_A_Jayasaro_Framing.mp3 Retrieved February 2, 2018.

Jayasaro, A. (2010). *On Love*. Thailand: Panyaprateep Foundation. This book is available for free download at: http://forestsanghapublications.org/viewBook.php?id=65&ref=vec

Jayasaro, A. (2011). *Mindfulness, precepts and crashing in the same car*. Bangkok, Thailand: Panyaprateep Foundation. This book is available for free download at: http://forestsanghapublications.org/viewBook.php?id=64&ref=vec

Jazaieri, H., Jinpa, G. T., McGonigal, K., et al. (2013). Enhancing compassion: A randomized controlled trial of a compassion cultivation training program. *Journal of Happiness Studies*, 14, 1113–1126.

Kabat-Zinn, J. (2005). Coming to our senses: Healing ourselves and the world through mindfulness. London: Piatkus.

Khalsa, S. S., Adolphs, R., Cameron, O. G., Critchley, H. D., Davenport, P. W., Feinstein, J. S., ...& The Interoception Summit 2016 Participants. (2018). Interoception and mental health: a roadmap. *Biological Psychiatry: Cognitive Neuroscience and Neuroimaging*. doi:10.1016/j.bpsc.2017.12.004

Kramer, G. (2007). *Insight Dialogue: The interpersonal path to freedom.* Boston, MA: Shambhala Publications.

Lutz, A., Brefczynski-Lewis, J., Johnstone, T., & Davidson, R. J. (2008). Regulation of the neural circuitry of emotion by compassion meditation: Effects of meditative practice. *PloS One*, 3, e1897.

Monteiro, L. (2016). Implicit ethics and mindfulness: Subtle assumptions that MBIs are values-neutral. *International Journal of Psychotherapy*, 20, 210–224.

Monteiro, L., & Musten, F. (2013). *Mindfulness stops here: An eight-week guide to skillful living.* Victoria, Canada: Friesen Press.

Neff, K. (2004). Self-compassion and psychological well-being. *Constructivism in the Human Sciences*, 9, 27–37.

Neff, K. (2011). *Self-compassion: The proven power of being kind to yourself.* New York: William Morrow.

Neil, D. P. (2015). Confluence: Adoption and adaptation of loving-kindness and compassion practice in Buddhist and secular contexts. *Dharma Drum Journal of Buddhist Studies*, 16, 95–121.

Rahula, W. (1974). *What the Buddha taught.* New York: Grove Press.

Rogers-Carter, M. M., Varela, J. A., Grobbons, K. B., Pierce, A. F., McGoey, M. T., Ritchey, M., & Christianson, J. P. (2018). Insular cortex mediates approach and avoidance responses to social affective stimuli. *Nature Neuroscience.* doi:10.1038/s41593-018-0071-y

Schopenhauer, A. (1903). *The Basis of Morality, Part III, Ch. VIII*, 4, pp. 213–214. London: S. Sonnenschein & Co.

Shonin, E., van Gordon, W., & Griffiths, M. D. (2015). Teaching ethics in mindfulness-based interventions. *Mindfulness.* doi:10.1007/s12671-015-0429-0

Session 10: Promoting Well-Being and Outgrowing Suffering

There is no duty we so much underrate as the duty of being happy.
—Robert Louis Stevenson, 1903

Introduction

This chapter summarizes the skills that your client has learned during the MiCBT program and describes ways to measure progress. It guides you in the process of reviewing the rationale for the sequence of meditation practices and the various behavioral techniques taught week by week. This will help to consolidate understanding and assist with commitment to ongoing practice, which will militate against potential relapse. The systemic or "holistic" approach of MiCBT teaches the development of self-regulation skills across the main dimensions of peoples' lives, including perceptual (Stage 1), behavioral (Stage 2), interpersonal (Stage 3) and transpersonal (Stage 4) systems. It teaches specific mindfulness meditation skills anchored in the theoretical framework of the co-emergence model of reinforcement. Since clients frequently ask about future directions for preserving well-being and promoting personal growth, this session also provides suggestions for the development of personal growth skills that are congruent with MiCBT and its theoretical underpinnings.

Checking Client Progress

How did your client do with the ethical challenges? Were they able to notice body sensations associated with an ethical challenge? Did they react to the experience of craving or aversion, or were they able to remain equanimous and abstain from the harmful behavior? Clarify with your client that the task was to study the emerging sensations during experiences of craving and aversion and prevent the

The Clinical Handbook of Mindfulness-integrated Cognitive Behavior Therapy: A Step-by-Step Guide for Therapists, First Edition. Bruno A. Cayoun, Sarah E. Francis, and Alice G. Shires.

Companion website: www.wiley.com/go/Cayoun/Mindfulness-integrated

response, so that reactions that are of a harmful nature are prevented. It will be helpful to reiterate that the goal is not to "become a good person"; it is to develop compassion for themselves and others every time they reappraise the consequence of harmful intentions and habits and prevent them from occurring. Check if they noted which intentions and behavior produced dissatisfaction or happiness in the past week, and whether or not they learned from these experiences. You will notice that as people's respect for ethical boundaries increases *in the absence of guilt and conceit*, their sense of self-worth and potential for well-being also increase. As mentioned in the last session, this can be reflected by life-changing decisions being made during this training stage.

Was your client able to practice their meditation regularly this week? Were they able to sweep in depth and then practice loving-kindness meditation? Could they remain equanimous? You will need to discuss potential problems that may arise this week as you review the program as a whole. Check if your client related to loving-kindness meditation. This can tell you a lot, including if they value kindness and compassion.

Summary of the Skills your Client has Learned

In Stage 1, for the first four weeks of the program, your client learned how to attend to internal experiences in order to develop awareness and equanimity. With mindfulness practice, your client learned to be less identified with their experiences and less reactive to them. In doing so, they learned to use their own mind to regulate attention and emotion. In Stage 2, your client learned to apply these skills to stressful external situations. The focus was on preventing avoidant behavior and increasing confidence and a sense of self-efficacy. They learned to regulate behavior. In Stage 3, your client broadened their external focus by applying their insight to their interactions with others. They progressively learned to take responsibility for their own reactions and to relinquish responsibility for the reactions of others. They learned to see the true nature of people's suffering and pave the way for empathy. They learned to regulate interpersonal dynamics. In Stage 4, your client learned to perceive the relationship between compassion, ethical action and minimization of harm. They developed compassion in order to prevent relapse, on the basis that compassion for oneself and others is incompatible with depression and anxiety. They used loving-kindness meditation and learned to consider and apply personal ethics to develop a sense of being connected both within themselves and with others. As part of loving-kindness meditation, your client learned to pair kind thoughts and pleasant sensations with the memory of people who may have displeased them or who could create future conflicts, which acted as counterconditioning. The impact of ethical behavior and compassion training extended their skills and understanding to a broader, transpersonal awareness. They learned to regulate their sense of self.

By the end of Stage 4, your client has developed sufficient levels of insight and experiential awareness to decrease their likelihood of relapse. You can now assist your client to reframe the notion of "relapse" from being a "failure" to simply being a "re-occurrence" of a familiar experience which is, in fact, a new experience to which one reacts in a familiar way.

Assessing Results

Behavioral Indicators

If you recall Session 1, one of the MiCBT protocols is to perform a "therapy contract." During this process, we identify the client's goals for commencing the program, which we divide into "targeted problems" and "success indicators." It is now time to review their goals by evaluating how well they were able to achieve the success indicators. Review each success indicator and tick the ones that have been achieved or score them using a scaling method, with 0 representing no progress at all and 10 representing the full achievement of this goal.

Clinical Measures

The measures you used at the commencement of the program to assess your client's distress or other tailored outcomes should be re-administered and reviewed at this stage. It can be very useful to share this information with your client. We typically anticipate significant improvements in standard measures of depression, anxiety, stress and mindfulness (Francis, 2009). In the context of research, it would be preferable to collect another dataset in at least three months from now.

Experiential Indicators

There are three re-occurring experiential indicators of a successful mindfulness-based program where equanimity is a central skill. These indicators are not affected by gender, age, culture, language, religion, social status, education, wealth or past experience with mindfulness, and are therefore good means of easily gauging clients' perceived benefits.

Equanimity.

Your client's progress in mindfulness meditation can be measured by their level of equanimity. The duration of your clients' reactivity is the best gauge of their progress in achieving equanimity, rather than the type, frequency, or strength of the reaction. For example, reactions to the loss of a loved one may continue to emerge with strong sadness, but the duration of each occurrence should progressively decrease. The less time the sadness lasts, the less likely it is to contribute to depression. Similarly, your client may be justifiably angry about a situation, but maintaining that anger can cause harm to them and possibly to others if it is vented aggressively. How long the reaction lasts is therefore a good gauge of equanimity. It reflects your client's ability to regain an equilibrium state in the system (Cayoun & Shires, submitted for publication). With ongoing practice, your client will be able to let go of reactivity within seconds.

Gratitude.

Based on the principle that "happiness is more than the absence of unhappiness" (Cayoun, 2015, p. 1), clients need to develop a better ability to enjoy the present moment despite their growing equanimity and other new abilities to cope with common stresses of daily life. Mindfulness training develops insight that humbles us and enables us to realize how many of the opportunities we have had in our lives have been facilitated by others. As a consequence of that insight, we tend to have gratitude, and your client may experience it for different aspects of their lives. Sometimes, clients say that they have gratitude for being able to learn MiCBT or even for the problems that brought them to learn mindfulness skills in the first place. Perhaps they feel gratitude towards family members or friends who may have supported them while they have been undertaking daily meditation practice. Above all, they may have gratitude toward you, their therapist and teacher for what made a genuine difference in their life.

Sharing benefits.

Your client may feel a strong desire to share their training with people they value and love most. This is understandable. If you try a dish and think it is the best dish you've ever eaten in your life, are you going to talk about it to others, especially those whom you care most about? Clients often want to pass it on. In traditional Buddhist teachings, this is known as *ehipassiko* in Pali, which is usually translated as "come and see" or "come and try."

Unrealistic expectations

Occasionally, some clients have unrealistic expectations of others, such as changing others' expectations of them, obtaining others' cooperation, validation or praise, or being more loved by someone. If this is the case with your client, explain that the skills they have learned can help them to have more control over their *own behavior* and to understand and relate better to others' experiences, but this program cannot teach them to control what *others* do or feel. Mindfully observing their own needs with *equanimity* will help your client have a more realistic self-appraisal and be less dependent on others to feel worthy.

When making important changes in our life, it is most helpful to balance changes made to the internal and external contexts of daily life. Change may require tolerance and patience (internal context) or a speedy action that involves some level of risk (external context). Some people want to take outwardly directed action for quick change in order to feel better. Others prefer to make changes internally. However, continually asking a family member or work colleague to change may be draining and disappointing, while tolerating an abusive relationship will be harmful. Being intolerant with ourselves when we fall short of our expectation is just as unhelpful. Extremes are usually unrealistic and unhelpful. Encourage your client to continue to develop their new skills, balancing the internal and the external contexts to create a sense of harmony and continuity, which is more likely to produce realistic and constructive outcomes.

Managing changes in relationships

As your client develops their mindfulness skills, they may already be noticing changes to some of their relationships. Some clients notice changes in their interest for some activities or the company of some of their friends or acquaintances or even partners. Because they have become more conscious of situations that promote unwholesome states of mind, they may begin to question why they continue to be in these situations. They may find it difficult to reconcile the nature of their actions and decisions with their ethical standards, and wonder if they are causing harm to themselves or to someone else.

Some relationships feed on emotional reactivity, conceit, addiction and other factors contributing to unhappiness and relapse. Even though a client may be under the impression that their newly learned interpersonal and empathic skills will suffice to address this, it is possible that their relationship is toxic and promotes relapse into a depressive or anxiety condition. This is a very useful discussion to have at this point because some clients can be a little unforthcoming with the necessary changes. Others may feel genuinely empowered for the first time in their life and can become a little extreme or even reckless with their decision-making. Practicing compassion and performing ethical actions will increase your client's sense of self-worth and self-compassion. In turn, this can help them decrease guilt and make skillful decisions that can transform their existing relationships, impact how they initiate new ones, and shape how they live their lives guiltlessly.

Supporting Personal Growth: Ten Maturing Factors

Having resolved the problems for which they sought therapy, clients who are about to be discharged from your service and are enthusiastic about this program will often ask where they go from here, and how best to support their ongoing work. There are a number of ways of living that will support your client's well-being and assist their journey towards psychological maturation. Here are the ten most important ones, all well-documented in Buddhist psychology, where they are traditionally called "The Ten Perfections" (see Cayoun, 2015, for a detailed description of these ten factors):

1. Deciding to be *generous* whenever possible—generous with our time, knowledge or resources.
2. Being willing to act with *virtuous* intentions, respecting ethical boundaries, and acting in ways that are wholesome and do not cause internal agitation.
3. Exercising the ability to *renounce* (*let go of*) things, people or behaviors that are no longer wholesome and are not contributing to well-being.
4. Continuing to develop understanding, *wisdom*, across all life experiences, including the understanding of how holding on to fixed ideas about *who we are* (our sense of self) may not be useful.
5. Making ongoing *effort* to maintain mindfulness skills, avoid engaging in unwholesome (harmful) activities, let go of reactive behaviors when they are based on craving or aversion, and avoid taking things personally.
6. Developing *patience*, a powerful attribute that supports all nine other maturing factors. For example, patience helps with being able to tolerate the unpleasant aspects of life; it also helps with the development of equanimity and wisdom.
7. Being able to see and uphold the *truth* about various situations (e.g., being truthful with ourselves or admitting being in the wrong instead of defending a lie).
8. Being able to maintain commitment and *determination* to work toward goals.
9. Being able to be *kind* and compassionate.
10. Developing and applying the non-reactive and detached attitude of *equanimity* to what is unfolding in the present.

Maintenance of Mindfulness Practice

Explain to your client that an ongoing commitment to mindfulness meditation practice is necessary to maintain their skills. During this program maintaining meditation practice enabled your client to train a mental state that is both sharp and relaxed. They have already developed a better understanding of what causes their reactivity and its long-term negative consequences on mood. They now need to maintain their ability to detect early cues of distress in order to prevent their proliferation. We find it helpful to use the body as an analogy for ongoing practice: "Just as regular fitness exercises are necessary for ongoing physical fitness, regular meditation is necessary for ongoing fitness in the mind." Explain to your client that they will need to continue to develop and maintain the skills they learned in order to accept the rough with the smooth in life.

Practice Avoidance: "I always found it difficult until I tried"

Whether we practice mindfulness of breath or any type of body scanning, mindfulness meditation is essentially an exposure approach. As such, it is not always a pleasant experience. This can be a deterrent to a client's maintenance of practice, especially if they still have a lot to deal with. Accordingly, some clients want "a break." In a non-judgmental way, explain to your client that when we lack motivation, we can create many barriers to our regular practice: we feel too tired or too energetic, we are too busy or too lazy, we feel too sick or it is too late, it is too hot or too cold, etc. It is easy for the therapist to get lost in their client's narrative and reduce their ability to assist the client by respectfully questioning their hindering beliefs using the Socratic method. Sometimes practice seems to become a chore, a mechanical process and hard work. If this happens for your client, suggest that they take a minute before each practice session to ask themselves why they have decided to practice; what is their purpose for practicing? Bringing to mind the intentions and goals of the practice will also be helpful if they find that they are becoming drowsy.

It is also useful to explain that we *love* sensory stimulation. We are so addicted to seeing, hearing, smelling, tasting, feeling, thinking, all of which are far more attractive than meditating, during which they are discouraged. A basic reason for craving sensory stimulation is that we associate the senses with our sense of self. Stimulating them makes us feel "alive;" a basic but powerful *self*-reinforcer—and reinforcer of consumerism. By contrast, shutting our senses down prevents sensory reinforcement and is synonymous to *self*-disappearance. Therefore, we crave stimulation to the extent that we are attached to our sense of self. Sensation-seeking is particularly prominent in adolescence and during hyperthymic and euphoric moods. Moreover, experiencing extreme depression or extreme elation is likely to hinder motivation to practice because equanimity is difficult to maintain with extreme aversion or craving. This discourages clients from practicing. Discuss applying effort and determination, as mentioned earlier, as one of the ways to overcome the resistance to mindfulness practice.

Change in Health as Motivational Factor

The prospect of maintaining or improving physical health can be a powerful motivating factor in your client's maintenance of practice. There is now a large body of evidence that mindfulness meditation improves health-related outcomes as well as our psychological health. For example, mindfulness interventions have been found to decrease chronic pain (Cayoun, Simmons, & Shires, 2017; Zeidan et al. 2011), improve sleep quality (Farrarelli et al. 2013), improve memory and other mental abilities (Luders et al. 2013), improve sugar control in Type 2 Diabetes (Rosenzweig et al. 2007), reduce smoking addiction (Tang., et al. 2013), improve blood pressure (Hughes et al., 2013), improve immune function (Davidson et al., 2003), and protect chromosomes and longevity by maintaining telomeres' length (Hoge et al., 2013), to cite a few.

Mindfulness skills enable your client to be more aware of their physical needs including what and when to eat, sleep, exercise etc. With a greater ability to feel body sensations, we can be aware of upcoming problems earlier and more accurately, becoming more sensitive to early cues of health problems. For example, it becomes easier to understand and recognize the mechanisms of addiction more clearly, enabling earlier treatment, a better chance of recovery, and potentially extended longevity (Langer 1989).

Practice Maintenance: Type and Schedule

When your client has finished the program, a daily 45-minute practice is a good approach to skill maintenance and well-being. The standard maintenance practice in MiCBT consists of 10 minutes of mindfulness of breath, 25 minutes of body scanning and 10 minutes of loving-kindness meditation at the end. Your client can use the "practice maintenance" audio instructions on track 19 for this purpose. The track lasts exactly 45 minutes so that the client need not be distracted by having to monitor the time.

Explain to your client that they can choose the type of body scanning practice depending on what they are able to practice on the day. A useful guideline is to use a scanning method that is likely to require some effort. This will prevent habituation and drowsiness and be helpful for progress. As your client progresses, they will increasingly use the same skills in life as they do in their meditation practice; after all we use the same brain all the time! For example, if your client is equanimous while experiencing disturbing thoughts or physical pain during their practice, they will start to find the same ability in daily life; their meditation practice is reflected in their life. It is worth reminding your client that purposeful ruminating or mind-wandering during practice, or not making sufficient effort to let go of thoughts, will always be an impediment to good practice.

However, when stress levels are very high, resuming a twice-daily practice is recommended, although this might require a great deal of effort. This is likely to help with mood management and improve sleep. With extreme stress, body scanning may not be possible, in which case advise your client to practice only mindfulness of breath. If this is too hard, then they should practice progressive muscle relaxation and loving-kindness for a few days until they can resume mindfulness of breath. When stress levels are extreme, your client may need to postpose their practice until the crisis subsides. They can then restart the meditation practice gently, beginning with mindfulness of breath.

The experience of "bliss" or "dissolution" was discussed in a previous chapter. If this happens regularly for your client, you can suggest that they scan through the spine transversally and then return to standard scanning. This is because older memories and associated conditioned responses are known to meditation teachers to be linked with this area of the body. They are working towards sweeping in depth through the whole body in a single breath; downward with an in-breath and upward with an out-breath. There is more to learn from the *Vipassana* meditation traditions, but this is clearly beyond the scope of a mindfulness-based intervention in clinical contexts. More can be learned during intensive courses in *Vipassana* meditation centers. Clients can take further training, such as a ten-day *Vipassana* course or a course run through meditation centers in the tradition of Sayagyi U Ba Khin (www.dhamma.org).

Application with Individual Clients

Session Aim

Session 10 consolidates Stage 4 and serves to recap the entire program, including a review of client's success indicators and clinical measures. It also addresses relapse prevention and future practice goals.

Review Homework and Progress

Conduct the feedback session on the home practice set last week: sweeping in depth practice, loving-kindness practice and ethical challenges. Check with your client if they were able to practice sweeping in depth. Discuss how they did with the ethical challenges. Could they prevent taking lives, such as killing a spider or an ant? Could they restrain themselves from saying something unkind or buying into politics at work? What about alcohol? How did they manage when trying not to use alcohol? Check also how the loving-kindness meditation went; were they able to generate loving and kind thoughts about themselves? Were they able to monitor the sensations co-emerging with both harmful and compassionate intentions before performing a verbal or physical action?

Program Revision

Summarize the key elements of MiCBT including:

Formal practice tools:

- Progressive Muscle Relaxation
- Mindfulness of breath

- Body scanning:
  - Part-by-part scanning
  - Symmetrical scanning
  - Partial sweeping
  - Sweeping en masse
  - Transversal scanning
  - Sweeping in depth
  - Loving kindness

Other tools:

- The co-emergence model of reinforcement
- Bipolar exposure—items listed on SUDS form
- Mindful assertiveness
- Ethical challenges

Assess Goals Achievement

Repeat clinical measures and compare results. Discuss your client's goals and treatment expectations and their progress in terms of their behavior, overall health and relationships. Discuss their levels of equanimity. This indicates their sense of self-efficacy.

Relapse-prevention Guidelines and Setting a Follow-up Session

Provide relapse-prevention guidelines: maintaining mindfulness and loving-kindness meditation practices, maintaining ethical boundaries, and reframing relapse.

Follow-up sessions can be useful to consolidate practice and reduce the risk of relapse. These could be offered as four sessions spread over a year following post-treatment, starting a month after the end of the program.

Practice Support Group

If appropriate, encourage the possibility of joining or forming a regular mindfulness practice group. This aids the maintenance of sitting practice, and fosters social networking.

Application with Groups

Session Aim

Session 10 consolidates Stage 4 and serves to recap the entire program, including a review of clients' success indicators and clinical measures. It also addresses relapse prevention and future practice goals.

Materials

Pens and paper, a "Certificate of Participation" (if possible), list of goals captured in the first session and clinical outcome measure questionnaires (if data were collected at the outset).

Review Homework and Progress

Conduct the feedback session on the home practice set last week: sweeping in depth practice, loving-kindness practice and ethical challenges. Check with participants if they were able to practice sweeping in depth. Discuss how they went with the ethical challenges. Could they prevent taking lives, such as killing a spider or an ant? Could they restrain themselves from saying something unkind or buying into politics at work? What about alcohol? How did they manage when trying not to use alcohol? Check also how the loving-kindness meditation went; were they able to generate loving and kind thoughts about themselves? Were they able to monitor the sensations co-emerging with both harmful and compassionate intentions before performing a verbal or physical action?

Program Revision

Summarize the key elements of MiCBT including:
Formal practice tools:

- Progressive Muscle Relaxation
- Mindfulness of breath
- Body scanning:
    - Part-by-part scanning
    - Symmetrical scanning
    - Partial sweeping
    - Sweeping en masse
    - Transversal scanning
    - Sweeping in depth
    - Loving kindness

Other tools:

- The co-emergence model of reinforcement
- Bipolar exposure—items listed on SUDS form
- Mindful assertiveness
- Ethical challenges

Assess Goals Achievement

Discuss participants' goals and expectations for treatment and how they evaluate their progress in terms of their behavior, overall health and relationships. Discuss their levels of equanimity. This provides an indication of their sense of self-efficacy. Using the whiteboard, discuss goal achievement as follows:

1 List on the board all initial generic goals and write the number of participants who endorsed them in session 1 (from the copy your participants kept).
2 Go through each item listed on the board one by one and ask participants who have been able to improve their skills (by a show of hands). Your participants are measuring their sense of self-efficacy.
3 Ask participants to check off which of their goals were achieved.

In-session Practice

Conduct a sweeping in depth practice (with no instruction) followed by a five-minute loving-kindness meditation; either in silence, using the script, or allowing participants to generate their own script.

Certificate of Participation

Present a Certificate of Participation to each participant. This can act as a positive reinforcer for attending follow-up sessions, which in turn stimulates the consolidation of skills.

Practice Support Group

If appropriate, encourage the possibility of joining or forming a regular mindfulness practice group. This aids maintenance of group cohesiveness, maintenance of sitting practice, and fosters social networking.

Fill in the last outcome-assessment forms if data are needed.

Outline of MiCBT Follow-up Sessions

Follow-up sessions can be useful to consolidate practice and reduce the risk of relapse. This could be offered as four sessions spread over a year starting a month after the end of the program.

Follow-up Sessions

- Welcome participants
- In-session practice:
    - Group mindfulness practice for 15 to 20 minutes (one-third of the time on breath awareness, two-thirds on body scanning)

Feedback on Maintaining Practice and Well-Being Since the Group Ended

1. Revisit initial goals set at the start of the program and how they rated their achievements at the end of the program.
2. Ask participants to rate out of ten the extent to which they have sustained their achievement.
3. If they have struggled to sustain their achievements, ask them to reflect on how much time and effort they have invested. Discuss maintaining an ongoing mindfulness practice.

Refreshing Key Issues

1. Interpersonal issues: role-play an interpersonal issue using assertive statements demonstrating equanimity.
2. Discuss the importance of impermanence.
3. In depth review of steps of experiential ownership.
4. Review of ethics, contextualized within the co-emergence model.

Setting Goals

1. Ask participants to select realistic goals:
    a. to achieve by the next session;
    b. longer-term goals.
2. Suggest a bipolar exposure visualization of achieving the goals.
3. Ask them to rate out of ten how realistic and feasible the goals are.
4. Visualize realistic short-term goals (to try to achieve by next session).

Practice of Stage 4

Reiterate the importance of practicing Stage 4 as part of their maintenance practice: compassion (loving-kindness meditation), adhering to their own ethical standards and ongoing mindfulness practice (one-third on breath awareness, two-thirds on body scanning).

Handout 10.1 MiCBT Program Overview

Internalizing skills

Stage 1
Personal stage

Behavioral task: Mindfulness training for deep levels of metacognitive and interoceptive awareness; acceptance of impermanence and egolessness of phenomena; increased equanimity and sense of self-efficacy; emphasis on practice commitment.

Meditative type:
Session 1*—Progressive muscle relaxation (14-minutes twice daily).*
Session 2*—Mindfulness of breath (MOB) (30 minutes twice-daily from here on).*
Session 3*—Part-by-part unilateral body Scanning.*
Session 4*—Unilateral body scanning without audio and applied practice.*

Externalizing skills

Stage 2
Exposure stage

Behavioral task: Exposure procedures: "bipolar exposure" (guided imagery with interoceptive exposure to SUDS targets while remaining equanimous) followed by in-vivo exposure applying equanimity.

Meditative type:
Session 5*—Bilateral body scanning to engage broader somatosensory networks symmetrically and rapidly; practice of bipolar exposure for 11 minutes after the 30-minute meditation.*
Session 6*—Partial sweeping by passing attention in a continuous manner, to "flow" through the body while preventing craving to pleasant sensations; practice of bipolar exposure for 11 minutes after the 30-minute meditation.*

Stage 3
Interpersonal stage

Behavioral task: "Experiential ownership" (interpersonal exposure to prevent avoidance and interpersonal conflicts; not reacting to others' reactions (seeing suffering); assertiveness.

Meditative type:
Session 7*—Sweeping en masse with "free flow" through the entire body in a single pass while remaining equanimous with pleasure.*
Session 8*—Transversal scanning by passing attention transversally through the body to feel the interior of the body with equanimity.*

Stage 4
Empathic stage

Behavioral task: Awareness of ethical boundaries and commitment to ethics; compassion for oneself and others; preventing relapse; maintaining gains.

Meditative type:
Session 9*—Sweeping in depth by passing attention with vertical free flow on the inside of the body with equanimity; loving-kindness meditation for eight minutes; mindful practice of five ethical precepts.*
Session 10*—Maintenance practice (once per day for 45 minutes) with 10 minutes MOB, 25 minutes body scanning, 10 minutes loving-kindness; program review.*

References

Cayoun, B. A. (2011). *Mindfulness-integrated CBT: Principles and practice.* Chichester, UK: Wiley.

Cayoun, B. A. (2015). *Mindfulness-integrated CBT for wellbeing and personal growth: Four steps to enhance inner calm, self-confidence and relationships.* Chichester, UK: Wiley.

Cayoun, B. A., & Shires, A. (submitted for publication). Co-emergence reinforcement: A proposed transdiagnostic mechanism in emotional disorders and their remediation through mindfulness and cognitive-behavioral interventions. Manuscript submitted for publication.

Cayoun, B. A., Simmons, A., & Shires, A. (2017). Immediate and lasting chronic pain reduction following a brief self-implemented mindfulness-based interoceptive exposure task: A pilot study. *Mindfulness*. 1–13. doi: 10.1007/s12671-017-0823-x

Farrarelli, F., Smith, R., Dentico, D., et al. (2013). Experienced mindfulness meditators exhibit higher parietal-occipital EEG gamma activity during NREM sleep. *PLoS ONE*, 8, e73417.

Hoge, E. A., Chen, M. M., Orr, E., et al. (2013). Loving-Kindness Meditation practice associated with longer telomeres in women. *Brain Behavior and Immunity*, 32, 159–163. doi:10.1016/j.bbi.2013.04.005

Francis, S. E. B. (2009). A study of the relationship between mindfulness and well-being (Unpublished Master Thesis). Swinburne University, Melbourne

Langer, E. J. (1989). *Mindfulness*. New-York: Addison-Wesley.

Luders, E., Thompson, P. M., Kurth, F., et al. (2013). Global and regional alterations of hippocampal anatomy in long-term meditation practitioners. *Human Brain Mapping*, 34, 3369–3375.

Rosenzweig, S., Reibel, D. K., Greeson, J. M., et al. (2007). Mindfulness-based stress reduction is associated with improved glycemic control in Type 2 Diabetes Mellitus: A pilot study. *Alternative Therapies*, 13, 36–38.

Stevenson, R. L. (1903). *Virginibus puerisque: An apology for idlers.* New York: Roycrofters.The details of Vipassana Meditation Centers can be found online at: www.dhamma.org

The details of International Meditation Centers can be found on line at: www.international-meditationcentre.org/global/index.html

Thorndike, E. L. (1898). Animal intelligence: An experimental study of the associative processes in animals. *Psychological Monographs: General and Applied*, 2, i–109.

Tang, Y., Tang, R., & Posner, M. (2013). Brief meditation training induces smoking reduction. *Proceedings of the National Academy of Sciences of the USA*, 110, 13971–13975.

Woodward, F. L. (1925). *Some sayings of the Buddha: According to the Pali Canon.* London: Oxford University Press.

Zeidan, F., Martucci, K. T., Kraft, R., et al. (2011). Brain mechanisms supporting the modulation of pain by mindfulness meditation. *The Journal of Neuroscience*, 31, 5540–5548. *PNAS, 110,* 13971–13975.

Part 3
Summary Checklists and MiCBT Scripts

Appendix 1

Summaries of Weekly Content

Session 1: Summary of weekly content—individuals

Application with individual clients	*Handouts for clients*
1. Discuss briefly that MiCBT integrates Eastern and Western psychologies and that it uses very specific mindfulness exercises	
2. Explain mindfulness	**Handout 1.1** What is Mindfulness?
3. Discuss and agree goals for therapy—create and sign therapy contract	**Handout 1.2** Therapy Contract
4. Readiness for change	**Handout 1.3** Readiness for Change and Requirement for Effort
5. Explain three complementary ways of learning about ourselves	**Handout 1.4** Three Ways of Learning
6. Briefly explain that MiCBT is a four-stage program *Mindfulness for self-awareness and acceptance, exposure to difficulties, improving relationships with others, and empathy grounded in ethical living*	**Handout 1.5** Program Structure: The Four Stages
7. Discuss the need for regular practice	**Handout 1.6** Why it is Important to Develop a Regular Practice

(*Continued*)

Application with individual clients	*Handouts for clients*
8. Present PMR and Mindfulness of Body Brief PMR practice	**Handout 1.7** Progressive Muscle Relaxation and Mindfulness of Body
9. List of tracks	**Handout 1.8** Audio Tracks for the MiCBT Program
10. Setting up home practice • Provide the Daily Practice Record of PMR practice • Read handouts and twice-daily practice of PMR • Practice mindfulness of the body as often as possible	**Handout 1.9** Daily Record of Progressive Muscle Relaxation

Session 1: Summary of weekly content—groups

Application with groups	*Handouts for clients*
1. Introduce participants and yourself	
2. Discuss briefly that MiCBT integrates Eastern and Western psychologies and that it uses very specific mindfulness exercises – addresses both content and processing of thoughts	
3. Explain three complementary ways of learning about ourselves	**Handout 1.4** Three Ways of Learning
4. Readiness for change	**Handout 1.3** Readiness for Change and Requirement for Effort
5. Discuss mindfulness—write definition on whiteboard	**Handout 1.1** What is Mindfulness?
6. Briefly explain that MiCBT is a 4-stage program *Mindfulness for self-awareness and acceptance, exposure to difficulties, improving relationships with others, and empathy grounded in ethical living*	**Handout 1.5** Program Structure: The Four Stages
7. Use whiteboard to set goals and empathy grounded in ethical living brainstorm and then consolidate long-list into list of 5–15	**Handout 1.2** Therapy Contract

Application with groups	*Handouts for clients*
8. Present PMR and Mindfulness of Body Brief PMR practice	**Handout 1.7** Progressive Muscle Relaxation and Mindfulness of Body
9. List of tracks	**Handout 1.8** Audio Tracks for the MiCBT Program
10. Discuss the need for regular practice	**Handout 1.6** Why it is Important to Develop a Regular Practice
11. Setting up home practice: • Provide the Daily Practice Record of PMR practice • Read handouts and twice daily practice of PMR • Practice mindfulness of the body as often as possible	**Handout 1.9** Daily Record of Progressive Muscle Relaxation

Session 2: Summary of weekly content—individuals

Application for individual clients	*Handouts for clients*
1. Review practice from last week and check readiness to proceed to MOB	**Handout 2.1** Typical Difficulties Encountered in Practice
2. Mindfulness of breath practice • Facilitate a brief practice then discuss practice set-up (location, scheduling, posture, clothing)	**Handout 2.2** Practice Tips
3. Discuss mindfulness of breath practice (three skills) • awareness of thoughts as "just thoughts" • learning to not buy into thoughts • being able to switch back to breath Apply the finger task	
4. Explain intrusive thinking • recency, frequency, co-emergence • fasting metaphor	

(Continued)

Application for individual clients	*Handouts for clients*
5. Set up home practice • Provide the daily practice record of MOB • Read handouts and twice-daily practice of MOB • Applied practice: breath and thought monitoring in daily life	**Handout 2.3** Homework exercises **Handout 2.4** Daily Record of Mindfulness Practice

Session 2: Summary of weekly content—groups

Application with groups	*Handouts for clients*
1. Mindfulness of breath practice • Run the practice session then discuss practice set-up (location, scheduling, posture, clothing)	**Handout 2.2.** Practice Tips
2. Review practice from last week • go around each group member • reinforce practice and use Socratic questioning to investigate barriers to practice	**Handout 2.1.** Typical Difficulties Encountered in Practice
3. Discuss mindfulness of breath practice (three skills) • awareness of thoughts as "just thoughts" • learning to not buy into thoughts • being able to switch attention back to the breath Apply the finger task	
4. Explain intrusive thinking • recency, frequency, co-emergence • fasting metaphor	
5. Set up the home practice • Provide daily practice record of MOB • Read handouts and twice-daily practice of MOB • Applied practice: breath and thought monitoring in daily life	**Handout 2.3** Homework Exercises **Handout 2.4** Daily Record of Mindfulness Practice

Session 3: Summary of weekly content—individuals

Application with individual clients	*Handouts for clients*
1. Review last week's practice and discuss any issues raised	
2. Present the rationale for body scanning using the Diary of Reactive Habits with an example	**Handout 3.1** Diary of Reactive Habits

Application with individual clients	*Handouts for clients*
3. Explain impermanence and how this enables a new relationship to experiences including difficult body sensations/emotions	
4. Discuss equanimity and how developing equanimity helps to regulate emotions and develop self-acceptance	**Handout 3.2** Body scanning: Understanding Feelings and Equanimity
5. Conduct a brief body-scanning practice and introduce the Interoceptive Awareness Indicator	**Handout 3.3** Interoceptive Awareness Indicator
6. Give out the Diary of Reactive Habits for use during the week with any stressful situations that occur	**Handout 3.1** Diary of Reactive Habits
7. Setting up home practice: body scanning using tracks 7 and 8.	**Handout 3.4** Daily Record of Mindfulness Practice

Session 3: Summary of weekly content—groups

Application with groups	*Handouts for clients*
1. Conduct a brief mindfulness of breath practice	
2. Review last week's practice and discuss any issues raised	
3. Present the rationale for body scanning using the Diary of Reactive Habits with an example	**Handout 3.1** Diary of Reactive Habits
4. Explain impermanence and how this enables a new relationship to experiences, including difficult body sensations/emotions	
5. Discuss equanimity and how developing equanimity helps to regulate emotions and develop self-acceptance	**Handout 3.2** Body scanning: Understanding Feelings and Equanimity
6. Conduct a body-scanning practice (30 minutes) and introduce the Interoceptive Awareness Indicator	**Handout 3.3** Interoceptive Awareness Indicator

(*Continued*)

Application with groups	*Handouts for clients*
7. Distribute copies of the Diary of Reactive Habits for use during the week with any stressful situations that occur	**Handout 3.1** Diary of Reactive Habits
8. Setting up home practice: body scanning using tracks 7 and 8.	**Handout 3.4** Daily Record of Mindfulness Meditation Practice

Session 4: Summary of weekly content—individuals

Application with individual clients	*Handouts for clients*
1. Review homework and check readiness to progress.	
2. Increasing practice efficacy: ● Discuss silent practice, immobility, equanimity, pacing the practice and effort in practice.	
3. Body scanning, ego and the development of insight	
4. Applying and measuring equanimity: ● Introduce the MISS and MIET. Ask clients to record the four characteristics and severity of sensations on the MISS every time they feel emotions.	**Handout 4.1** Mindfulness-based Interoceptive Signature Scale (MISS)
5. Discuss the need for regular practice: ● Discuss maintaining interoceptive awareness and equanimity as much and as often as possible throughout the day, from the moment they wake up until the moment they fall asleep	
6. Setting up home practice: ● Practice without audio instructions, in complete immobility and faster. ● Read handout with homework ● Provide Daily Record of Mindfulness Meditation Practice form ● Provide Interoceptive Awareness Indicator form (introduced in Session 3)	**Handout 4.2** Applied Practice **Handout 4.3** Daily Record of Mindfulness Meditation Practice **Handout 3.3** Interoceptive Awareness Indicator

Session 4: Summary of weekly content—groups

Application with groups	*Handouts for clients*
1. Conduct a group practice of unilateral body scanning	
2. Review homework and check readiness to progress.	
3. Increasing practice efficacy: • Discuss silent practice, immobility, equanimity, pacing the practice and effort in practice.	
4. Body scanning, ego and the development of insight.	
5. Applying and measuring equanimity: • Introduce the MISS and MIET. Ask clients to record the 4 characteristics and severity of sensations on the MISS every time they feel emotions.	**Handout 4.1** Mindfulness-based Interoceptive Signature Scale (MISS)
6. Discuss the need for regular practice: • Discuss maintaining interoceptive awareness and equanimity as much and as often as possible throughout the day, from the moment they wake up until the moment they fall asleep.	
7. Setting up home practice: • Practice without audio instructions, in complete immobility and faster. • Read handout with homework • Provide Record of Mindfulness Practice form • Provide Interoceptive Awareness Indicator form (introduced in Session 3)	**Handout 4.2** Applied Practice **Handout 4.3** Daily Record of Mindfulness Meditation Practice **Handout 3.3** Interoceptive Awareness Indicator

Session 5: Summary of weekly content—individuals

Application with individual clients	*Handouts for clients*
1. Review last week's practice	
2. Introduce symmetrical scanning	**Handout 5.1** Symmetrical Scanning

(*Continued*)

Application with individual clients	*Handouts for clients*
3. Introduce exposure: • Identify avoided situations and fill out Exposure Record Sheet (SUDS form) in session or at home	**Handout 5.2** The Nature of Avoidance **Handout 5.3** Instructions for Bipolar Exposure **Handout 5.4** Exposure Record Sheet: Subjective Units of Distress (SUDS) **Handout 5.5** Practice of in-vivo Exposure
4. Explain home exercises • Symmetrical scanning • In-vivo and bipolar exposure • Fill out mindfulness practice sheet	**Handout 5.6** Homework Exercises **Handout 5.7** Daily Record of Mindfulness Meditation Practice

Session 5: Summary of weekly content—groups

Application with groups	*Handouts for clients*
1. Conduct in-session practice of unilateral part-by-part body scanning	
2. Review last week's practice.	
3. Introduce symmetrical scanning • Conduct short practice	**Handout 5.1** Symmetrical Scanning
4. Introduce bipolar exposure task • Participants identify avoided situations and fill out SUDS form	**Handout 5.2** The Nature of Avoidance **Handout 5.3** Instructions for Bipolar Exposure **Handout 5.4** Exposure Record Sheet: Subjective Units of Distress (SUDS) **Handout 5.5** Practice of in-vivo Exposure
5. Explain home exercises • Symmetrical scanning • In-vivo and bipolar exposure • Fill out mindfulness practice sheet	**Handout 5.6** Homework Exercises **Handout 5.7** Daily Record of Mindfulness Meditation Practice

Session 6: Summary of weekly content—individuals

Application for individual clients	*Handouts for clients*
1. Review mindfulness practice and provide feedback • Check for 80% coverage when using symmetrical scanning. • Check progress with SUDS items and discuss this week's exposure items	
2. Introduce partial sweeping	**Handout 6.1** Partial Sweeping
3. Measuring progress with desensitization • Clients re-rate all SUDS items including those not yet addressed with exposure	**Handout 6.2** Measuring Progress with Desensitization
4. Discuss generalization of avoidance	**Handout 6.3** The Generalizing Effects of Avoidance and Desensitization
5. Explain homework for this week • Partial sweeping (tracks 11 and 12) • Exposure task using SUDS items: implement bipolar exposure with remaining items • Fill out mindfulness practice sheet	**Handout 6.4** Exposure Record Sheet: Subjective Units of Distress (SUDS) **Handout 6.5** Homework Exercises **Handout 6.6** Daily Record of Mindfulness Meditation Practice

Session 6: Summary of weekly content—groups

Application with groups	*Handouts for clients*
1. Review mindfulness practice and provide feedback • Check for 80% coverage when using symmetrical scanning. • Check progress with SUDS items and discuss this week's exposure items	
2. Introduce partial sweeping scanning	**Handout 6.1** Partial Sweeping
3. Measuring progress with desensitization • Clients re-rate all SUDS items including those not yet addressed with exposure	**Handout 6.2** Measuring Progress with Desensitization

(Continued)

Application with groups	*Handouts for clients*
4. Discuss generalization of avoidance	**Handout 6.3** The Generalizing Effects of Avoidance and Desensitization
5. Explain homework for this week • Partial sweeping (track 10) • Exposure task using SUDS items—implement bipolar exposure with remaining items • Fill out mindfulness practice sheet	**Handout 6.4** Exposure Record Sheet Subjective Units of Distress (SUDS) **Handout 6.5** Homework Exercises **Handout 6.6** Daily Record of Mindfulness Meditation Practice

Session 7: Summary of weekly content—individuals

Application with individual clients	*Handouts*
1. Review homework and progress with SUDS items	
2. Introduce sweeping en masse	**Handout 7.1** Sweeping en masse
3. Introduce Stage 3 • Explain experiential ownership: taking full responsibility for our thoughts and body sensations and disowning those of others while remaining empathic about their suffering • Ask your client to select some situations for the experiential ownership practice	**Handout 7.2** Experiential Ownership **Handout 7.3** The Practice of Experiential Ownership
4. Explain homework exercises • Sweeping en masse (audio tracks 13 and 14) • Bipolar and in-vivo exposure to interpersonal issues using experiential ownership • Fill out mindfulness practice sheet	**Handout 7.4** Homework Exercises **Handout 7.5** Daily Record of Mindfulness Meditation Practice

Session 7: Summary of weekly content—groups

Application with groups	*Handouts*
1. Review homework and progress with SUDS items • Check in with participants on ability to maintain twice-daily practice	

Application with groups	*Handouts*
2. Introduce sweeping en masse • Conduct a 15-minute practice session to introduce sweeping en masse with track 14	**Handout 7.1** Sweeping en masse
3. Introduce Stage 3 • Explain experiential ownership: taking full responsibility for our thoughts and body sensations and disowning those of others while remaining empathic about their suffering • Ask participants to select some situations for the experiential ownership practice	**Handout 7.2** Experiential Ownership **Handout 7.3** The Practice of Experiential Ownership
4. Explain homework exercises • Sweeping en masse (audio tracks 13 and 14) • Bipolar and in-vivo exposure to interpersonal issues using experiential ownership • Fill out mindfulness practice sheet	**Handout 74** Homework Exercises **Handout 7.5** Daily Record of Mindfulness Meditation Practice

Session 8: Summary of weekly content—individuals

Application with individual clients	*Handouts*
1. Check with your client on ability to maintain twice-daily practice	
2. Review homework and progress with SUDS items – interpersonal items	
3. Conduct a short practice session to introduce transversal scanning with track 15 & 16	**Handout 8.1** Transversal Scanning
4. Introduce mindful assertiveness • Explain what is meant by mindful assertiveness; relationship between depression and assertiveness • Ask client to select a situation for mindful assertiveness practice • Discuss the seven assertive statements: starting with the facts, how "I" feel, how "I" think, acknowledging the other, what "I" want, how to reward cooperation or compromise for a win–win solution.	**Handout 8.2** Assertiveness Training Task

(Continued)

Application with individual clients	*Handouts*
5. Explain homework exercises • Twice-daily practice of transversal scanning (audio tracks 15 and 16) • Choose situations to practice being assertive, expressing needs assertively, in a considerate respectful way. • Clients may have items listed on their SUDS form that they can use.	
6. Fill out mindfulness practice monitoring form	**Handout 8.3** Daily Record of Mindfulness Meditation Practice

Session 8: Summary of weekly content—groups

Application with groups	*Handouts*
1. Review homework and progress with SUDS items - interpersonal items • Check in with participants on ability to maintain twice-daily practice	
2. Introduce transversal scanning • Conduct a 15-minute group practice session to introduce transversal with track 15 & 16	**Handout 8.1** Transversal Scanning
3. Introduce mindful assertiveness • Explain what is meant by mindful assertiveness, relationship between depression and assertiveness • Ask participants to select a situation for mindful assertiveness practice • Write the seven assertive statements: starting with the facts, how "I" feel, how "I" think, acknowledging the other, what "I" want, how to reward cooperation or compromise for a win–win solution.	**Handout 8.2** Assertiveness Training Task
4. Explain homework exercises • Twice-daily practice of transversal scanning (audio tracks 15 and 16) • Choose situations to practice being assertive, expressing needs assertively, in a considerate respectful way. • Clients may have items listed on their SUDS form that they can use.	

Application with groups	*Handouts*
5. Fill out mindfulness practice monitoring form	**Handout 8.3** Daily Record of Mindfulness Meditation Practice

Session 9: Summary of weekly content—individuals

Application with individual clients	*Handouts*
1. Review practice from last week • Check readiness to proceed • Check on assertiveness task	
2. Introduce sweeping in depth	**Handout 9.1** The Practice of Sweeping in Depth **Handout 9.5** Daily Record of Mindfulness Meditation Practice
3. Introduce loving-kindness meditation	**Handout 9.2** Loving-kindness Meditation
4. Introduce five ethical challenges. • Describe the five ethical challenges (preventing lying, killing, stealing, becoming intoxicated and inappropriate sexual activity).	**Handout 9.3** Five Ethical Challenges **Handout 9.4** Record of Ethical Challenges
5. Set homework • Sweeping in depth practice • Loving-kindness practice • Five ethical challenges	**Handout 9.1** The Practice of Sweeping in Depth **Handout 9.2** Loving-kindness Meditation **Handout 9.3** Five Ethical Challenges **Handout 9.4** Record of Ethical Challenges **Handout 9.5** Daily Record of Mindfulness Meditation Practice

Session 9: Summary of weekly content—groups

Application with groups	*Handouts*
1. Review practice from last week • Check readiness to proceed • Check on assertiveness task	
2. Introduce sweeping in depth	**Handout 9.1** The Practice of Sweeping In Depth **Handout 9.5** Daily Record of Mindfulness Meditation Practice
3. Introduce loving-kindness meditation	**Handout 9.2** Loving-Kindness Meditation
4. Introduce five ethical challenges. • Describe the five ethical challenges (preventing lying, killing, stealing, becoming intoxicated and inappropriate sexual activity).	**Handout 9.3** Five Ethical Challenges **Handout 9.4** Record of Ethical Challenges
5. Set homework • Sweeping in depth practice • Loving-kindness practice • Five ethical challenges	**Handout 9.1** The practice of sweeping in depth **Handout 9.2** Loving-Kindness Meditation **Handout 9.3** Five Ethical Challenges **Handout 9.4** Record of Ethical Challenges **Handout 9.5** Daily Record of Mindfulness Meditation Practice

Session 10: Summary of weekly content—individuals

Application with individual clients	*Handouts*
1. Review last week's homework • Sweeping in depth practice • Loving kindness practice • Ethical challenges	

Application with individual clients	*Handouts*
2. Program revision Stage 1 • PMR, Mindfulness of breath and part-by-part body scan • Co-emergence model of reinforcement Stage 2 • Advanced scanning • Exposure methods; developing equanimity Stage 3 • Advanced scanning (sweeping methods) • Mindful interpersonal communication Stage 4 • Advanced scanning (sweeping in depth) • Mindfulness and ethics • Loving kindness meditation	**Handout 10.1** MiCBT Program overview
3. Revisit original goals from session 1. • Review in the context of expectations being realistic • Discuss future maintenance practice	
4. Fill in final outcome assessment forms	

Session 10: Summary of weekly content—groups

Application with groups	*Handouts*
1. Review last week's homework • Sweeping in depth practice • Loving kindness practice • Ethical challenges	
2. Program revision Stage 1 • PMR, Mindfulness of breath and part by part body scan • Co-emergence model of reinforcement Stage 2 • Advanced scanning • Exposure methods; developing equanimity Stage 3 • Advanced scanning (sweeping methods) • Mindful interpersonal communication Stage 4 • Advanced scanning (sweeping in depth) • Mindfulness and ethics • Loving kindness meditation	**Handout 10.1** Program overview

(*Continued*)

Application with groups	*Handouts*
3. Revisit original goals from session one. • Feedback on practice and general functioning since the group started • Discuss in the context of expectations being realistic	
4. In session practice • Sweeping in depth and loving-kindness • Discuss future maintenance practice	
5. Deliver a "Certificate of Participation" to each participant	
6. Fill in final outcome assessment forms	

Appendix 2
Audio Instruction Scripts for Therapists

Guidelines for Therapists

The following scripts are approximate transcripts of Dr. Cayoun's recorded instructions, which clients listen to during daily practice. These instructions are adapted from those of Eastern teachers of the Burmese *Vipassana* tradition, such as Sayagyi U Ba khin, Mother Sayamagyi and S. N. Goenka during ten-day meditation courses. Note that instructions are given once the client is relatively relaxed. If they are too agitated, they need to relax a little first. These instructions are given in a slow and peaceful but assertive manner by a trained professional. Note also that " ... " means pause of about 5 seconds, that " ...... " means a pause about twice longer, and that a 30-second pause is denoted by an underscore "_". These pausing notations appear at the end of the word just preceding the pause. In any case, pauses should be sufficiently long to enable the client to scan the targeted body part. Some words are italicized, marking an emphasis. The client hears all instructions in each script below with closed eyes, sitting up with neck and back straight.

Timing protocol on scripts for audio instructions

"..." = about 5 seconds
" __ " = about 30 seconds

General Introduction

Script duration is about 1.5 minutes

Welcome to this training in mindfulness meditation in the ancient Burmese *Vipassana* tradition, which has benefitted thousands of people from all walks of life. It is a wonderful way of letting go of unhelpful habits of thinking, feeling and

The Clinical Handbook of Mindfulness-integrated Cognitive Behavior Therapy: A Step-by-Step Guide for Therapists, First Edition. Bruno A. Cayoun, Sarah E. Francis, and Alice G. Shires.

Companion website: www.wiley.com/go/Cayoun/Mindfulness-integrated

behaving. In case you are currently experiencing severe psychological distress, or you have been diagnosed with a chronic mental health condition, it is important that you take this training with the supervision of a qualified and registered mental health professional who is also well trained in mindfulness meditation. If this is relevant to you, please ask your doctor for a referral or for advice, or perhaps speak directly to your psychiatrist, psychologist or counsellor, if you have one. If this is not relevant to you, the guidance from these audio instructions will be sufficient to help you develop invaluable mindfulness skills.

Rationale for Mindfulness Training

Script duration is about 11 minutes

Before we begin, I'd like to take a few minutes to provide an important reason for using mindfulness meditation. It is not just about being in the present moment per se. A cat in front of a mousehole is very focused in the present. A sniper ready to kill is also very focused in the present; but neither is mindful. Mindfulness is a tool, not a goal. It is a tool that we develop to discover how we process information in daily life, how we can be more aware of the *mechanism* of thinking, feeling and reacting, and regain a sense of control in the way we conduct our life. It is about making conscious and wise choices with daily experiences, so that our intentions and actions are skillful, leading to decreasing dissatisfaction and increasing well-being. Let's have a quick look at how we process information, and briefly consider how mindfulness training can help us process information in a way that promotes a sense of peace and contentment.

Once a situation has arisen in our consciousness, we may become aware of it through our senses. For example, in the environment, we use our senses to see, hear, touch and smell that something is changing; perhaps it is raining. Within our body, we may experience tightness in the stomach and heat in the cheeks; perhaps we are hungry or anxious. With experiences perceived within the body, we can *feel* the tightness. In the mind, we may experience an unplanned thought, like a spontaneous memory. What enables us to perceive this thought is called *metacognitive awareness*. Both our physical senses and metacognitive awareness form the so-called *sensory perception* aspect of how we process information. It permits us to make contact with the world within and outside ourselves. This step is extremely rapid and usually subconscious.

As soon as we sense that a situation has occurred, very rapidly, in less than a second, it is evaluated by our mind, so we can quickly make sense of the world; recognize things like threats and other important aspects of survival. It is categorized and compartmentalized. Rain becomes rain, not just water falling from the sky. Say that it is raining, and we are preparing a barbecue, we are not just a neutral observer of the rain. We make a judgment of the situation. We might find it unacceptable and think, "This is terrible, it is raining, and I won't have a barbecue with my friends this afternoon." Now see the difference between *this* interpretation and the interpretation of a farmer in a dry paddock. It starts to rain, is perceived, categorized as rain, and straight away judged as a blessing. He might think, "This is wonderful for my crop!" The same situation for two different people will produce very different experiences. This is the *judgmental* part of the mind; the so-called *evaluation* aspect of how we process information.

You may have noticed that when we judge that the situation we encounter has some personal implication, it creates a sensation in the body. The more we judge that the situation is *personally* important, the *stronger* the body sensation becomes. In other words, when we take things personally, the basic elements for emotions are stimulated and felt in the body. This is the feeling part of the mind; the so-called *interoception* aspect of how we process information.

If we are untrained in mindfulness practice, these experiences in the body are not easily felt and we can't manage them skillfully. We assume that we feel what we do because of the situation, the trigger. We then react automatically to the situation to make ourselves feel better. This is the reactive part of the mind, the so-called *reaction* aspect of information processing. If the body sensations are pleasant, we tend to crave for more. If they are unpleasant, we tend to react with aversion, with resentment towards these sensations. We typically try to avoid feeling unpleasant sensations by either distracting our mind or reacting in a way that helps to reduce them. Our reaction leads us to feel a little better, either because we distract our mind with activities or intoxicants, like drinking alcohol, or we feel a little relieved because we react to the external situation to gain a sense of control. Next time this kind of problem arises, we'll use the same method of coping. This is called reinforcement. Our behavior is reinforced, and we are very likely to repeat it in similar future situations. It becomes a habit pattern, and we even call it part of who we are.

On the other hand, if we are trained in mindfulness, we become increasingly able to notice the skillful or unskillful nature of our thoughts and *feel* body sensations, even very subtle ones. As soon as we think that the rain is unacceptable, we can easily feel the unpleasant body sensations caused by the thought. As a result, we can be more aware that we are about to react because of these sensations, and not because of the rain. The rain is not an experience for us. Our experience can *only* be the sensations we feel in the body. Therefore, our reactions are *always* because of body sensations, which often result from our *interpretation* of the situation, and not the situation itself. What produces our instant reaction is the habit of reacting to body sensations.

In mindfulness training, we learn not to judge and not to react. We focus as much as possible with an objective attitude, an objective mind, with an unbiased perception of the way things are. Observing what passes by, without making judgments, from moment to moment. By learning to prevent reactivity, we train our brain to reduce the connections that are responsible for producing stress hormones. Progressively, our nervous system learns to change its habit of processing information. It becomes less judgmental, less reactive, more objective, providing us with more opportunities to cope healthily with life, whatever problem presents itself. In a nutshell, the purpose of practicing mindfulness meditation is to develop a degree of awareness and acceptance towards our experience, so that we can make more informed choices about our behavior. When things seem acceptable from within, it seems that people find things more acceptable in daily life as well. The world becomes a better place.

So, let us now turn to the training itself. This training requires a strong commitment on your part. If you decide to give it a real chance, you need to commit for at least an entire week to the first exercise. If you benefit from it, then commit to the next exercise for an entire week, etc. Success will depend on three conditions: sufficient frequency of practice (which means twice daily), sufficient duration of practice (which means 30 minutes per session) and sufficient accuracy of practice (which means as per these audio instructions). Without strong commitment to these three aspects of training, the nervous system will not learn to reconnect itself and change unhelpful habits that have been there for years, sometimes decades. To change years of habits, you must give this training a fair trial.

Introduction to Progressive Muscle Relaxation Script (Session 1)

Script duration is about 2.5 minutes

Progressive muscle relaxation, or PMR, is not a mindfulness practice but it is used in MiCBT to prepare and teach our nervous system to relax before starting mindfulness practice. This method has been well researched since the 1970s and there is empirical evidence for its effectiveness as a short-term stand-alone technique to address discomfort associated with stress, muscle tension, headaches and anxiety. It is the relaxation method of choice because it grounds you in the present 'reality' of your experience, rather than teaching you to dissociate from the body and use your imagination to find a peaceful place. PMR relaxes you while restoring the connection between your mind and body.

PMR requires you to contract and relax all major muscle groups successively. Practicing PMR this week will produce several benefits. Besides the ability to relax, you may feel more grounded and present, and more committed to self-care. Committing to care for yourself twice a day, while practicing an immediately rewarding relaxation method, will prepare you for the next step, next week.

For this, you need to sit comfortably in a chair or armchair and gently close your eyes. The sitting posture will help you perform the stretches, which are difficult to perform if you lie down. Therefore, avoid lying down. This will also prevent you from falling asleep. It is important that you learn to be relaxed while awake and attentive, so you can carry this ability in your daily life. Remember, always closed eyes, never lie down.

Progressive Muscle Relaxation Script (Session 1)

Script duration is about 14 minutes

Relax as you take two or three slow and deep breaths, deep in your stomach... deep breath... pause.... Now, as you let the rest of your body relax, clench your fists and bend them back at the wrists, tighter and tighter... keep breathing and feel the tension in your fists and forearms... Now relax... Feel the looseness in your hands and forearms. Notice the contrast between tension and relaxation...

Now bend your elbows and tense your biceps, tense... tense them firmly and observe the feeling of tautness... Let your arms drop down now and relax, feel the difference between tension and relaxation in your biceps...

Now turn your attention to your head and wrinkle your forehead... as tight as you can, tight, feel the tension, and keep breathing. Feel the tension in the forehead and scalp... and relax and smooth it out. Feel your entire forehead and scalp becoming smooth and rested...

Now frown and notice the strain spreading throughout your forehead... Keep breathing and let go, relax, allow your brow to become smooth again.

Now squeeze your eyes closed, squeeze your eyes closed, tighter, keep breathing... and relax your eyes, let them remain gently and comfortably closed.

Now open your mouth wide and feel the tension in your jaw... and relax your jaw. When the jaw is relaxed, your lips are slightly parted. Notice the contrast between tension and relaxation in your jaw.

Now press your tongue against the roof of your mouth. Experience the ache at the back of your mouth... Keep breathing through your nose... and relax.

Press your lips now, purse them into an 'o' shape... and now relax your lips. Feel the relaxation in your forehead, scalp, eyes, jaw, tongue and lips... Let go more and more...

Now roll your head slowly around your neck, you might need to sit up a little straighter for that. Feel the point of tension shifting as your head moves... and now slowly roll your head the other way... Keep breathing, now relax, allowing your head to return to a comfortable position...

Now, shrug your shoulders, bring your shoulders up towards your ears... hold it tight... now keep breathing and drop your shoulders back down, and feel the relaxation spreading through your neck, throat and shoulders... Pure relaxation, feel more and more relaxed, deeply relaxed while remaining awake.

Now breathe in, filling up your lungs completely and hold your breath... experience the tension... now exhale and let your chest become loose... Try again, filling your lungs completely and holding your breath, experience the tension... you might even feel sensations in your cheeks and face... now exhale. Continue relaxing letting your breath come freely and gently... Notice the tension draining out of your muscles with each exhalation...

Next, tighten your stomach and hold... keep breathing, feel the tension... and relax...

Now place your hands on your stomach, breathe deeply into your stomach pushing your hands upward against your stomach... hold... and relax... Feel the sensation of relaxation in the abdomen area...

Now arch your back, stretching it without straining, and keep the rest of your body as relaxed as possible. Focus on the tension in your lower back... now relax, let the tension pass away...

Now tighten your buttocks and thighs... strong... stronger. Keep breathing, feel the tension... and relax and feel the difference. Try again. Tighten your buttocks and thighs strongly, keep breathing... feel the tension and relax.

Now straighten your back a little and tense your legs, curling your toes downwards... Keep breathing, experience the tension... and relax...

Again, straighten and contract your legs, but this time bend your toes towards your face, bend your toes towards your face... tighter, keep breathing and feel the tension... and relax. Feel the comfortable warmth and heaviness of deep relaxation throughout your entire body, as you continue to breathe slowly and deeply...

You can relax even more as you move up through your body, letting go of the last bit of tension in your body. Start with the feet...and relax your feet.

Move up... and relax your ankles... relax your calves... relax your shins... your knees... your thighs and buttocks.... Let the relaxation spread through your stomach to your lower back... to your chest... Let go more and more...

Feel the relaxation deepening in your shoulders, in your arms and in your hands, deeper and deeper... Notice the feeling of looseness and relaxation in your neck, your jaw, your face and your head... Continue to breathe slowly and deeply, down in your stomach. Allow your entire body to be comfortably loose and relaxed, calm and rested.

Introduction to Mindfulness of Breath Script (Session 2)

Script duration is about 2.5 minutes

Now that you have trained yourself to relax, consider that *changing* our experience, which is what we often try to do when we try to relax, is quite different from *accepting* our experience. When we feel stressed or experience an unpleasant emotion, we can't always *change* the unpleasant reality that takes place in our mind and body. In fact, trying to do so is often impractical and it can sometimes make things worse, as it is easy to become habitually avoidant of unpleasant experiences ... The answer is acceptance. When we are able to accept an unwanted experience, it doesn't bother us anymore. Feeling relaxed becomes a consequence of acceptance, and not an escape from discomfort.

You are about to learn skills that will help you accept your experiences, as they occur from moment to moment ... You will start by learning to pay attention to your breath. This is an *attentional* exercise, not a *breathing* exercise. It is part of what is known as *mindfulness training*, which teaches you to observe things objectively, *just* the way they are, without adding anything to your experience or subtracting anything from it. This is beneficial in itself, but it will also prepare you for the next method. Our mind is often stressed and over-thinking, repeating over and over thoughts that are unhelpful. Mindfulness of breath will teach you to become immediately aware of what your mind is doing and help you from being caught up in unhelpful thoughts and attitudes. It will give you a sense of control over your own mind by helping you focus on what you choose to and to let go of the rest.

Mindfulness of Breath Script (Session 2)

Script duration is about 20 minutes

Let us now start with the practice ... Sit comfortably, either cross-legged on the floor if you are used to sitting in this way, or on a chair, without leaning against the back of the chair. Your knees should be lower than your buttocks, so you might need to sit on top of one or more cushions. Your neck and back must be kept straight. Neck straight, back straight, comfortably seated, focus all your attention at the entrance of your nostrils. Be aware of the breath coming in, going out ... simple breath ... non-controlled breath ... natural breath ... breathe as you need to breathe, without controlling the breath_.

If the air in the environment is very warm or very cold, you may feel the temperature of the air, touching the outer ring or the inner walls of the nostrils, and at other times you won't. That's OK. Then be simply aware that the air is flowing continuously at the entrance of your nostrils ... Notice if it comes more though the left or right nostril ...if it is deep or shallow ... fast or slow_. When you are aware of the incoming and outgoing breath, there is no past or future ... you are in the present moment, from moment to moment ... Time almost doesn't exist _ _.

Your mind is not used to staying in the present moment. It is used to wandering in the past ... wandering in the future ... but very rarely staying in the present moment ... There are reasons why this occurs. When parts of the brain are constantly activated, by habit or because there is a memory that is more or less stressful, the strength of this activation in the brain is such that we tend to repeat the thought or the memory. And because of this repetition, these pathways in the brain are facilitated and the thoughts related to these pathways keep on intruding. They keep on intruding over and over and over again, until you stop nurturing them by not *thinking* them ... Your big challenge during this exercise is to withdraw your attention from an ongoing thought, understanding this is *just* a thought_.

Keep breathing consciously_. Very alert, very attentive ... Every time a thought arises, see it for what it is, just a thought. Not the truth, not you ... Although there may be true issues within that thought, the thought is just a thought ... Learn to see thoughts for what they are. Practice now for a few minutes, to see thoughts for what there are, without reacting or engaging with them, without identifying yourself with them ... with a degree of detachment. And look at the incoming and outgoing breath, as it comes in, as it goes out. Do your best_ _ _ _.

Keep on focusing steadily on the in- and outgoing breath... trying to sustain your attention towards your breath for as long as you can_ _ _. There is no need to count or to put any strategy into your mind because you would focus on the strategy and forget about the breath ... You might start saying "one two, one two" or "in out, in out" and forget all about what you are actually doing ... So just *observe* what actually happens rather than *thinking* about what happens_. Learn about your mind by focusing on your breath, from moment to moment, without judging, evaluating, or reacting to the experience ... Keep practicing. The longer you practice, the more changes you will notice in your daily activities or you will be able to focus better, gain time on the job, be less bothered by intrusive thoughts and develop a degree of self-confidence and self-control_ _.

Keep practicing steadily, focusing on your incoming and outgoing breath ... Every time your mind wanders, do not feel disappointed or defeated. Bring it back smilingly to the awareness of respiration, at the entrance of the nostrils ... and keep on developing your awareness of breath ... mastering your own mind, bit by bit, progressively ... Keep practicing confidently_ _ _.

You may be able to feel a sensation of coldness on the inner walls of the nostrils as you breathe in, and maybe a little sensation of warmth on the inner walls of the nostrils as you breathe out, and maybe a little feeling of the air touching the skin below the nostrils on the area above the upper lips, on the area of the moustache ... If you don't feel anything, breathe slightly harder for a few seconds just to feel the touch of the breath and then quickly come back to normal breathing, natural breathing. Remember we are not trying to regulate the breath, we are just observing and accepting it as it is_ _.

Sometimes your mind will wander because it doesn't like to stay in the present moment; it is not used to it ... It will wander either in the past or in the future. Bring it back to the present moment ... smilingly ... without resenting the fact that it has wandered despite your effort to keep it steady ... Each time it wanders, gently bring it back to the awareness of respiration_ _.

Keep on focusing on the in- and outgoing breath, trying to sustain your attention for as long as you can_ _ _.

Keep breathing consciously ... very alert, very attentive ... Every time a thought arises, see it for what it is, just a thought ... in the present moment, from momentto moment ...

Some of you may already feel sensations somewhere around the nose perhaps, on the face, or elsewhere on the body. This is normal. Whether they are pleasant or unpleasant, feeling these sensations is absolutely normal ... The more relaxed you are, the more sensitive to your processes you become, because you are not distracted ...

Very alert, keep on focusing consciously on the in- and outgoing breath for as long as you can_. If you are using the MP3 version, continue practicing in silence until the bell rings. If you are using the CD version, you can now stop the CD and continue practicing without the CD for another 10 minutes. The more you practice, the more benefits you will gain.

Introduction to Part-by-Part Body Scanning Script (Session 3)

Script duration is about 1.5 minute

In daily life, we typically try to get rid of unpleasant experiences and attract pleasant ones. The purpose of the following practice, commonly called body scanning, is to train you to realize and accept the impermanent and impersonal nature of all experiences, so you become less caught up in emotional reactivity in your daily life. For this, you will develop awareness of thought, awareness of body, and *equanimity*, which means balance or evenness of mind, composure, equilibrium. It means not getting personally involved with the current experience. This includes not reacting with desire for what is pleasant, or aversion for what is not pleasant. Equanimity is a form of acceptance of the situation, unconditional acceptance ... Relaxation becomes a by-product of that, because when you are more able to accept your experience, you relax. You relax but not to fall asleep or sleep better. You do so to remain alert, attentive and as objective as possible.

Part-by-Part Body Scanning Script (Session 3)

Script duration is about 31.5 minutes

Keep your eyes closed, keep breathing peacefully, calmly and attentively_. Start by focusing all your attention on your nostrils and focus on the incoming and outgoing breath, as it comes in ... as it goes out ... without changing anything retraining the breath to relax. We are learning to be equanimous, non-reactive, neutral_. Now shift *all* your attention, *all* your attention to the top of your head, to the top of your head, and observe whatever sensation you feel at the top of your head ... You may not feel any sensation yet ... Certainly you will not feel the subtle ones, even though there are millions of sensations on the top of your head, but your mind hasn't been trained enough, it is not concentrated and subtle enough to feel them ... In time, this will become easier if you persevere ... For now, you may feel perhaps some gross sensations like itching or ants crawling, pressure, and temperature of some type ... anything ... or maybe you feel nothing. It doesn't matter as not feeling anything is still an experience, therefore just observe... No reaction. Stay there at the top of your head ... As you observe the top of your head, if you feel nothing, you may feel something somewhere else on your body ... don't allow yourself to be distracted. *You* are "the master of the house"... therefore *you* decide where you put your attention ... At this moment, you are in control of your attention ...

Having made sure that there are no more sensations to perceive on top of your head, start moving further and survey the entire scalp area, bit by bit, part-by-part ... If you feel you have difficulties feeling any sensation at all, then use larger parts of your head, so you may feel something if you scan a larger portion at a time ... maybe 10- to 15-centimeter diameter areas at a time. If you stay in an area and you feel nothing there for about half a minute, then move further and as soon as you feel a sensation, again move further straight away ... avoid getting stuck with *any* sensation, whether pleasant or unpleasant ...

If any thought overpowers you, maybe a recurring thought, then go back to the awareness of breathing in and breathing out for a few seconds, even half a minute if you can. If it is still overpowering, breathe slightly harder, not too hard, just slightly harder or you might hyperventilate ... and then as soon as you are aware of your breathing again, and the thought is gone, then start slowing down your breathing and go back to the body sensation where you left off and continue scanning the entire scalp area ...

Now move to the forehead and survey the entire forehead area. Survey the eyebrows; starting with one, continuing with the other ... Then move your attention to the nose. Look at any sensations on the nose ... Move further down to the mouth and survey the lips for any sensations ... feel the tongue, any sensations on the tongue? ... Of course, your mouth is closed or the lips gently parted, but you are breathing through the nose ... Move your attention to the chin for any sensations in on your chin ... Move up to the left cheek and then move aside to the right cheek ... If you feel any sensation, avoid getting attached to it in any way, just move further ... No clinging ... Move up to the left ear and then to the right ear ... Now survey the throat area. Any sensation in the throat area? ...

It can be anything, pain, strain, tingling sensation, itching sensation, pulling, throbbing, sweating ... any sensation is an experience; therefore, we just observe it ... objectively ... without judging it or reacting to it ... It is not *yours*, it is not *you*. It merely arises to pass away, *just* to pass away ... It is the same with your thoughts, they arise and pass away if you don't nourish them, feed them with more thoughts ...

When you finish surveying the throat area, keep moving and survey the entire neck area ... any sensation in the neck? ... Keep moving and try to feel sensations on your left shoulder ... part-by-part, not reacting to any type of sensation whether subtle, gross, pleasant or unpleasant ... If you feel any discomfort it is absolutely normal, so just observe smilingly, peacefully, progressively moving down to the left arm, surveying the entire left arm and left elbow ... Patiently and calmly, survey the entire left wrist and left hand ...

... Then move up to the right shoulder, the *right shoulder* and survey the *entire* shoulder, moving as soon as you feel a sensation ... If there are no sensations for about half a minute, then move further anyway ... Maybe when you go back to this shoulder in the next round you might feel something there... There is no need to feel defeated or annoyed by what you experience. The whole exercise is to develop equanimity, balance of the mind, the opposite of reactivity ... Now move down to the right arm and the right elbow_. Move to the right forearm and down to the right wrist and the right hand_. Then move your attention up to the chest, from the upper chest to the lower chest area, and try to feel sensations in this area part-by-part ... Try to scan in a vertical order _ _. Keep the same order of scanning each time you scan your body parts ...

If you feel your heart beat and you interpret it as your heart beat, then you are not simply feeling sensations, you are *interpreting* sensations. It is important that you try to remain with the task of *pure* observation ... *no* evaluation ... *no* interpretation ... *just* observation. It is a *very* specific task ... *mere* observation. The basic *experience* of the heartbeat is just a body sensation ... Pleasant or unpleasant makes no difference, try to just observe ... If you are not evaluating it, then it is bound to subside progressively although it may increase at first, simply because you are aware of it ... in fact it doesn't really increase, it is your awareness of it which increases ... The sensation will subside and then pass away, however long it takes, because this is the nature of *all* sensations ... As soon as it is reinforced, as soon as it is reacted to, when the next similar sensation arises you will react to it similarly or even more strongly ... So, we start learning not to react to sensations, even benign sensations, or even pleasurable sensations ... no reaction and your mind will get very skilled at this ... and this skill will be transferred in your daily life, but first you will need to train very seriously ...

Now move down and survey the entire abdomen area, part-by-part, without any reaction whatsoever ... try not to miss any part, including genitals_ _. Now move up to the upper back area, the upper back area and feel any sensation you may come across in your *upper back area* ... always very calmly, equanimously_ _. Then move down to the lower back area_.

Try not to get caught in your thoughts ... as soon as you think something, and this is bound to happen over and over, quickly go back to the awareness of any sensation you were looking at and *move* further ... maybe you haven't felt a sensation for some time, so, in a manner of speaking, the mind gets bored ... Remain optimistic, this is just the beginning but you will get better at it with practice ...

Now keep moving down to the buttocks and survey the entire buttocks area. Start with the left and once it is surveyed move to the right buttock_ _. Move down to the left thigh and survey the entire *left thigh*, part-by-part down to the left knee_ _.

Now move down to the left leg, the *left leg* ... Even though there may be some gross sensations, like pressure, tension, or even pain perhaps, especially if you are sitting crossed legged on the floor, be very still, accepting *every* experience ... Within the most painful sensations, in case you encounter any today or another day, you will find there is an underlying current inside that sensation ... it is like an underlying sensation in which there is no pain ... a flow of very tiny sensations ... so always try to remain very still and attempt to feel this underlying current_.

Now move your attention down to the left ankle, and the entire left foot, to the tips of the left toes, the left foot, to the tip of the toes_. Now go up to the right thigh, the *right thigh* and survey the entire right thigh, part-by-part, in the same way_.

Keep moving down to the right knee, the right leg, the right ankle and the right foot_ _. You have now surveyed the entire body, from the top of your head to the tips of your toes. Now start from the tips of your toes and move back up to the top of your head. Start from the left foot and move up to the left leg, left thigh and left buttock _. Similarly, from the right foot, move up progressively to the right leg, the right thigh and survey the right buttock_.

Continue scanning your body calmly and equanimously, focusing on the lower back ..., followed by the upper back_ _. Now survey the entire abdomen and chest areas, patiently and calmly_ _. From the upper chest move up to the throat area ...

From the left hand move up to the left shoulder ... From the right hand then move up to the right shoulder ... Survey then the entire neck area and then the face ... part-by-part ... and then do the same with the entire scalp area_ _.

And again, from the top of the head go down to the tip of your toes and scan your body entirely, as long as you can give it time ... As you practice correctly, your mind will become increasingly and profoundly detached, at the level of body sensations ... Remember, the most important thing to keep in mind is that all body sensations and all thoughts are impermanent by nature ... The impression that they remain is because we react to them, we reinforce them ... Each time you come across a sensation, especially those that are very pleasant or very unpleasant, just remember their nature, their *impermanent* nature. Reacting to it only increases the reinforcement of our habits in daily life ...

What you do during this training will be reflected in your daily life ... it is a very effective technique... Of course, sometimes you will react during your practice, but watch that you react less and less and the results in daily life will be surprising ... Now, you can practice without instructions, in silence, if you have some time ... If you are using the CD version, you can now stop the CD ... the more you practice the more you will benefit _.

Withdrawing Audio Instructions Script (Session 4)

Script duration is about 3.5 minutes

I have provided the necessary instructions you need for this first part of your training, but as you develop mindfulness skills, these instructions will become a distraction. They will become a hindrance to your progress. Therefore, it is important not to be too attached to instructions for support. Generally, people benefit from using the instructions when practicing twice daily for a week. After a week of body scanning practice with instructions, continue scanning the body part-by-part for at least another week without instructions, in silence. You will notice that when you are not distracted by instructions, you can experience more intrusive thoughts during practice. This is very normal, but it can be challenging sometimes. It is because your mind is not busy hearing the instruction, so nothing stops thoughts to surface in consciousness. Learn to deal with them. In fact, these thoughts are also useful because it is through learning to let them go during our practice that we learn the skill to let go outside the practice in our daily life. The new brain connections that we created so far during practice can now be used in daily life.

It is also important not to use the instructions once we've learned the techniques because we cannot play the instructions in daily life, while interacting with people at work or at social events, and it is important to become self-sufficient and apply the skills in daily situations. Your skills must become portable, easy to use.

So, the schedule is as follows: once you have practiced body scanning with the instructions for a whole week, repeat the same 30-minute long practice twice daily for another week, but without audio instructions. During that week, make sure you also apply your skills, your awareness of sensations and equanimity, all day long, as much and as often as possible with all situations. After one week of practice without instructions, as soon as you can feel about 80 % of the body surface during body scanning, start advanced scanning with the instructions.

Introduction to Advanced Scanning Script (Session 5)

Script duration is about 3 minutes

Until now, you were asked to use a unilateral part-by-part scanning method. Although it is very profound and beneficial in itself, unilateral scanning is the first step to prepare you for more advanced methods. These methods help us develop an ability to feel more and more body parts simultaneously, which, in turn, allows us to detect very early and subtle signs indicating that an emotion is about to come up. So, these methods are extremely useful tools to regulate our emotions. You are now ready to learn the first advanced scanning method, provided of course, that you can feel sensations in most parts of your body without too much difficulty, and without too much effort. To double-check whether you are ready for advanced scanning, pay attention to what you feel in your right shoulder right now. Any sensation?...Note whether you can feel something straight away...Now cross check at random, for example on your left thigh...towards the knee...any sensation there?...On the right ankle...the left elbow...the forehead...the center of the abdomen...If you can feel sensations relatively easily, start practicing advanced scanning methods. The first one is called bilateral scanning, or symmetrical scanning. As you did with unilateral scanning, you will survey every part of the body, but this time, you will pay attention to both sides of the body at the same time. For this, please follow the instructions on the next track.

Symmetrical Scanning Script (Session 5)

Script duration is about 13 minutes

Practice Instructions

Once you are sitting up with your eyes closed and neck and back straight, peacefully, quietly, begin your practice. Focus your attention on both sides of the body at the same time, as you scan the body downwards, and then upwards, part-by-part, with spots of attention of about 5 centimeters in diameter. Start from the top of your head, focusing on both sides of your scalp at once, part-by-part. __ __ Pay equal attention to both sides of your body symmetrically, continue surveying the rest of the head...both ears at once...... both sides of the forehead...... both eyebrows and eyes at once...the entire nose and mouth at once...... the chin...both cheeks at once, part-by-part.........then scan the left and right parts of the throat at once...... Now do the same with the neck and shoulders. Both shoulders at once __ both arms __ both elbows...... both forearms __ both wrists and hands at once, part-by-part __ Then move back to the base of the throat and survey the entire chest area symmetrically, moving downward part-by-part toward the abdomen __ Then move down, focusing on both sides, part-by-part, surveying the entire abdomen __ __ Now move to the upper back and survey from the upper back downward symmetrically, part-by-part __...... Then move down to the lower back area, very calmly and equanimously __...... Now keep moving down to the buttocks and survey the both buttocks part-by-part, symmetrically __ __ Continue passing your attention on both thighs at once, moving down towards the tip of the toes, with equanimity...... No reaction, no judgment, keep moving __ Once you reach the tips of the toes, move back up in exactly the same fashion: feeling both feet, both ankles, both legs, up to the top of the head __ __ __ __ No reaction, no judgment, and keep your attention moving __ __ __ __ From now on, twice a day, practice symmetrical scanning with awareness and equanimity for a whole week. Now you can stop this audio recording and practice in silence, on your own, for at least 30 minutes.

Introduction to Partial Sweeping Script (Session 6)

Script duration is about 1.5 minute

Now a week of hard work has passed, where you have tried and practiced the first advanced scanning method. Up until now, you were moving through every part of the body, one part at a time, symmetrically. With the next advanced method of scanning, we will be focusing our attention in a way that makes more of the brain work at the same time. From now on, you will scan the body in a *sweeping* fashion, which means in a continuous fashion, rather than part-by-part. You will 'sweep' body parts, feeling very subtle warm vibrations, like a flow of pleasant tingling sensations. For example, if you are able to focus on a shoulder and at the same time feel this and the surrounding parts of the body, such as the whole arm, vibrating all at once without needing to scan through it, then it is time for you to engage in the training of sweeping methods, starting with partial sweeping.

Partial Sweeping Script (Session 6)

Script duration is about 14.5 minutes

Once you are sitting up with your eyes closed and neck and back straight, peacefully, quietly, begin your practice. Start by focusing all your attention on the top of your head and begin to scan the body downward. If you feel parts that vibrate freely, pass your attention in a continuous flow, as if you were *sweeping* through the entire part at once, without interruption, starting with the entire head __ As you scan downwards, and then upwards on both sides of the body symmetrically, sweep freely through vibrating parts of the body with a free flow of attention __ The sensations may be tingling, vibrating, and appear to be pleasant and warm...Remember, whether pleasant or unpleasant, they indicate an experience of change, so there is no need to be attached to something which is continually changing...Keep moving downwards equanimously...... Sensations will be more enjoyable in some parts of the body, as they are generally associated with pleasures...Try not to further associate any sensation with any attitude except equanimity, neutrality, balance of the mind.........No craving for the pleasant flow, and no aversion towards less pleasant sensations or blank spots you may come across __ The flow of sensations is not dictated by anybody, it takes place whenever it is ready to take place. There are at least three reasons for which we can't feel free flow in certain parts. One is that the brain cells which allow us to feel sensations are not yet connected enough to let us feel free flow and we simply need more training. Another is that we may be feeling tired or not very attentive, and the other possible reason is that we may be reacting with craving or aversion to these sensations or because of the thoughts we have at this moment...So if you feel parts in which you can sweep, then sweep through the entire parts...It may be the entire head, or it may be both arms, symmetrically, or both buttocks, or the legs __ During this week, sweep wherever you can sweep, and after one or two sweepings of these parts, go back to surveying the entire body part-by-part symmetrically, paying particular attention to the parts where there is no free flow, equanimously, with a calm mind. __ No reaction, no judgment, and keep moving __ __ __ __ No reaction, and keep moving, keep moving __ __ __ __ There are often blank areas to discover...or there are stronger and unpleasant sensations that can emerge at times, so scanning part-by-part is also important when you come across these experiences.........For the remainder of your sessions this week, practice partial sweeping for about two body cycles, which means head to toe and toe to head twice, and then practice part-by-part scanning for one cycle before sweeping again...and this with equanimity, and awareness of the impermanence of body sensations. This means practicing with wisdom...Now you can stop the audio instructions and practice in silence, on your own, until the total duration of this practice session is at least 30 minutes.

Introduction to Sweeping en masse Script (Session 7)

Script duration is about 2 minutes

Now that you have practiced partial sweeping for at least a whole week, you have learned to scan most body parts quickly and in a single flow of attention. You might have noticed that more and more parts are vibrating with free flow. Tingling sensations may now appear in many parts of the body, although you may have already felt it a week or two ago. Some people feel this flow very early in their training and others later in their training. So many tiny parts of the brain, which we call nerve cells, or neurons, are now sufficiently connected to allow you to feel whole sections of the body without hindrance. This is the result of your commitment and continuous effort to progress…This week, a more advanced scanning method will require you to sweep en masse through the entire body from the top of the head to the tips of the toes, combining arms and torso. As for last week, this part of your training can be quite pleasant at times, and experiences can be addictive at times. Make sure you do not get attached to any free flow of sensations, as those tend to come with pleasant thoughts, sometimes even memories of pleasant events. This is not a stoic path, but it is not a path of craving and attachment either. So it is important that you remain conscious and realistic about the true nature of these sensations. All sensations are impermanent, and none belong to you; even the pleasant flow of energy will change at times. It will come and go. Remaining aware of this during your practice will lead to wisdom in daily life.

Sweeping en masse Script (Session 7)

Script duration is about 13.5 minutes

Once you are sitting with your eyes closed and neck and back straight, peacefully, with a quiet mind, begin your practice. From the top of the head, down to the tips of the toes, sweep en masse…passing your uninterrupted attention through the entire body, with free flow, as many parts as you can at once…… remain very attentive, very calm, and very equanimous, as you sweep the whole body vertically, from head to toe and from toe to head, continuously, in a loop…… Some people report feeling as if they are pouring a bowl of honey on top of their head. Your attention will flow from head to toe through the entire body. Later on, you may feel your attention flowing more like water you pour on top of your head. You will be able to sweep through the body in a single flow very quickly, while feeling all body parts simultaneously as you move your attention downwards __ __ Because of your dedicated practice, it won't take long to survey the entire body several times during your 30-minute sessions. Once you have swept through the entire body two to three times, then pass your attention through the parts that you've missed during sweeping, one at a time, without frustration, very patiently and equanimously __ __ In case you can't feel any sensation in some parts, pause on these parts for up to about half a minute, calmly and patiently, and then move on to the next part, part-by-part __ __ __ __ Very alert, very equanimous…Every time a thought arises, see it for what it is, just a thought, remaining very attentive __ __ __ __ As we sweep through large areas of the body, it is common for more thoughts to emerge in the mind. Let this not be a problem. It doesn't mean that you are losing your skills. Just refocus on the body part where you were, trying to sweep through the entire body with free flow, as many parts as you can at once __ __ __ __ Keep on moving your attention in order throughout the body, remaining very alert, with a degree of detachment __ __ __ __ No reaction, no judgment, and keep moving __ __ __ __ Practice wisely, sweep en masse with equanimity and awareness of the impermanence of body sensations, for the remainder of your sessions this week…Now you can stop the audio instructions and practice in silence, on your own, until the total duration of this practice session is at least 30 minutes.

Introduction to Transversal Scanning Script (Session 8)

Script duration is about 1.5 minute

As you have been training to sweep en masse through the entire body for at least a whole week, your equanimity and awareness have increased, and your experiences in daily life may have changed to some extent. Being less reactive, you can now perceive things a little more the way they are, more objectively. You are now going to deepen your objectivity using a more advanced scanning method called transversal scanning. If you have reached the stage of experiencing free flow of subtle sensations at the surface of most body parts, and perhaps a little bit inside some body parts, cross check anywhere in the body if there is a free flow of tingling, soft vibrations. If you can feel subtle sensations in most body parts you look at randomly, you are ready to start the practice of transversal scanning.

Transversal Scanning Script (Session 8)

Script duration is about 16.5 minutes

Once you are sitting with your eyes closed and neck and back straight, with a peaceful and quiet mind, begin your practice. Start scanning the body part-by-part again, with spots of attention about 5 centimeters in diameter, but this time, passing your attention to the inside of the body, traversing the body horizontally instead of scanning the surface vertically. Starting at the forehead, pass your attention piercingly and penetratingly toward the inside, through the entire head, slowly and progressively, until you reach the back…try to feel every sensation within the head…It doesn't mean that you're trying to feel or visualize your brain, your blood vessels or your bones. Not at all. We are only interested in the experience of sensations, which are just energy __ Once you have scanned across the head at the level of the forehead, move down to eye level and scan through to the other side of the head, in the same way, with 5-centimeter diameter spots of attention. Slowly and progressively, reach the other side towards the scalp __ Survey the entire head, from the face to the back of the head __ Once you have completed scanning the whole head from front to back, repeat scanning the head in the opposite direction, from the back of the head through to the face __ Then survey the throat in the same way, passing your attention part-by-part through the throat and reaching the back of the neck, in 2 or 3 spots __ Then pass your attention in the opposite direction, from the back of the neck slowly towards the throat, feeling every possible sensation in the middle __ Later in your training, you can also scan from side to side…Now scan the shoulders and arms, piercingly, penetratingly, reaching the other side, with equanimity and a degree of detachment __ Then survey the entire torso and abdomen. With a piercing and penetrating attention, reach the upper back, part-by-part __ Sometimes, all sorts of experiences can arise, such as aches or emotions, or deep blockages that prevent us to feel anything…Work with them in the same way you used at the beginning of this training, when you were scanning part-by-part for the first time…… Practice with equanimity, which means without reacting or judging the experience, and keep moving your attention __ When you scan through the abdomen, reach the lower back __ Keep moving down to the buttocks and survey the entire buttocks area, piercingly and penetratingly, with equanimity __ Then move down to the left thigh, and survey the entire thigh transversally, down to the left knee __ Then move down to the left leg, __ Piercingly and penetratingly, move down to the left foot, surveying the entire left foot, down to the tip of the toes __ Now start with the right thigh, and survey the entire right thigh in the same way, piercingly and penetratingly, down to the right knee __ Then the right leg, the right ankle and the right foot, with a degree of equanimity and detachment __ __ You have now surveyed the entire body, from the top of your head to the tip of your toes... Now, start from the tip of your toes and move back up to the top of your head in the same way...surveying the entire body transversally __ No reaction, no judgment, and keep moving __ In the following weeks, you will be ready to sweep in depth, vertically, through the inside of the body. This will require you to sweep en masse vertically, as you did before transversal scanning, but this time on the inside of the body. But not now. You must first ensure that you can feel most internal sensations when scanning through the body transversally part-by-part... Eventually, in a few months, you may be able to sweep and feel the entire body with every breath. Because this can bring up some unresolved emotions, the supervision of your teacher or therapist, if you have one, can be very useful. Now you can stop the audio instructions and practice in silence, on your own, until the total duration of this practice session is at least 30 minutes.

Note on Session 9

Please note that Session 9 requires practicing "sweeping in depth," which combines sweeping en masse and transversal scanning. Since both of these methods are already known to the meditator, there is no recording. Please see specific instructions in the Session 9 chapter.

Introduction to Loving-Kindness Meditation Script (Session 9)

Script duration is about 3 minutes

As your awareness further deepens into the nature of your reactivity and that of others, you learn to see people in a different way, more mindfully. You also learn to see yourself and others with more tolerance, patience and acceptance because you understand that we all react to body sensations without realizing it. We can be unreasonable and reactive because we are unaware, rather than profoundly unworthy or evil. Accordingly, at this stage of your training, it is important to develop a degree of compassion for yourself and others. For this, we now draw on a very ancient technique widely practiced in the east, called loving-kindness meditation, which uses meaningful and genuine positive affirmations grounded in the peaceful sensations we feel in the body. You will train your brain to connect itself in a way that makes it easier to think skillfully. In the first step, you will start by generating a sense of unconditional acceptance of yourself. You will then share your merits, your virtues and your compassion with others. In the second step, you will share it with people you love, people you care for and cherish.

In the third step, you will share it with those with whom you have less connection or for whom you have less affection, including people with whom there may have been conflicts, or with whom you may fear potential conflict in the future. Perhaps their insight and equanimity are not as developed as yours, but they can change, just as you are changing. Accordingly, you will send your goodwill to those who need it most.

The affirmations used in this recording are my own and follow closely traditional methods. After a week or two of practicing in this way, you may continue using these words or you may prefer to use your own words, those that resonate more for you according to your current situation. This is a skillful, calming and compassionate mental state, not wishful thinking, so you will need to be sincere and really mean what you think by feeling it in your body. Let us start Loving Kindness meditation, which I encourage you to practice every day for about 10 minutes after each sitting practice.

Loving-Kindness Meditation Script (Session 9)

Script duration is about 8 minutes

Keeping your eyes closed, relax your posture and any tension you may feel in the body…and start focusing all your attention on the center of the chest, the area we call the heart, with each incoming breath…You may feel a free flow of sensations in the chest, so focus on this part of the body, on the heart…If you find it difficult to focus on the chest, then focus on any part of the body that vibrates with a peaceful free flow of sensations, such as the palm of the hands…and with each outgoing breath, feel the pleasant flow of sensations expanding and taking more and more space in the body…… Feeling the entire body as you breathe out, start to generate kind and friendly thoughts about yourself, and good wishes for yourself…May I be peaceful…May I be free from agitation…May I feel safe and free from unhelpful thoughts and emotions…so that I develop real peace, real harmony in my life…patience and tolerance towards myself…May I be kind to myself and accept myself as I am…May I continue to grow in equanimity and wisdom…May I feel joy and contentment __.

Keep feeling the chest area as you breathe in, but now, as you breathe out, let the free flow of tingling sensations pour out of your body, and reach people that are most important to you, those you love and care for…Visualize these people and send them good wishes. Share your merits and good will with them. You can also visualize the sensations you send if it is easier or you may simply feel them, but make sure your intention is that they receive them and benefit from them… You can now address them directly:…May you also develop equanimity and wisdom…May you learn to see things more the way they are…May you experience *real* peace, *real* tranquility…May I share my merits with you, my love and compassion with you…… May you be happy __.

Keep feeling the sensations in the chest as you breathe in, but now, as you breathe out, let these peaceful sensations move further out of your body, radiating in all directions, reaching all beings, humans and non-humans, near and far…… Now share your merits and good will with all beings, including people who are not so close to you, and those who may have been in conflict with you or with other people in the past,...or those with whom there is potential for conflict in the future...Understanding that lack of awareness leads to suffering for everyone, which is the *real* cause of conflict...May they develop better awareness of their thoughts and behavior. May they develop equanimity...peace...and tranquility... May I share my merits and compassion with them...... May I share my goodwill, my joy and compassion with all beings...*all* beings...May all beings be free from suffering...May all beings experience real peace...may all beings be content __.

Index

The Clinical Handbook of Mindfulness-integrated Cognitive Behavior Therapy: A Step-by-Step Guide for Therapists, First Edition. Bruno A. Cayoun, Sarah E. Francis, and Alice G. Shires.

Companion website: www.wiley.com/go/Cayoun/Mindfulness-integrated

Printed and bound by CPI Group (UK) Ltd, Croydon, CR0 4YY
17/09/2026
14964306-0001